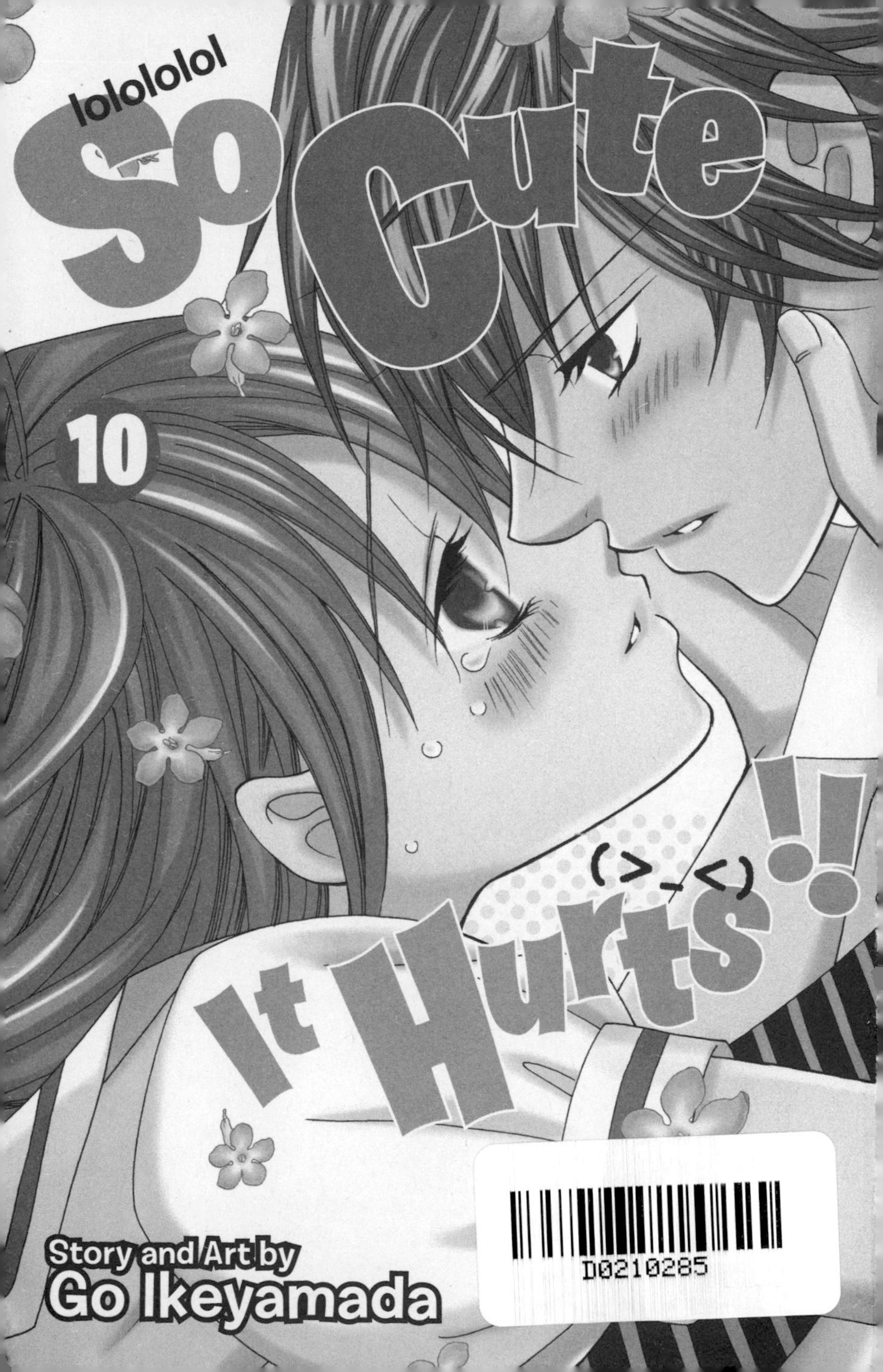
lolololol
So Cute It Hurts!!
(>_<)
10
Story and Art by
Go Ikeyamada

CHARACTERS

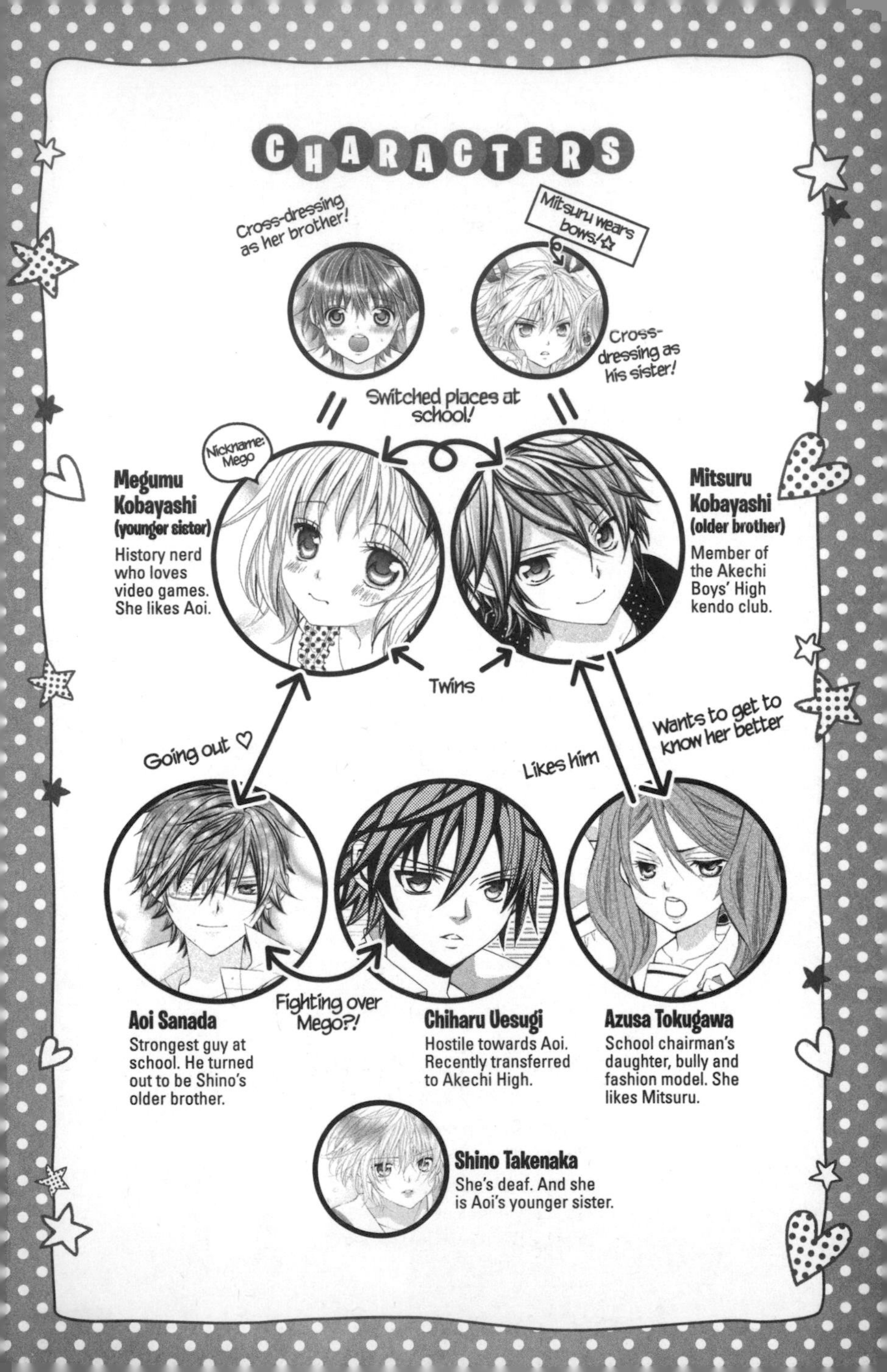
Cross-dressing as her brother!
Mitsuru wears bows!☆
Cross-dressing as his sister!
Switched places at school!
Nickname: Mego
Megumu Kobayashi (younger sister)
History nerd who loves video games. She likes Aoi.
Mitsuru Kobayashi (older brother)
Member of the Akechi Boys' High kendo club.
Twins
Going out ♡
Likes him
Wants to get to know her better
Aoi Sanada
Strongest guy at school. He turned out to be Shino's older brother.
Fighting over Mego?!
Chiharu Uesugi
Hostile towards Aoi. Recently transferred to Akechi High.
Azusa Tokugawa
School chairman's daughter, bully and fashion model. She likes Mitsuru.
Shino Takenaka
She's deaf. And she is Aoi's younger sister.

STORY

★ Mitsuru and Megumu are twins. One day they switch places and go to each other's school for a week! That's when Megumu falls in love with Aoi and Mitsuru falls in love with Shino. Azusa and Aoi both discover the twins' ruse but keep quiet for reasons of their own. When the week is over, Megumu declares her love for Aoi, and they start dating. They need to stay two feet apart because of Aoi's extreme discomfort around women, but they plan to work on it. Mitsuru is rejected by Shino, but Azusa starts to have feelings for him.

★ Azusa tells Mitsuru that she likes him after she sees him doing all he can to help others. She then declares she'll make him fall in love with her and beg to date her. Mitsuru slowly becomes attracted to the headstrong Azusa.

★ Then a mysterious boy named Uesugi transfers to Akechi High. He and Aoi used to be friends but are now seemingly enemies. Their antagonism disappears, however, when they face their shared past honestly. But when Uesugi declares he's fallen in love with Megumu, an unexpected love triangle is born!

★ One day a group of delinquents attacks Megumu, believing that she is Uesugi's girlfriend. Aoi, Uesugi and Mitsuru decide to rescue Megumu together. Aoi saves Megumu before she's hurt, but his eye patch falls off in the scuffle and Megumu finally sees what Aoi's been hiding!

CONTENTS

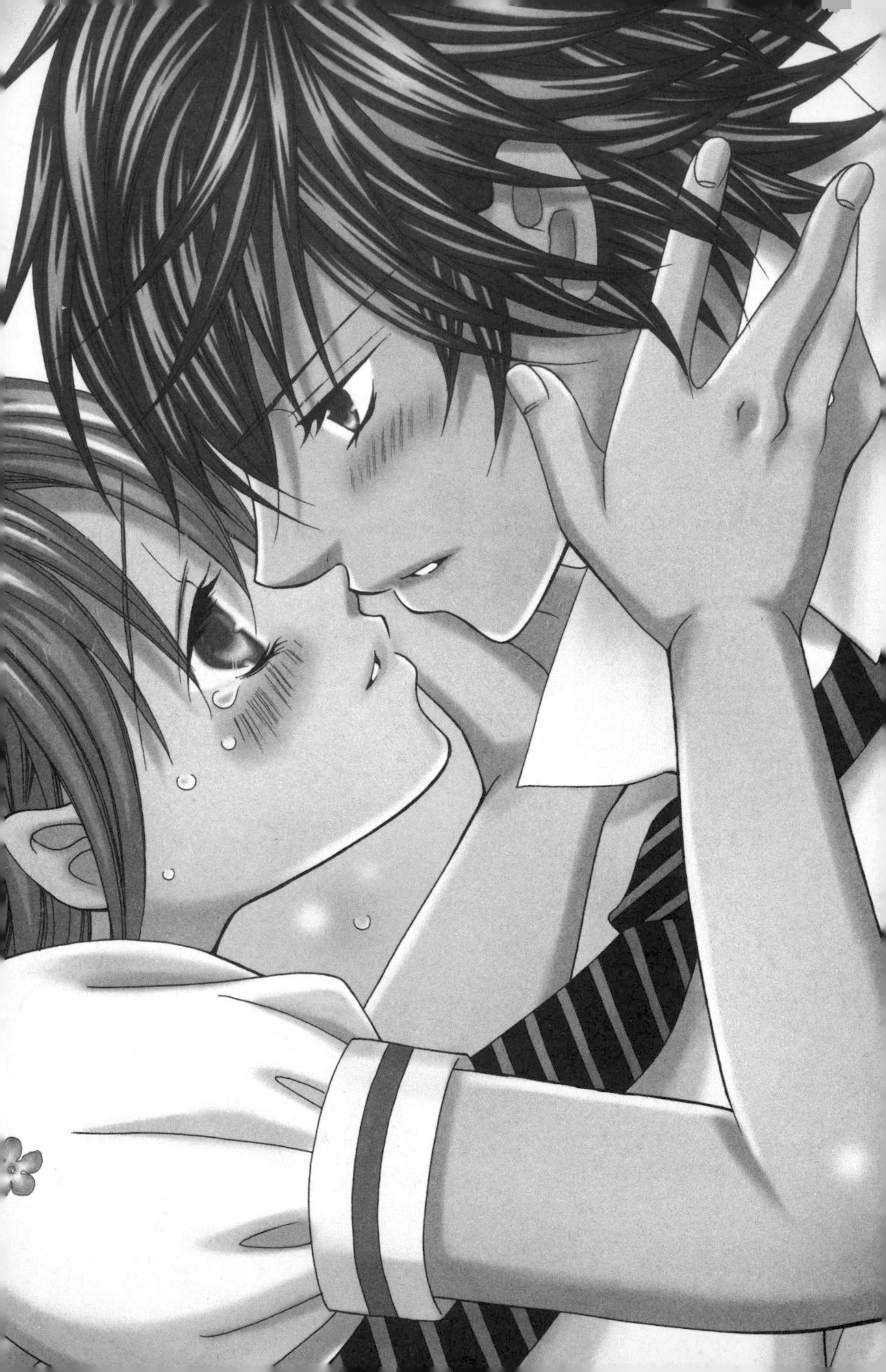

Chapter 46

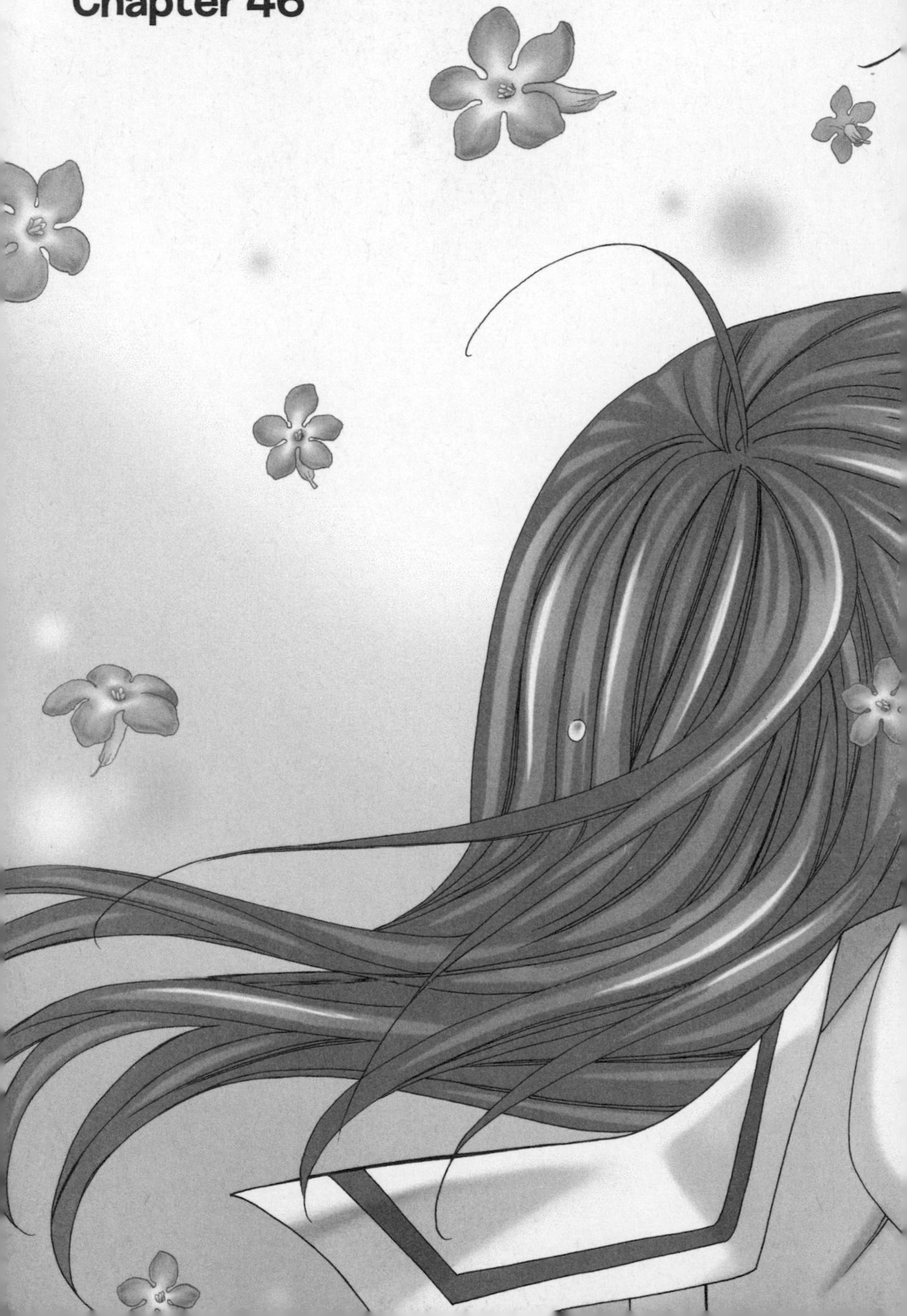

So Cute It Hurts!! (>_<)

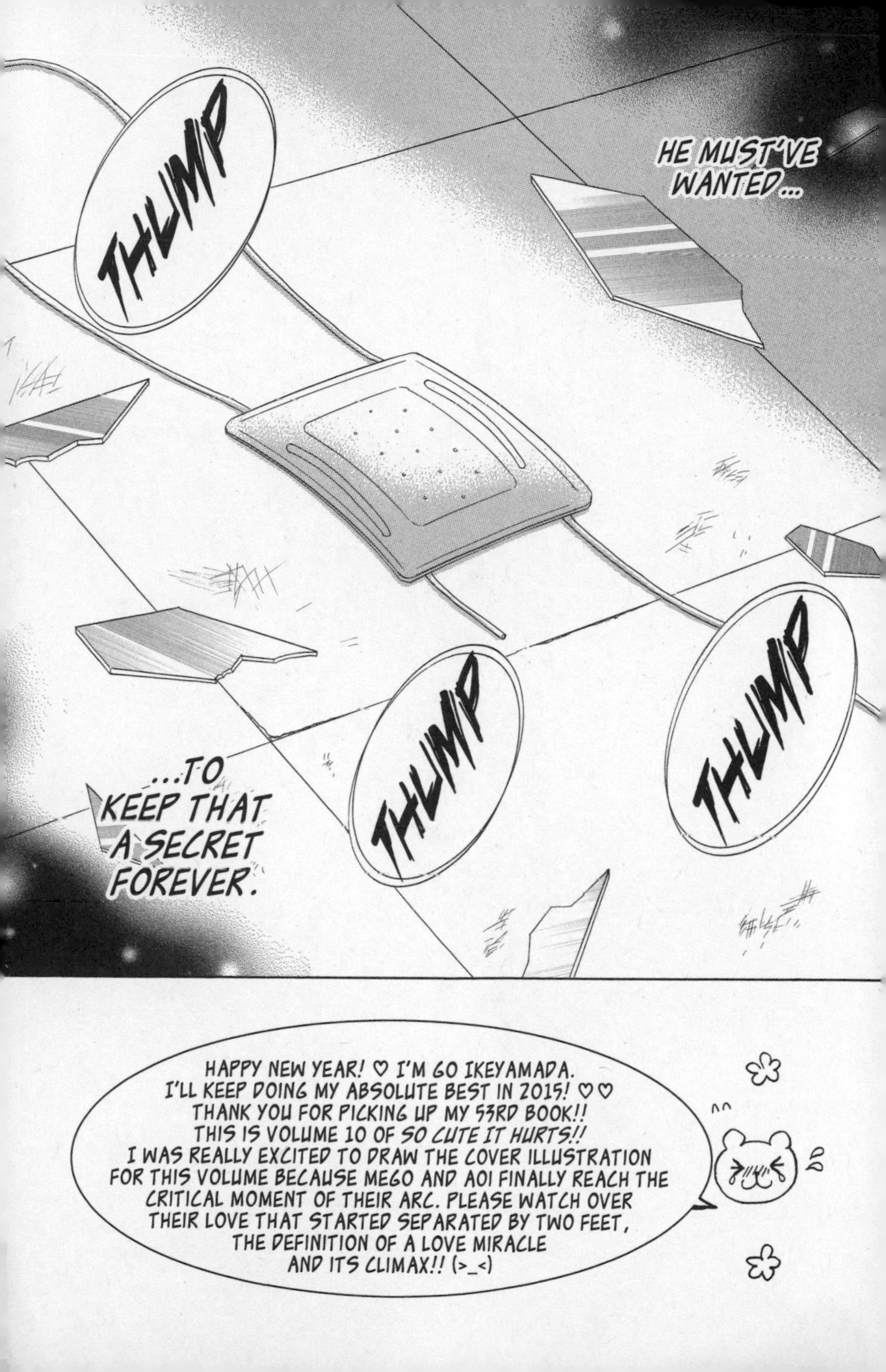
HE MUST'VE WANTED...
THUMP
THUMP
THUMP
...TO KEEP THAT A SECRET FOREVER.
HAPPY NEW YEAR! ♡ I'M GO IKEYAMADA.
I'LL KEEP DOING MY ABSOLUTE BEST IN 2015! ♡♡
THANK YOU FOR PICKING UP MY 53RD BOOK!!
THIS IS VOLUME 10 OF SO CUTE IT HURTS!!
I WAS REALLY EXCITED TO DRAW THE COVER ILLUSTRATION FOR THIS VOLUME BECAUSE MEGO AND AOI FINALLY REACH THE CRITICAL MOMENT OF THEIR ARC. PLEASE WATCH OVER THEIR LOVE THAT STARTED SEPARATED BY TWO FEET, THE DEFINITION OF A LOVE MIRACLE AND ITS CLIMAX!! (>_<)

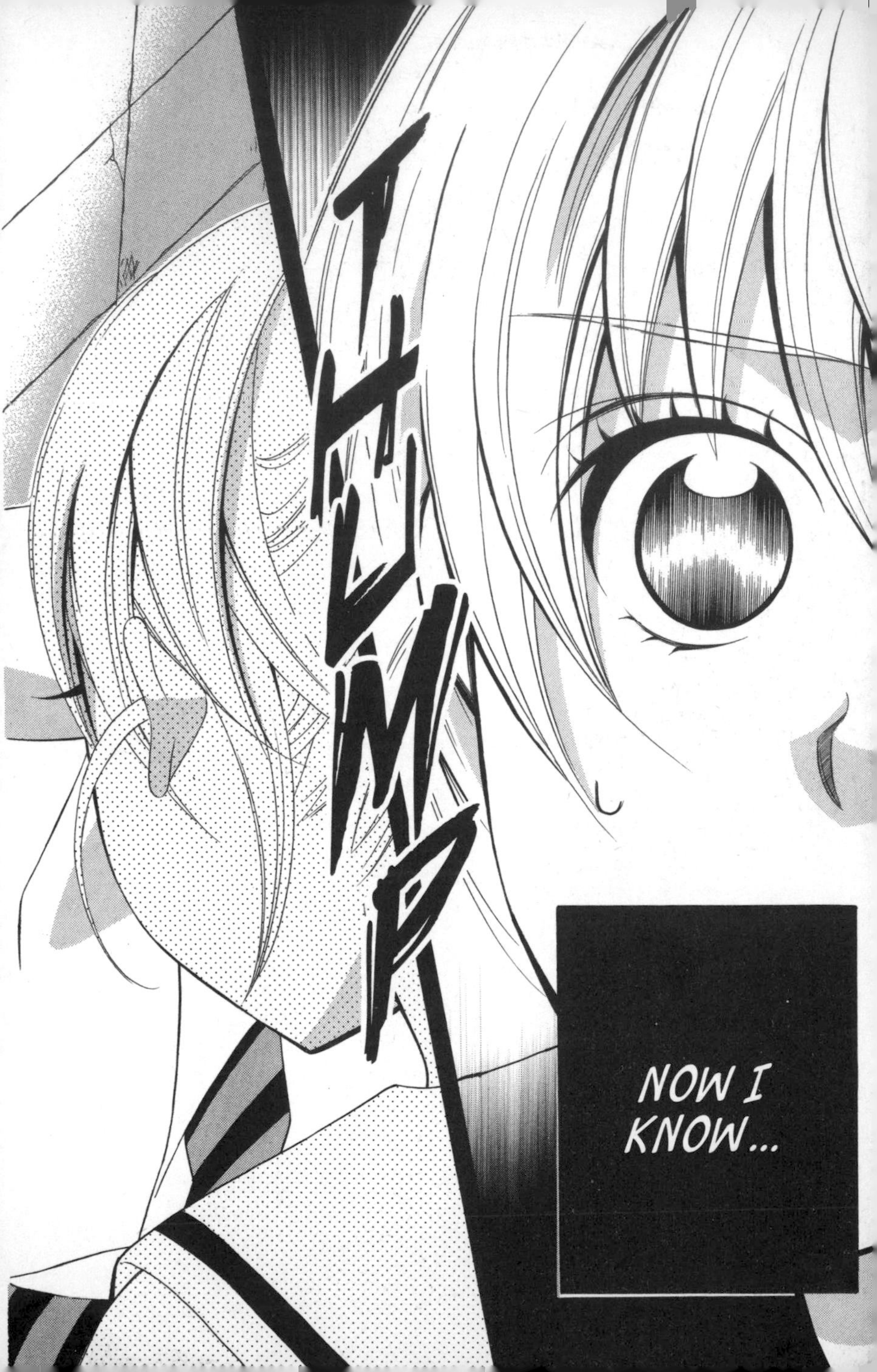
THUMP
NOW I KNOW...

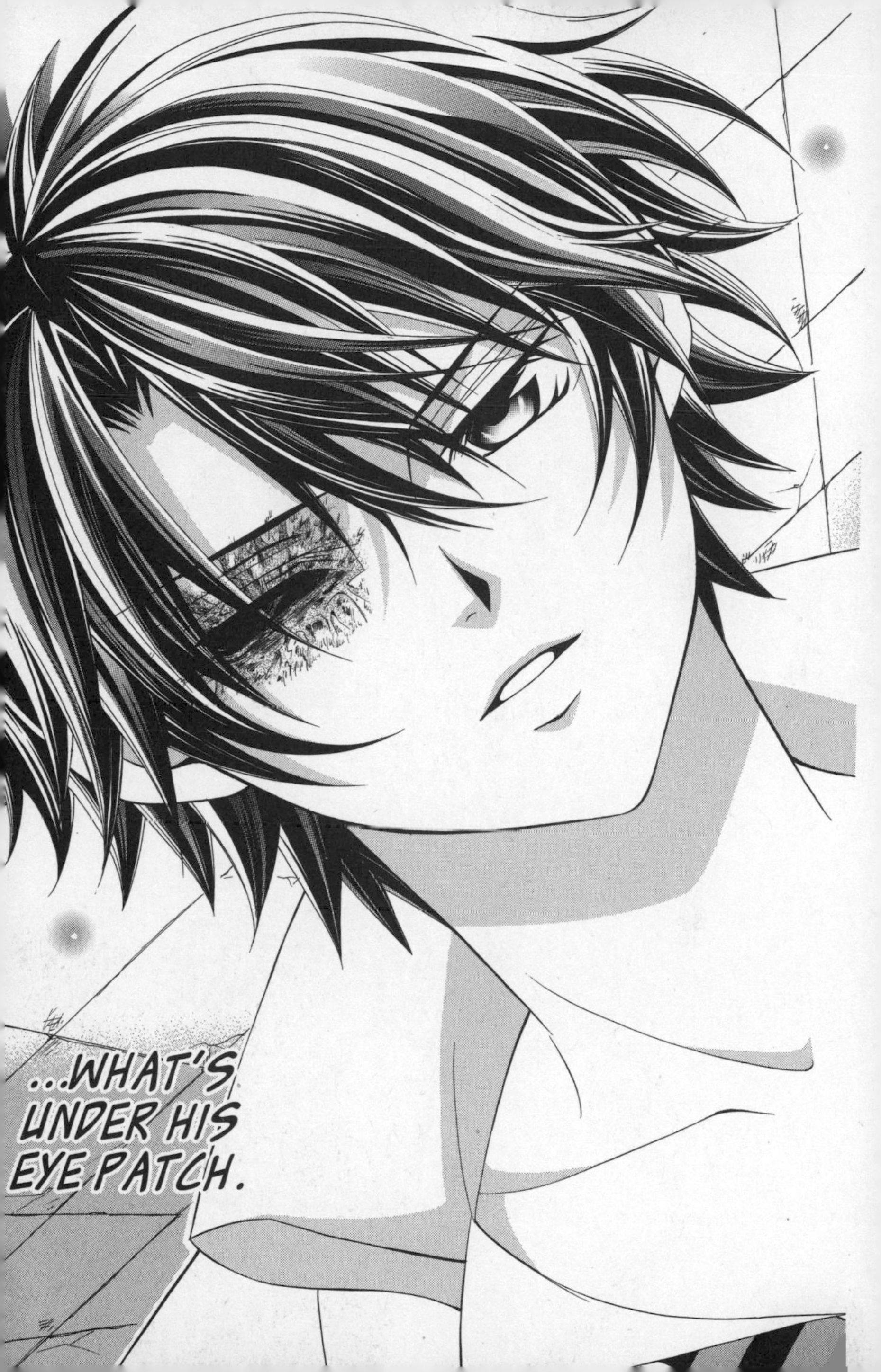
...WHAT'S UNDER HIS EYE PATCH.

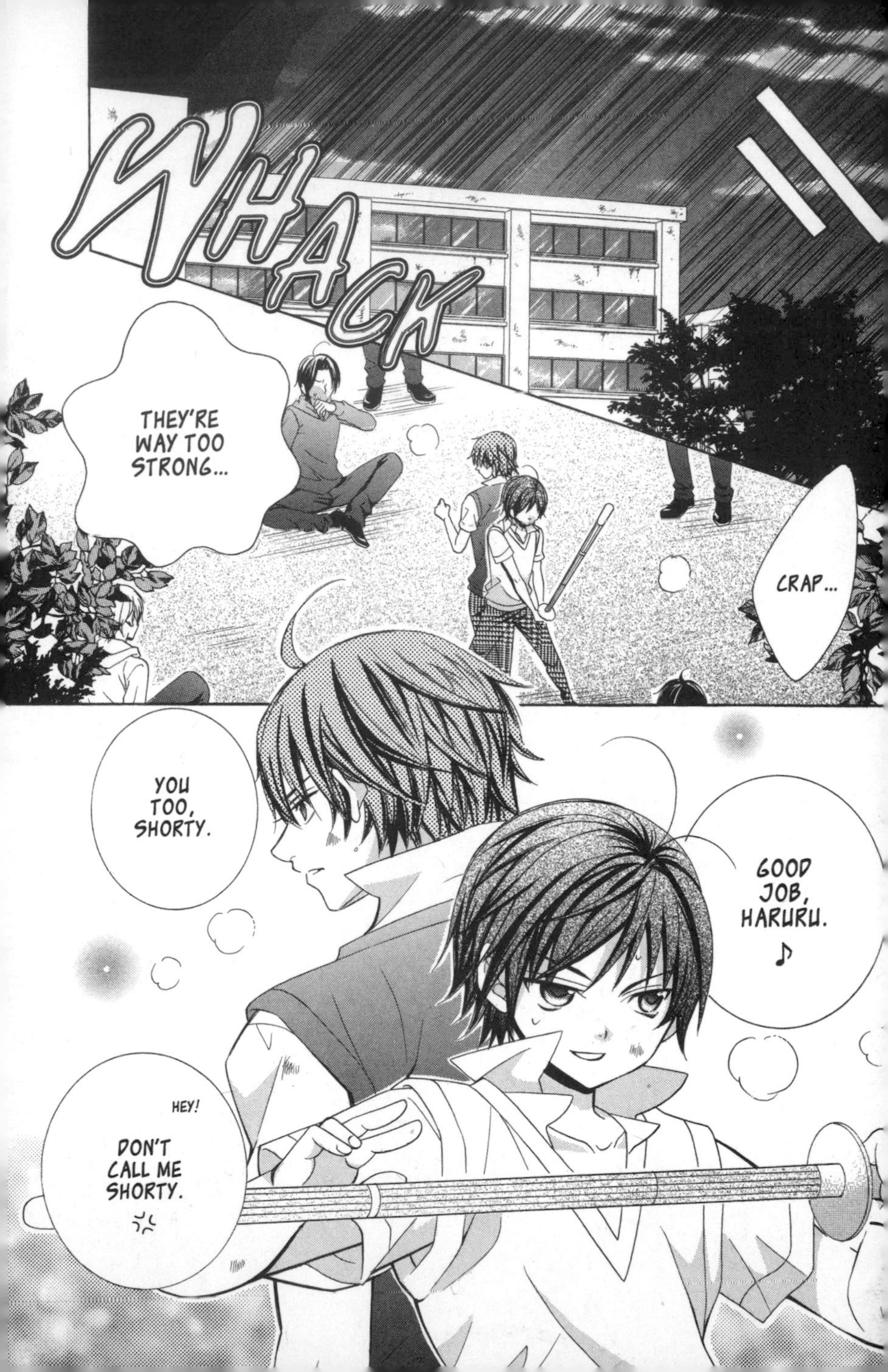
WHACK
CRAP...
THEY'RE WAY TOO STRONG...
GOOD JOB, HARURU. ♪
YOU TOO, SHORTY.
HEY!
DON'T CALL ME SHORTY.

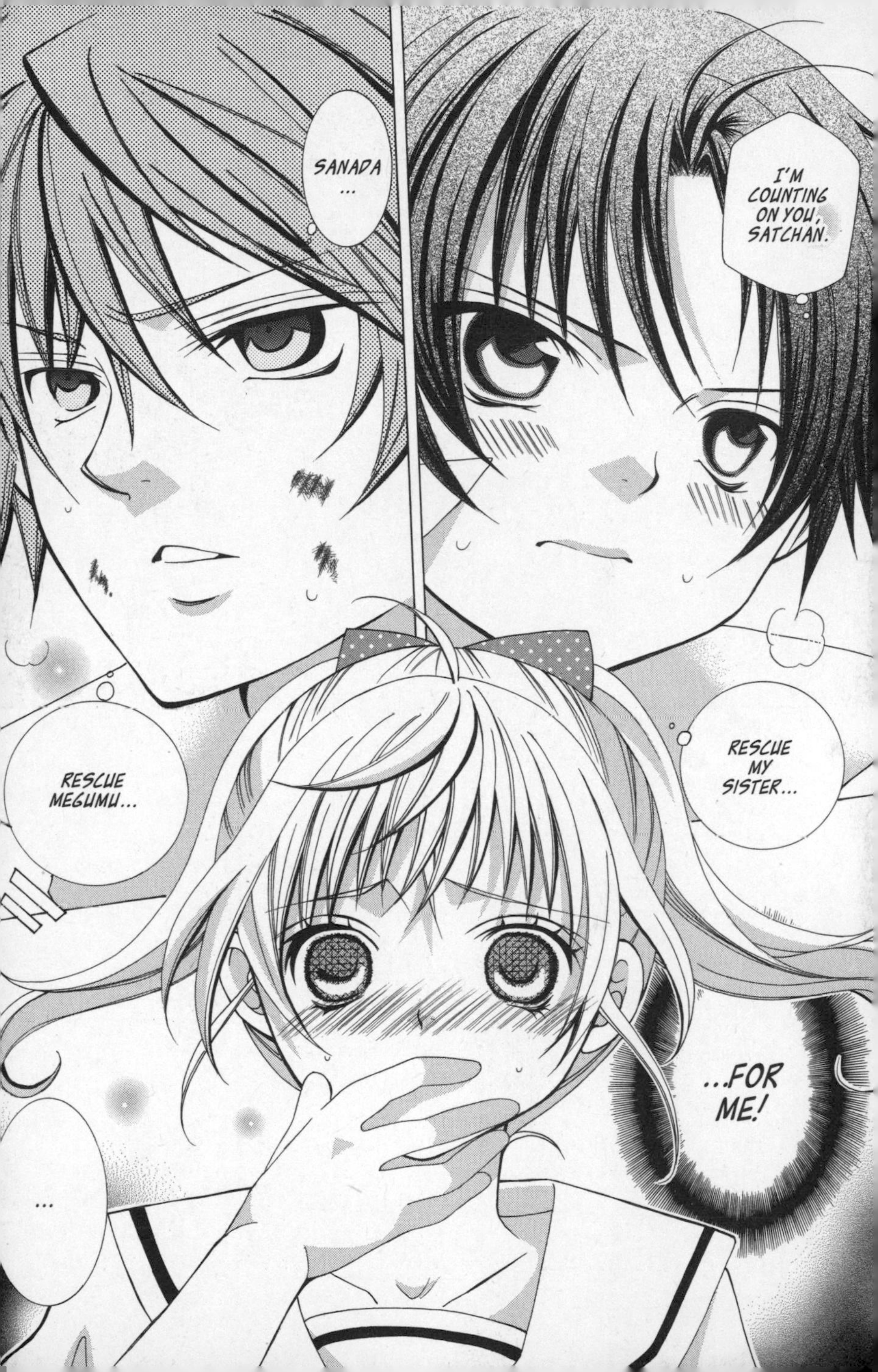
I'M COUNTING ON YOU, SATCHAN.
SANADA ...
RESCUE MY SISTER...
RESCUE MEGUMU...
...FOR ME!
...

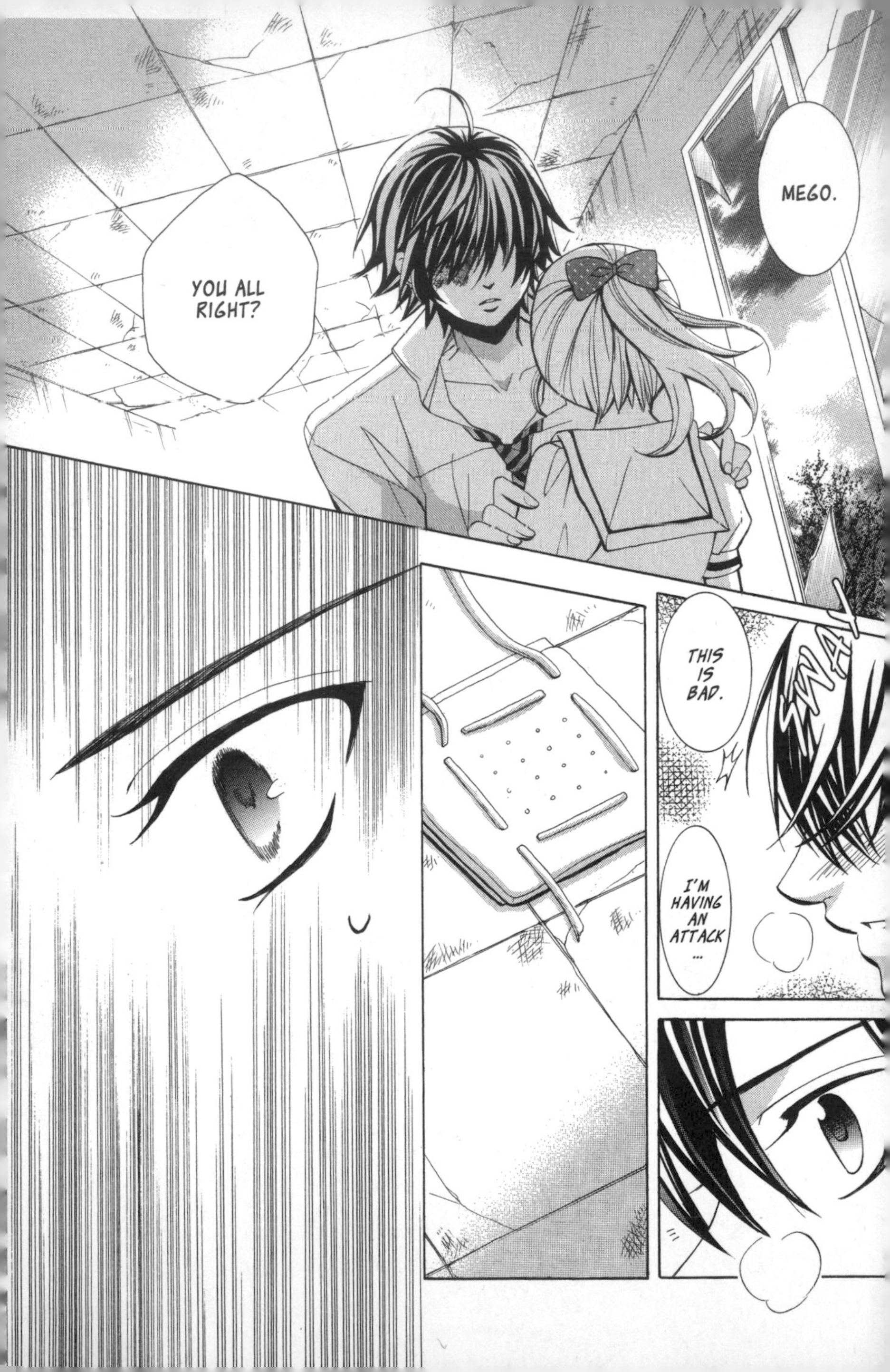
MEGO.
YOU ALL RIGHT?
SWAY
THIS IS BAD.
I'M HAVING AN ATTACK...

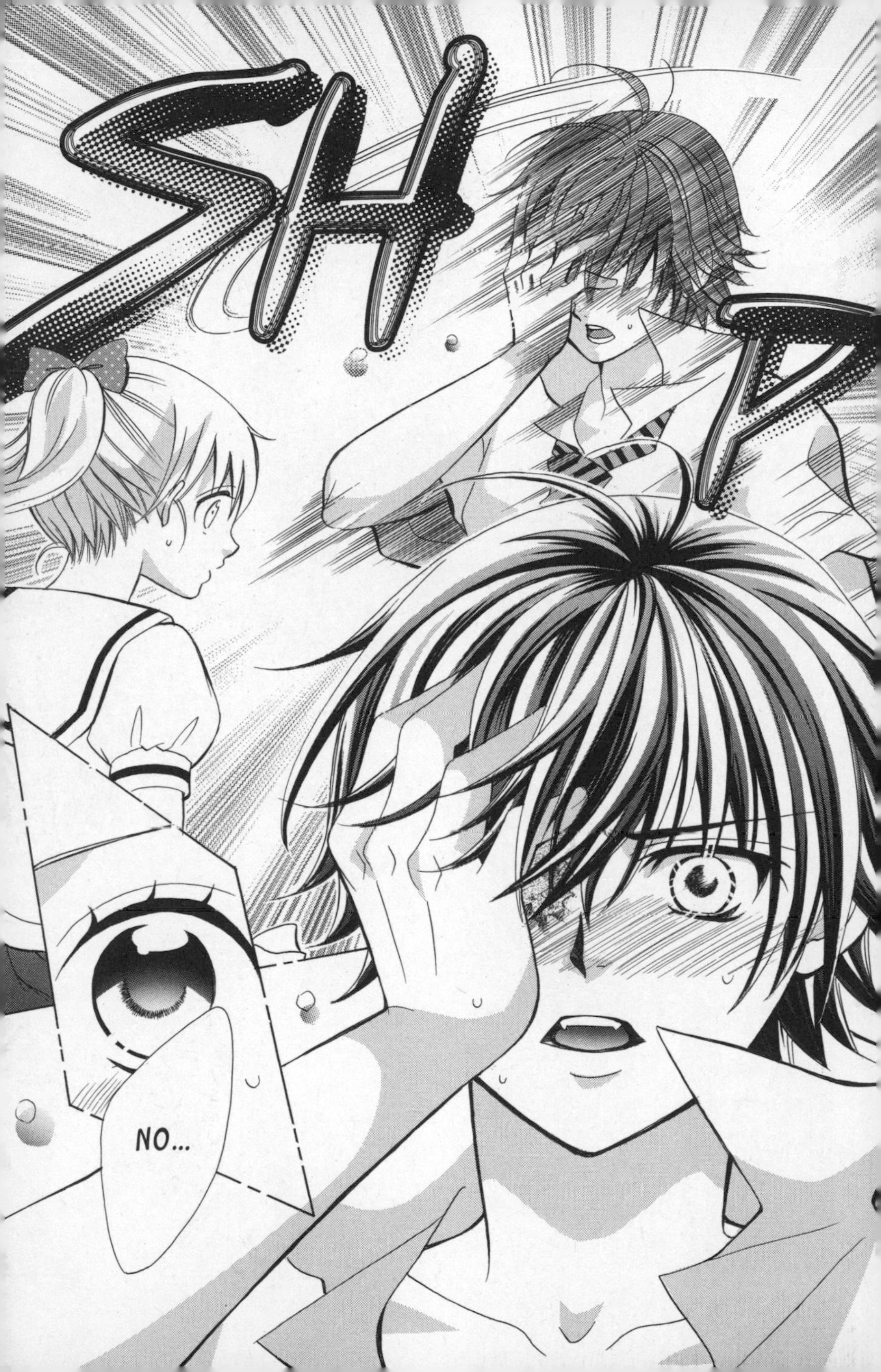
SHP
NO...

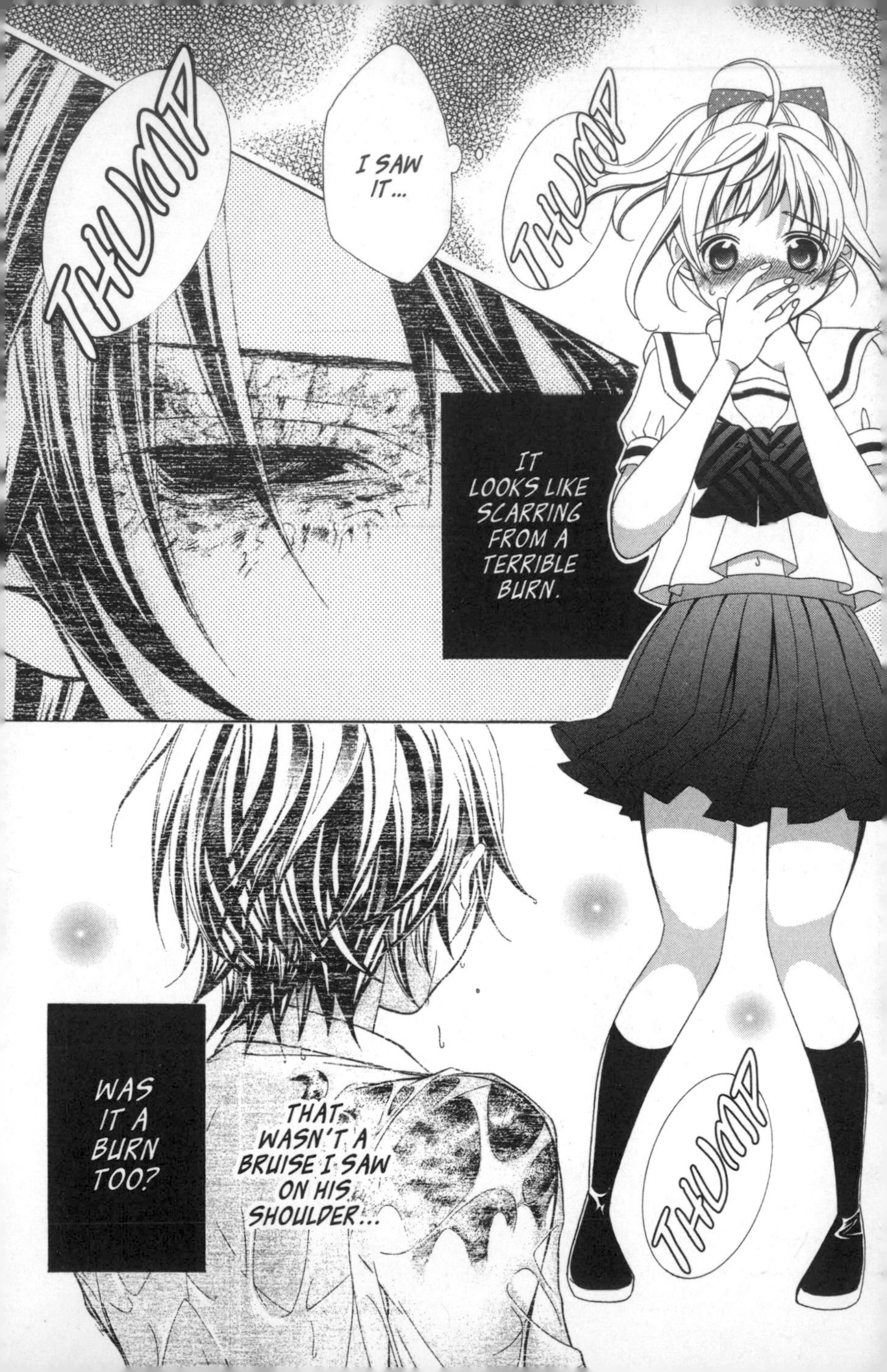
THUMP
I SAW IT...
THUMP
IT LOOKS LIKE SCARRING FROM A TERRIBLE BURN.
THAT WASN'T A BRUISE I SAW ON HIS SHOULDER...
WAS IT A BURN TOO?
THUMP

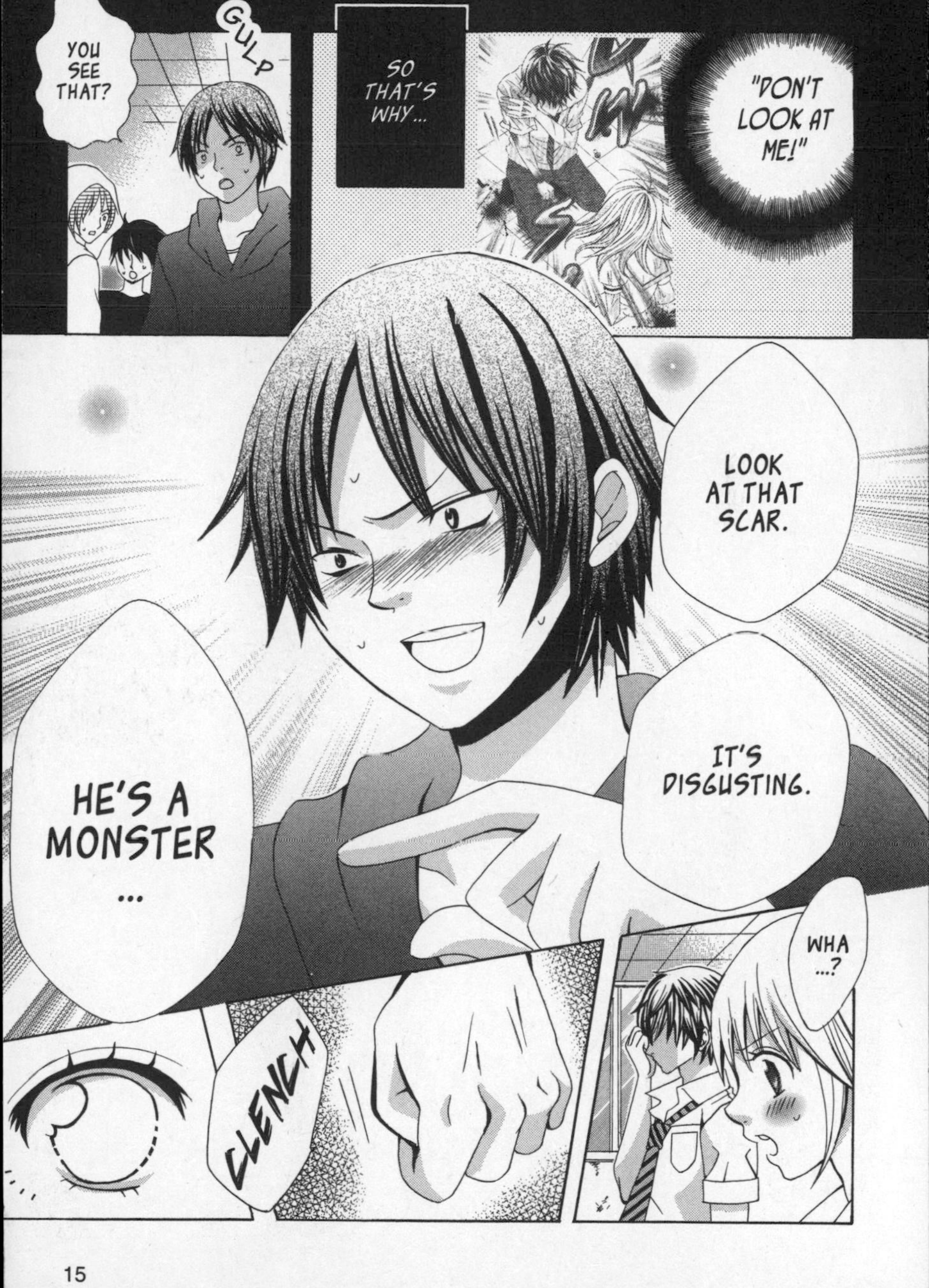
"DON'T LOOK AT ME!"
SO THAT'S WHY...
YOU SEE THAT?
GULP
LOOK AT THAT SCAR.
IT'S DISGUSTING.
HE'S A MONSTER ...
WHA ...?
CLENCH
....

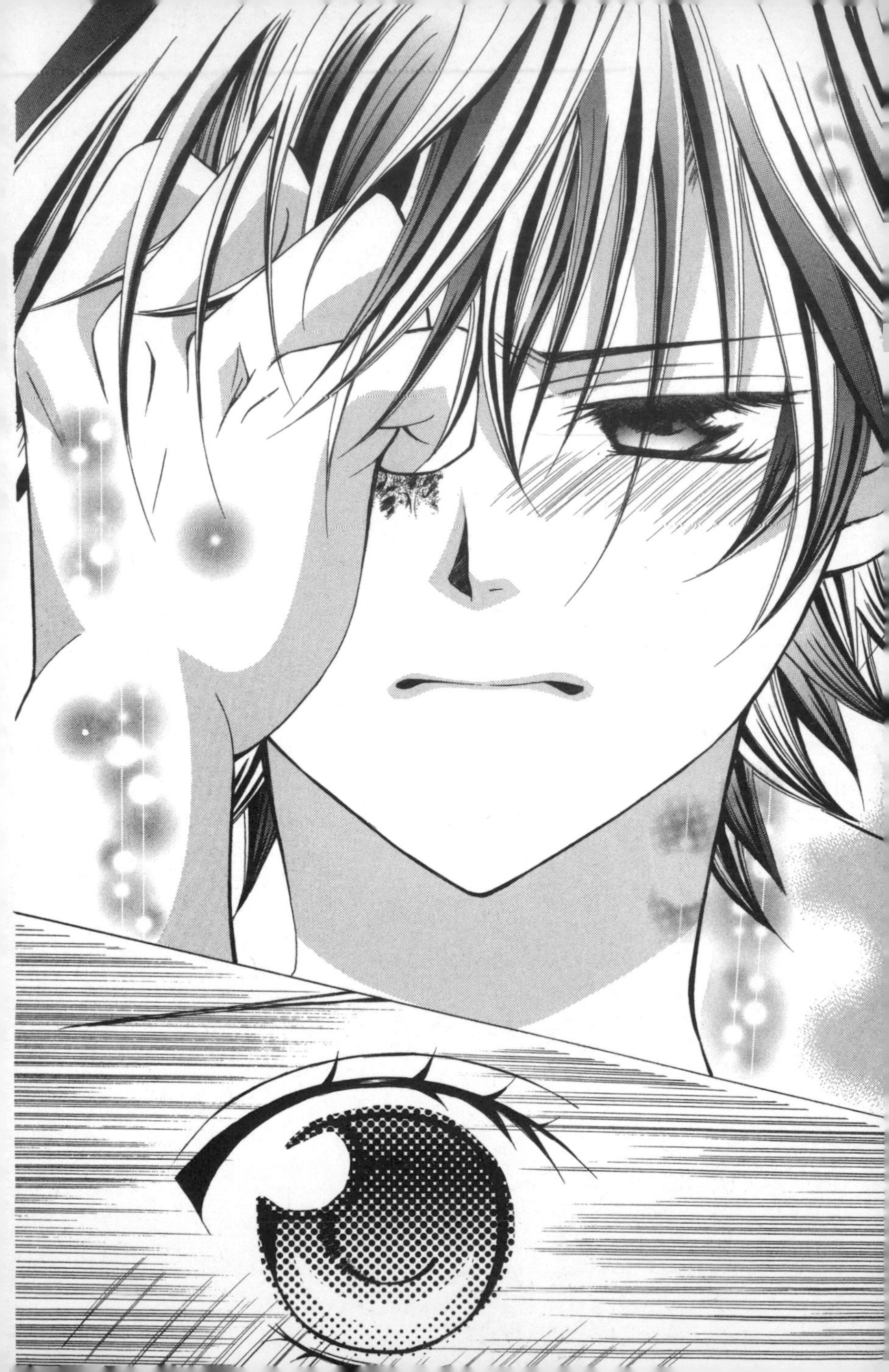

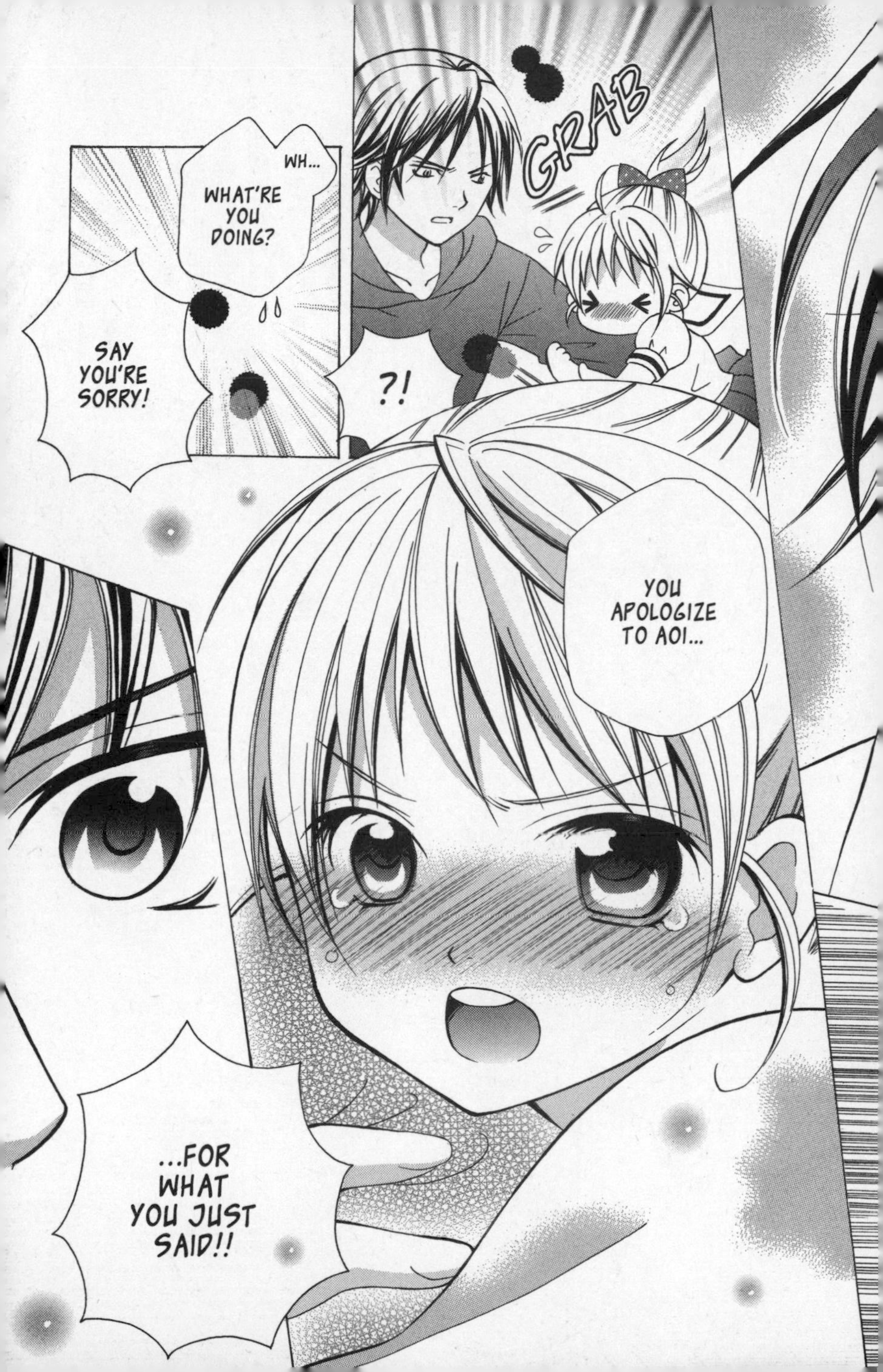
GRAB
?!
WH... WHAT'RE YOU DOING?
SAY YOU'RE SORRY!
YOU APOLOGIZE TO AOI...
...FOR WHAT YOU JUST SAID!!

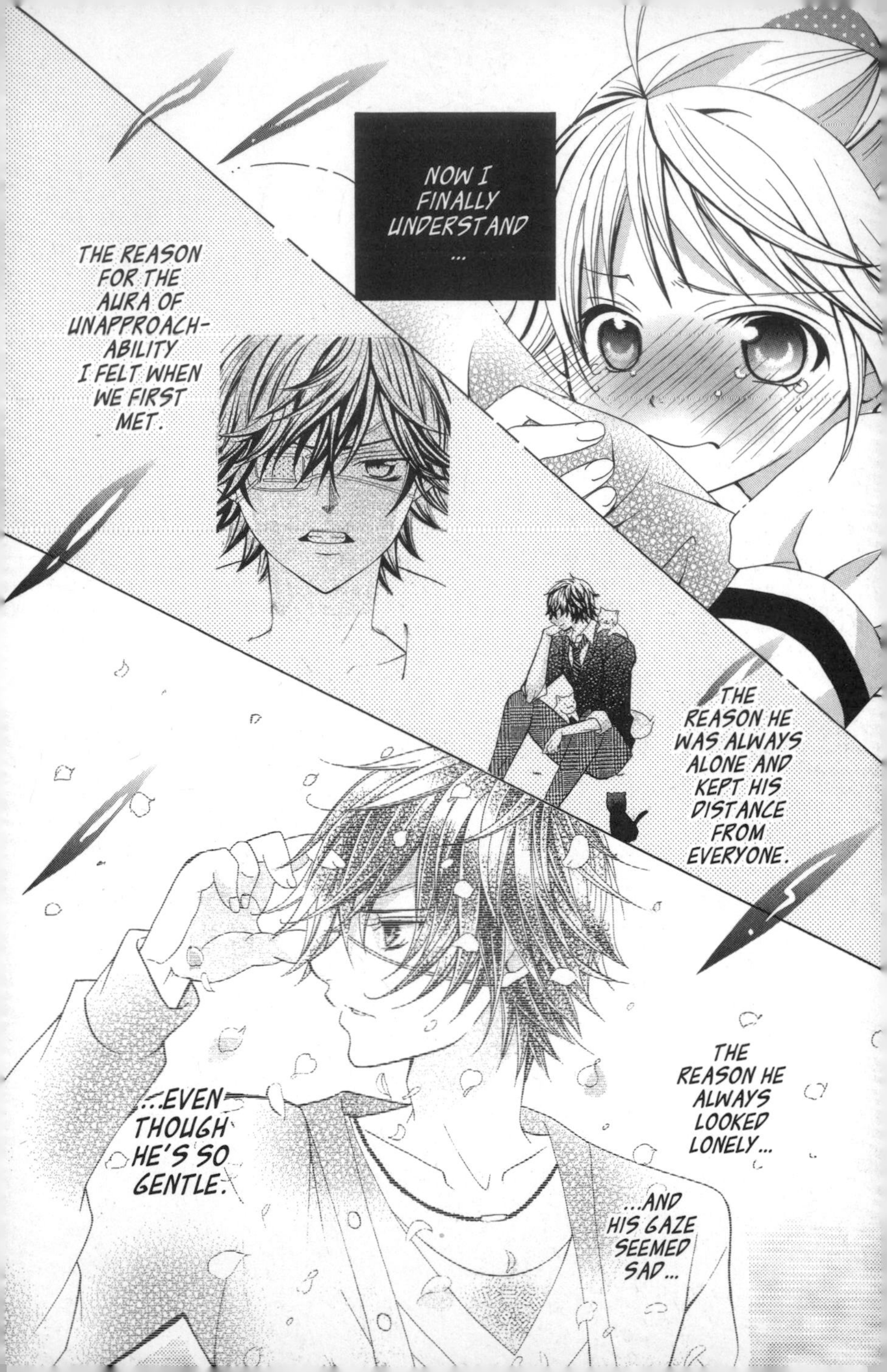
NOW I FINALLY UNDERSTAND ...
THE REASON FOR THE AURA OF UNAPPROACH-ABILITY I FELT WHEN WE FIRST MET.
THE REASON HE WAS ALWAYS ALONE AND KEPT HIS DISTANCE FROM EVERYONE.
THE REASON HE ALWAYS LOOKED LONELY...
...AND HIS GAZE SEEMED SAD...
...EVEN THOUGH HE'S SO GENTLE.

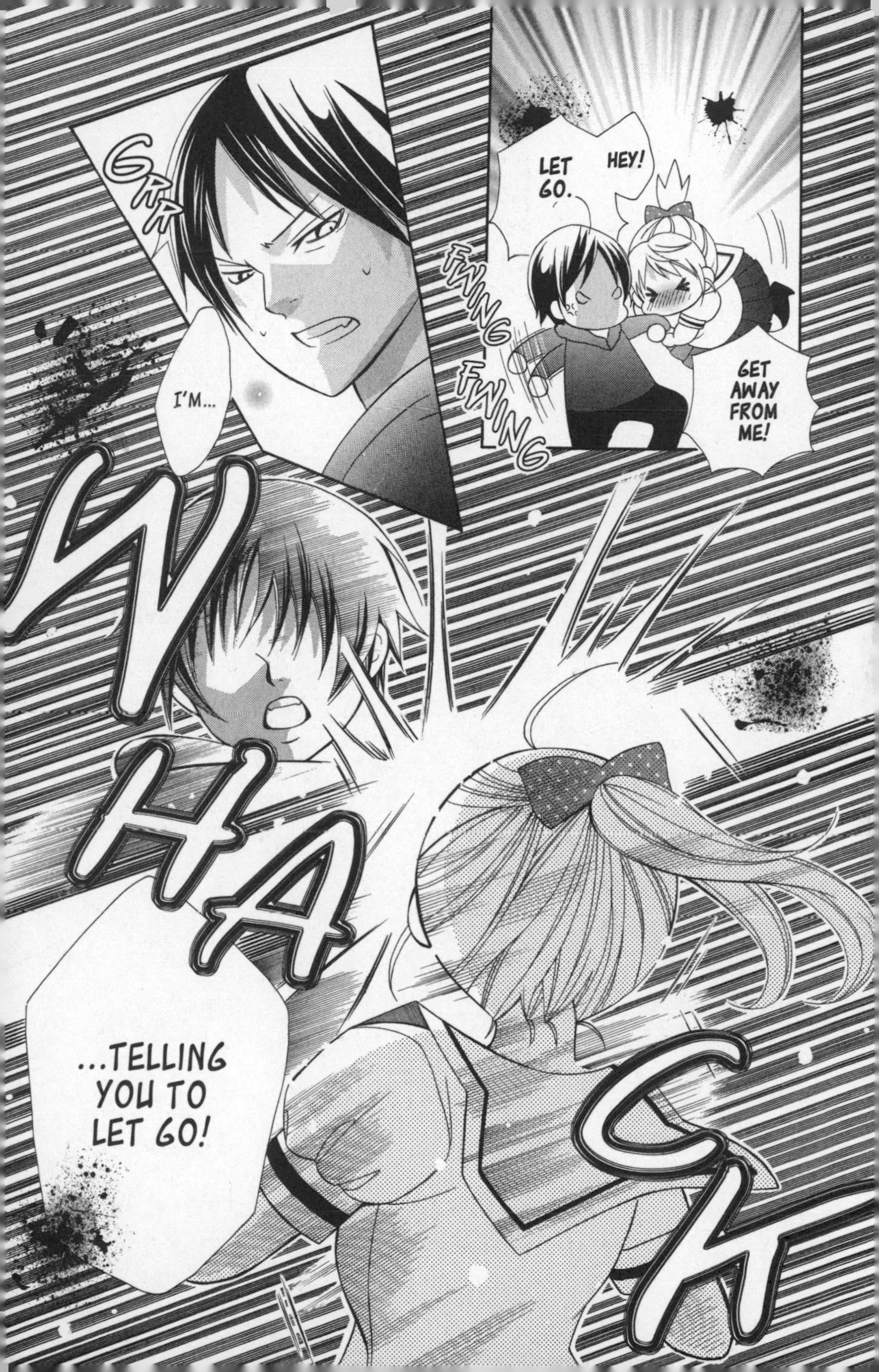
HEY!
LET GO.
GET AWAY FROM ME!
FWING FWING
GRR
I'M...
WHACK
...TELLING YOU TO LET GO!

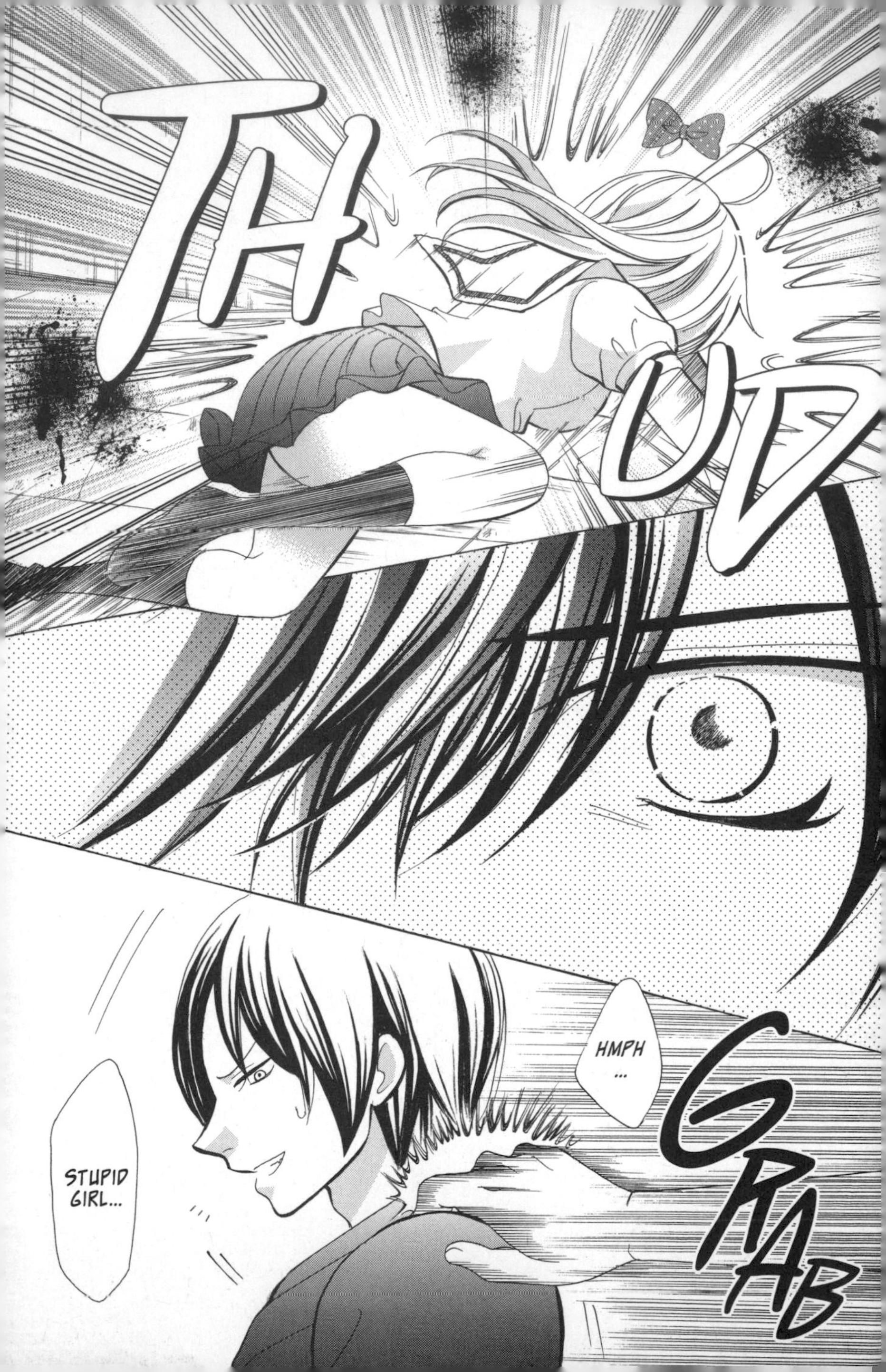
THUD
HMPH ...
GRAB
STUPID GIRL...

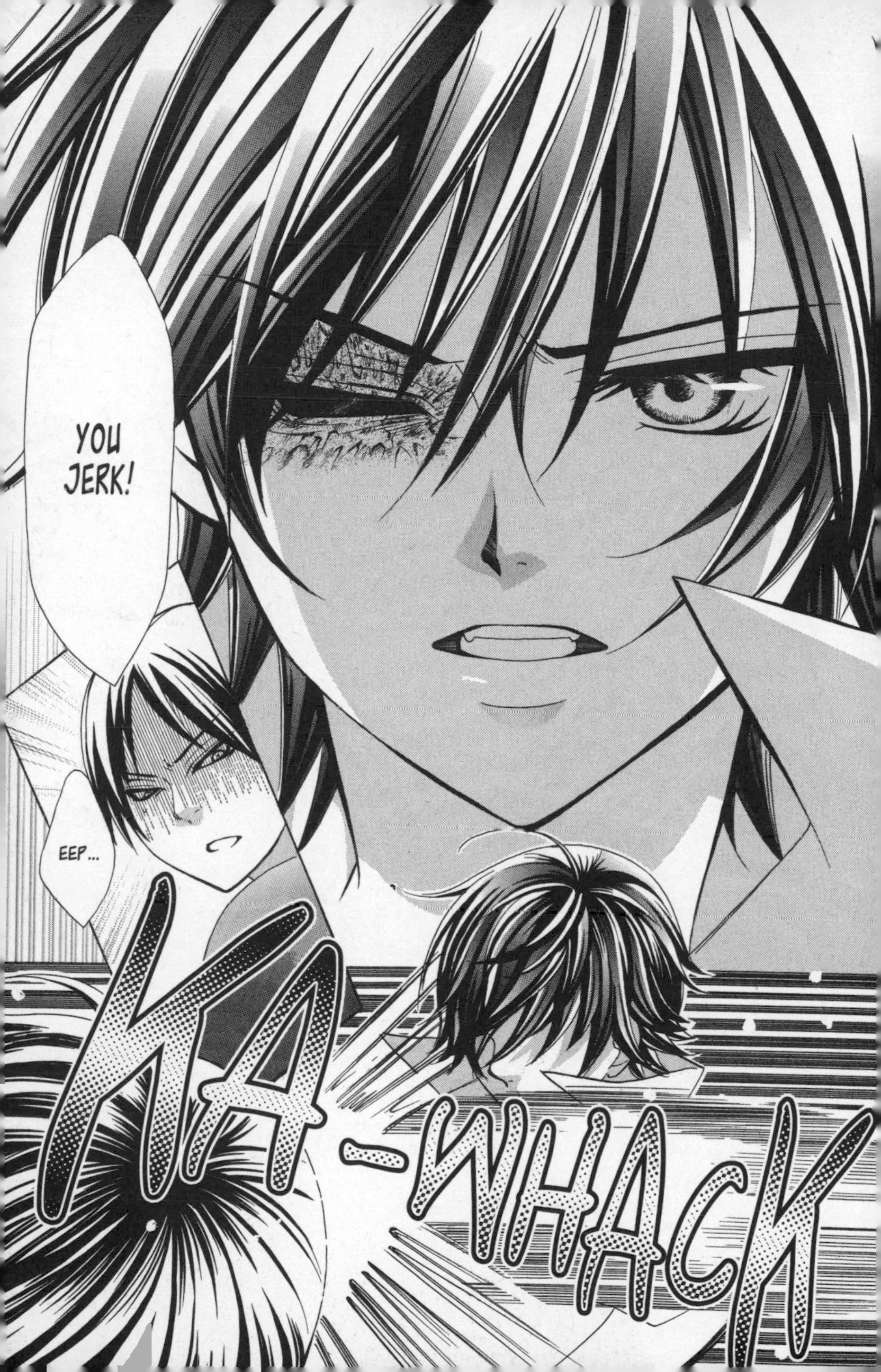
YOU JERK!
EEP...
KA-WHACK

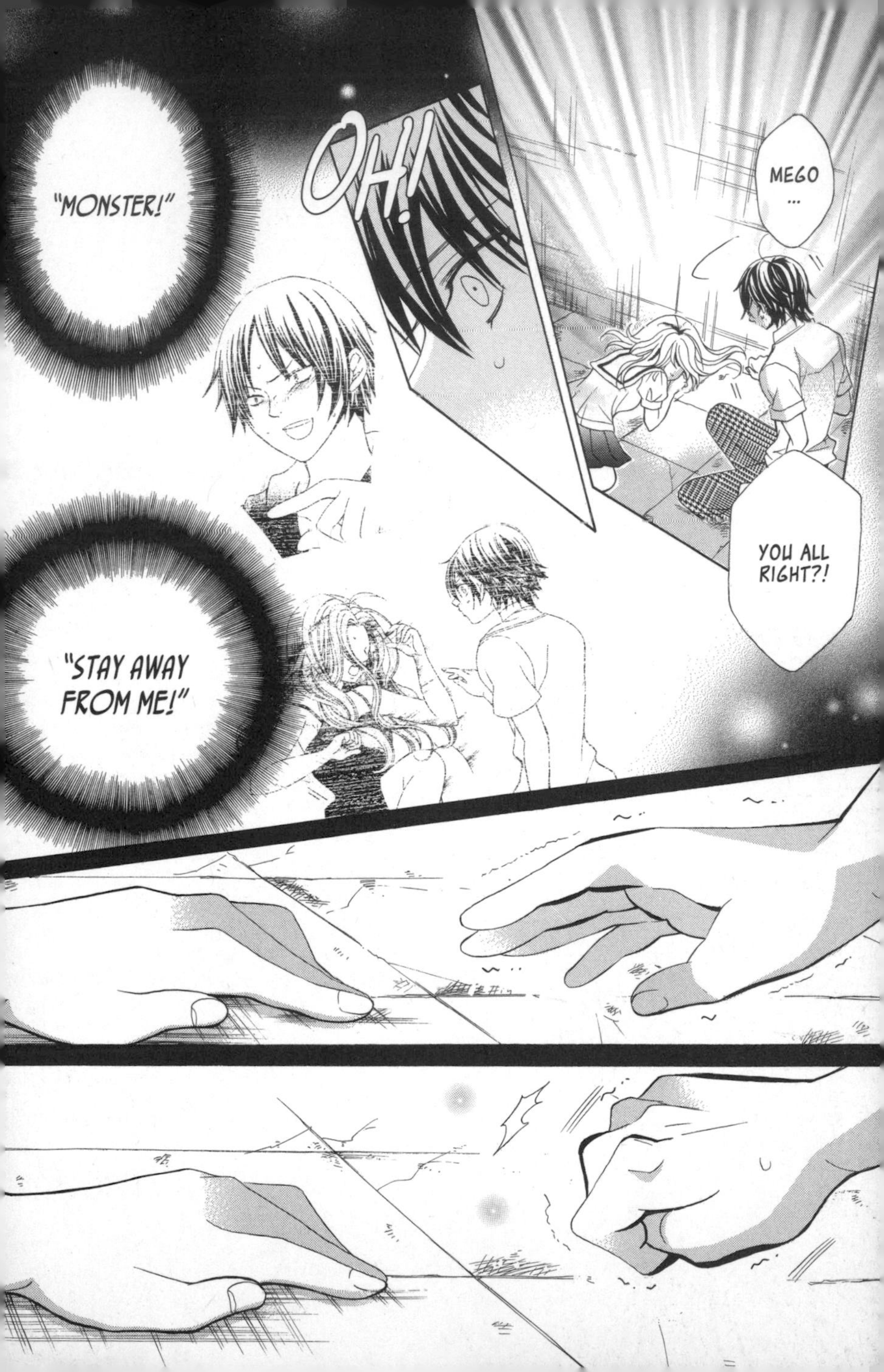
MEGO ...
YOU ALL RIGHT?!
OH!
"MONSTER!"
"STAY AWAY FROM ME!"

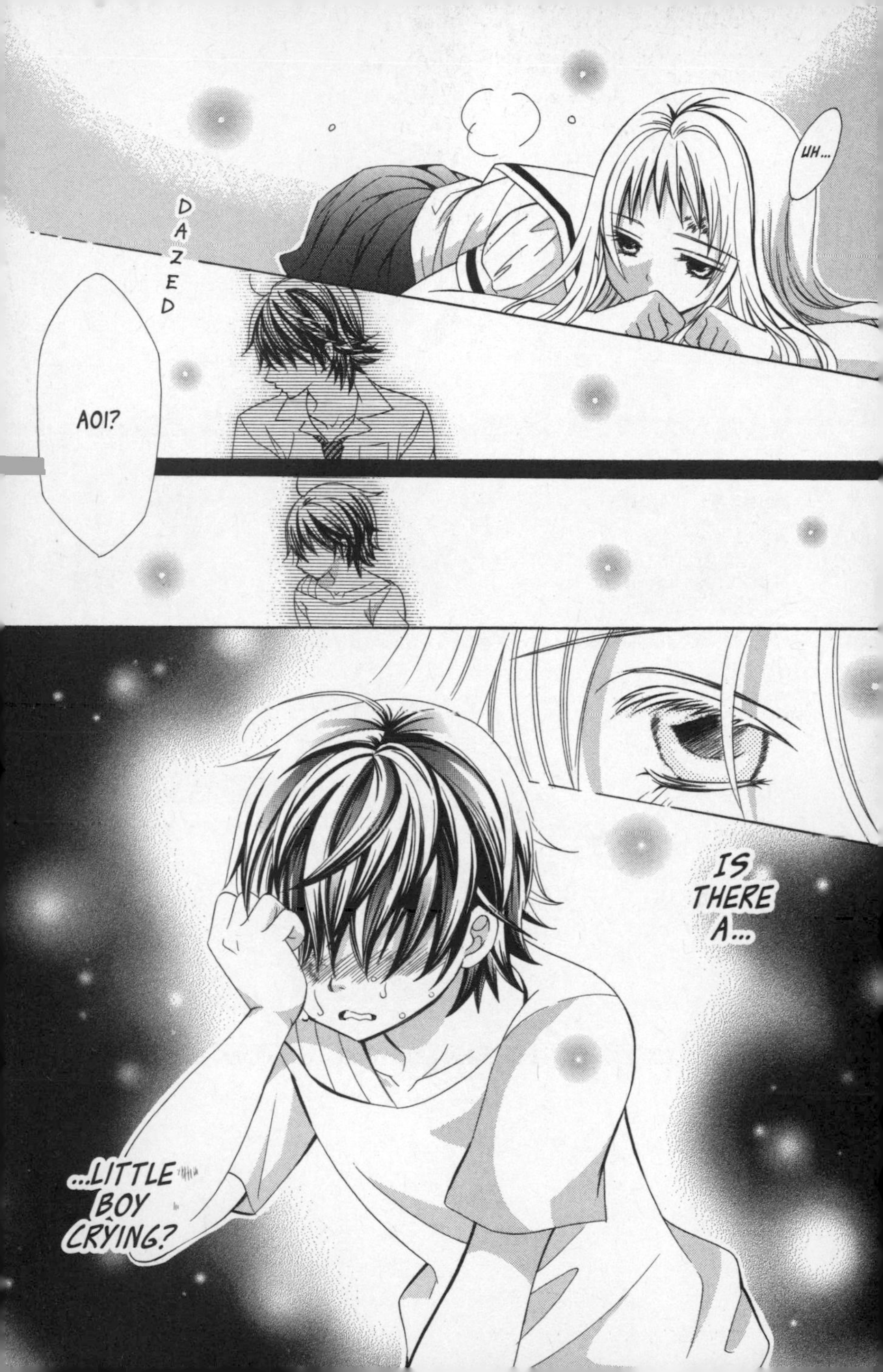
UH...
DAZED
AOI?
IS THERE A...
...LITTLE BOY CRYING?

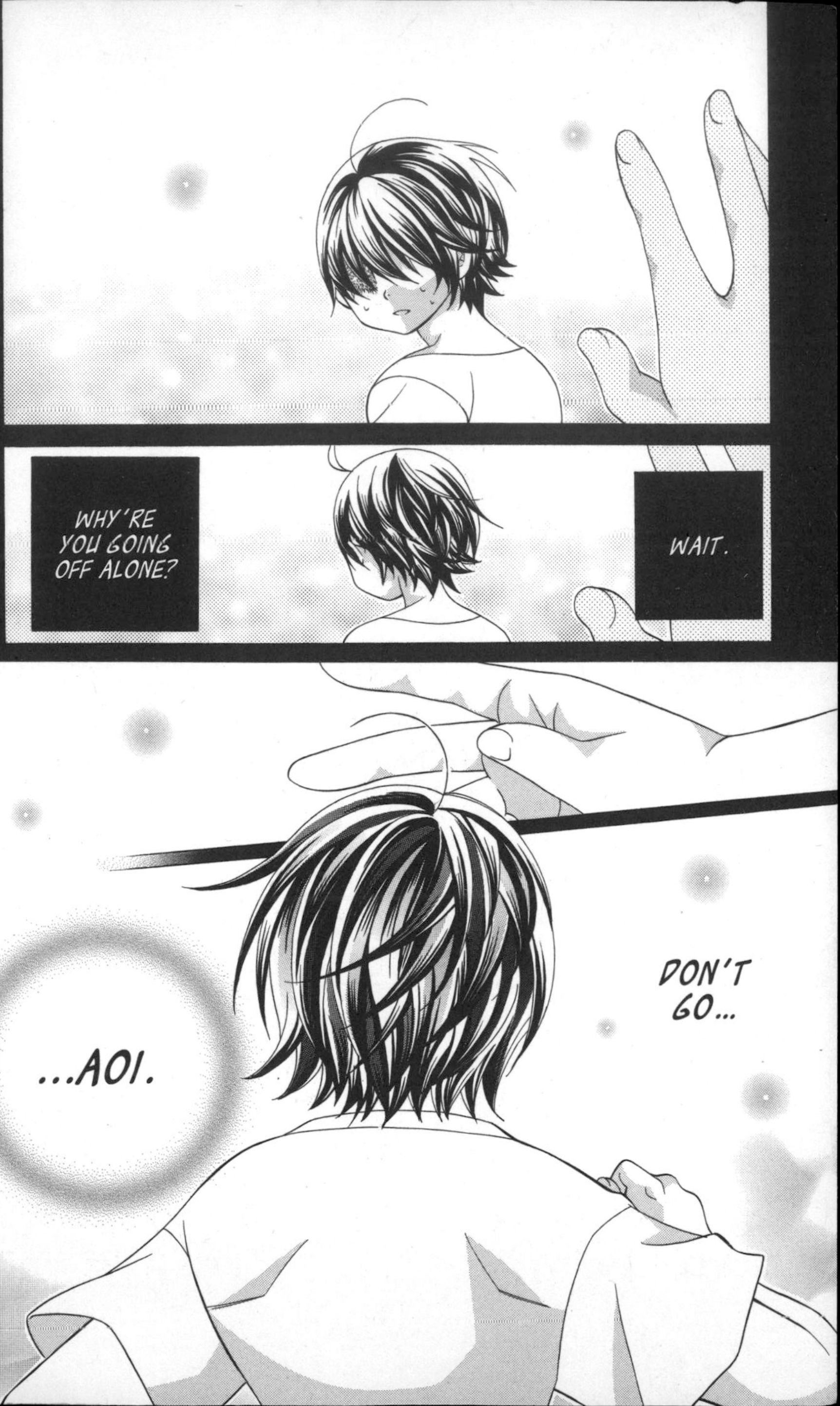
WAIT.
WHY'RE YOU GOING OFF ALONE?
DON'T GO...
...AOI.

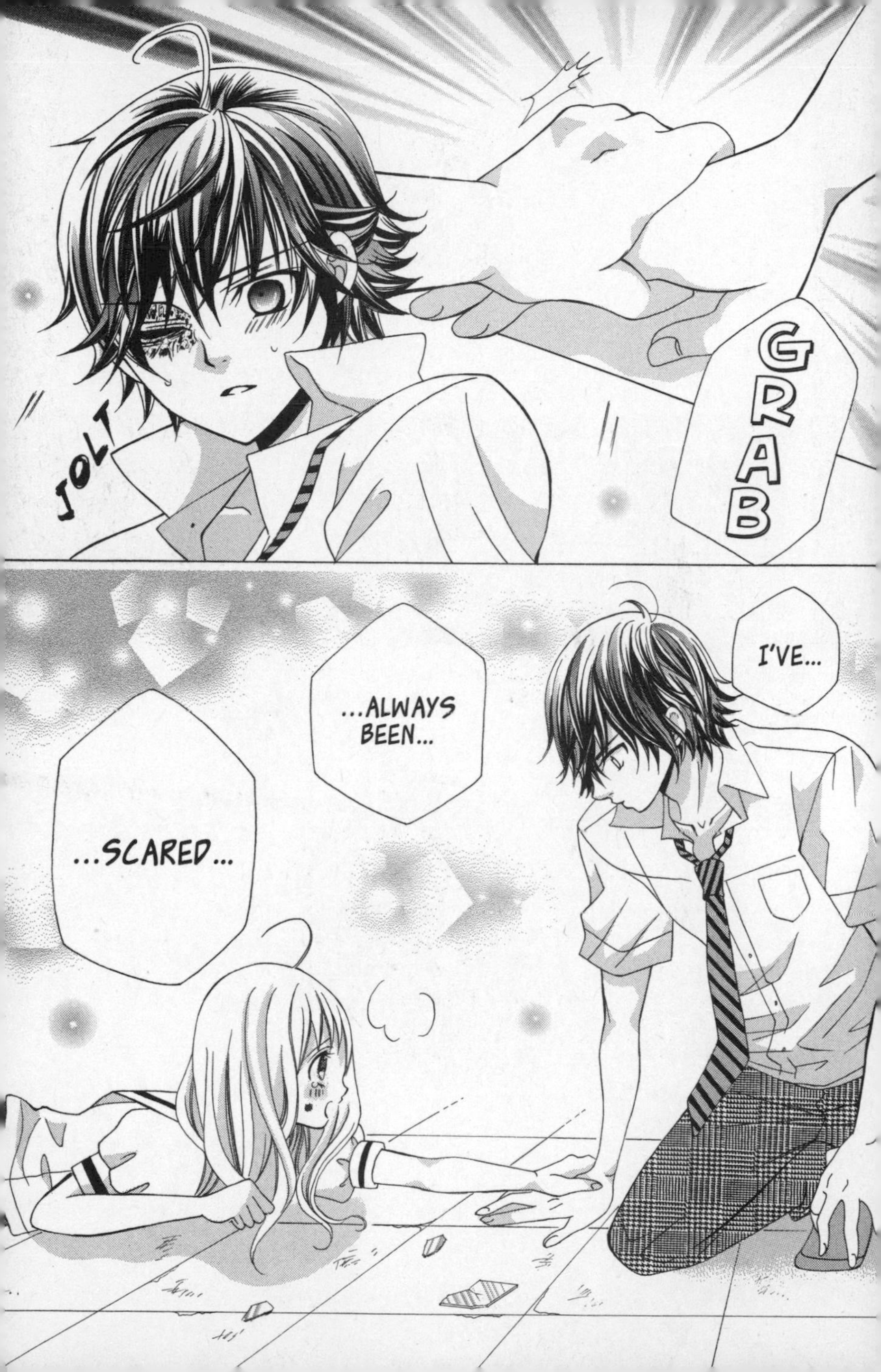
GRAB
JOLT
I'VE...
...ALWAYS BEEN...
...SCARED...

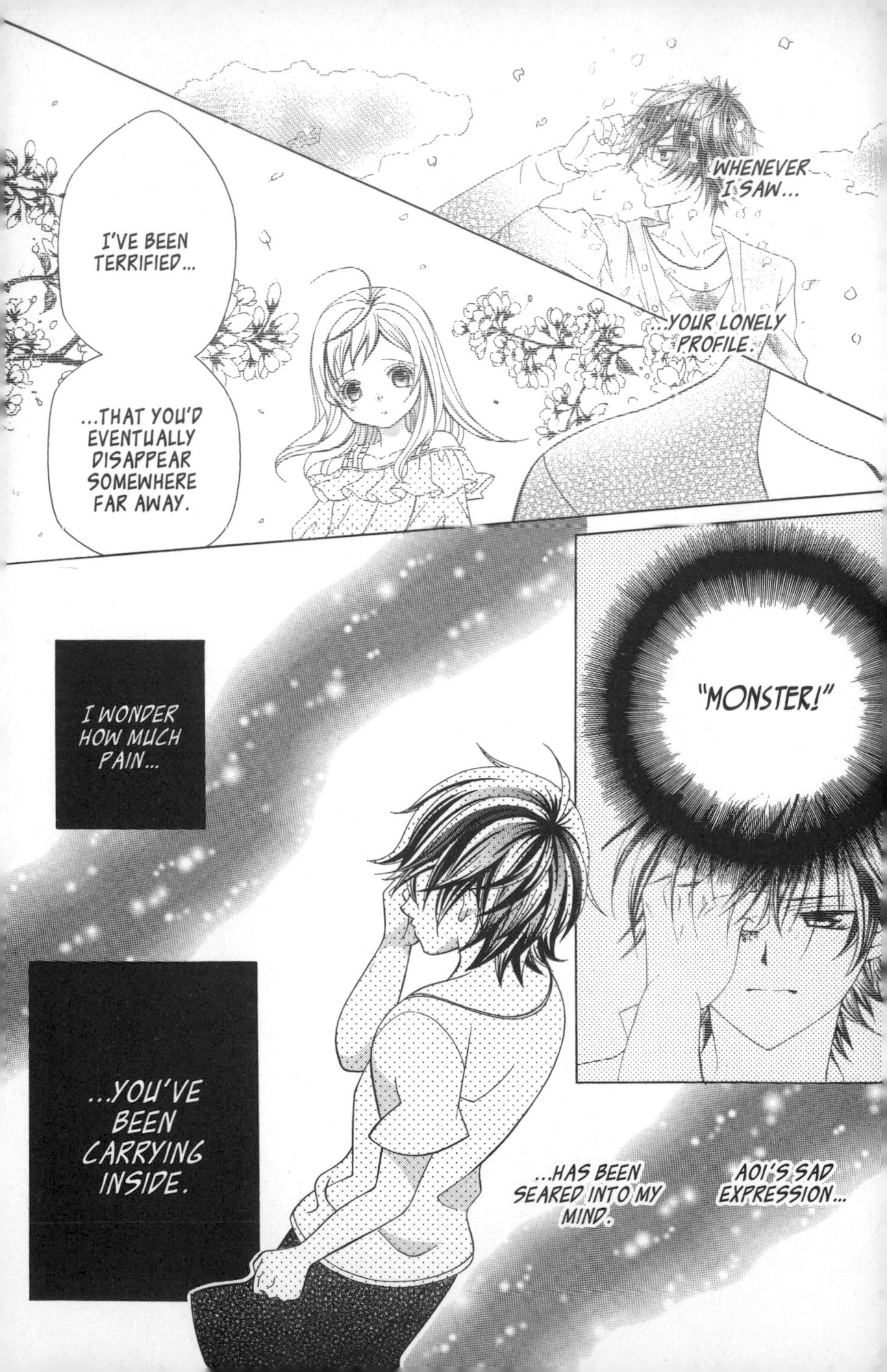
WHENEVER I SAW...
...YOUR LONELY PROFILE.
I'VE BEEN TERRIFIED...
...THAT YOU'D EVENTUALLY DISAPPEAR SOMEWHERE FAR AWAY.
"MONSTER!"
AOI'S SAD EXPRESSION...
...HAS BEEN SEARED INTO MY MIND.
I WONDER HOW MUCH PAIN...
...YOU'VE BEEN CARRYING INSIDE.

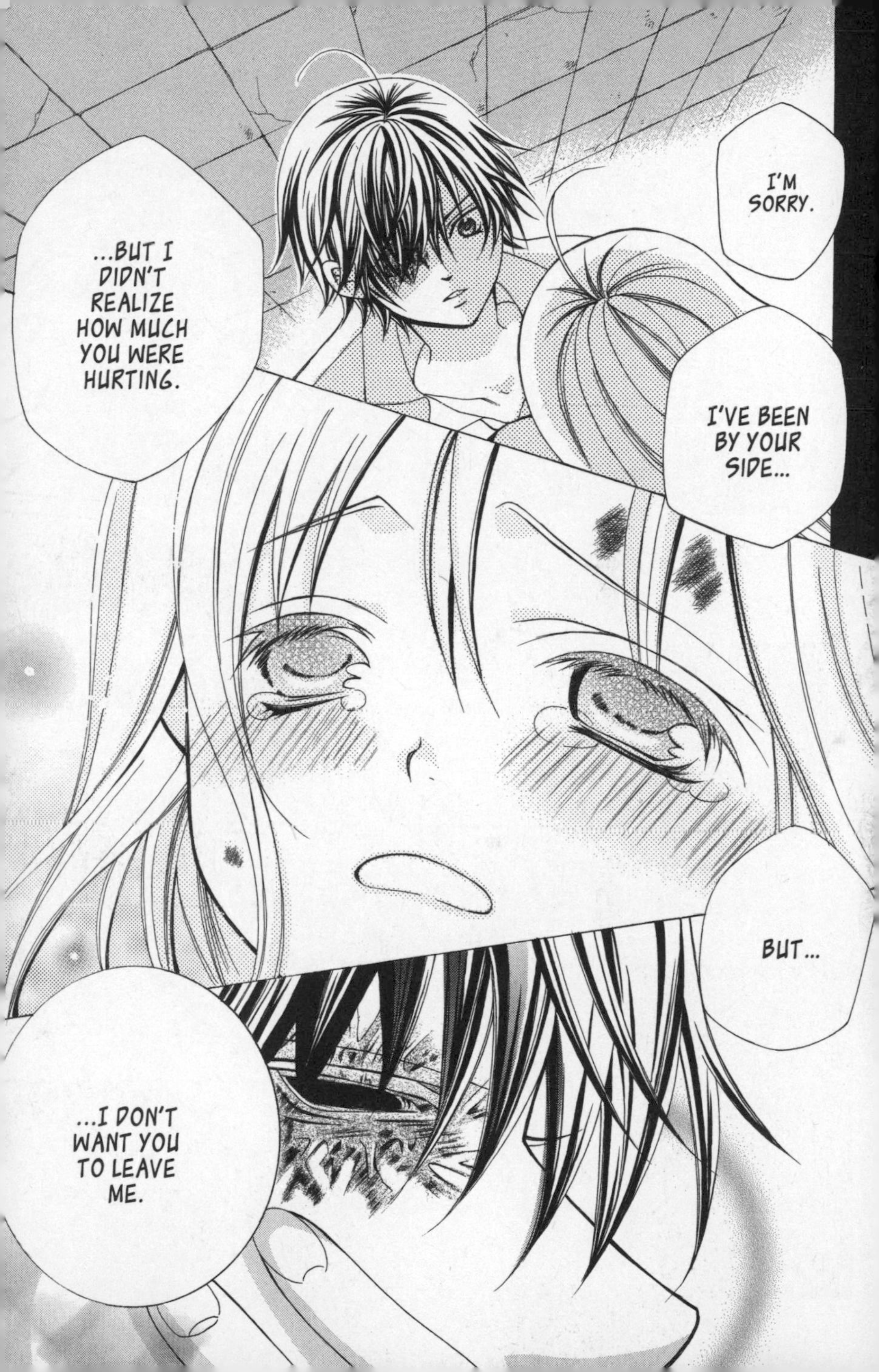
I'M SORRY.
I'VE BEEN BY YOUR SIDE...
...BUT I DIDN'T REALIZE HOW MUCH YOU WERE HURTING.
BUT...
...I DON'T WANT YOU TO LEAVE ME.

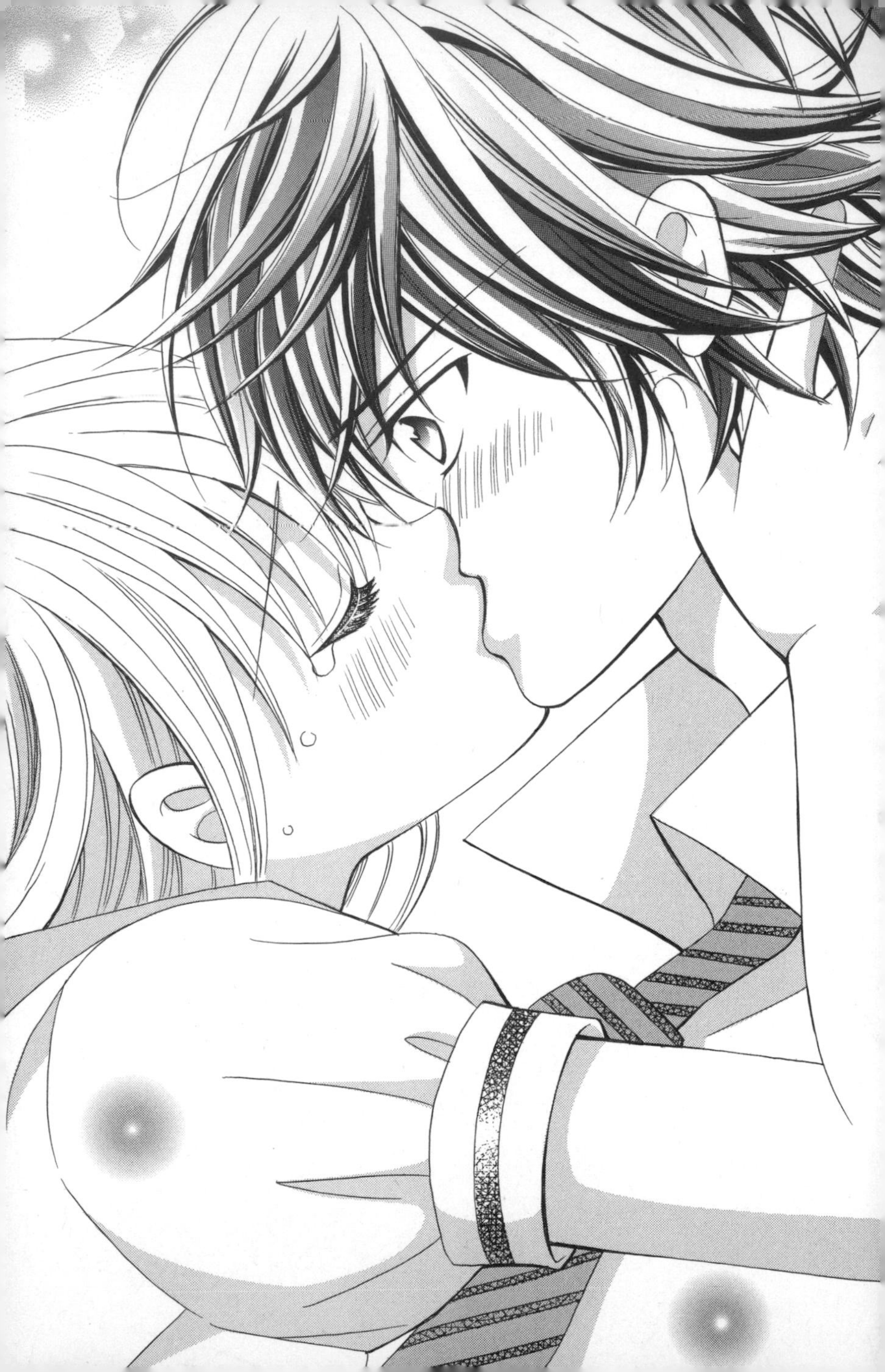

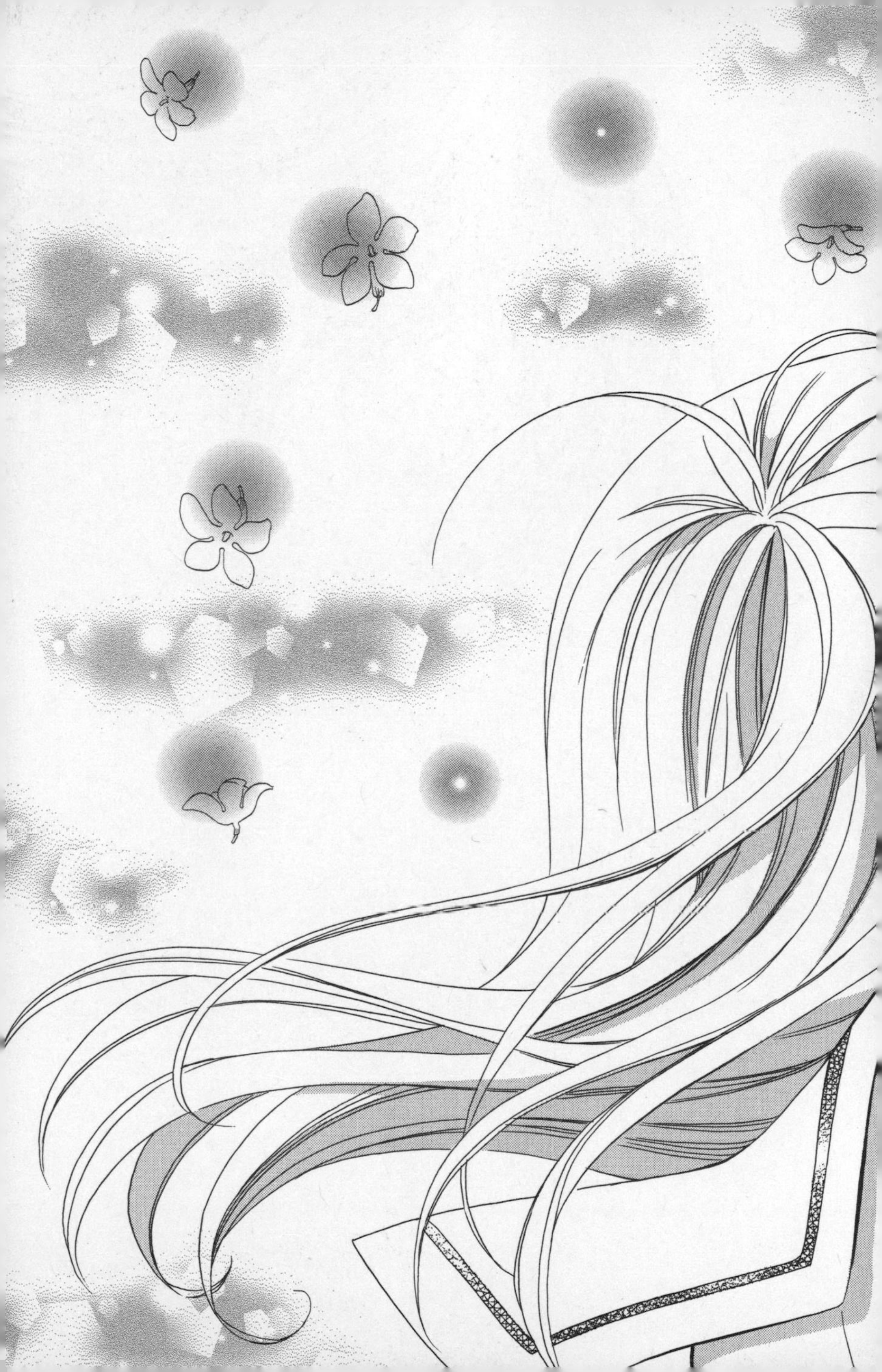

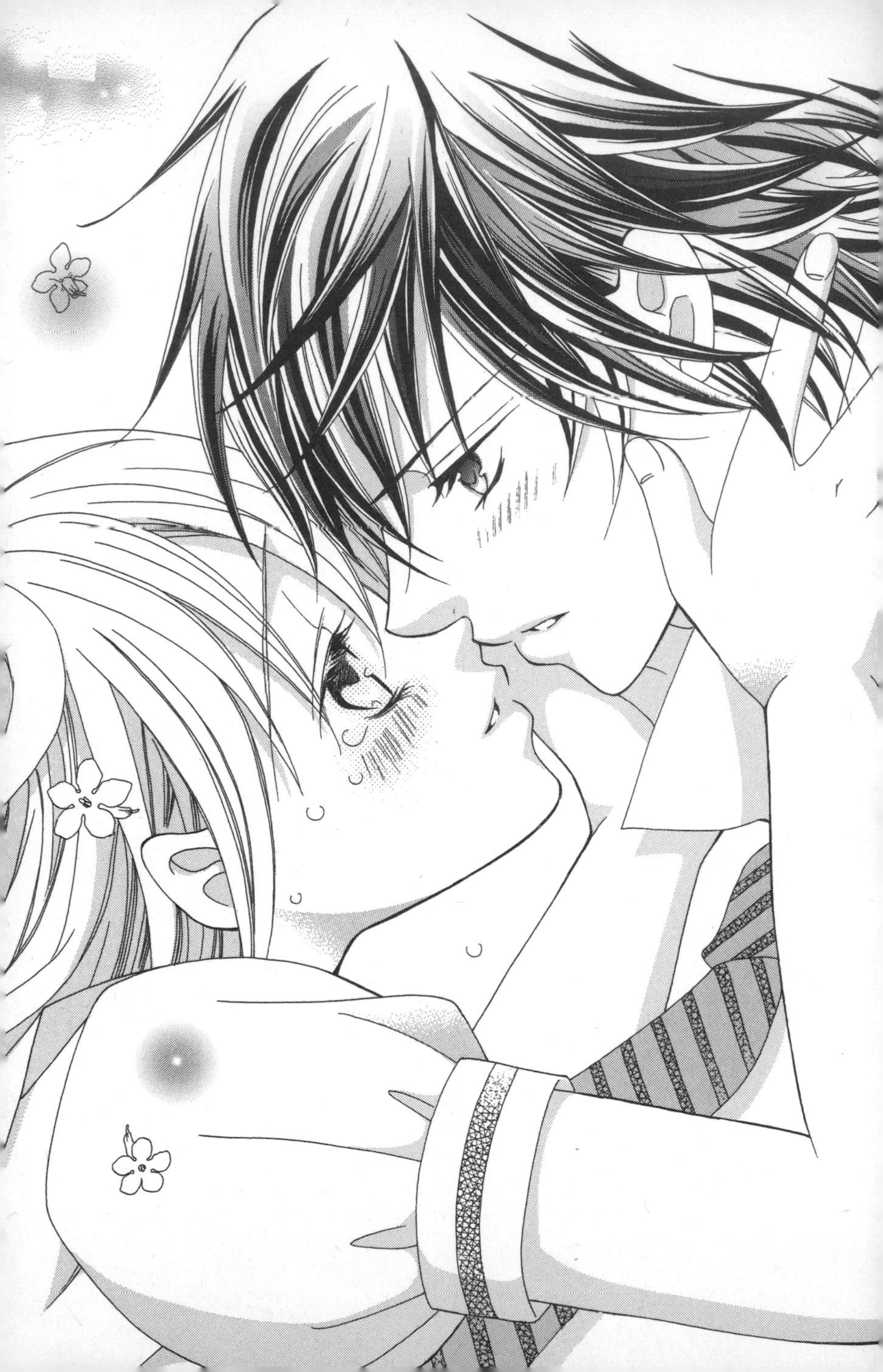

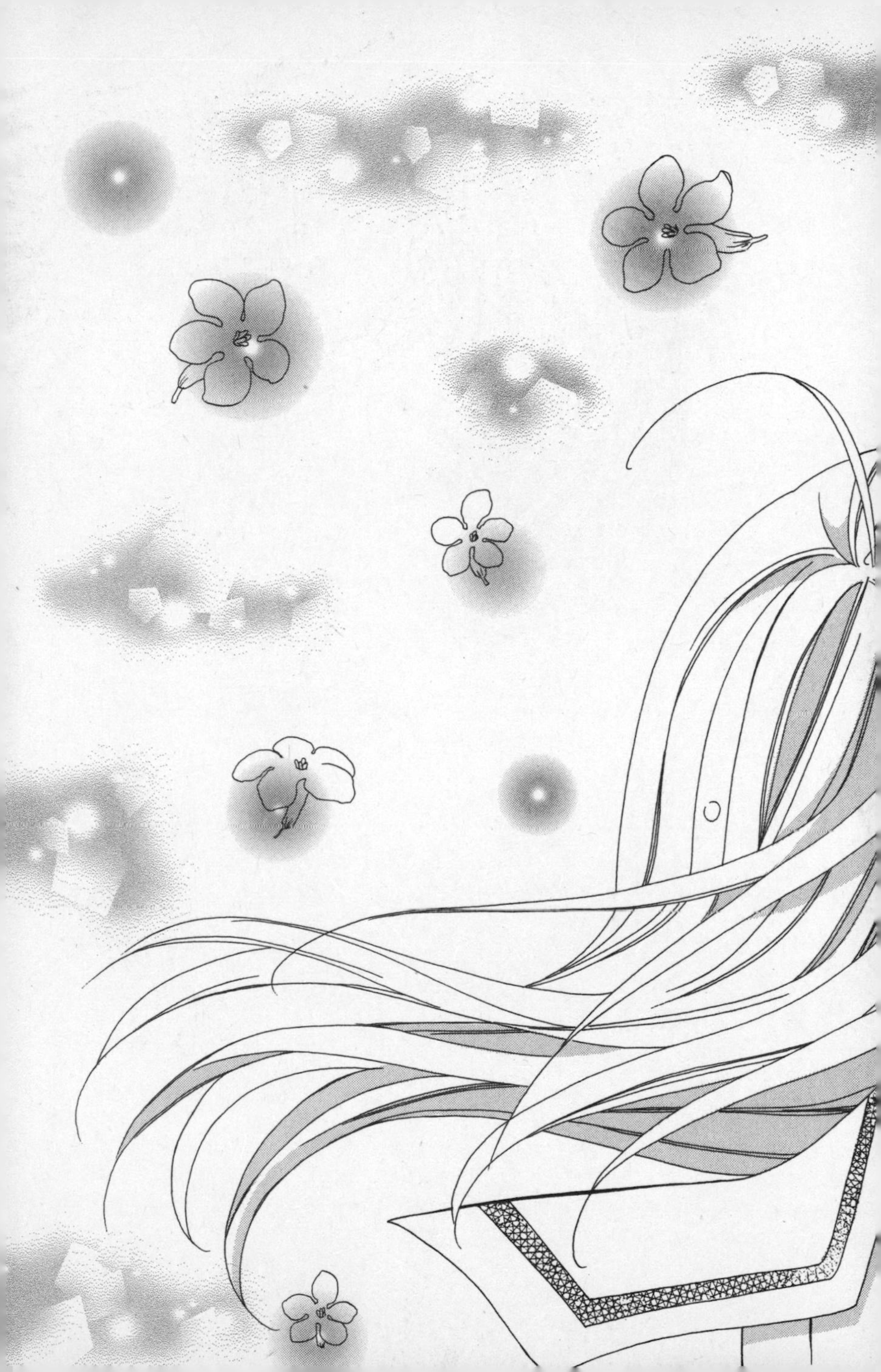

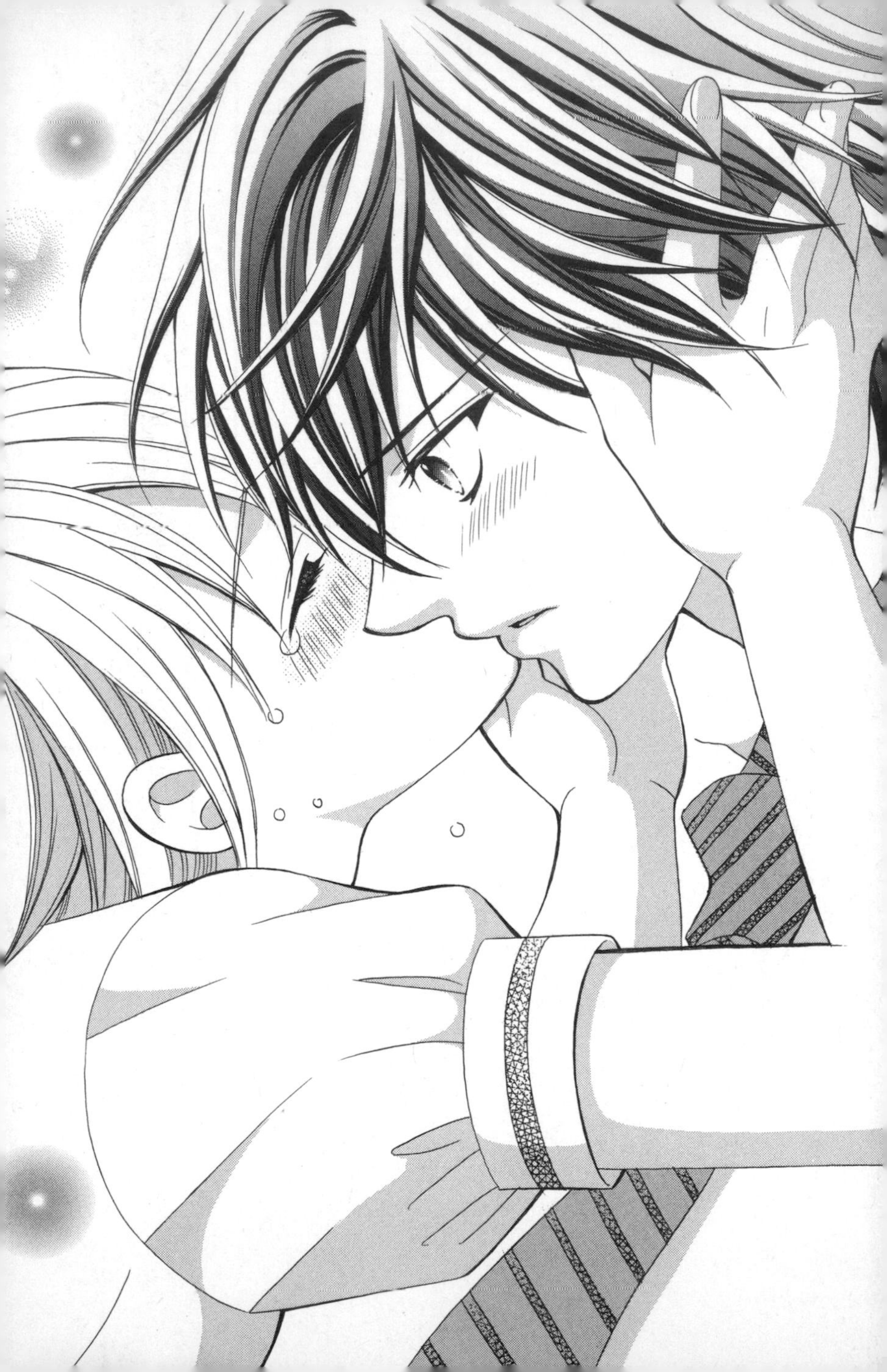

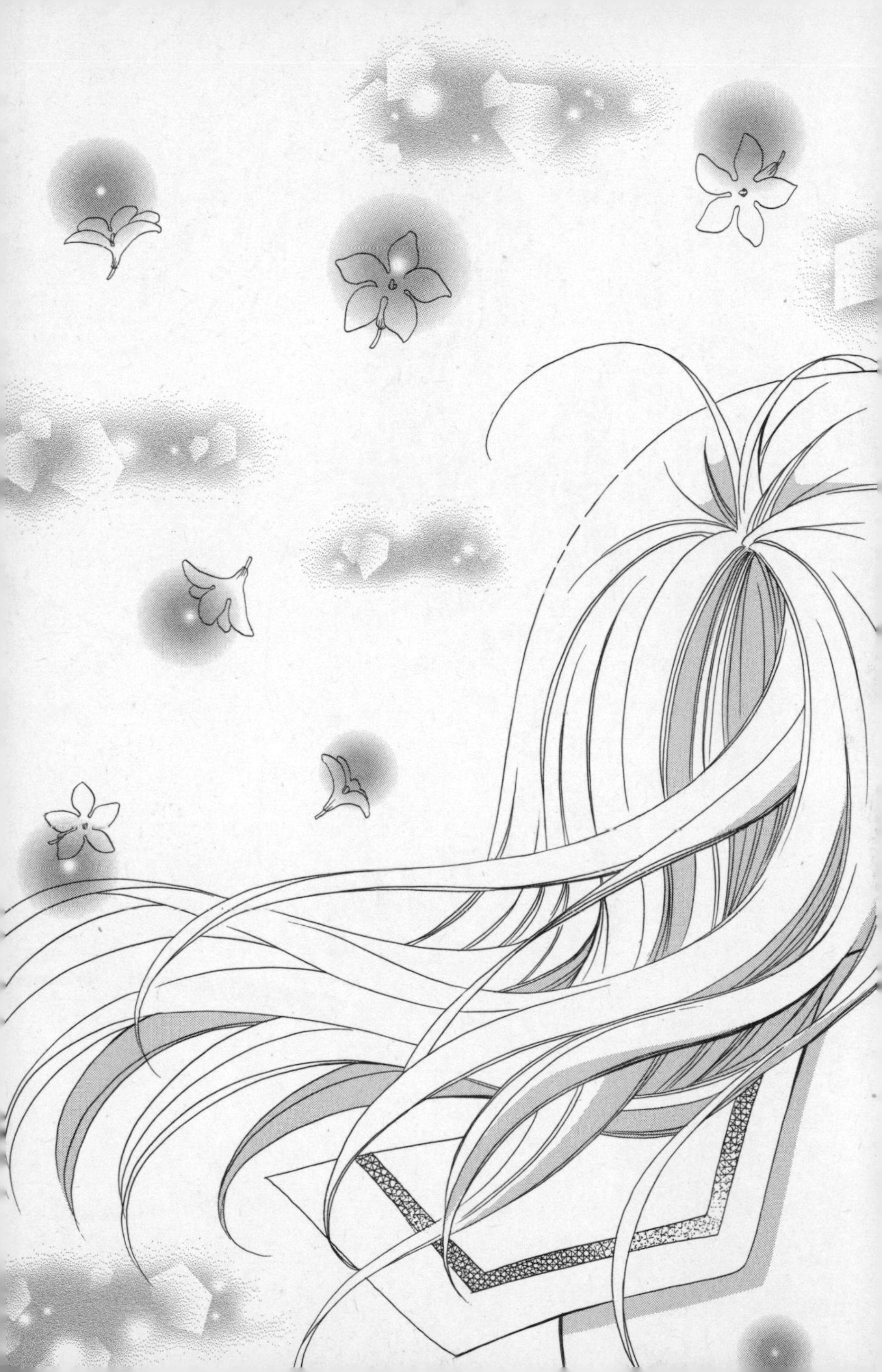

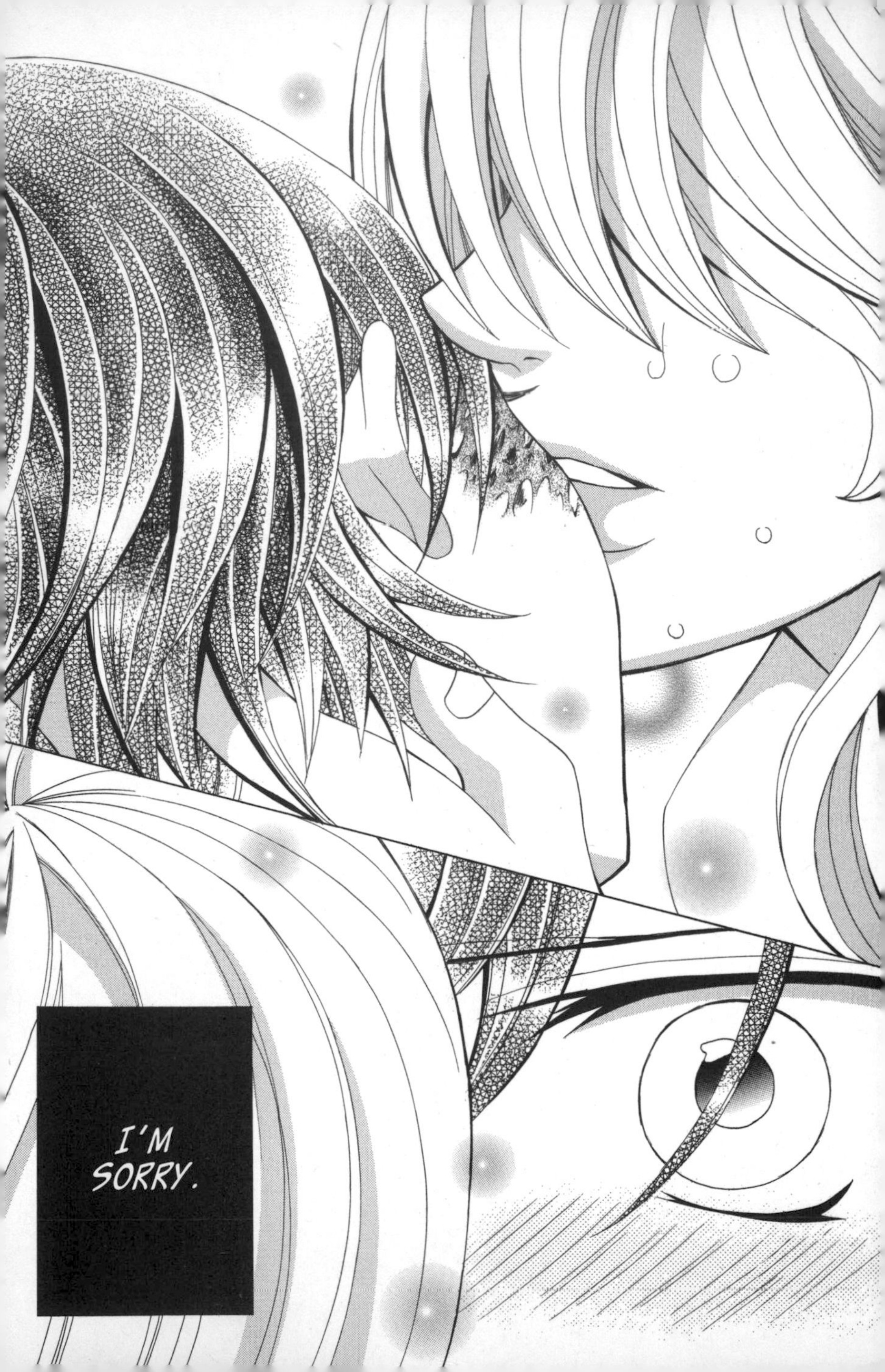
I'M SORRY.

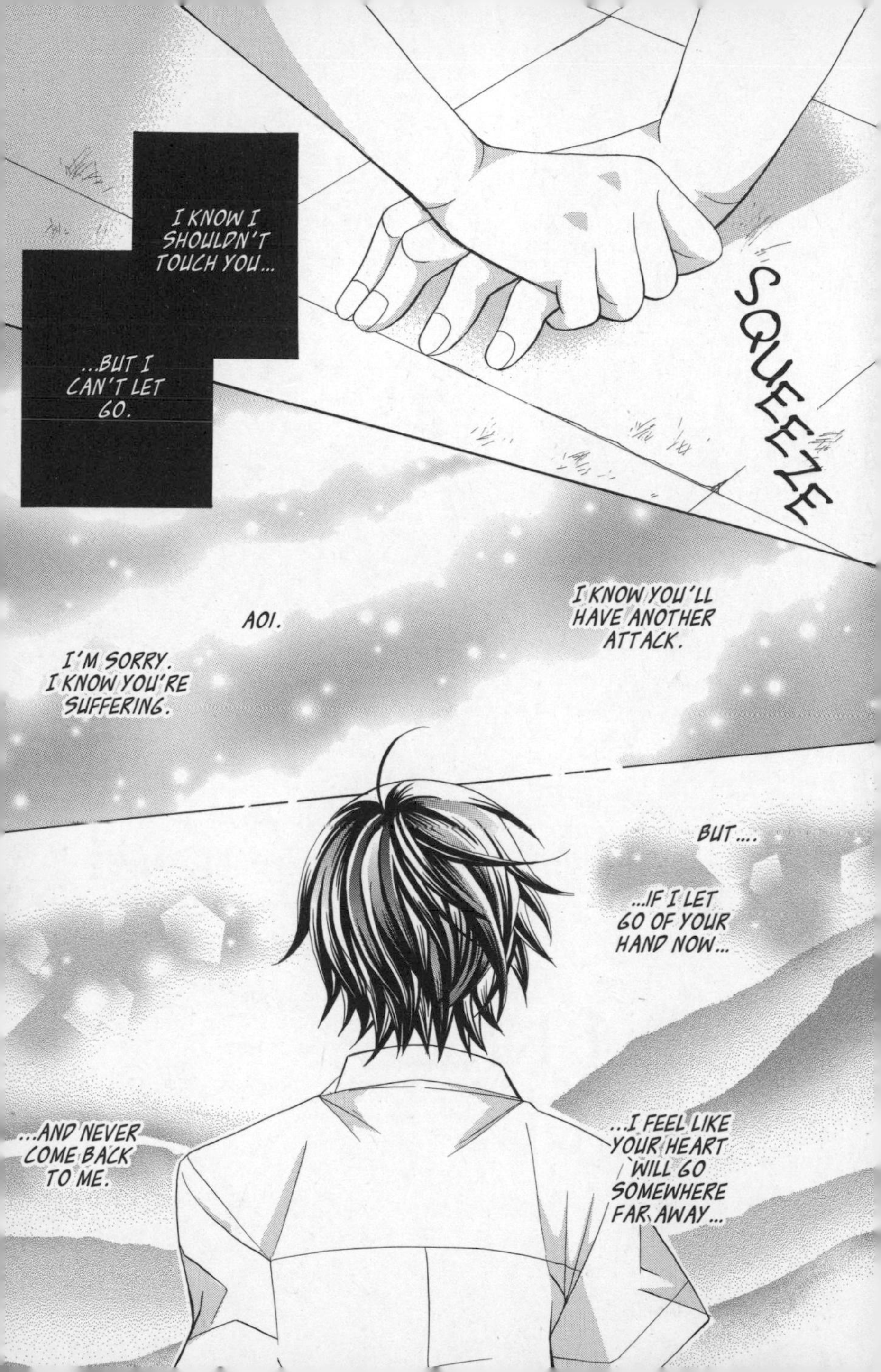
SQUEEZE
I KNOW I SHOULDN'T TOUCH YOU...
...BUT I CAN'T LET GO.
I KNOW YOU'LL HAVE ANOTHER ATTACK.
AOI.
I'M SORRY. I KNOW YOU'RE SUFFERING.
BUT....
...IF I LET GO OF YOUR HAND NOW...
...I FEEL LIKE YOUR HEART WILL GO SOMEWHERE FAR AWAY...
...AND NEVER COME BACK TO ME.

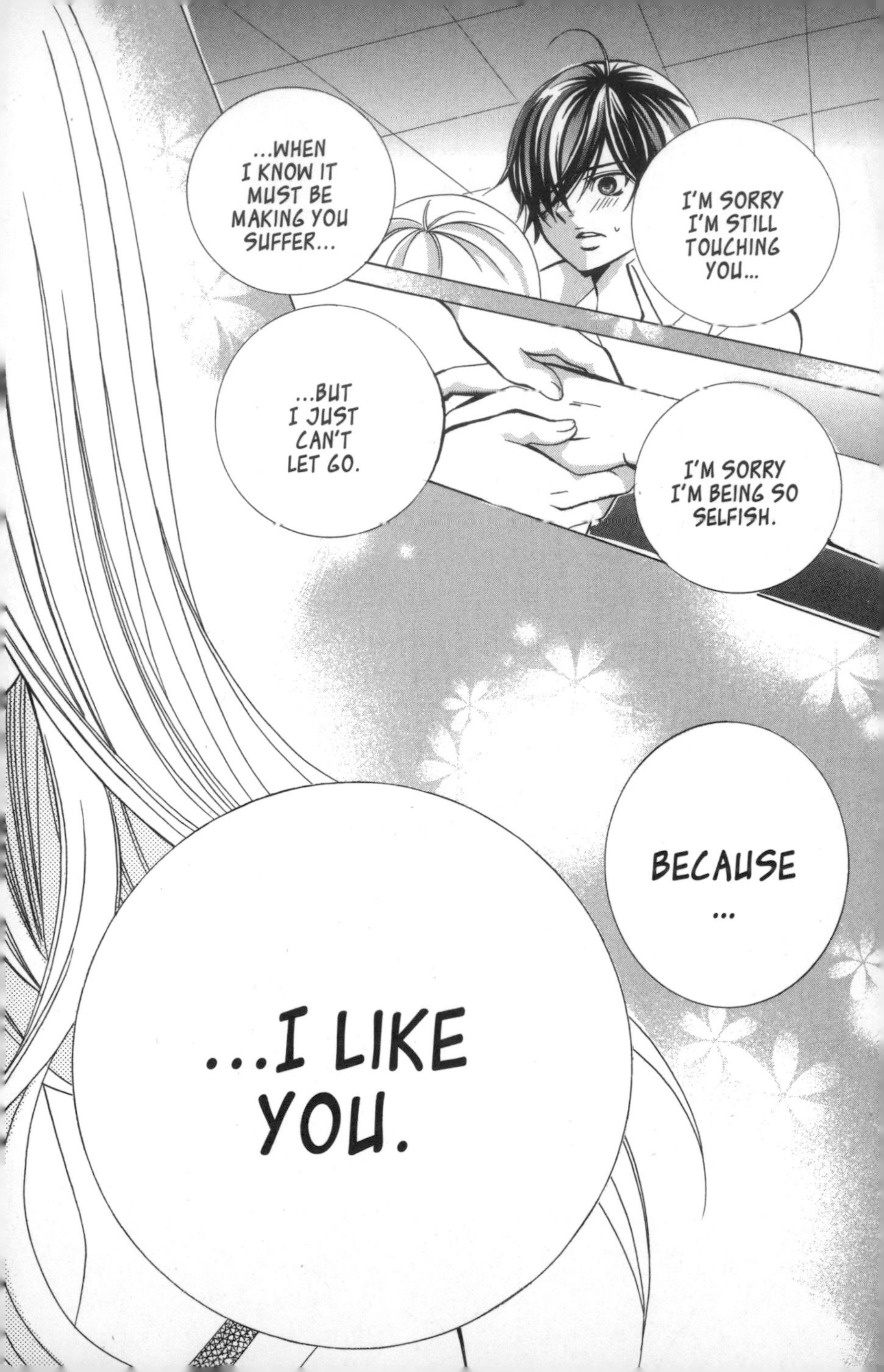
I'M SORRY I'M STILL TOUCHING YOU...
...WHEN I KNOW IT MUST BE MAKING YOU SUFFER...
I'M SORRY I'M BEING SO SELFISH.
...BUT I JUST CAN'T LET GO.
BECAUSE ...
...I LIKE YOU.

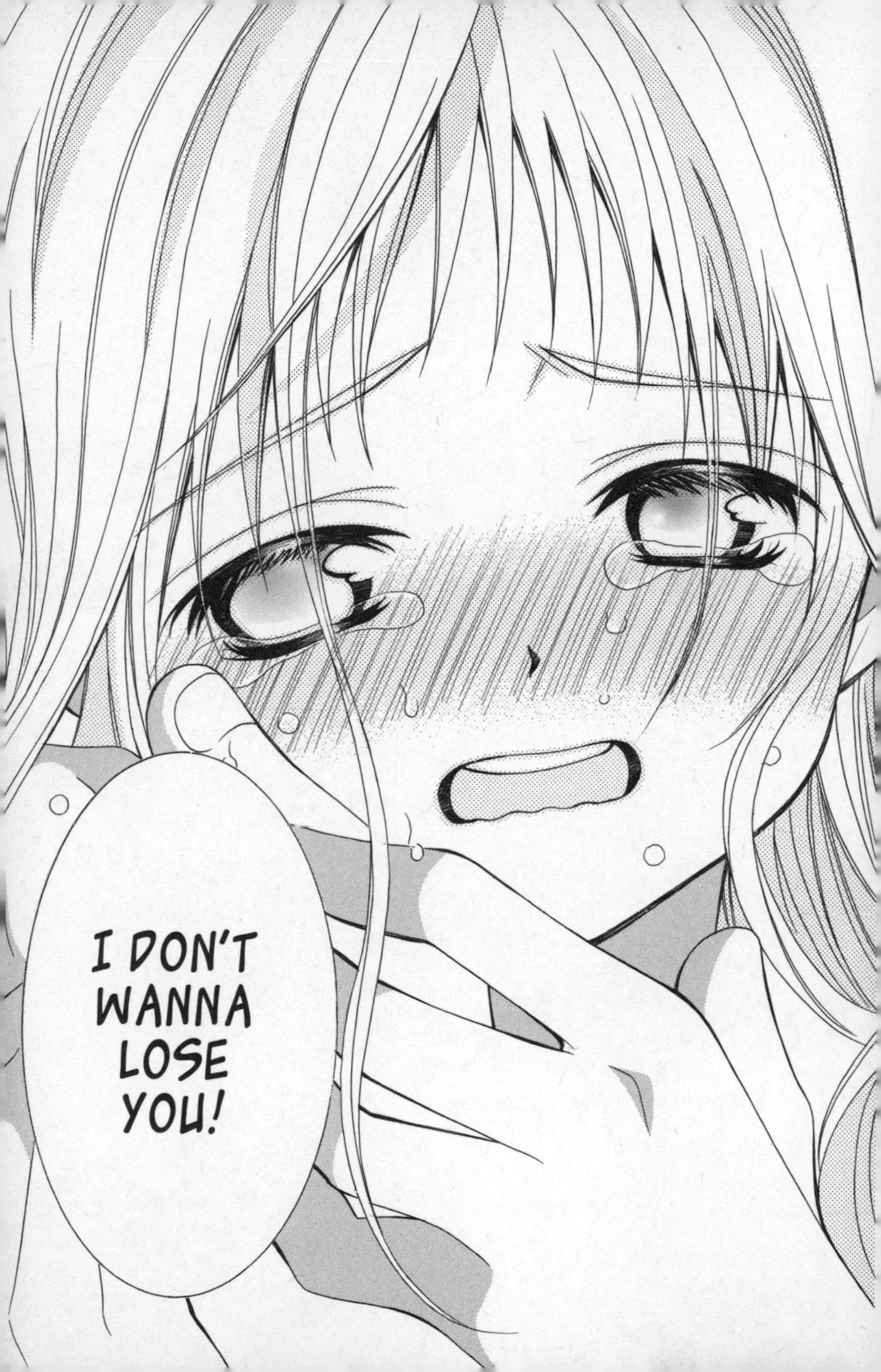
I DON'T WANNA LOSE YOU!

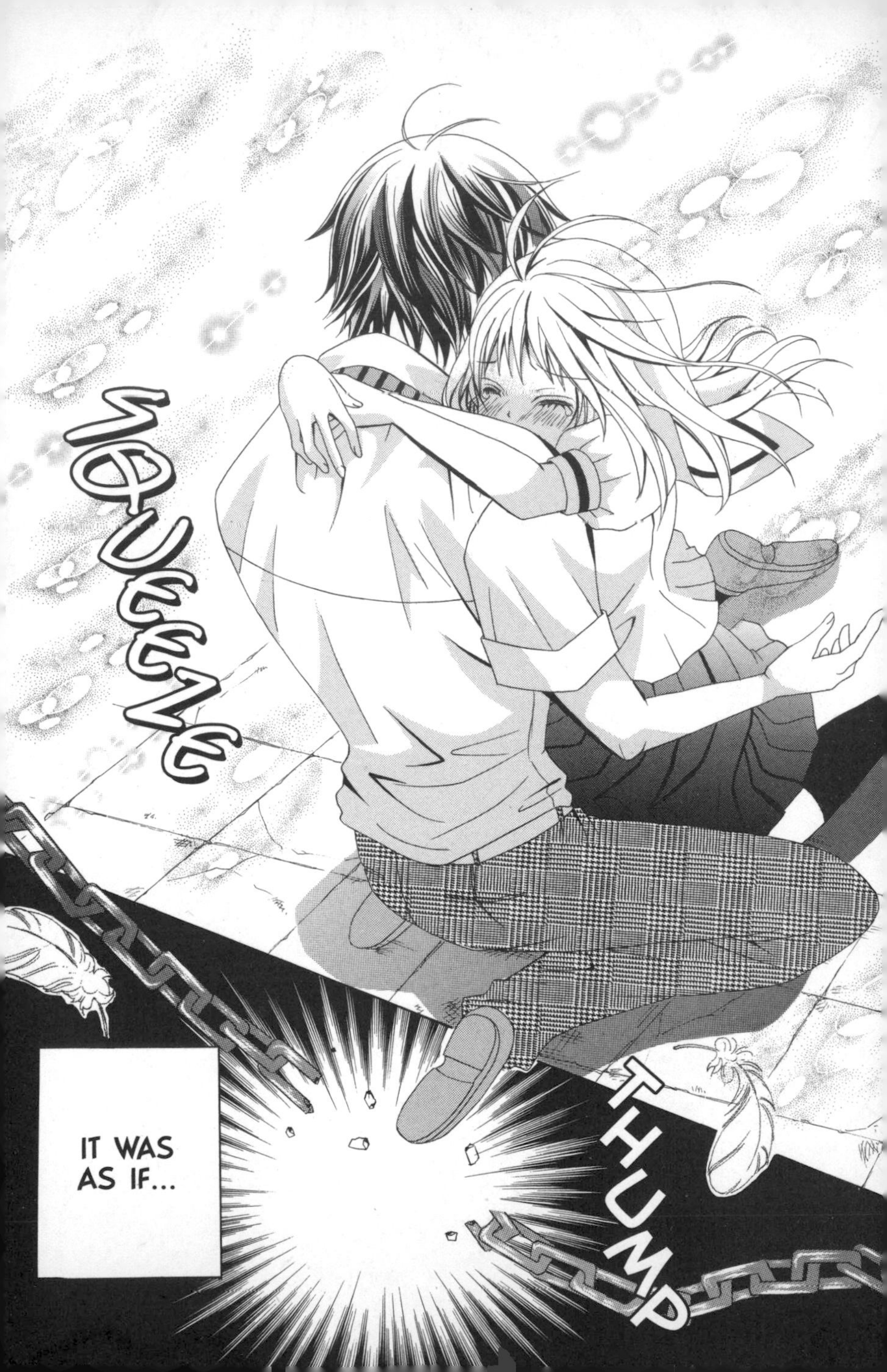
SQUEEZE
THUMP
IT WAS AS IF...

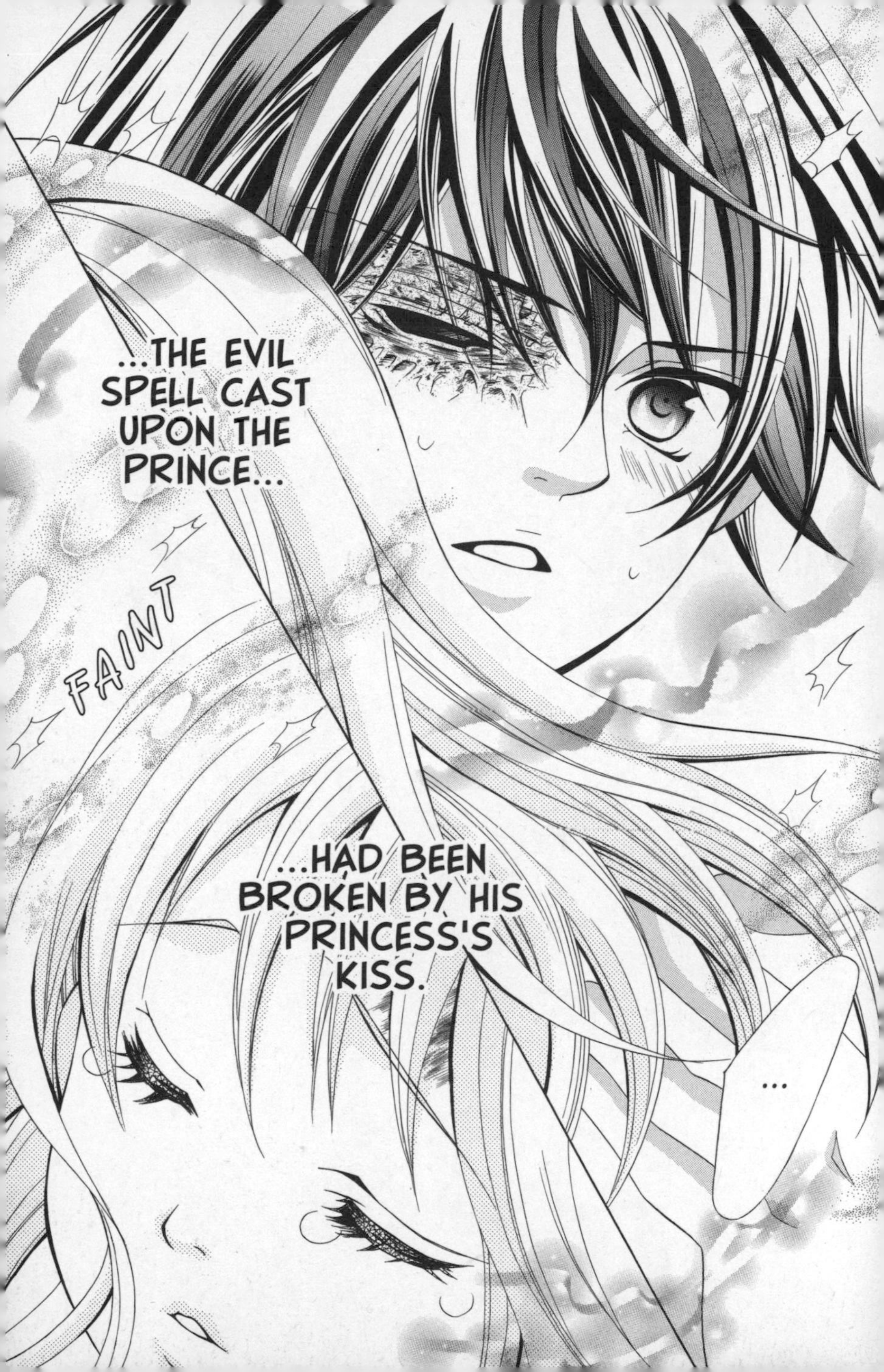
...THE EVIL SPELL CAST UPON THE PRINCE...
FAINT
...HAD BEEN BROKEN BY HIS PRINCESS'S KISS.
...

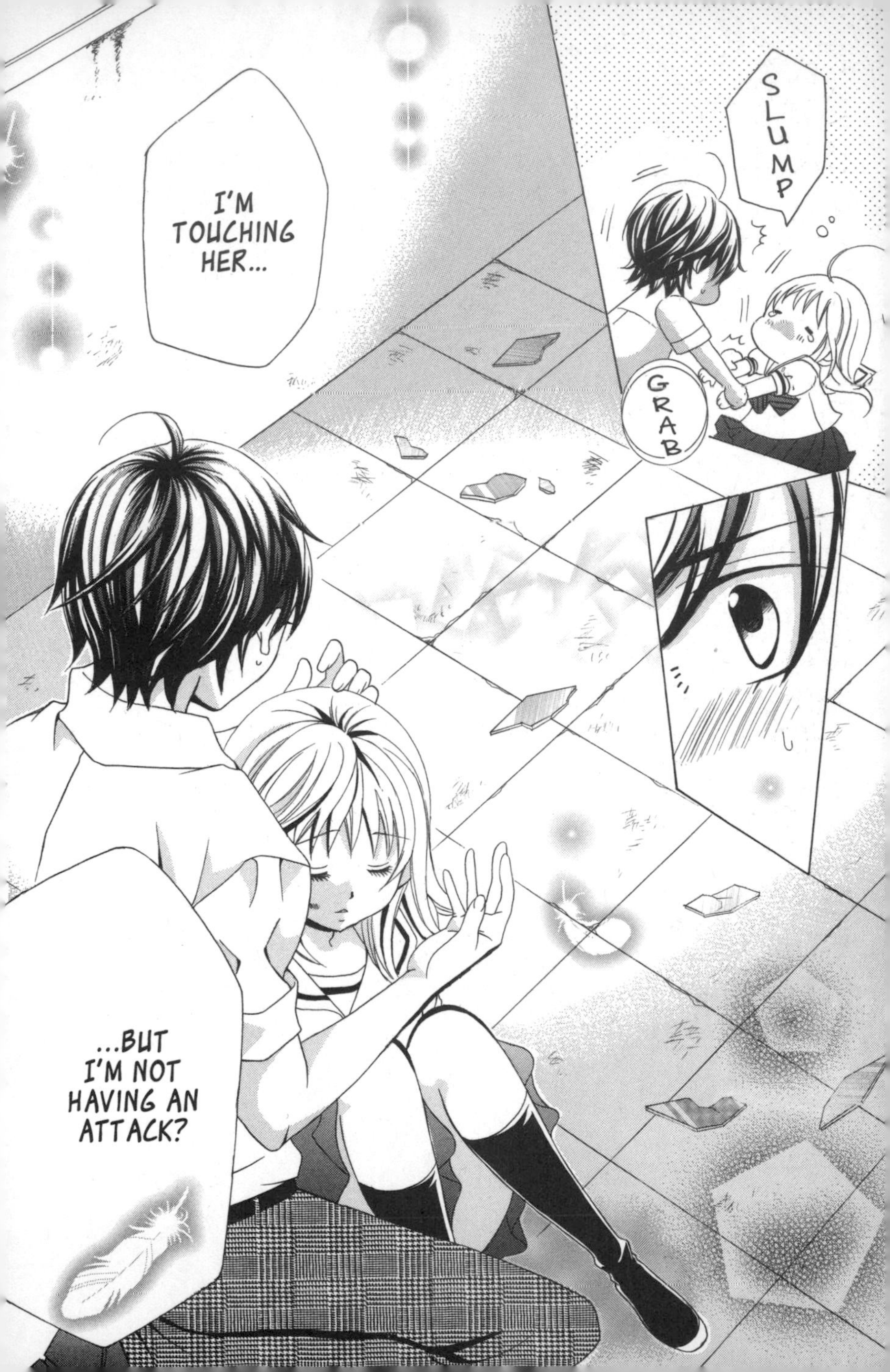
SLUMP
GRAB
I'M TOUCHING HER...
...BUT I'M NOT HAVING AN ATTACK?

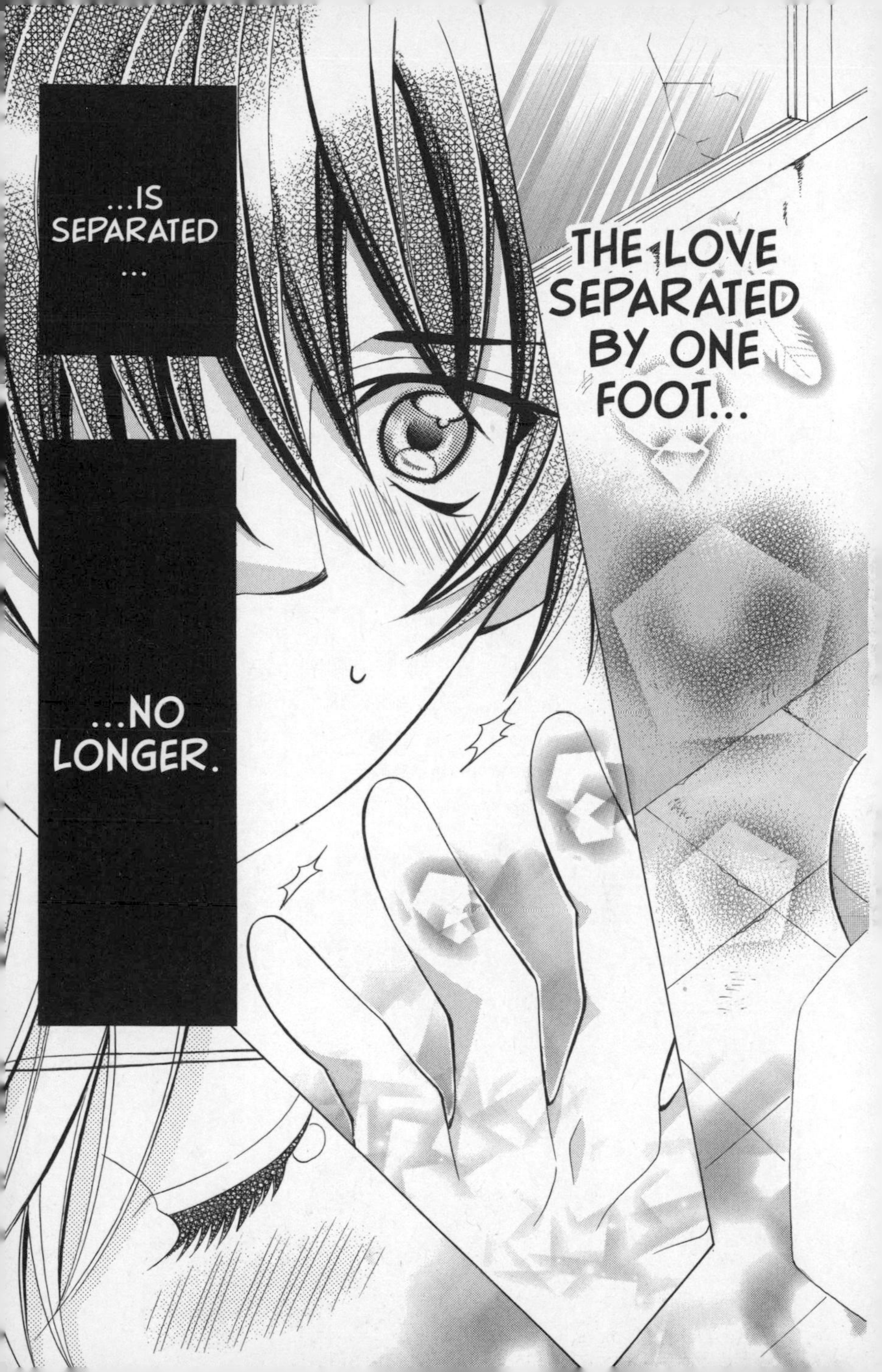
THE LOVE SEPARATED BY ONE FOOT...
...IS SEPARATED ...
...NO LONGER.

EVERYONE'S DRAWINGS ARE SO CUTE, THEY HURT!!

So Cute! Fan Art Feature ♥

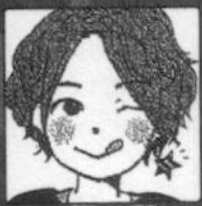

Shoji

Editor Shoji has commented on each one this time!!

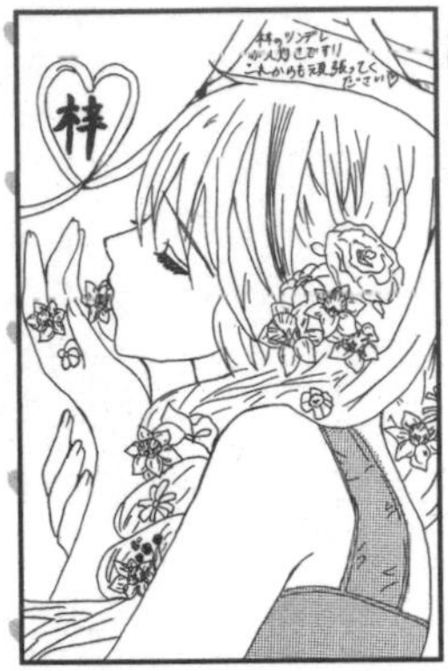

梓

Azuchin (Gunma) ←
Ed.: Even Mitsuru would fall in love with her beauty!!

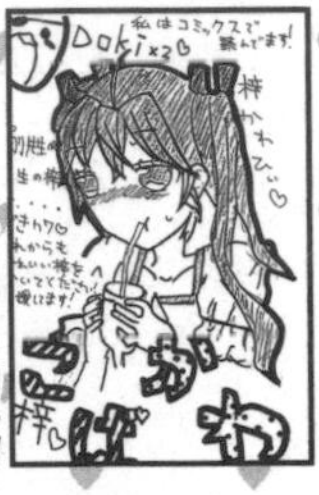

Doki x2
梓かわいい

Reika Nishiwaki (Osaka) →
Ed.: The blushing Azusa is super cute!

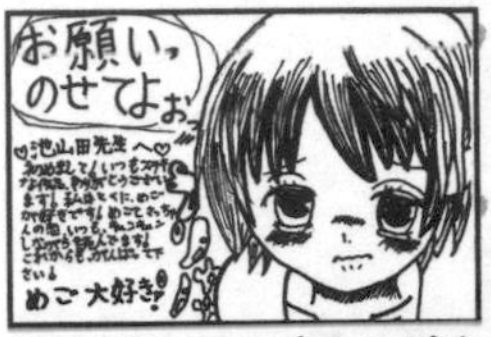

お願いっのせてよぉ
めご大好き

Ayumi Matsuoka (Ibaraki) ↑
Ed.: My heart flutters seeing the pretty Mego. ♥

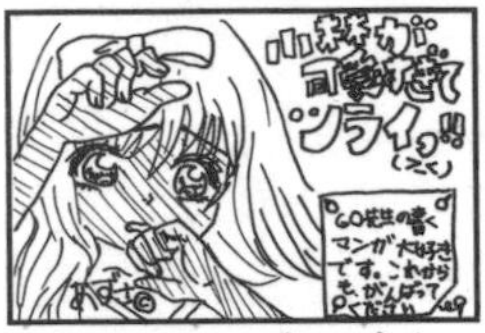

小林が。可愛すぎてツライっ!!

Manaka Sasaki (Saga) ↑
Ed.: Is Azusa a tsundere deredere now?

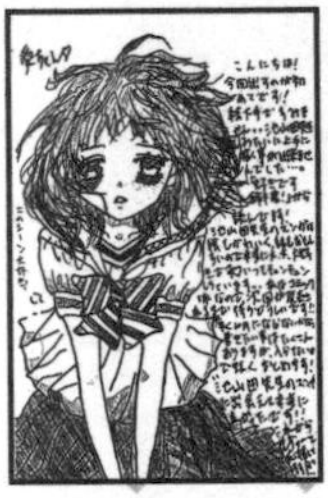

Seri (Saitama) ←
Ed.: You can't help but watch over Megumu's love after you see her look like this.

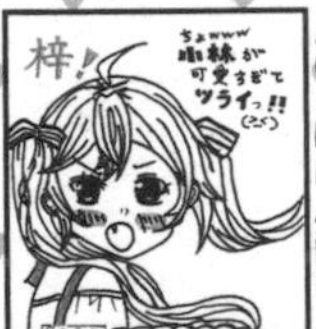

梓!
ちょwww 小林が可愛すぎてツライっ!!
コミカワ大好きです!
コミックス派です～
特に梓ちゃんが好きで～す
これからもがんばってください!!

Apple (Chiba) ←
Ed.: Azusa is becoming more and more popular!! Don't let her go, Mitsuru!

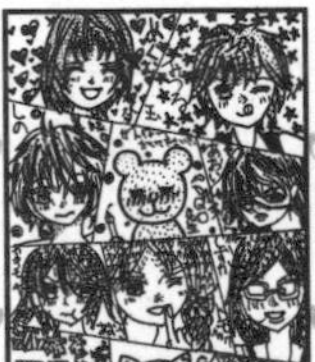

Shion Higashi (Osaka) ←
Ed.: Ooh! The otaku friends are here!!

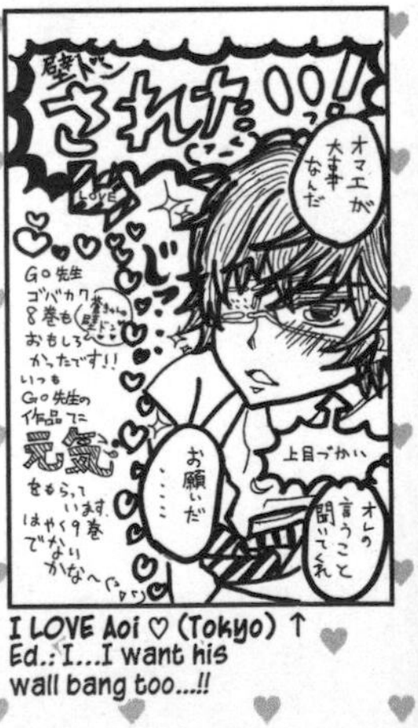

壁ドンされた!!
オマエが大事なんだ
LOVE
GO先生 ゴバカワ8巻もおもしろかったです!!
いつもGO先生の作品に元気をもらっています。
はやく9巻でないかな～
お願いだ……
上目づかい
オレの言うこと聞いてくれ

I LOVE Aoi ♡ (Tokyo) ↑
Ed.: I...I want his wall bang too...!!

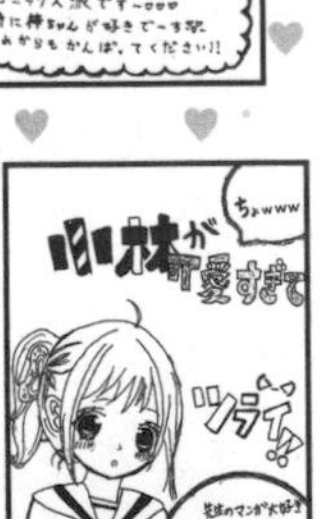

ちょwww
小林が可愛すぎて
ツライ!!

Haruka Morishita (Wakayama) ↑
Ed.: The butterfly hair clip looks great on her!!

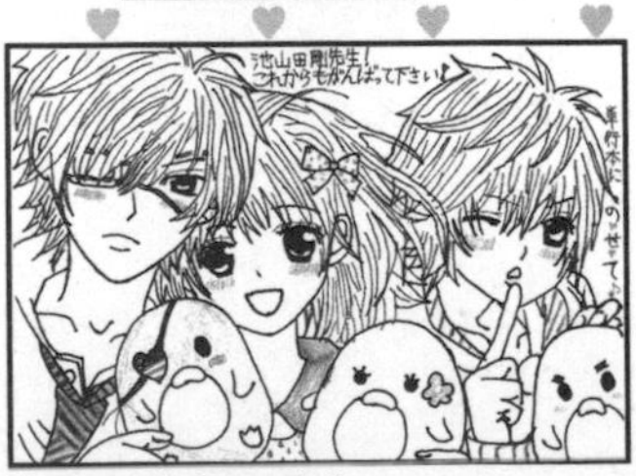

池山田剛先生! これからもがんばって下さい!

☆ Fuuka ☆ (Tokyo) ↑
Ed.: The three look cute, but the penguins look cute too!!

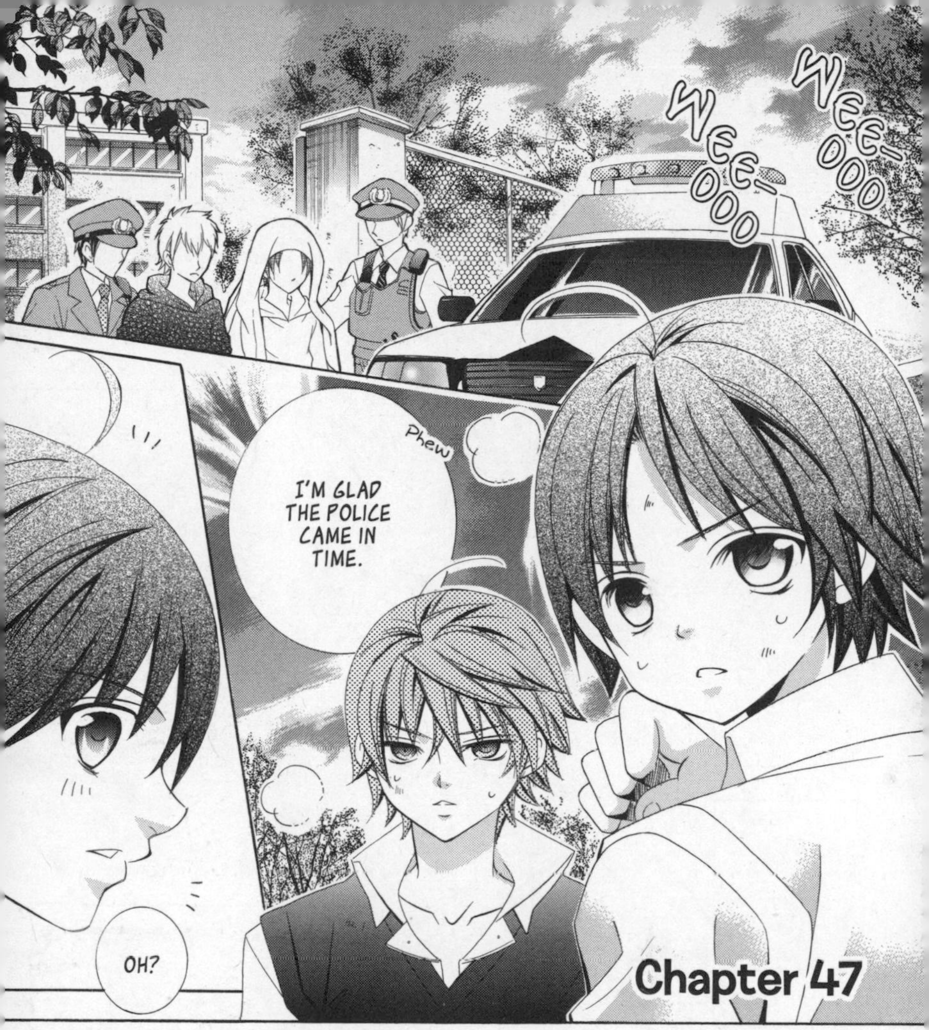
WEE-OOO
WEE-OOO
Phew
I'M GLAD THE POLICE CAME IN TIME.
Chapter 47
OH?

THANK YOU FOR SENDING ME LOVELY LETTERS AND DRAWINGS. ♡ THANK YOU FOR YOUR NEW YEAR'S CARDS AND CHRISTMAS GIFTS! I REALLY, REALLY APPRECIATE THEM!! ♡♡ I HOPE YOU SEND YOUR THOUGHTS AND DRAWINGS AFTER READING VOLUME 10. ♡

GO IKEYAMADA
C/O SHOJO BEAT
VIZ MEDIA, LLC
P.O. BOX 77010
SAN FRANCISCO, CA
94107 (^o^)

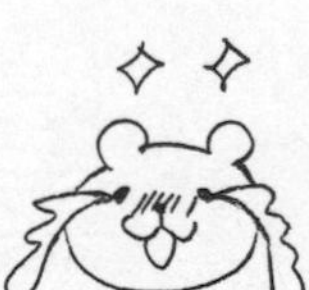

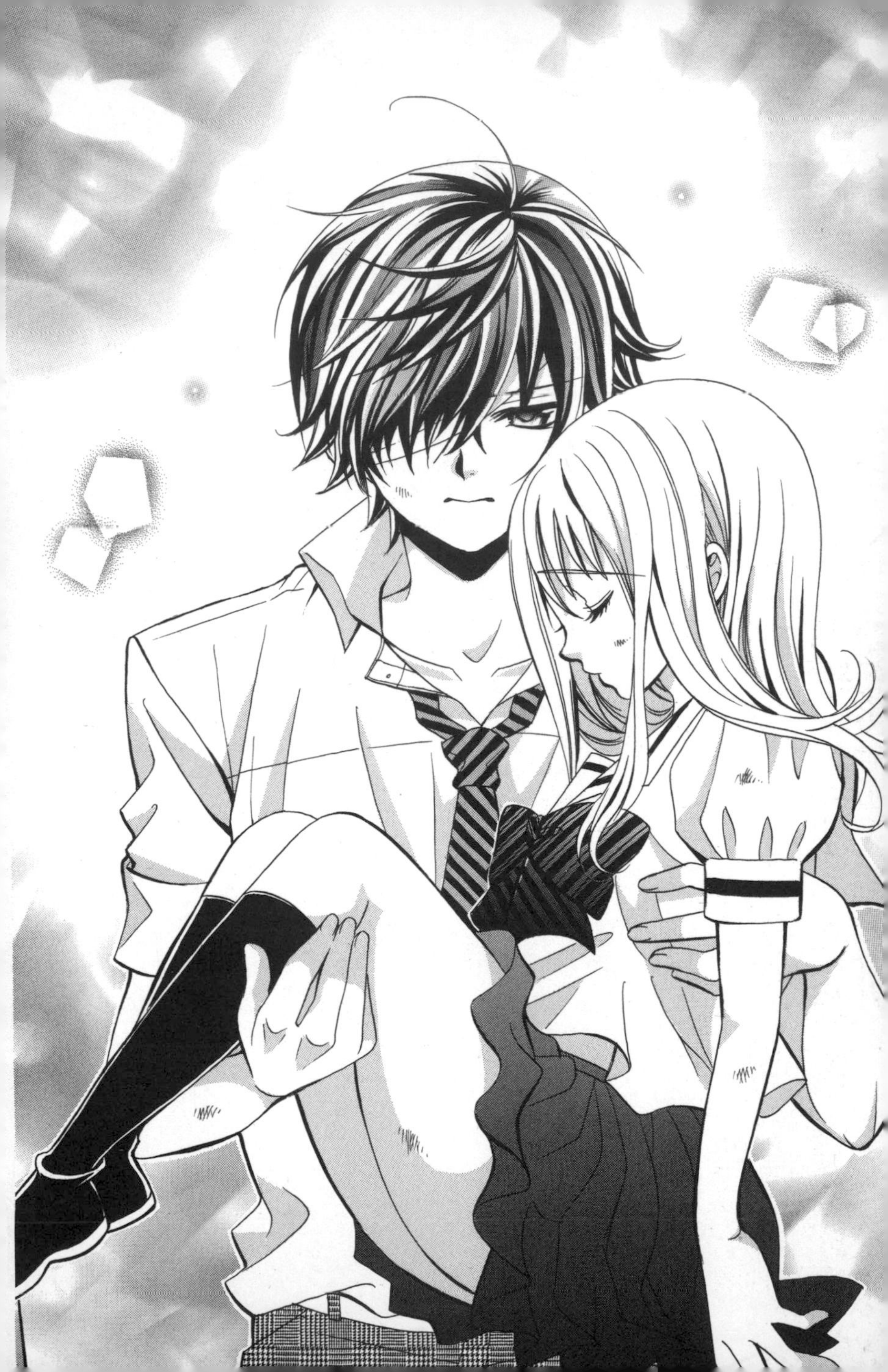

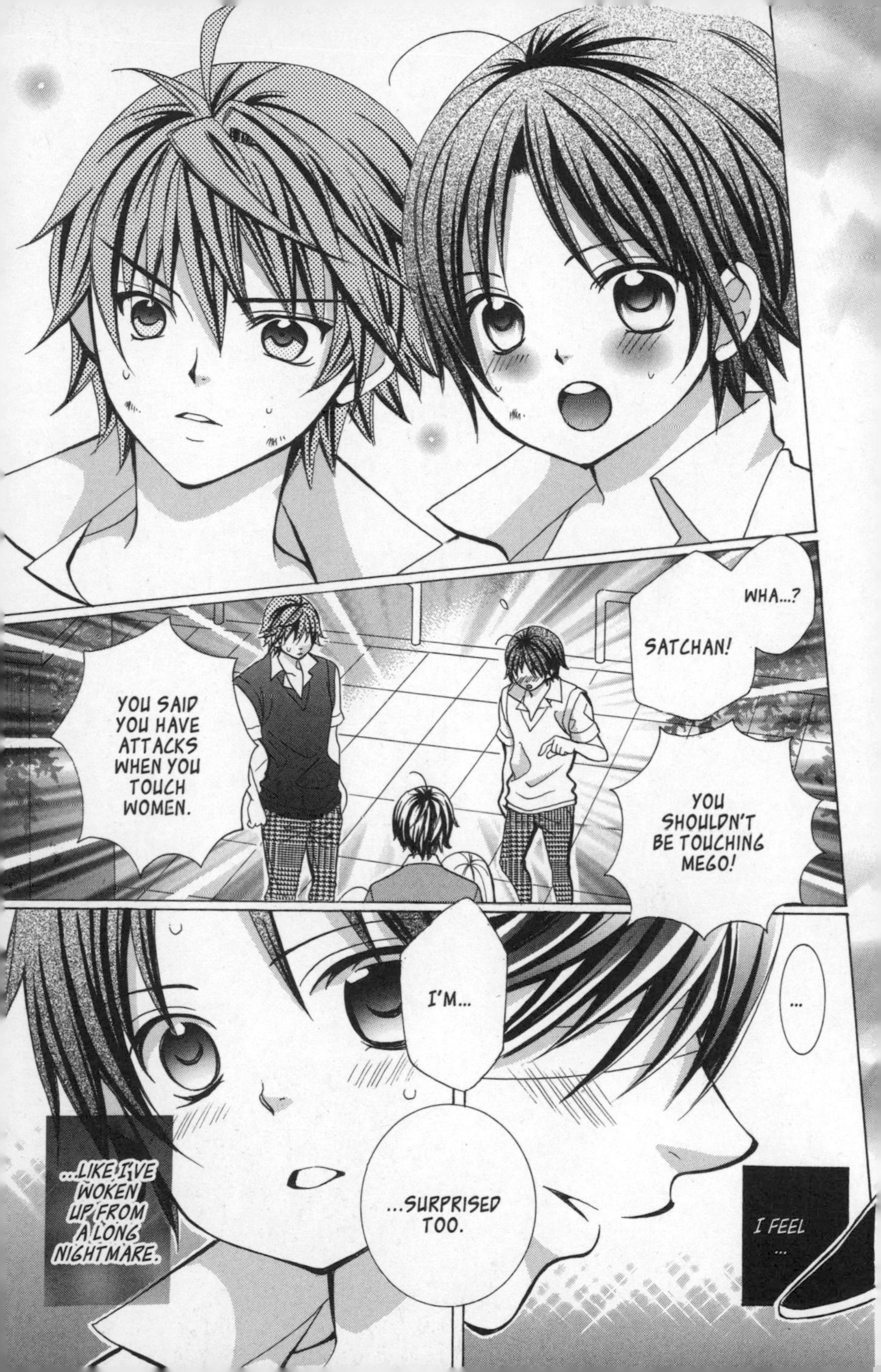
WHA...?
SATCHAN!
YOU SHOULDN'T BE TOUCHING MEGO!
YOU SAID YOU HAVE ATTACKS WHEN YOU TOUCH WOMEN.
...
I'M...
...SURPRISED TOO.
I FEEL ...
...LIKE I'VE WOKEN UP FROM A LONG NIGHTMARE.

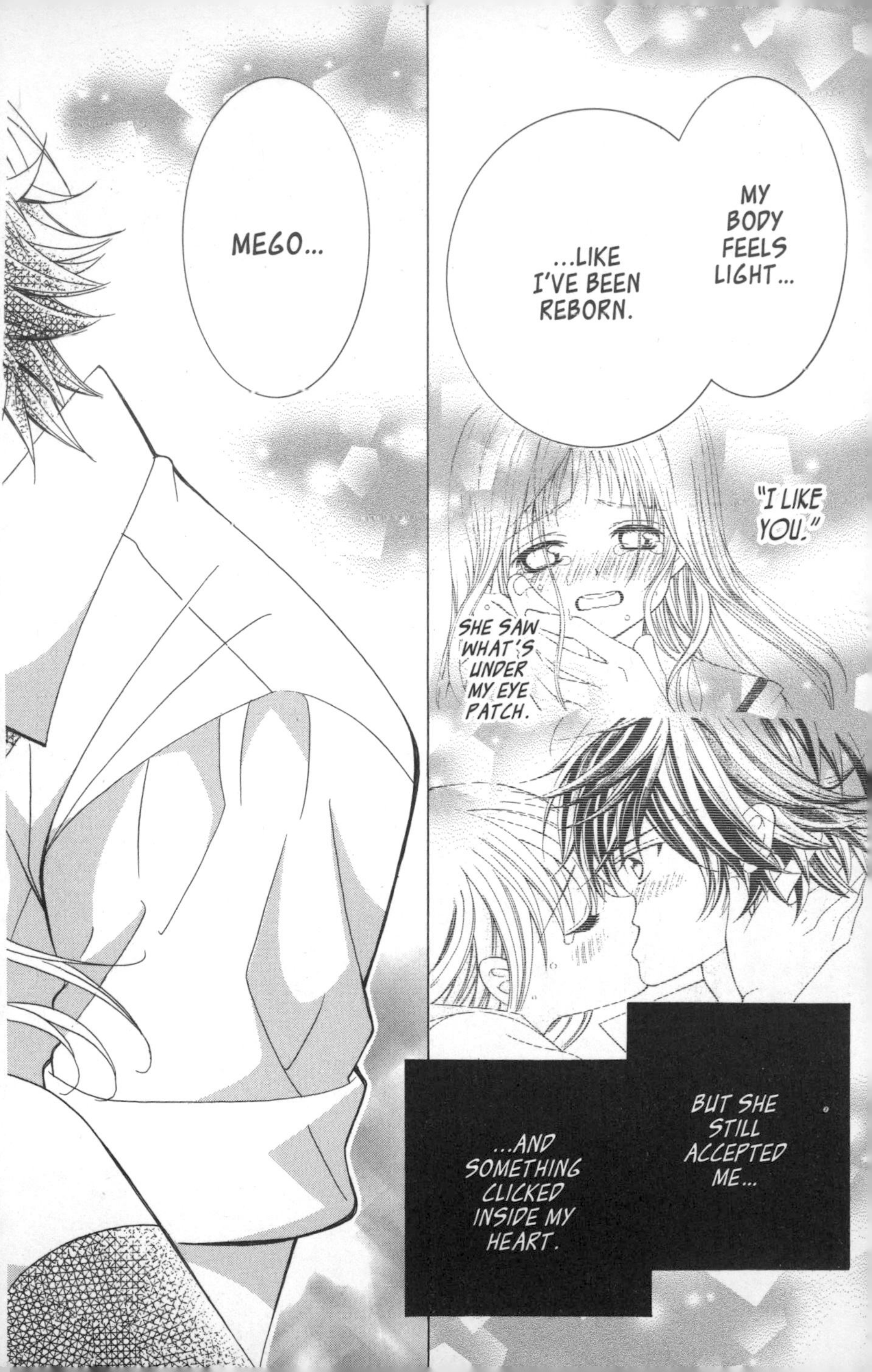
MY BODY FEELS LIGHT...
...LIKE I'VE BEEN REBORN.
"I LIKE YOU."
SHE SAW WHAT'S UNDER MY EYE PATCH.
BUT SHE STILL ACCEPTED ME...
...AND SOMETHING CLICKED INSIDE MY HEART.
MEGO...

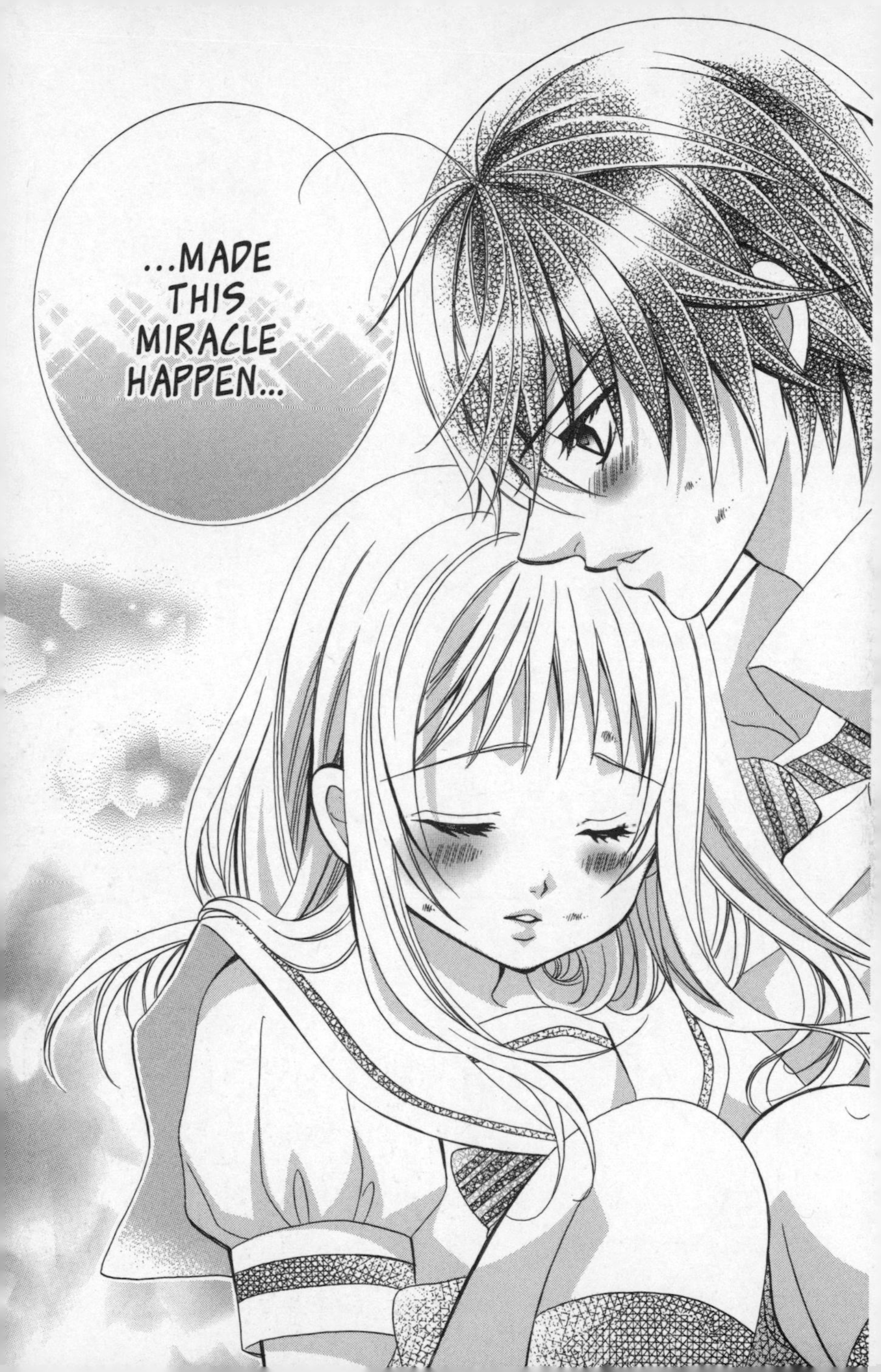
...MADE THIS MIRACLE HAPPEN...

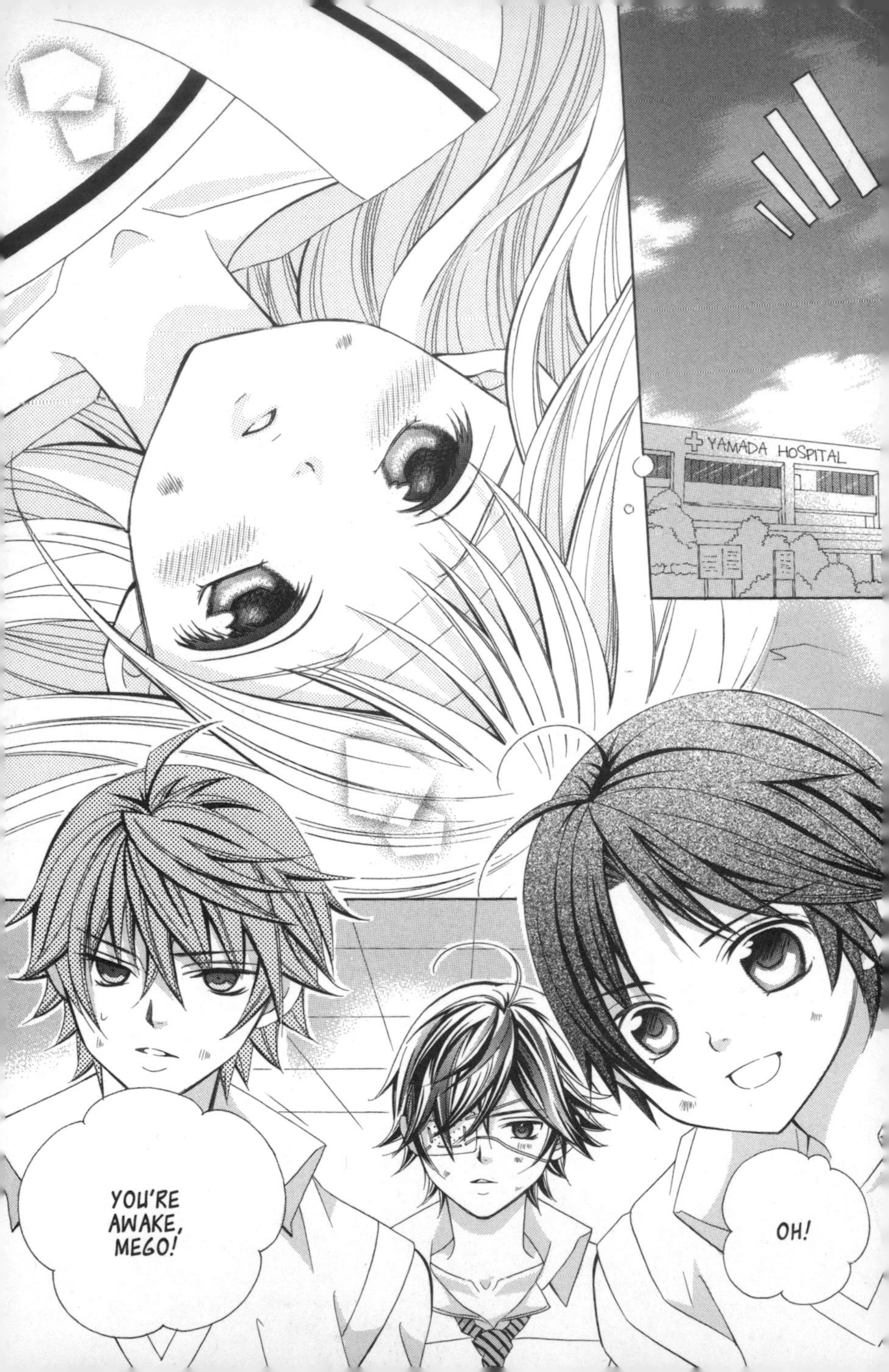
YAMADA HOSPITAL
OH!
YOU'RE AWAKE, MEGO!

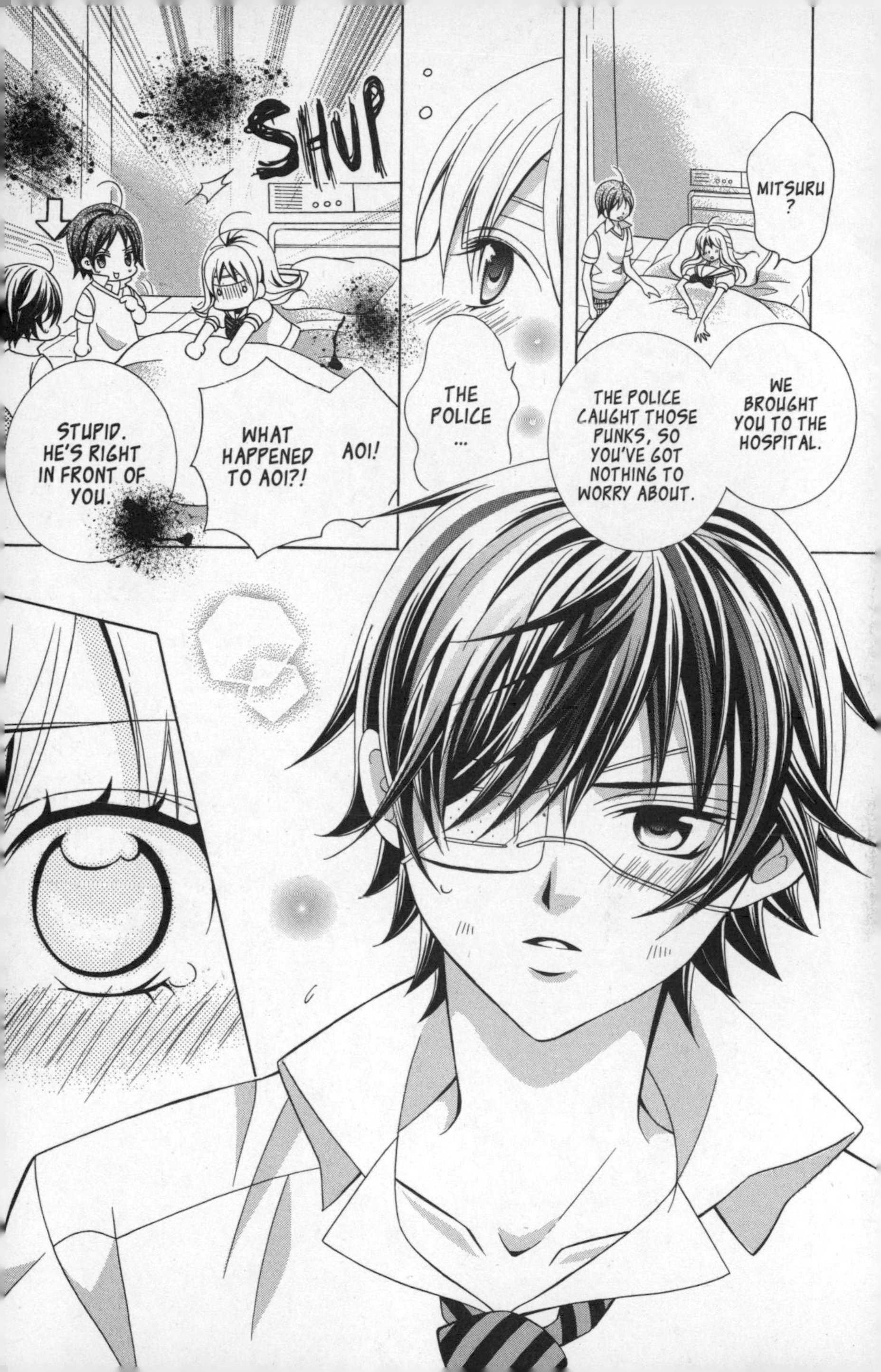
MITSURU?
WE BROUGHT YOU TO THE HOSPITAL.
THE POLICE CAUGHT THOSE PUNKS, SO YOU'VE GOT NOTHING TO WORRY ABOUT.
THE POLICE ...
SHUP
AOI!
WHAT HAPPENED TO AOI?!
STUPID. HE'S RIGHT IN FRONT OF YOU.

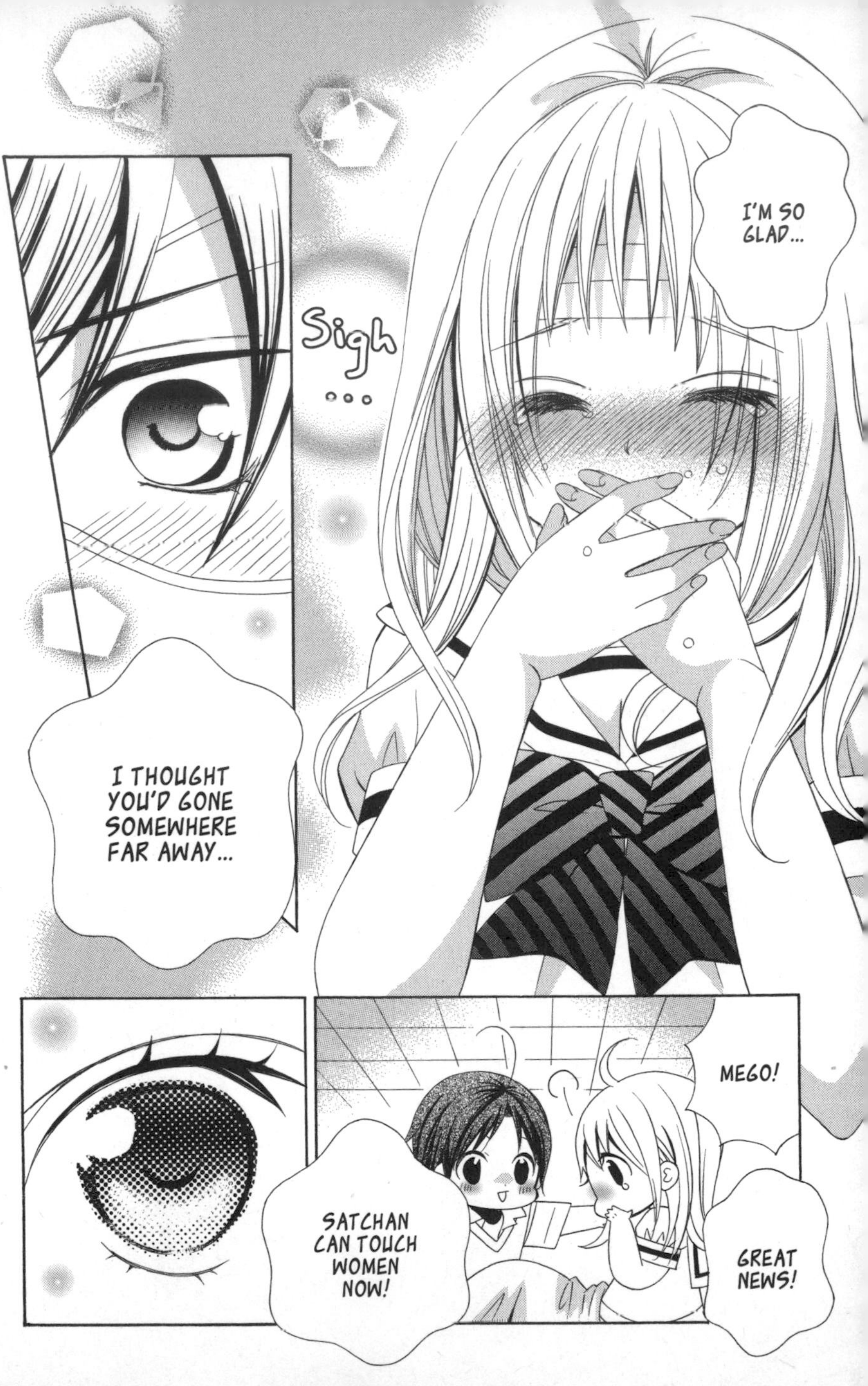
I'M SO GLAD...
Sigh...
I THOUGHT YOU'D GONE SOMEWHERE FAR AWAY...
MEGO!
SATCHAN CAN TOUCH WOMEN NOW!
GREAT NEWS!

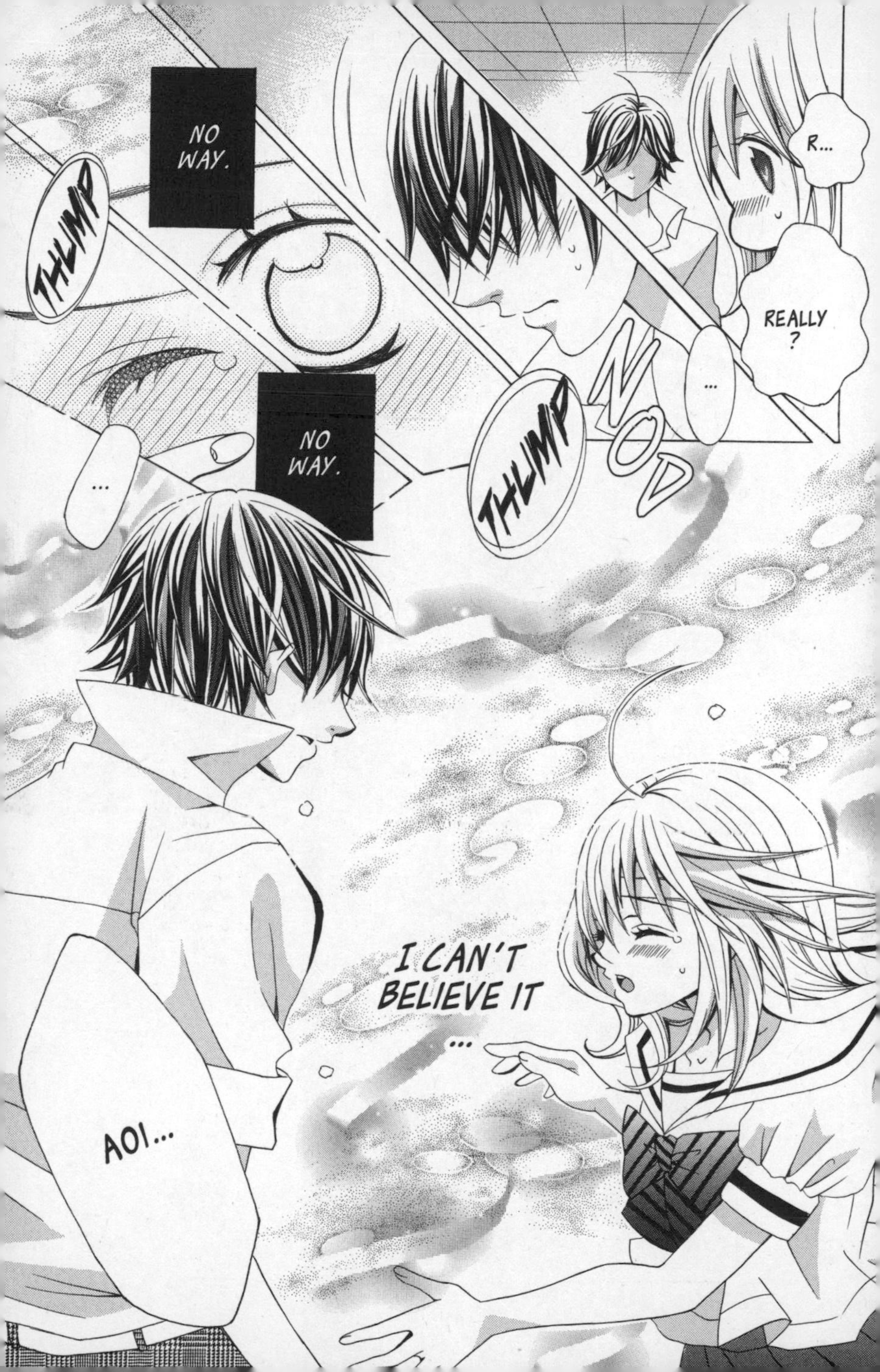
R...
REALLY?
...
NOD
THUMP
NO WAY.
THUMP
NO WAY.
...
I CAN'T BELIEVE IT ...
AOI...

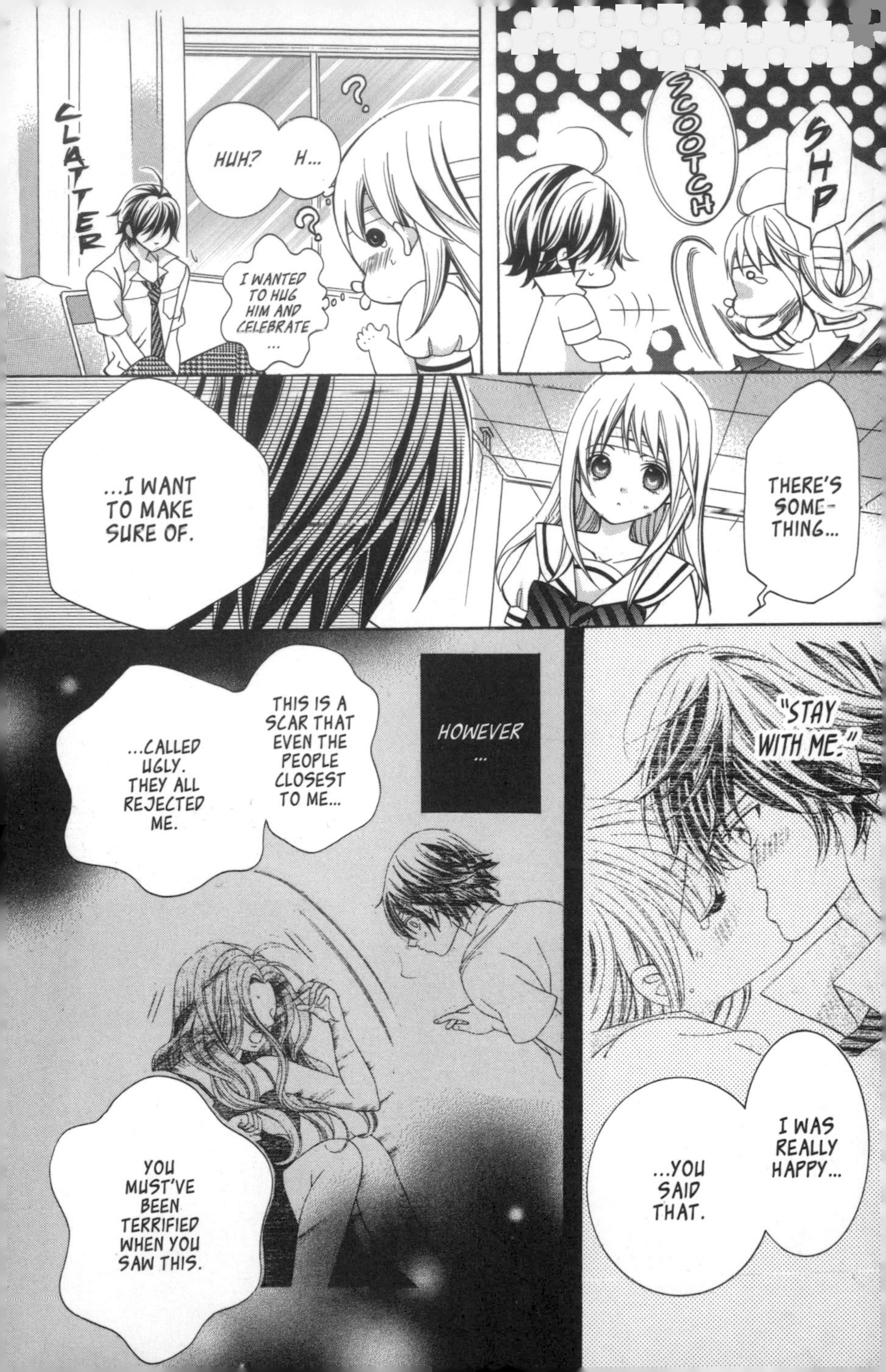
SCOOTCH
SHP
HUH? H...
I WANTED TO HUG HIM AND CELEBRATE ...
CLATTER
THERE'S SOME-THING...
...I WANT TO MAKE SURE OF.
"STAY WITH ME."
I WAS REALLY HAPPY...
...YOU SAID THAT.
HOWEVER ...
THIS IS A SCAR THAT EVEN THE PEOPLE CLOSEST TO ME...
...CALLED UGLY. THEY ALL REJECTED ME.
YOU MUST'VE BEEN TERRIFIED WHEN YOU SAW THIS.

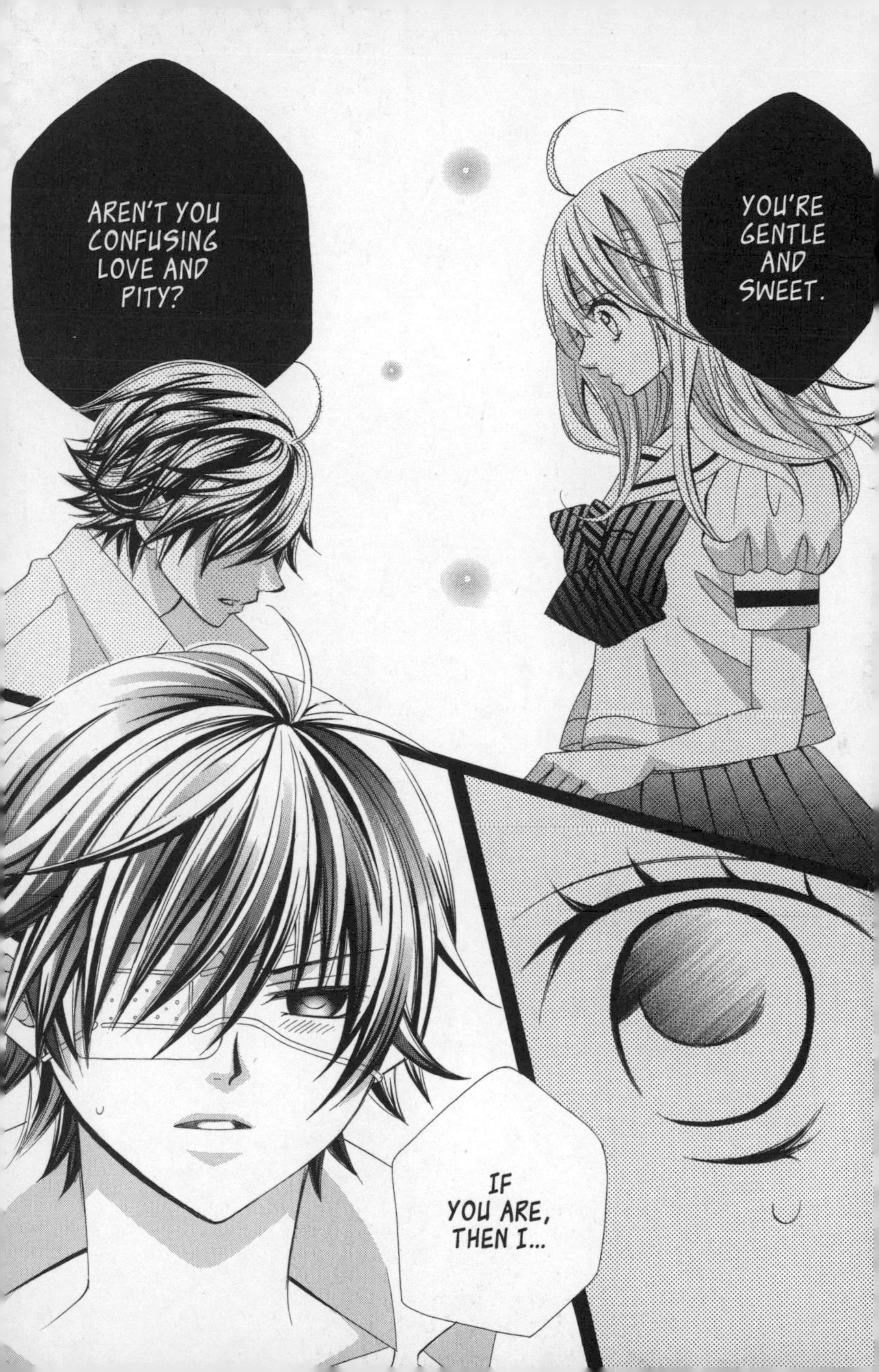
YOU'RE GENTLE AND SWEET.
AREN'T YOU CONFUSING LOVE AND PITY?
IF YOU ARE, THEN I...

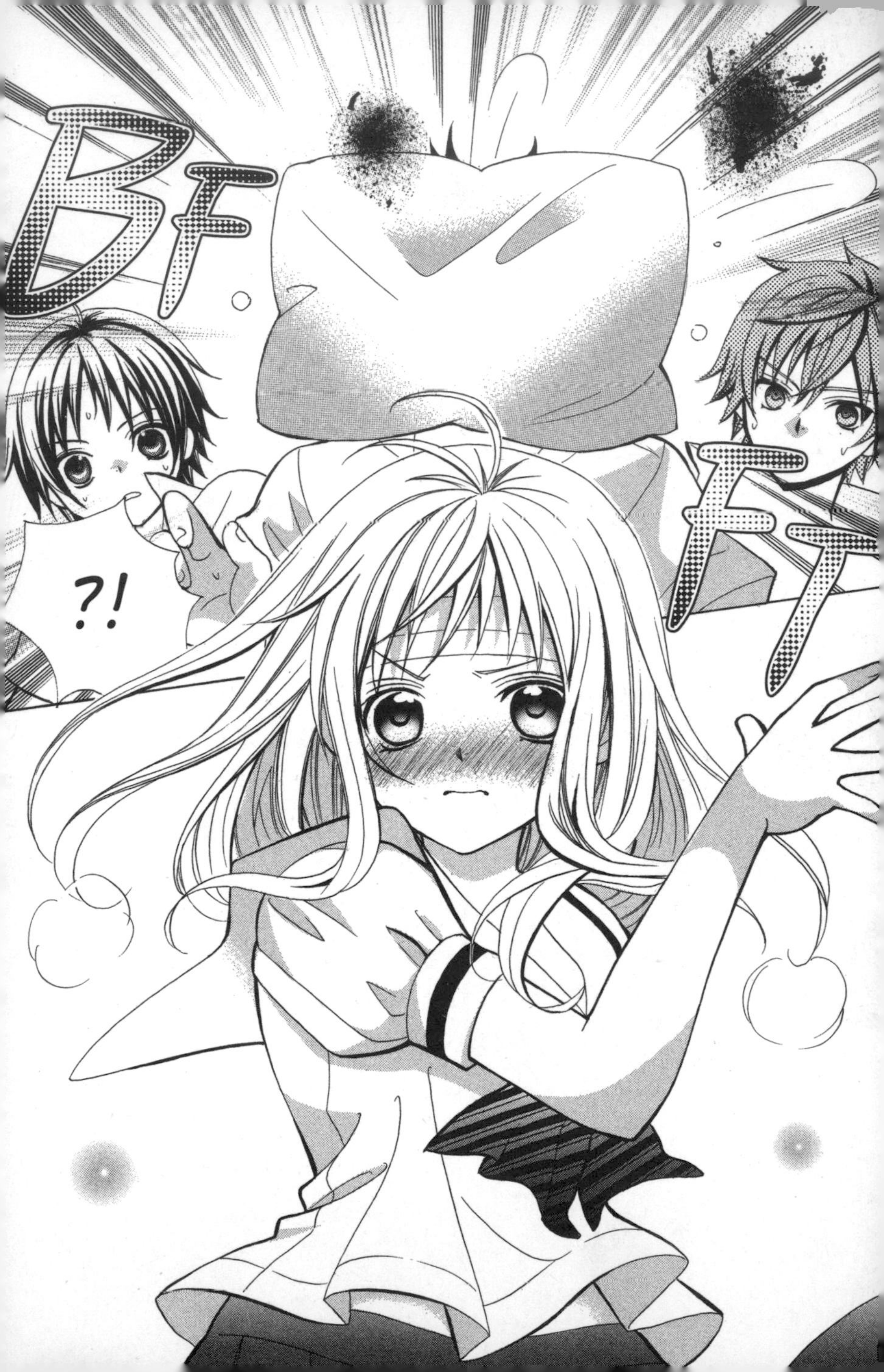
BF
FT
?!

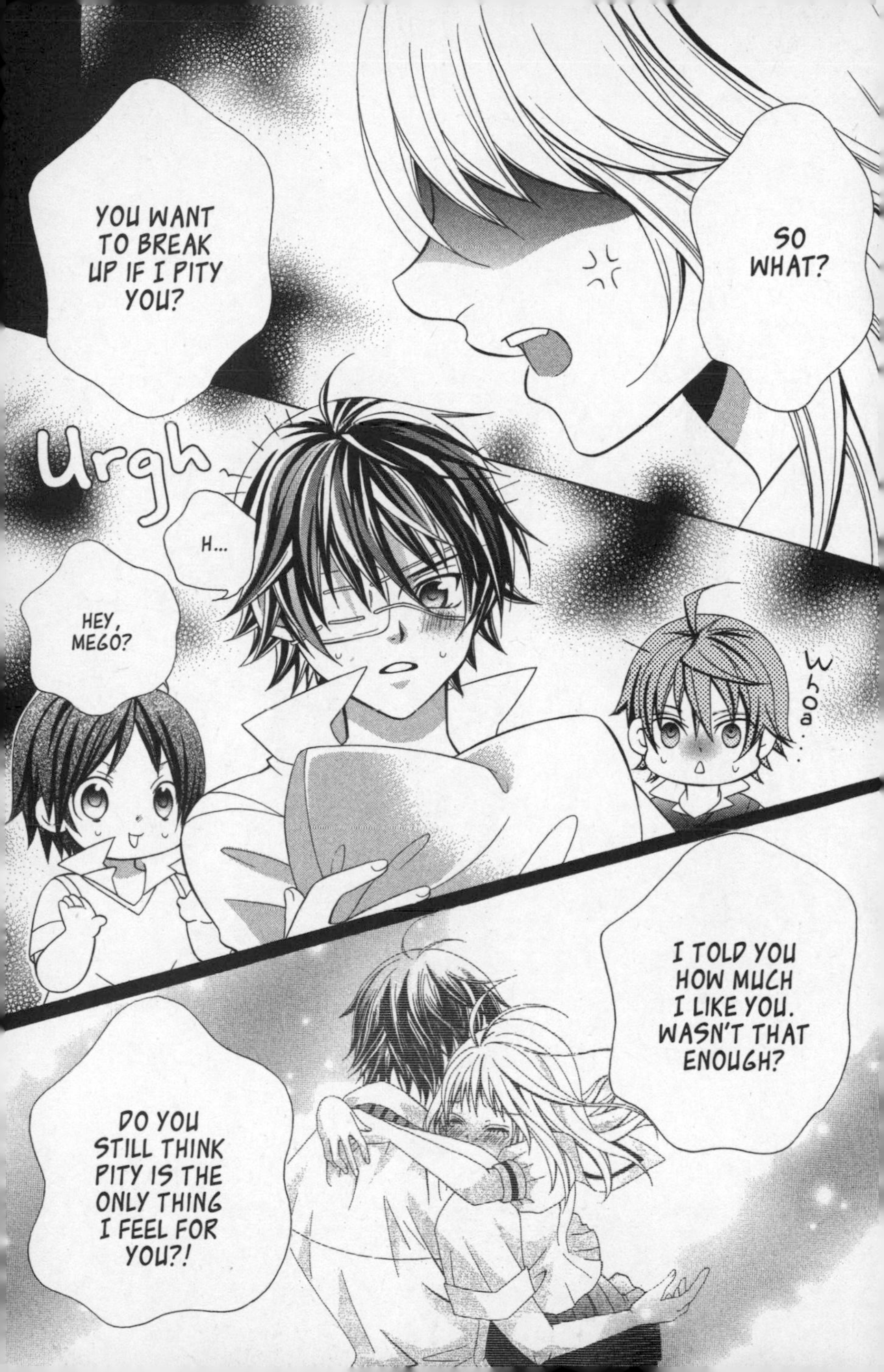
SO WHAT?
YOU WANT TO BREAK UP IF I PITY YOU?
Urgh
H...
Whoa...
HEY, MEGO?
I TOLD YOU HOW MUCH I LIKE YOU. WASN'T THAT ENOUGH?
DO YOU STILL THINK PITY IS THE ONLY THING I FEEL FOR YOU?!

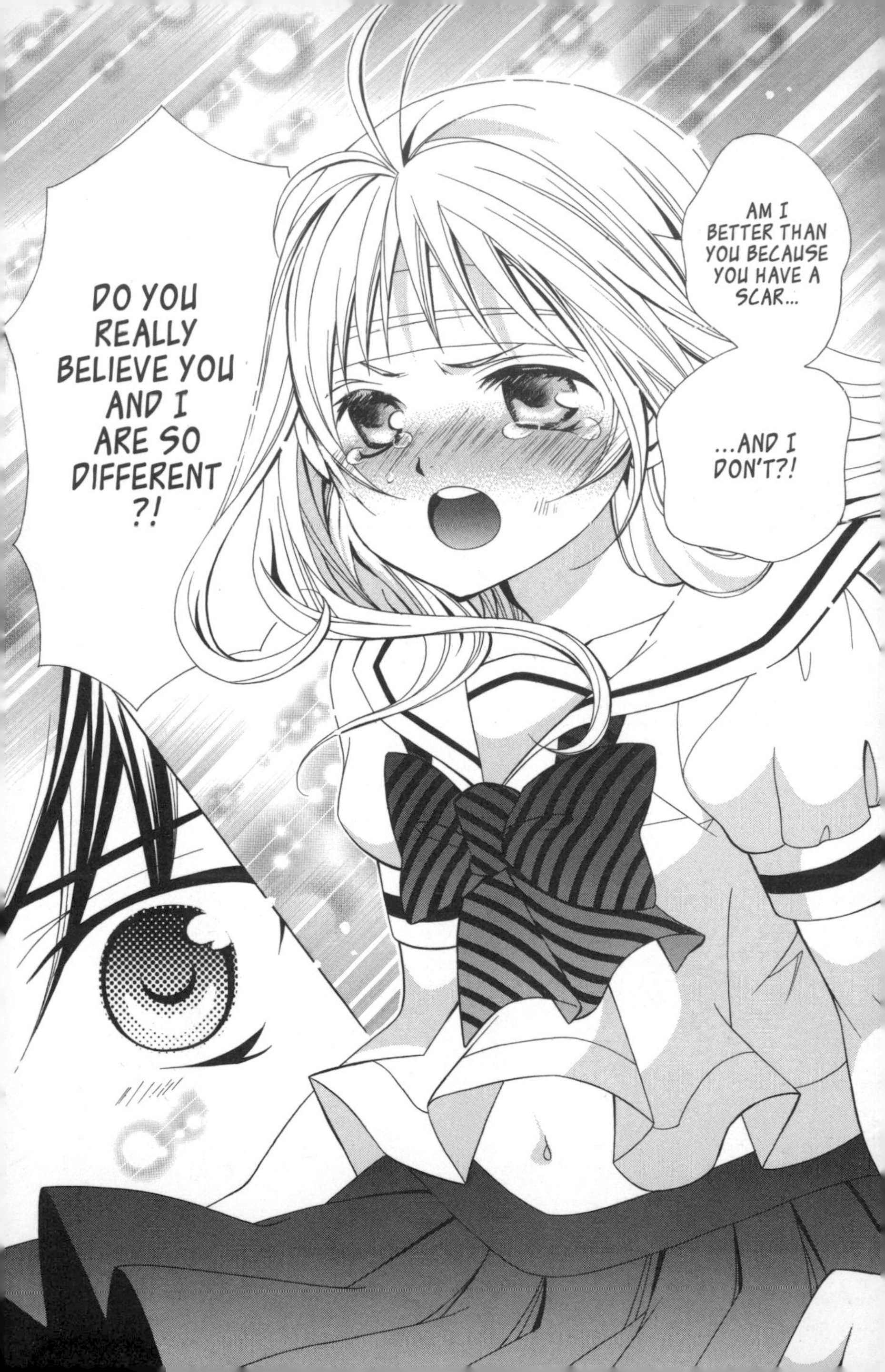
AM I BETTER THAN YOU BECAUSE YOU HAVE A SCAR...
...AND I DON'T?!
DO YOU REALLY BELIEVE YOU AND I ARE SO DIFFERENT ?!

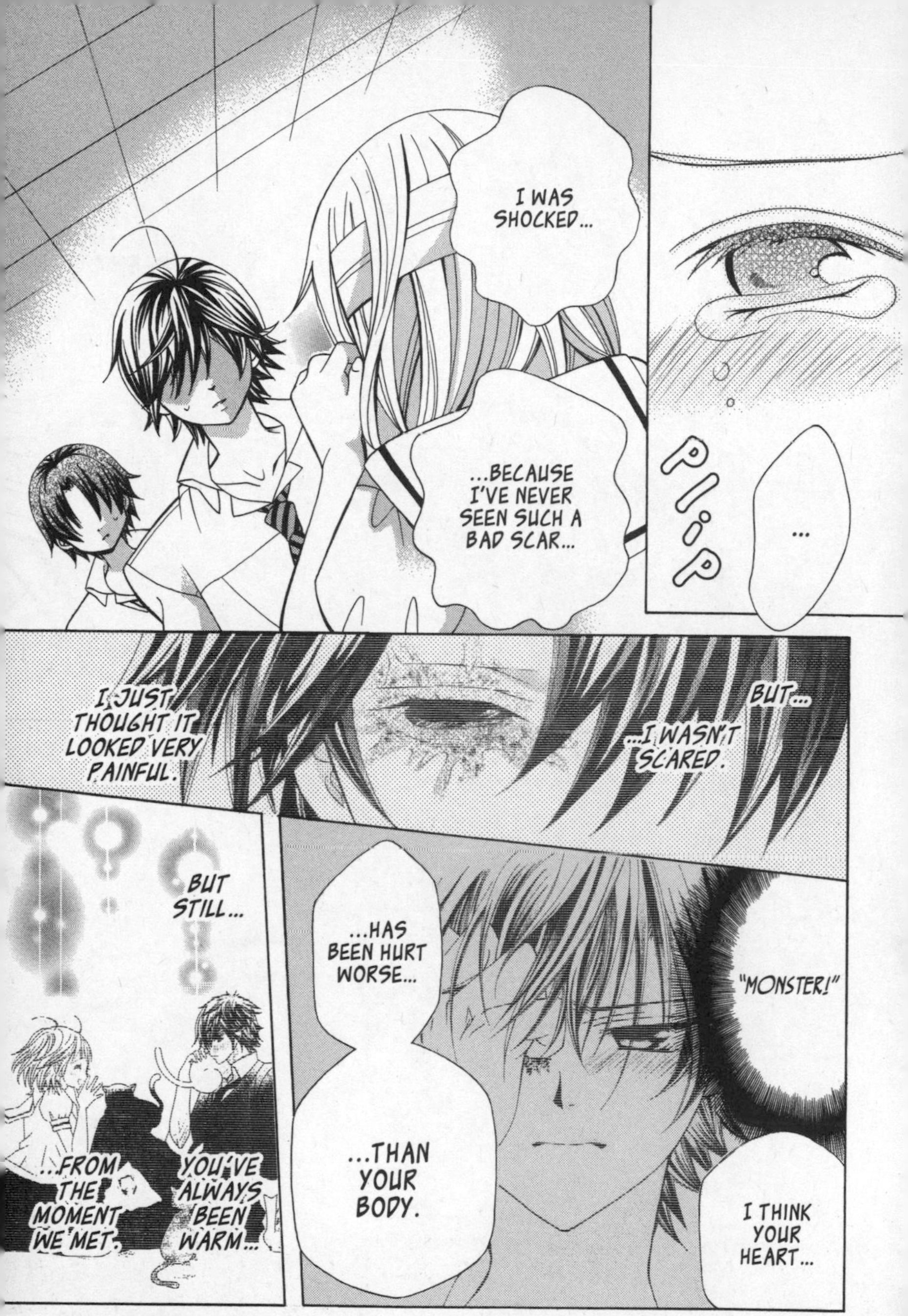
PLIP
...
I WAS SHOCKED...
...BECAUSE I'VE NEVER SEEN SUCH A BAD SCAR...
BUT...
...I WASN'T SCARED.
I JUST THOUGHT IT LOOKED VERY PAINFUL.
"MONSTER!"
I THINK YOUR HEART...
...HAS BEEN HURT WORSE...
...THAN YOUR BODY.
BUT STILL...
YOU'VE ALWAYS BEEN WARM...
...FROM THE MOMENT WE MET.

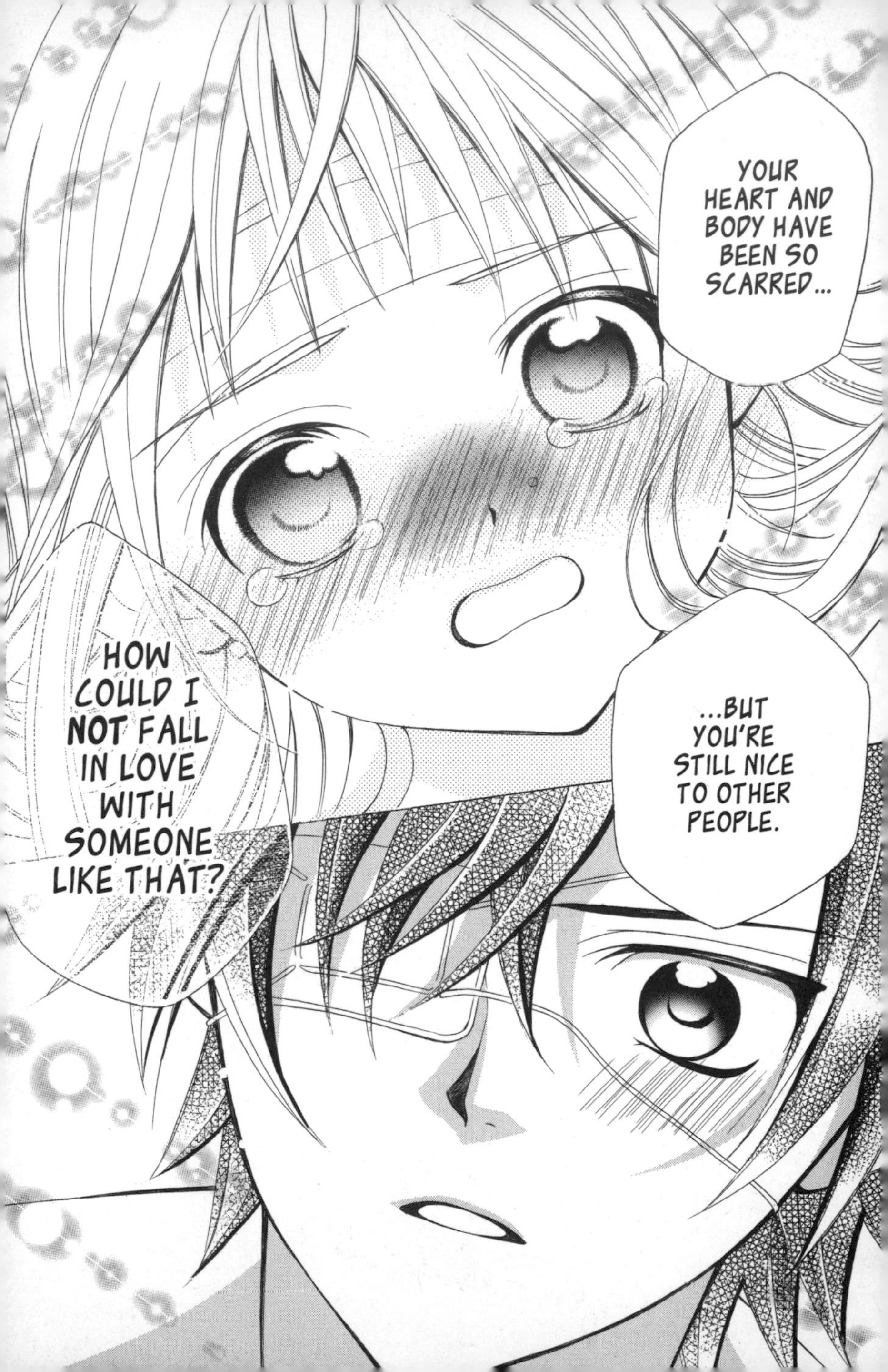
YOUR HEART AND BODY HAVE BEEN SO SCARRED...
...BUT YOU'RE STILL NICE TO OTHER PEOPLE.
HOW COULD I **NOT** FALL IN LOVE WITH SOMEONE LIKE THAT?

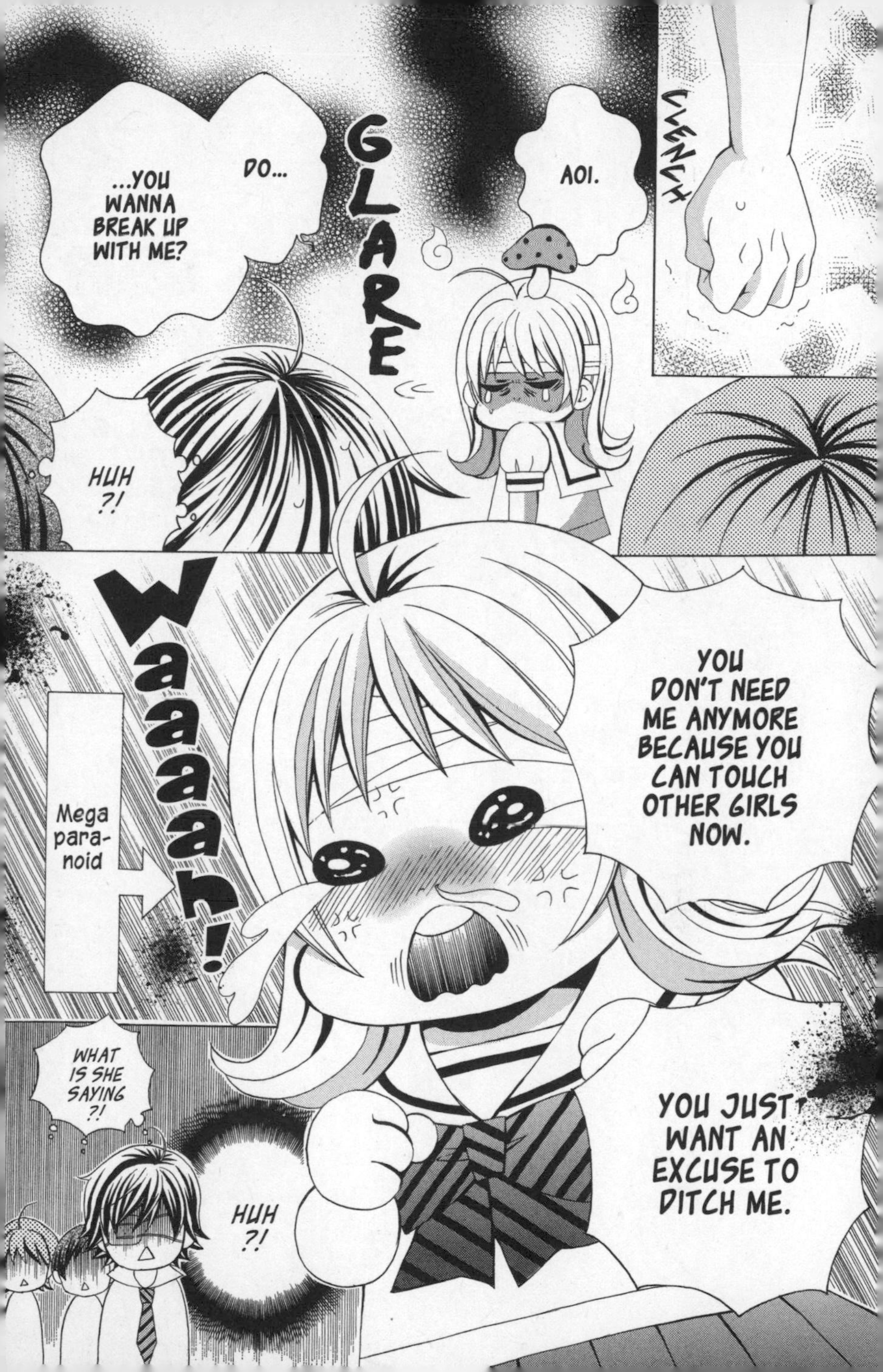
CLENCH
AOI.
GLARE
DO...
...YOU WANNA BREAK UP WITH ME?
HUH ?!
YOU DON'T NEED ME ANYMORE BECAUSE YOU CAN TOUCH OTHER GIRLS NOW.
Waaaah!
Mega para-noid
YOU JUST WANT AN EXCUSE TO DITCH ME.
HUH ?!
WHAT IS SHE SAYING ?!

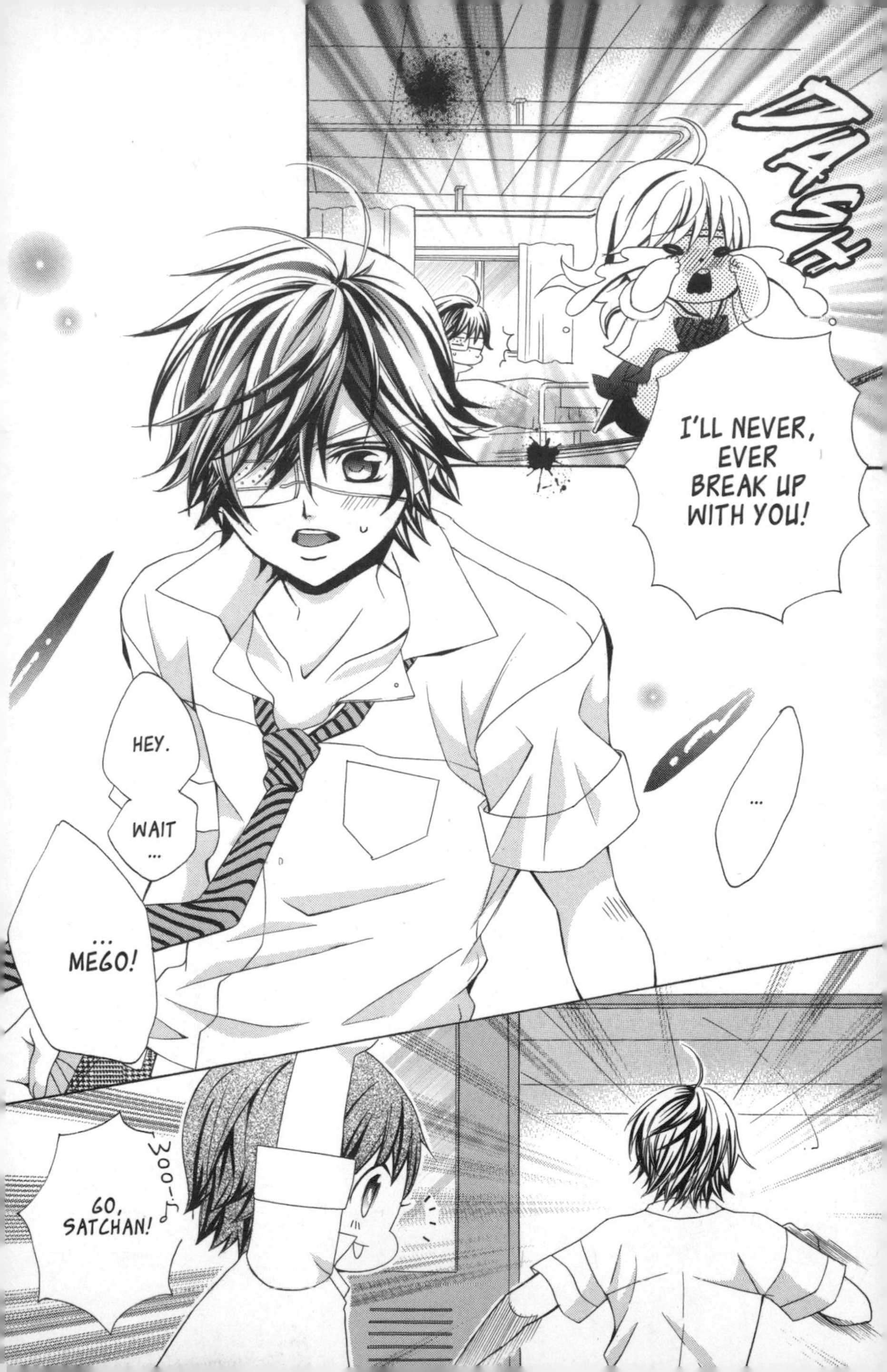
DASH
I'LL NEVER, EVER BREAK UP WITH YOU!
...
HEY.
WAIT ...
... MEGO!
WOO-!♪
GO, SATCHAN!

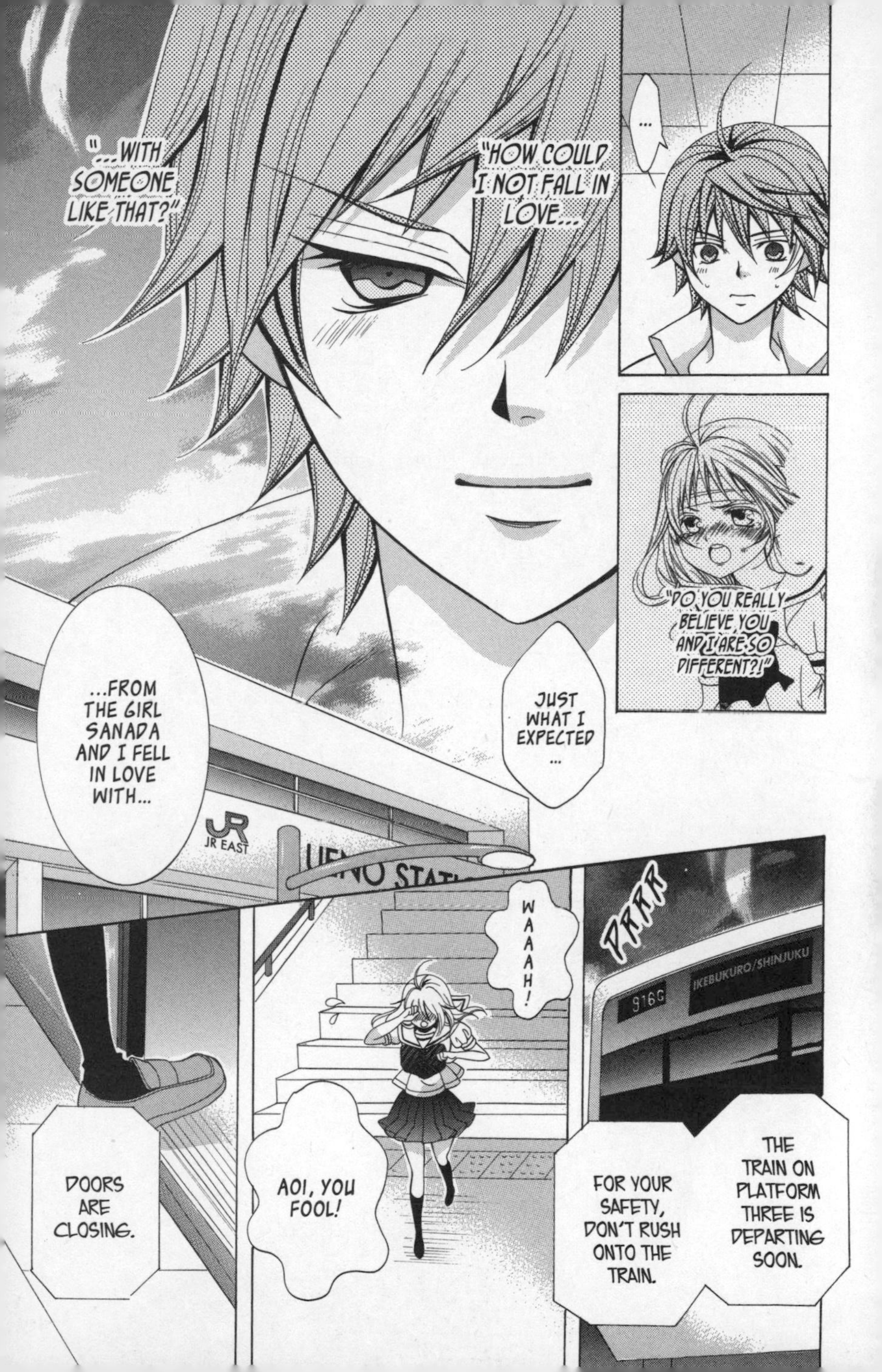
...
"DO YOU REALLY BELIEVE YOU AND I ARE SO DIFFERENT?!"
"HOW COULD I NOT FALL IN LOVE...
"...WITH SOMEONE LIKE THAT?"
JUST WHAT I EXPECTED...
...FROM THE GIRL SANADA AND I FELL IN LOVE WITH...
JR
JR EAST
PRRR
IKEBUKURO/SHINJUKU
916G
THE TRAIN ON PLATFORM THREE IS DEPARTING SOON.
FOR YOUR SAFETY, DON'T RUSH ONTO THE TRAIN.
WAAAAH!
AOI, YOU FOOL!
DOORS ARE CLOSING.

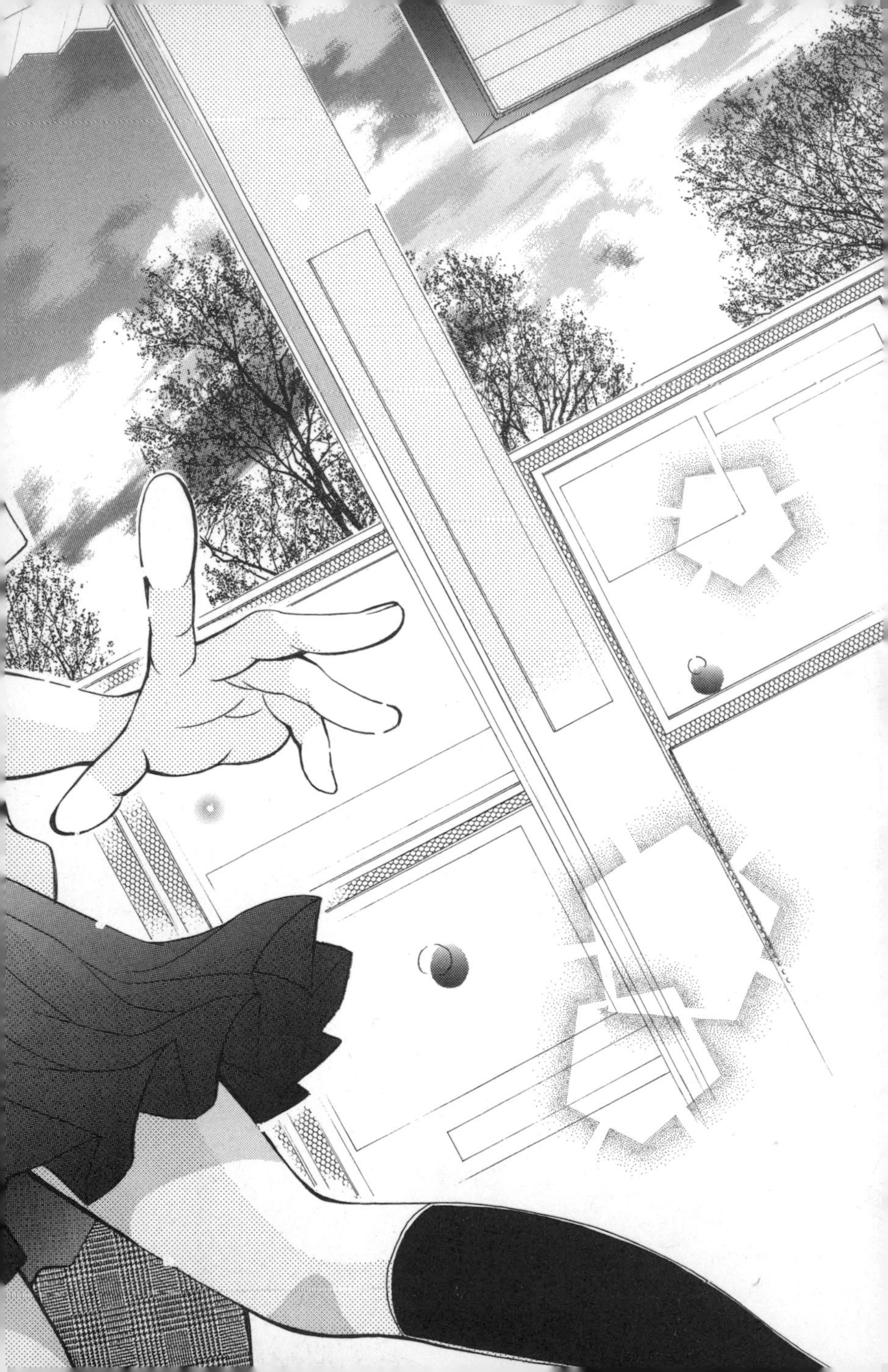

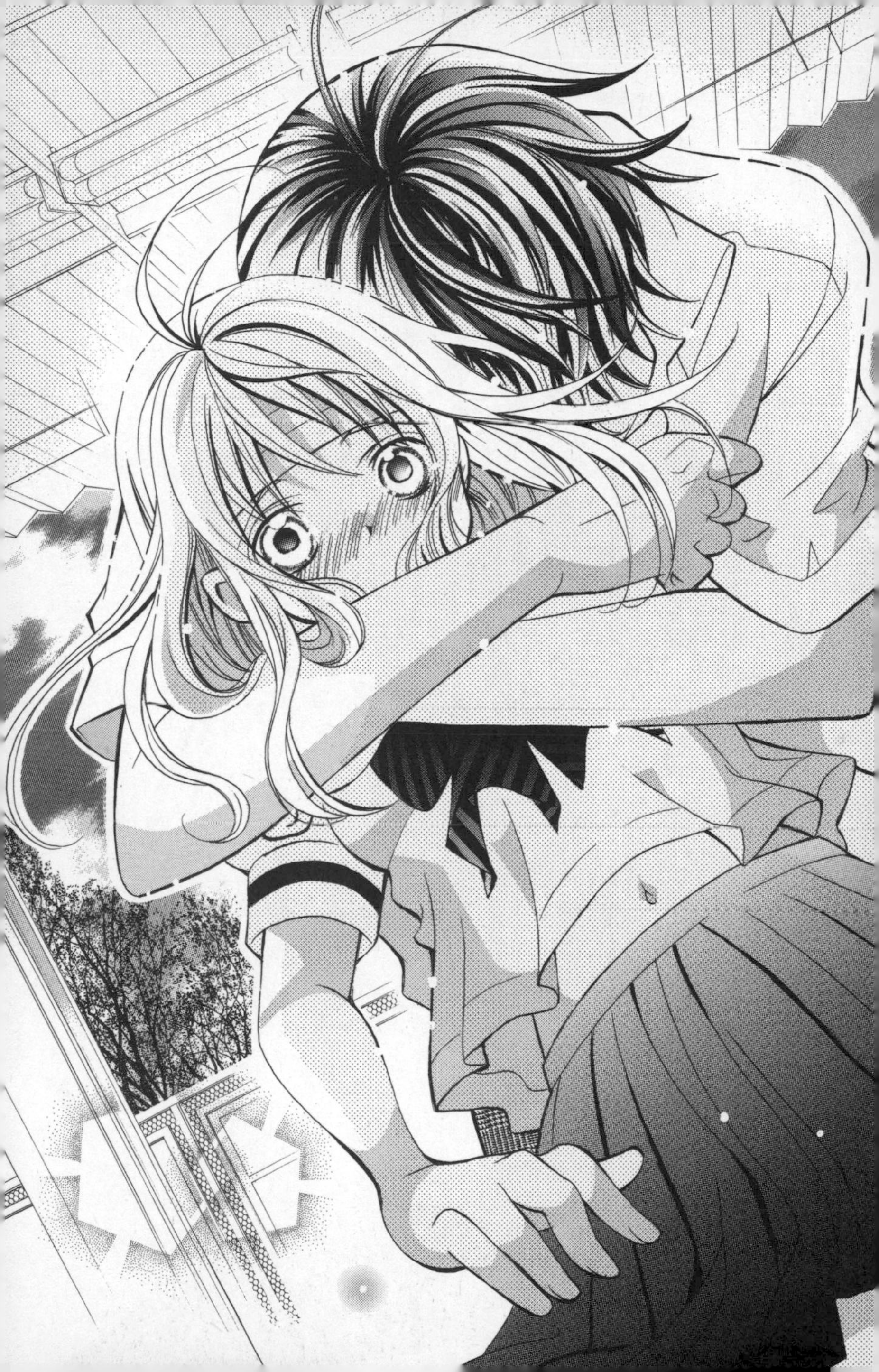

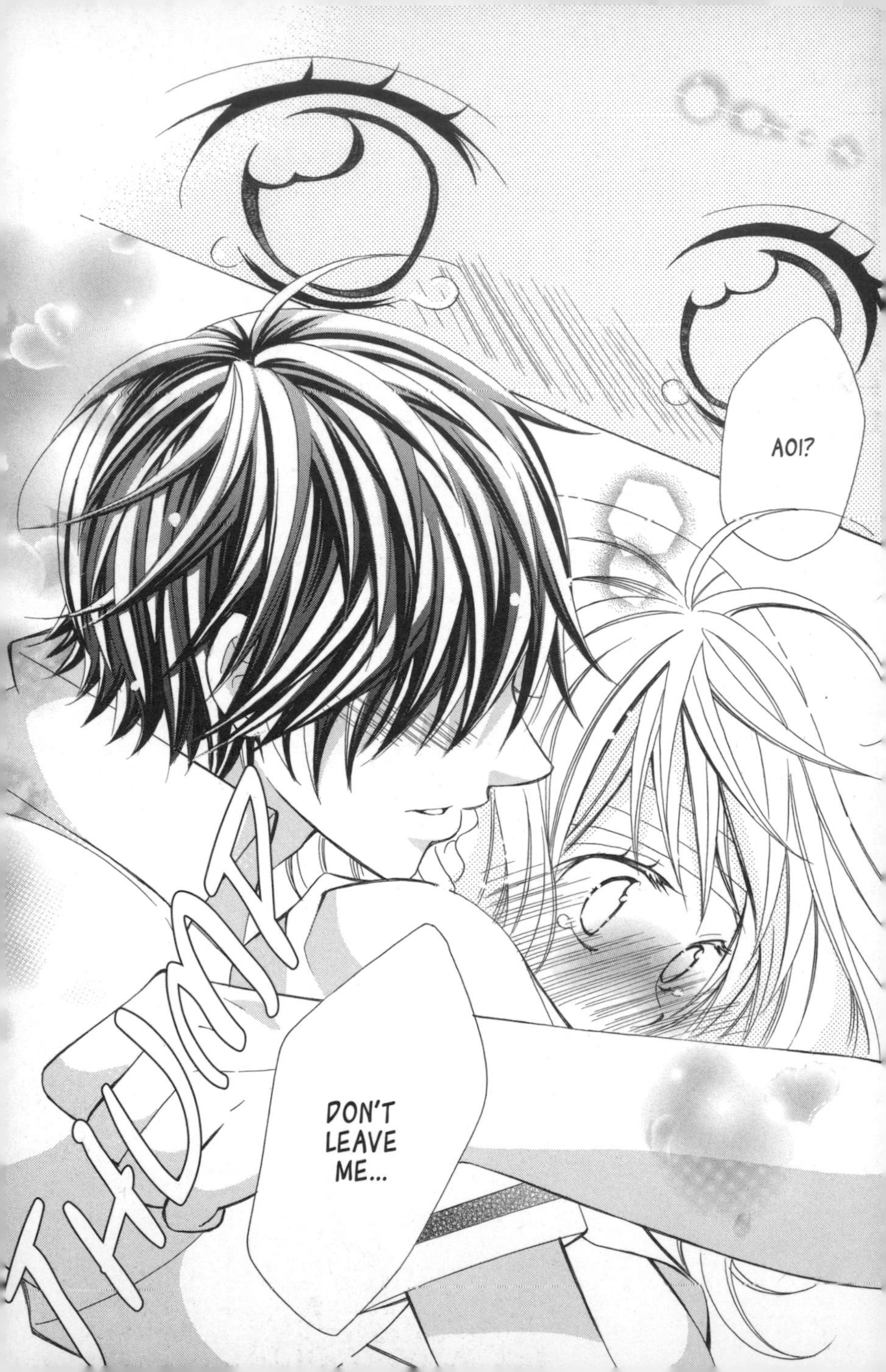
AOI?
THUMP
DON'T LEAVE ME...

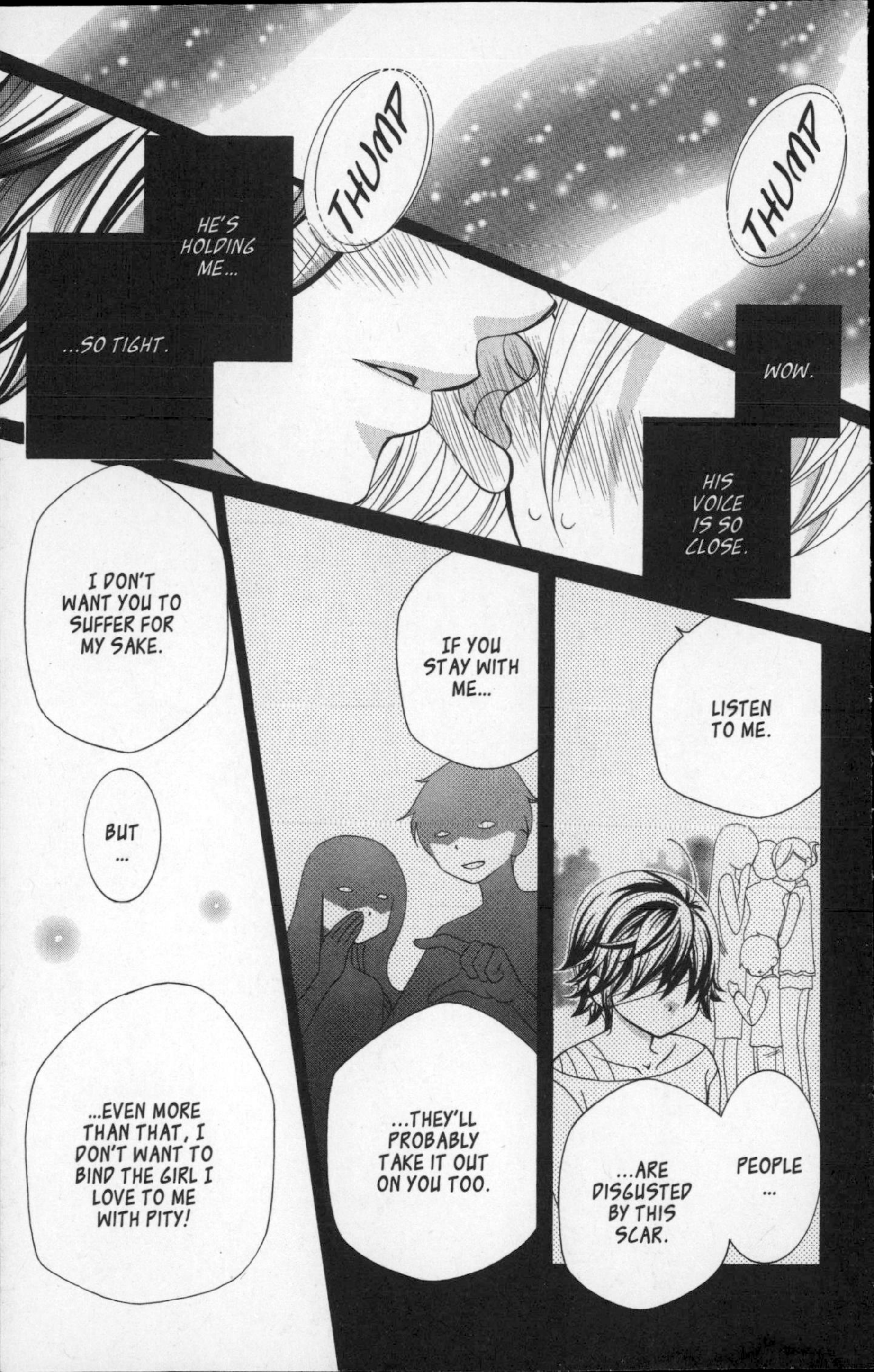
THUMP
THUMP
HE'S HOLDING ME...
...SO TIGHT.
WOW.
HIS VOICE IS SO CLOSE.
LISTEN TO ME.
PEOPLE ...
...ARE DISGUSTED BY THIS SCAR.
IF YOU STAY WITH ME...
...THEY'LL PROBABLY TAKE IT OUT ON YOU TOO.
I DON'T WANT YOU TO SUFFER FOR MY SAKE.
BUT ...
...EVEN MORE THAN THAT, I DON'T WANT TO BIND THE GIRL I LOVE TO ME WITH PITY!

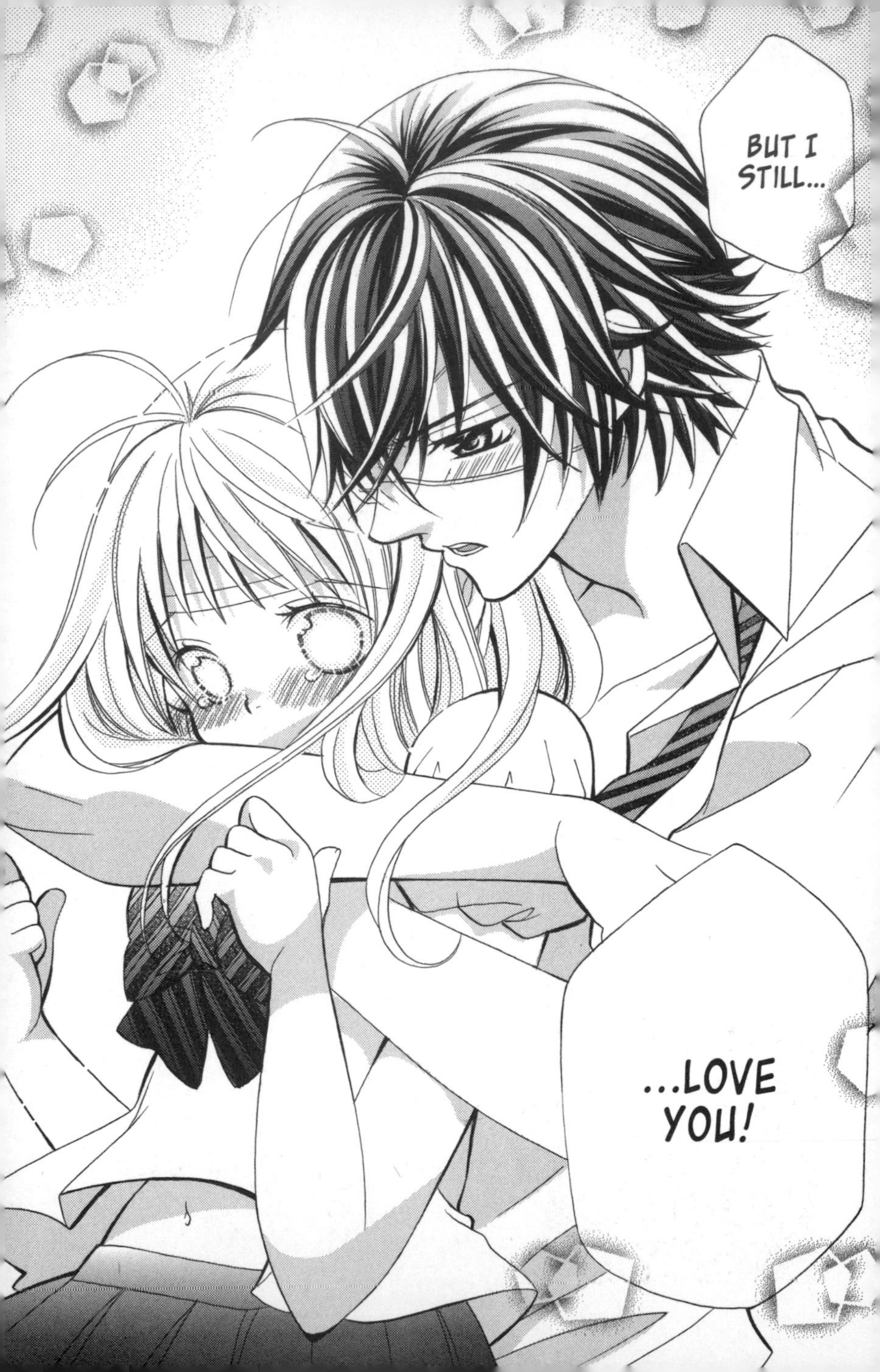
BUT I STILL...
...LOVE YOU!

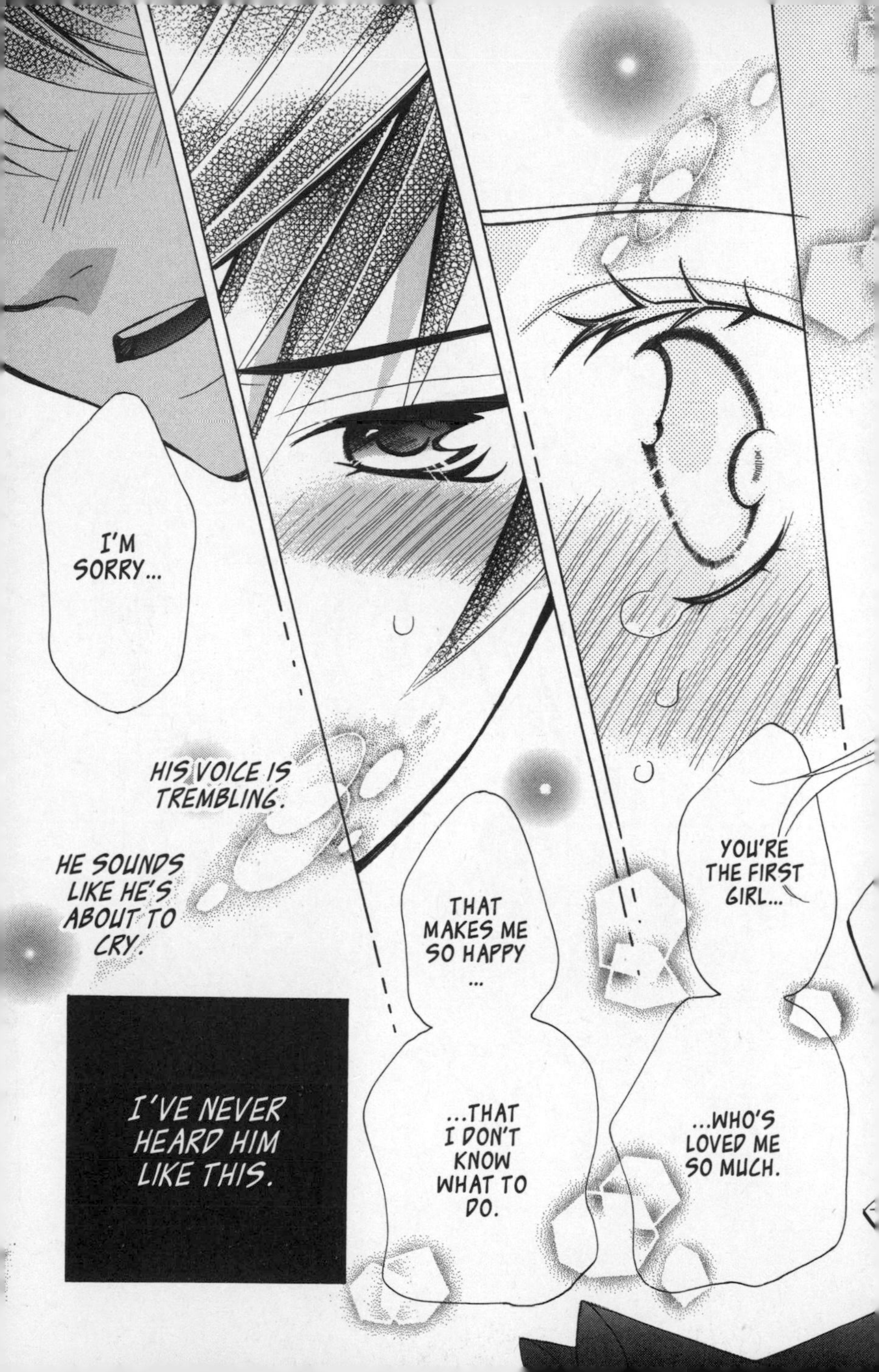
YOU'RE THE FIRST GIRL...
...WHO'S LOVED ME SO MUCH.
THAT MAKES ME SO HAPPY ...
...THAT I DON'T KNOW WHAT TO DO.
I'M SORRY...
HIS VOICE IS TREMBLING.
HE SOUNDS LIKE HE'S ABOUT TO CRY.
I'VE NEVER HEARD HIM LIKE THIS.

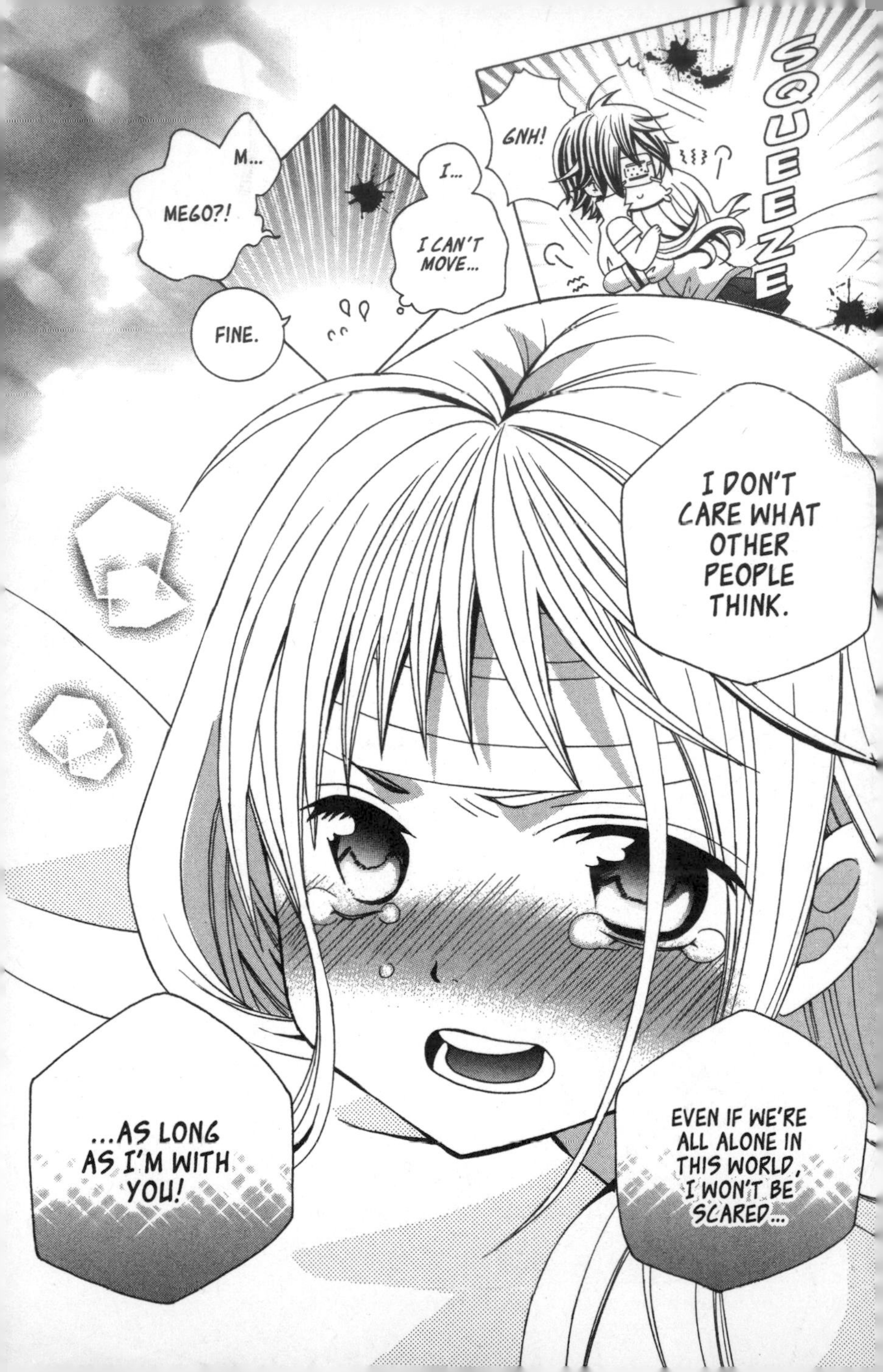
SQUEEZE
GNH!
I...
I CAN'T MOVE...
M...
MEGO?!
FINE.
I DON'T CARE WHAT OTHER PEOPLE THINK.
EVEN IF WE'RE ALL ALONE IN THIS WORLD, I WON'T BE SCARED...
...AS LONG AS I'M WITH YOU!

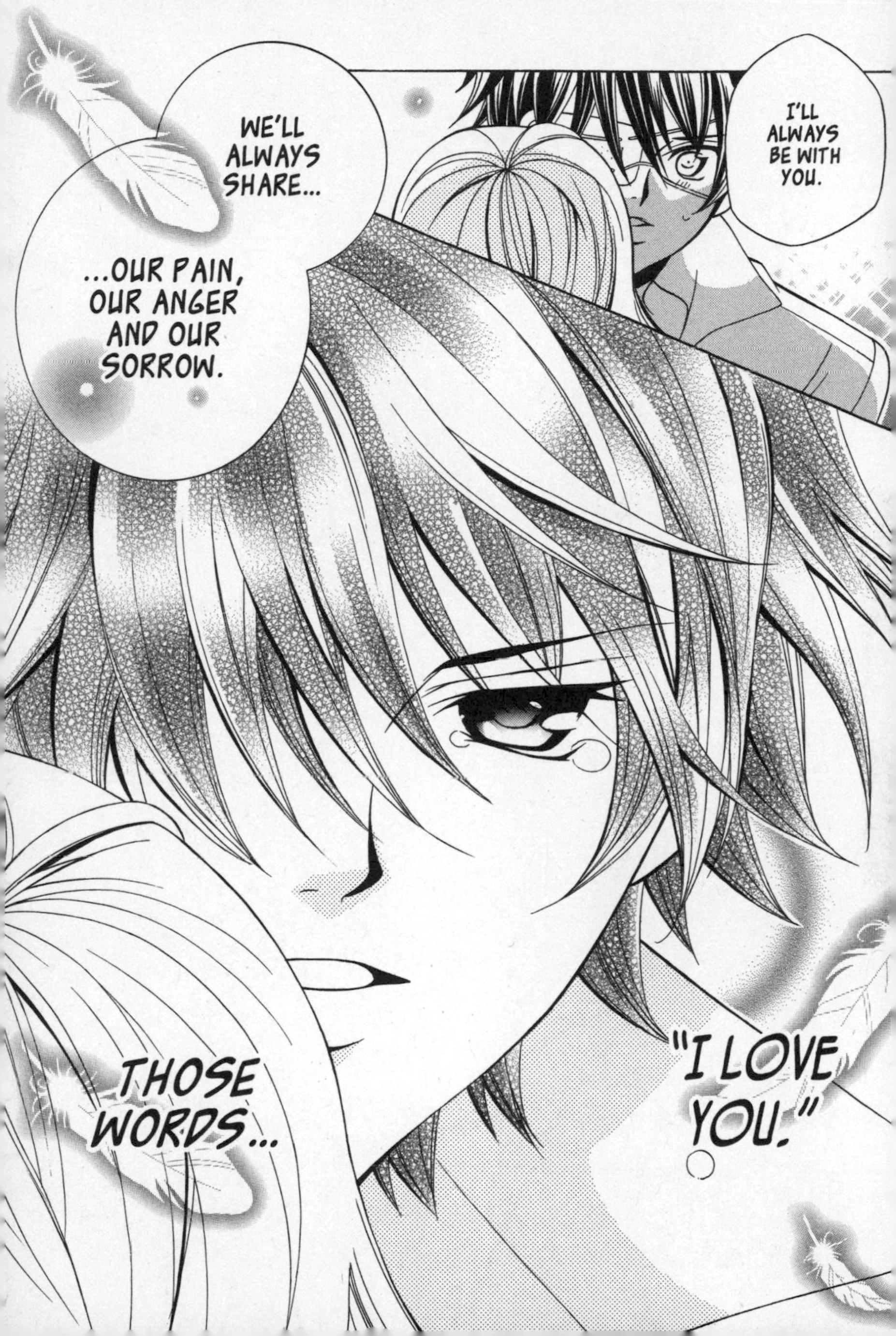
I'LL ALWAYS BE WITH YOU.
WE'LL ALWAYS SHARE...
...OUR PAIN, OUR ANGER AND OUR SORROW.
"I LOVE YOU."
THOSE WORDS...

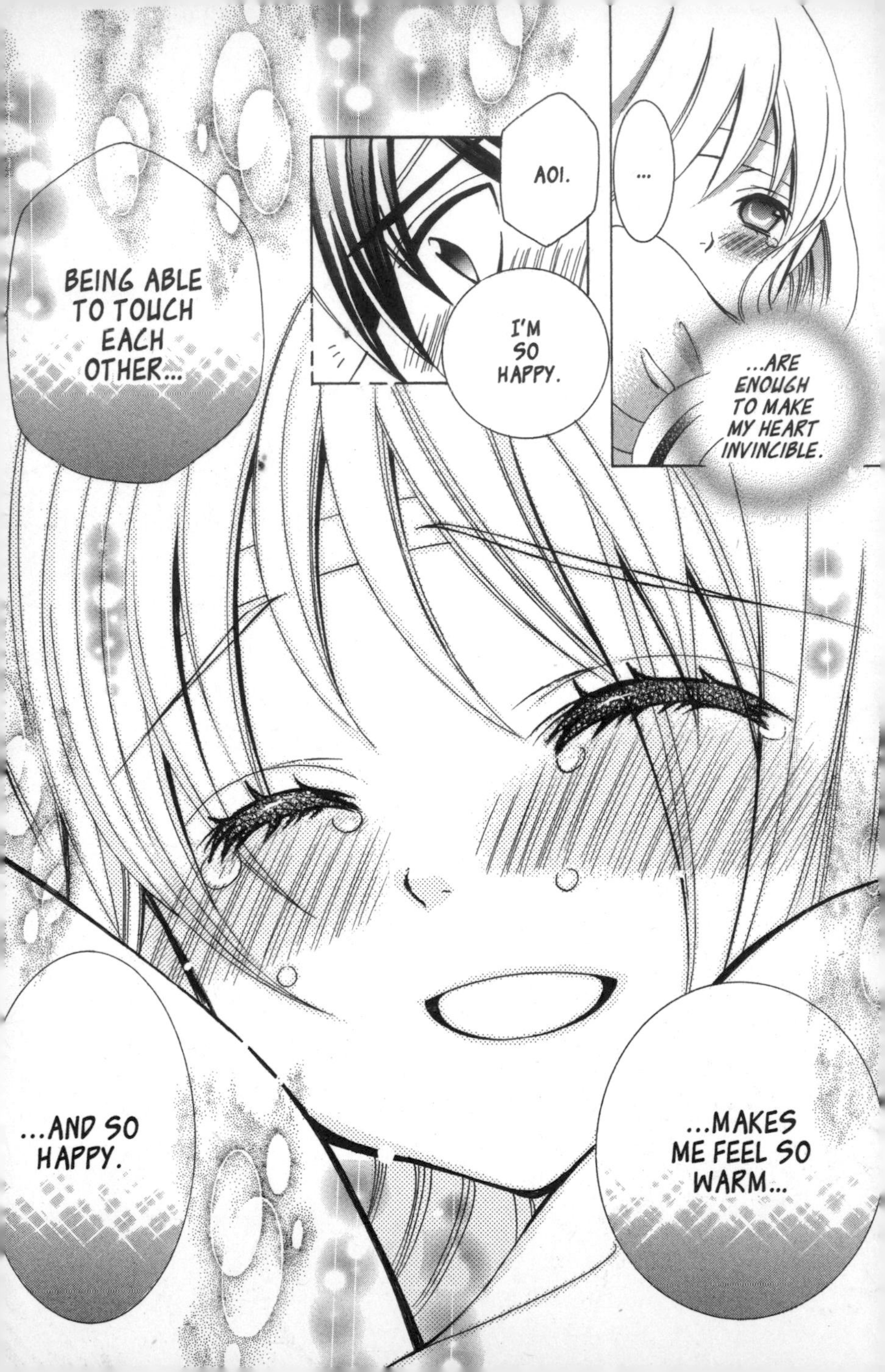
...
AOI.
I'M SO HAPPY.
BEING ABLE TO TOUCH EACH OTHER...
...ARE ENOUGH TO MAKE MY HEART INVINCIBLE.
...MAKES ME FEEL SO WARM...
...AND SO HAPPY.

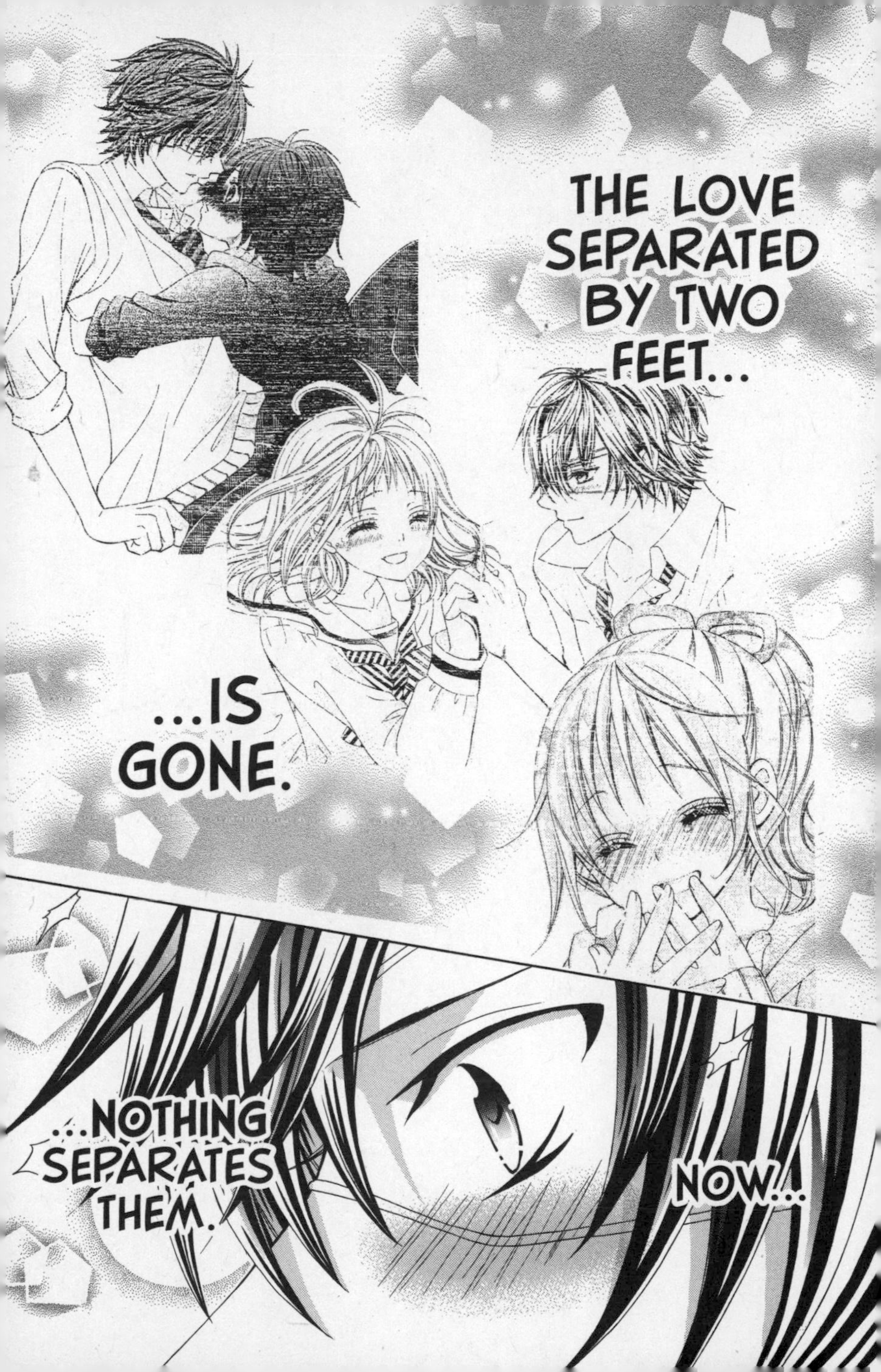
THE LOVE SEPARATED BY TWO FEET...
...IS GONE.
NOW...
...NOTHING SEPARATES THEM.

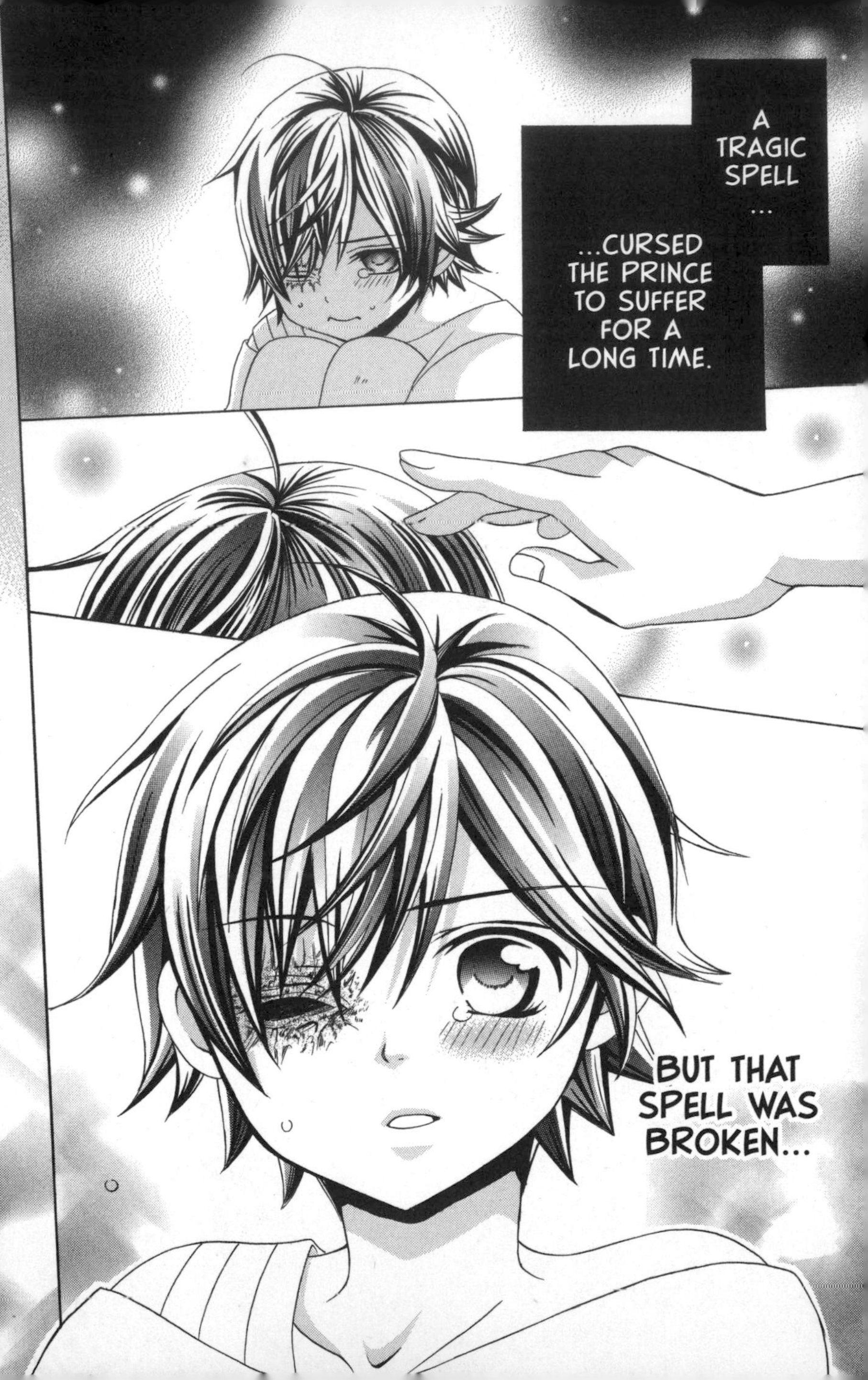
A TRAGIC SPELL ...
...CURSED THE PRINCE TO SUFFER FOR A LONG TIME.
BUT THAT SPELL WAS BROKEN...

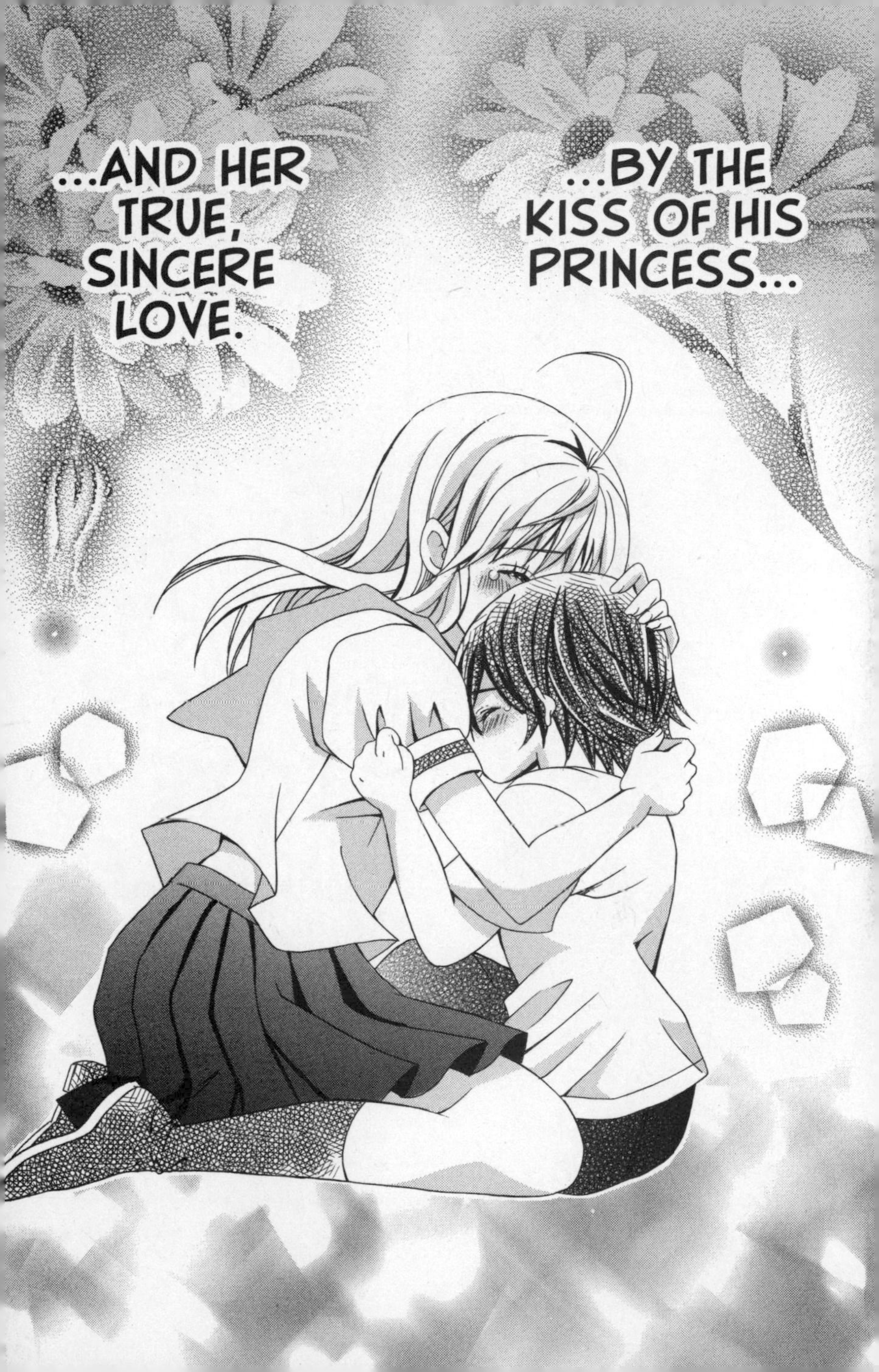
...BY THE KISS OF HIS PRINCESS...
...AND HER TRUE, SINCERE LOVE.

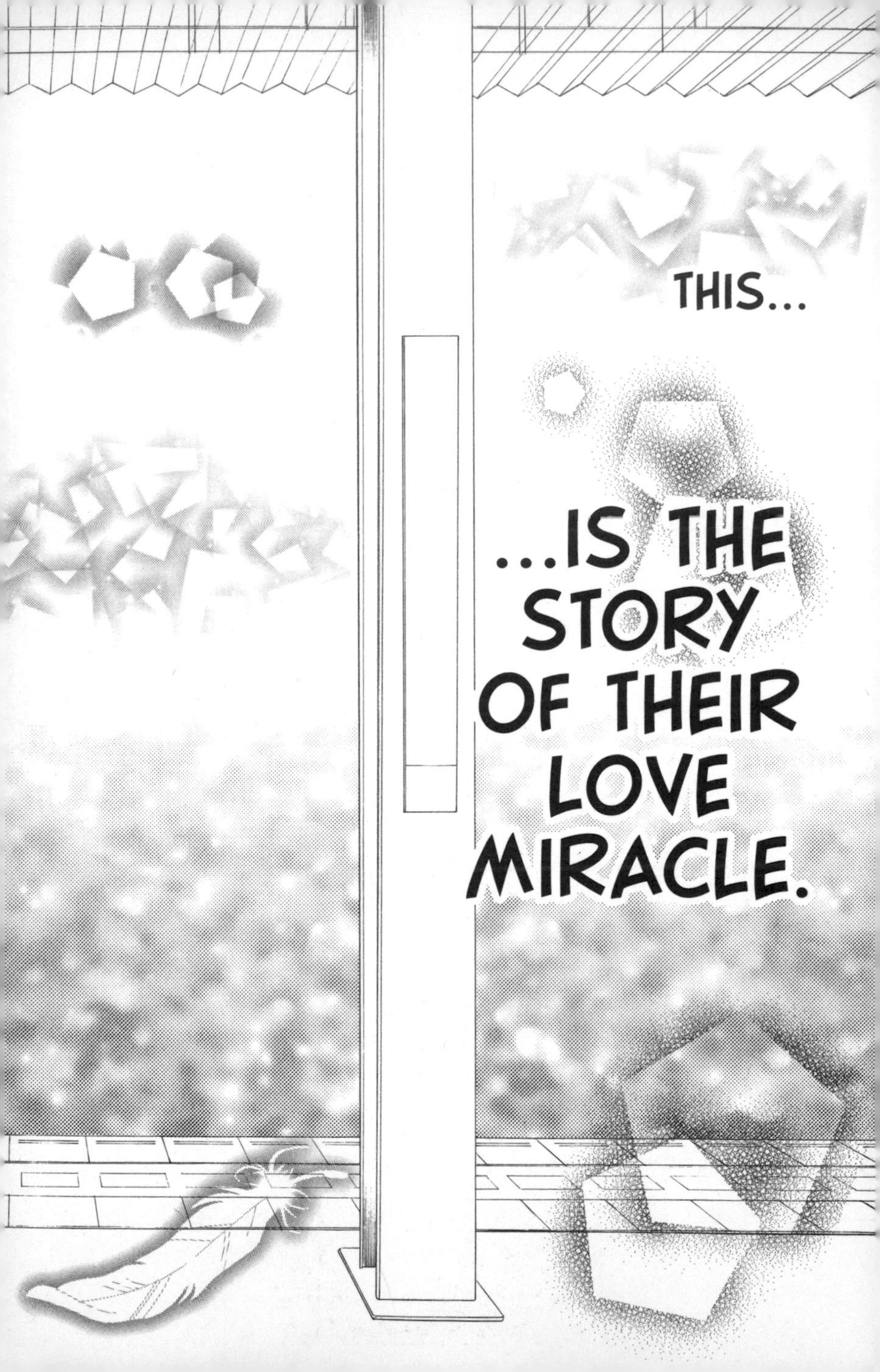
THIS...
...IS THE STORY OF THEIR LOVE MIRACLE.

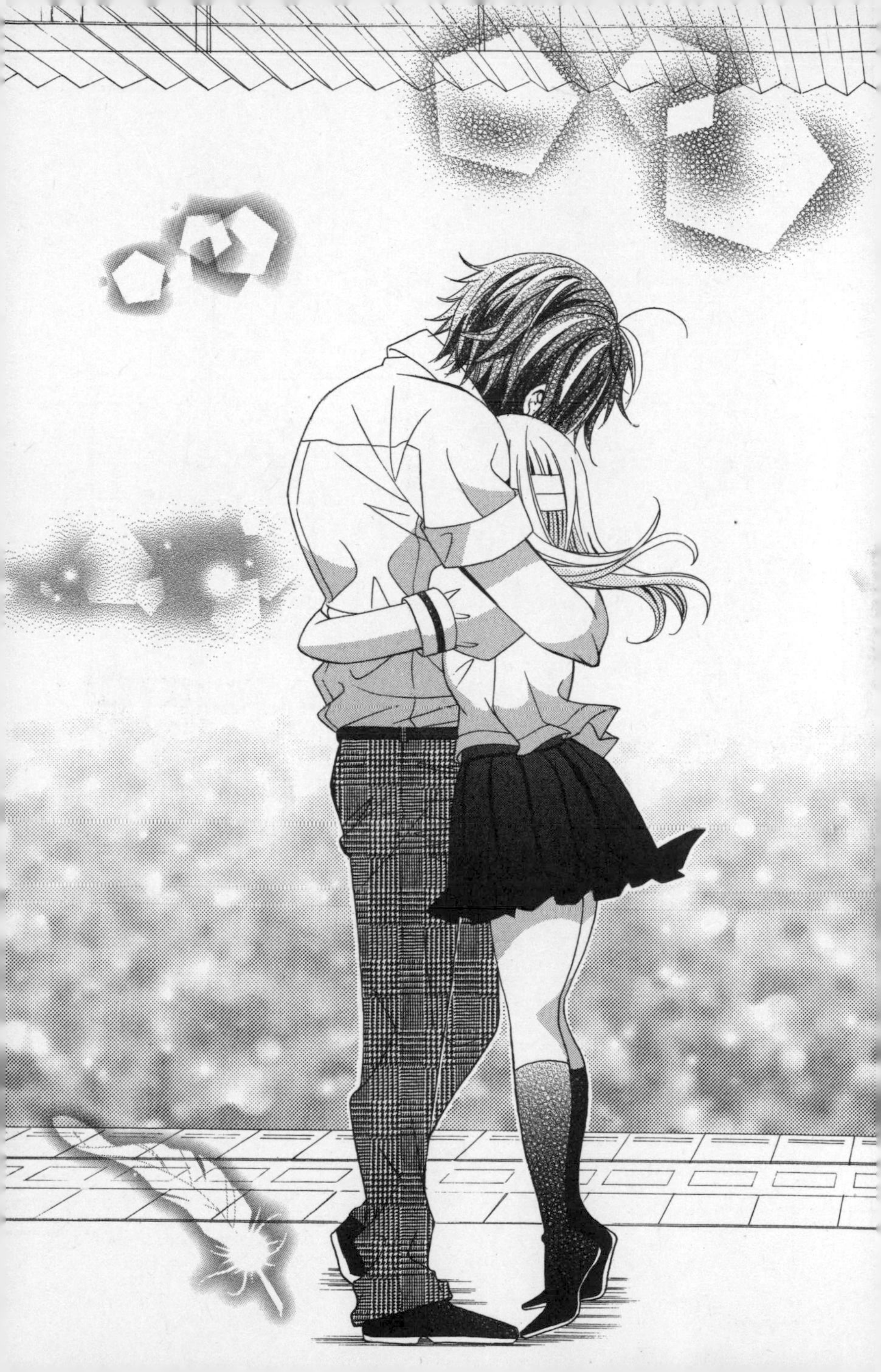

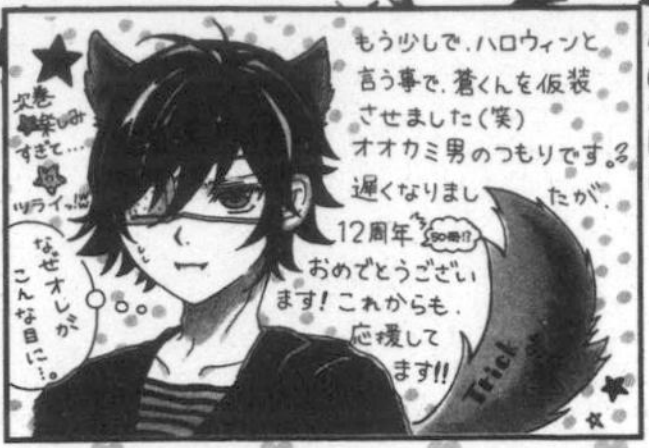
もう少しで、ハロウィンと言う事で、蒼くんを仮装させました(笑)
オオカミ男のつもりです。
遅くなりましたが、12周年おめでとうございます! これからも、応援してます!!
なぜオレがこんな目に…。
Trick

Atsuhiro Miyaji (Wakayama) ←
Ed.: Aoi the fox is cool!

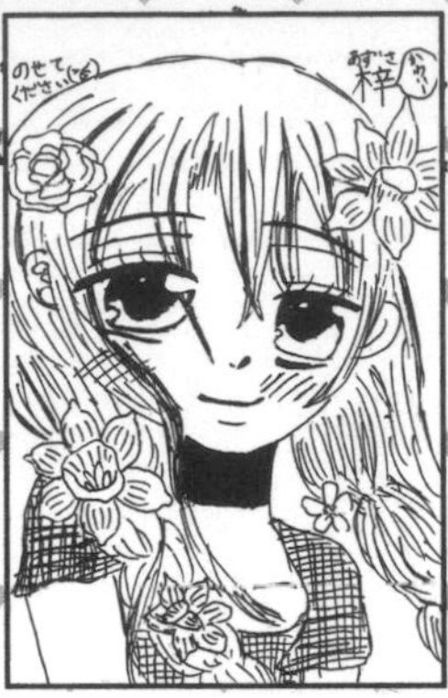
梓

Tamai Yamada (Tottori) ←
Ed.: Flowers look good on Ms. Azusa. ♥

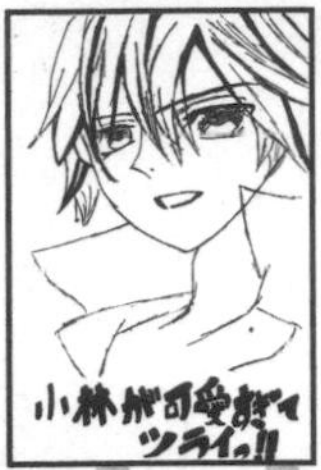
小林が可愛すぎてツライっ!!

Ami Sakuma (Saitama) ←
Ed.: He looks cool!

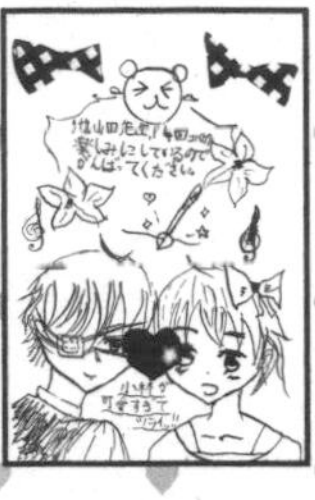

Ran Watanabe (Shizuoka) →
Ed.: These two are so in love. ♥

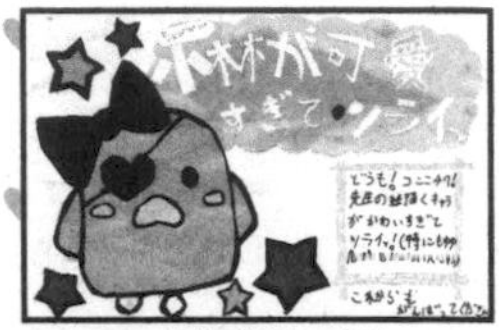
小林が可愛すぎてツライ

Sannen Milk (Ehime) ↑
Ed.: Readers really like the penguins!!

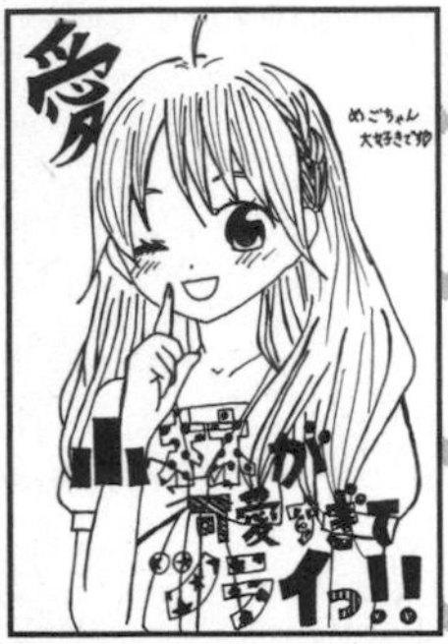
愛
小林が可愛すぎてツライっ!!

Natsuki Uchida (Aichi) ←
Ed.: Watching Mego makes me smile!!

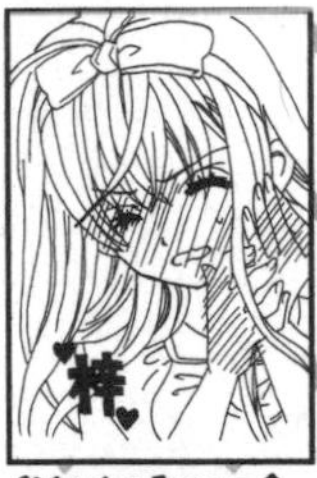
梓

Chizuka Inoue ↑ **(Hyogo)**
Ed.: I like Azusa no matter what she does.

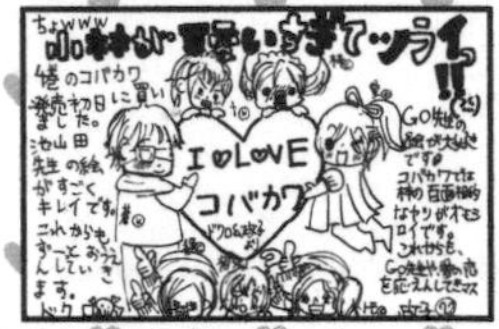
I ♥ LOVE
コバカワ

Dokuro & Masako ↑ **(Kanagawa)**
Ed.: Readers really like Tomo and Shizuka too!

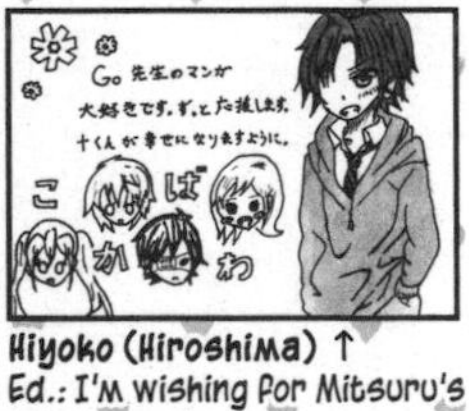
Go先生のマンガ大好きです。ずっと応援します。
十くんが幸せになりますように。
こばかわ

Hiyoko (Hiroshima) ↑
Ed.: I'm wishing for Mitsuru's happiness too!

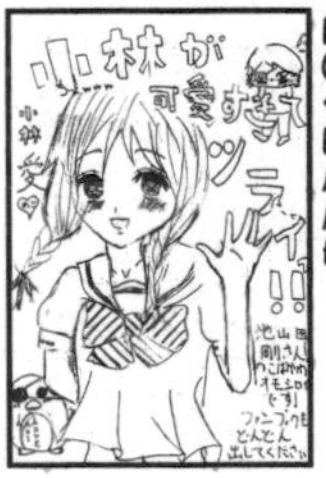
小林が可愛すぎてツライ!!

Neko Neko♡ (Yamagata) ←
Ed.: Aoi would melt seeing Mego like this...

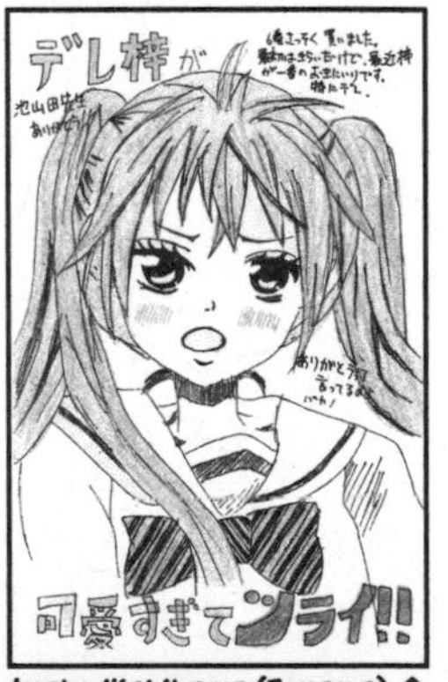
デレ梓が
可愛すぎてツライ!!

Ayako Nishikawa (Toyama) ↑
Ed.: Seeing Azusa act sweet makes my heart flutter!!

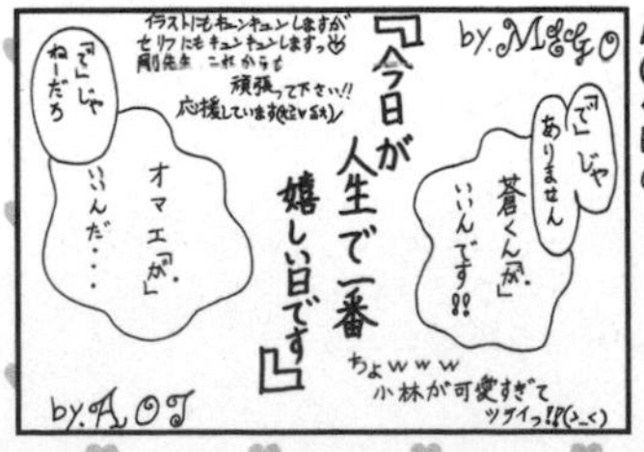
by. Mego
『今日が人生で一番嬉しい日です』
「で」じゃねーだろ
オマエ「が」いいんだ・・・
「で」じゃありません
蒼くん「が」いいんです!!
ちょwww 小林が可愛すぎてツライっ!!
by. AOT

Angel (Tokyo) ←
Ed.: The power of words!!

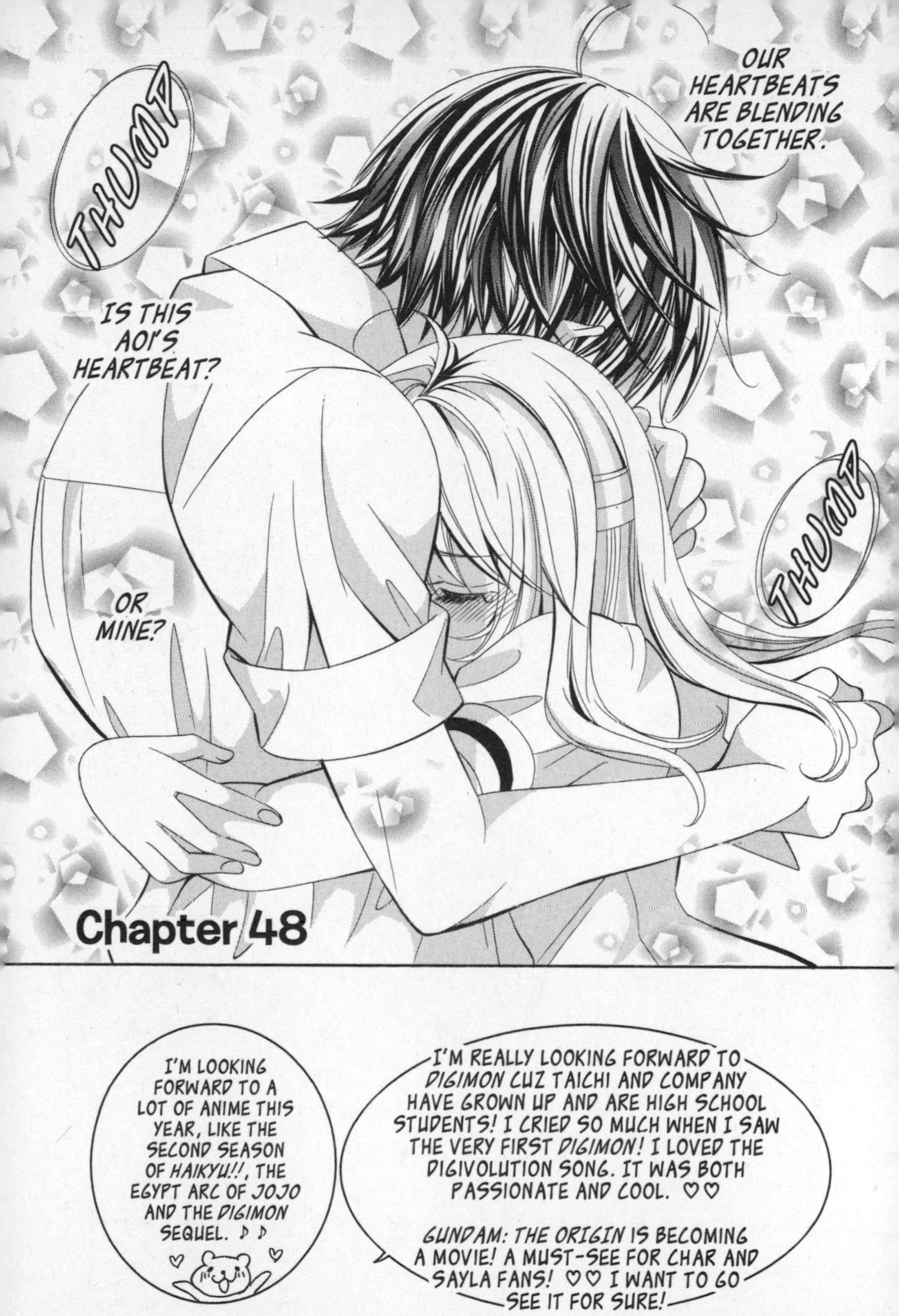
OUR HEARTBEATS ARE BLENDING TOGETHER.
THUMP
IS THIS AOI'S HEARTBEAT?
THUMP
OR MINE?

Chapter 48

I'M LOOKING FORWARD TO A LOT OF ANIME THIS YEAR, LIKE THE SECOND SEASON OF *HAIKYU!!*, THE EGYPT ARC OF JOJO AND THE *DIGIMON* SEQUEL. ♪♪

I'M REALLY LOOKING FORWARD TO *DIGIMON* CUZ TAICHI AND COMPANY HAVE GROWN UP AND ARE HIGH SCHOOL STUDENTS! I CRIED SO MUCH WHEN I SAW THE VERY FIRST *DIGIMON*! I LOVED THE DIGIVOLUTION SONG. IT WAS BOTH PASSIONATE AND COOL. ♡♡

GUNDAM: THE ORIGIN IS BECOMING A MOVIE! A MUST-SEE FOR CHAR AND SAYLA FANS! ♡♡ I WANT TO GO SEE IT FOR SURE!

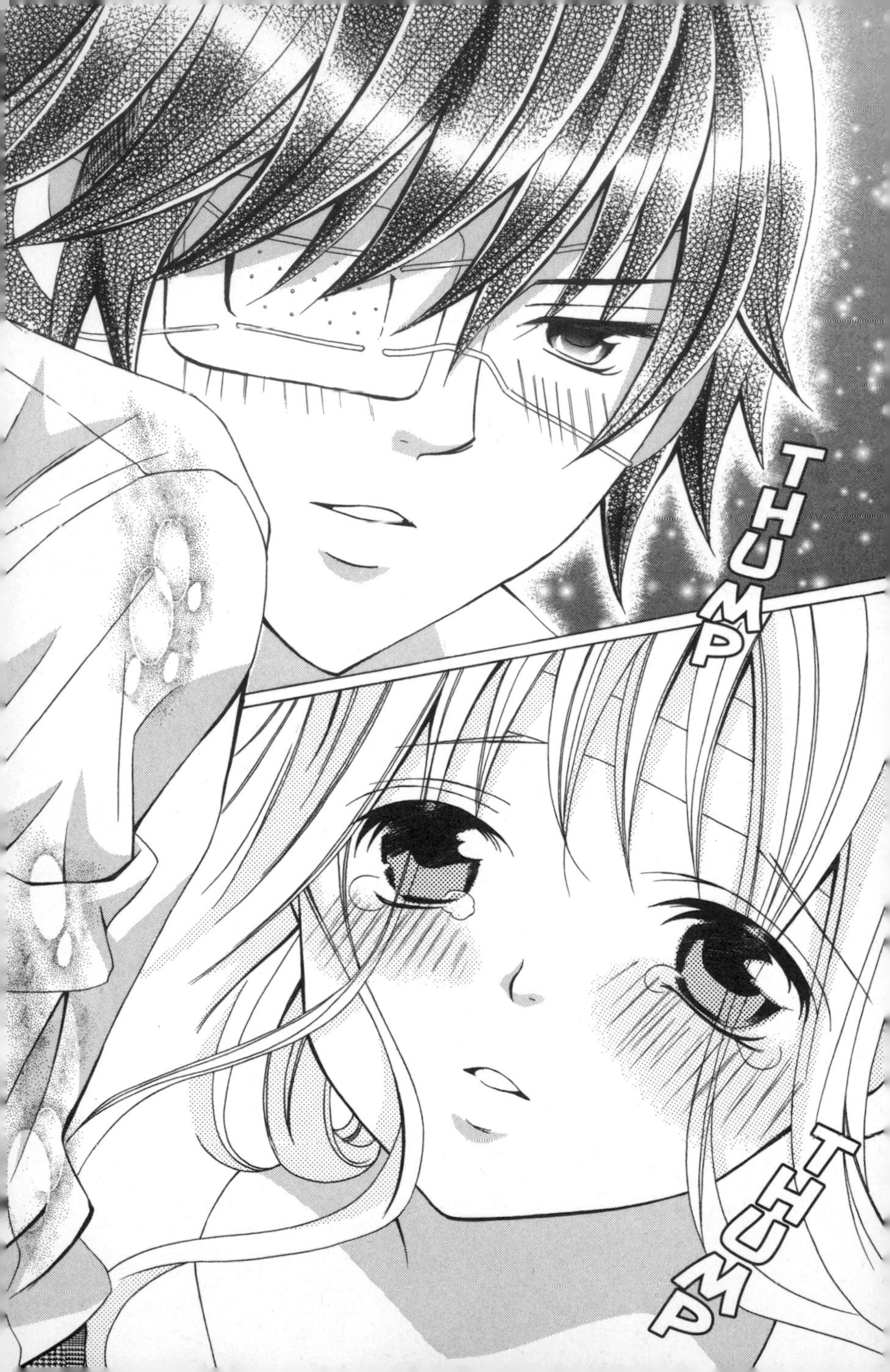
THUMP
THUMP

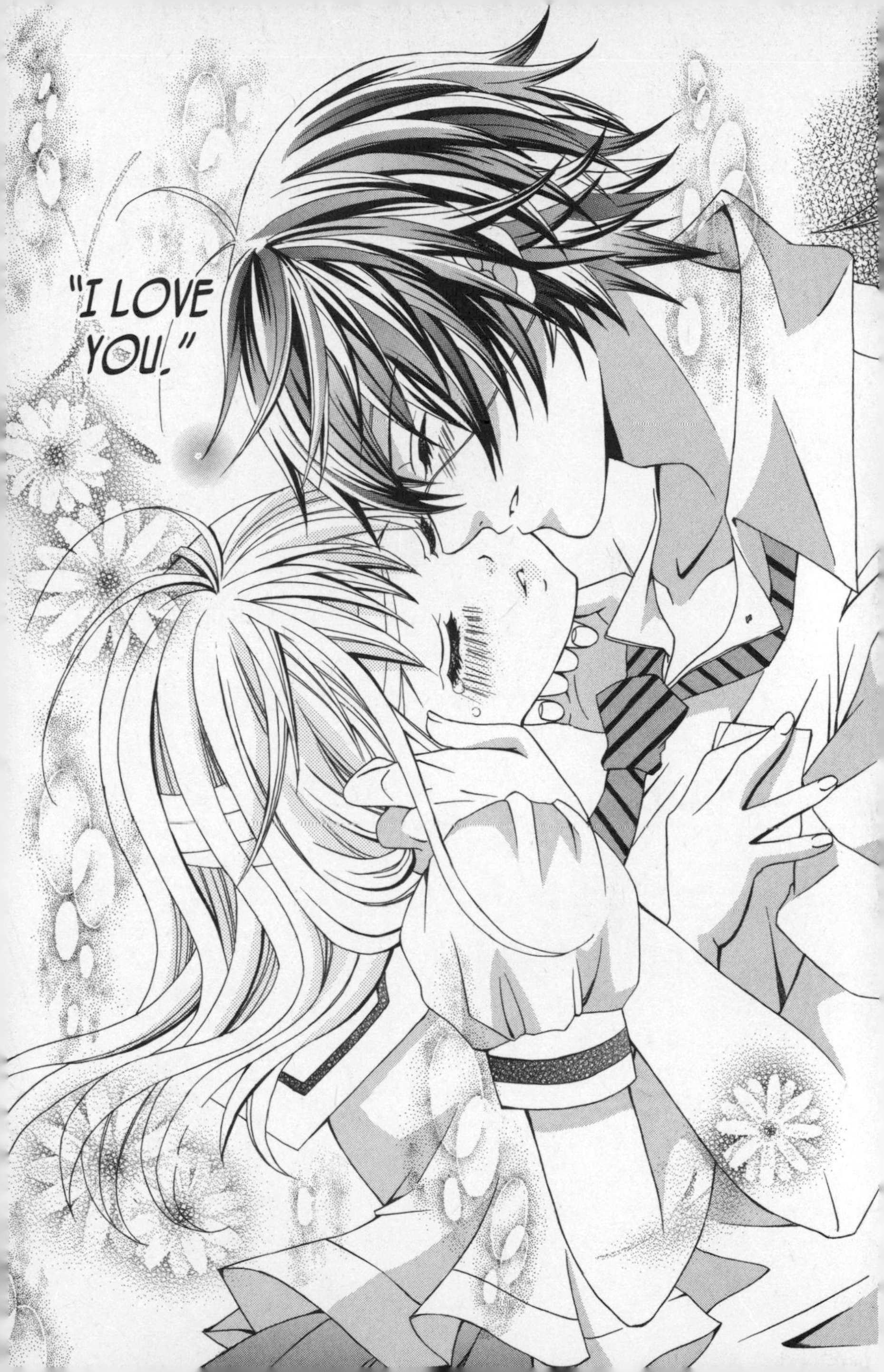
"I LOVE YOU."

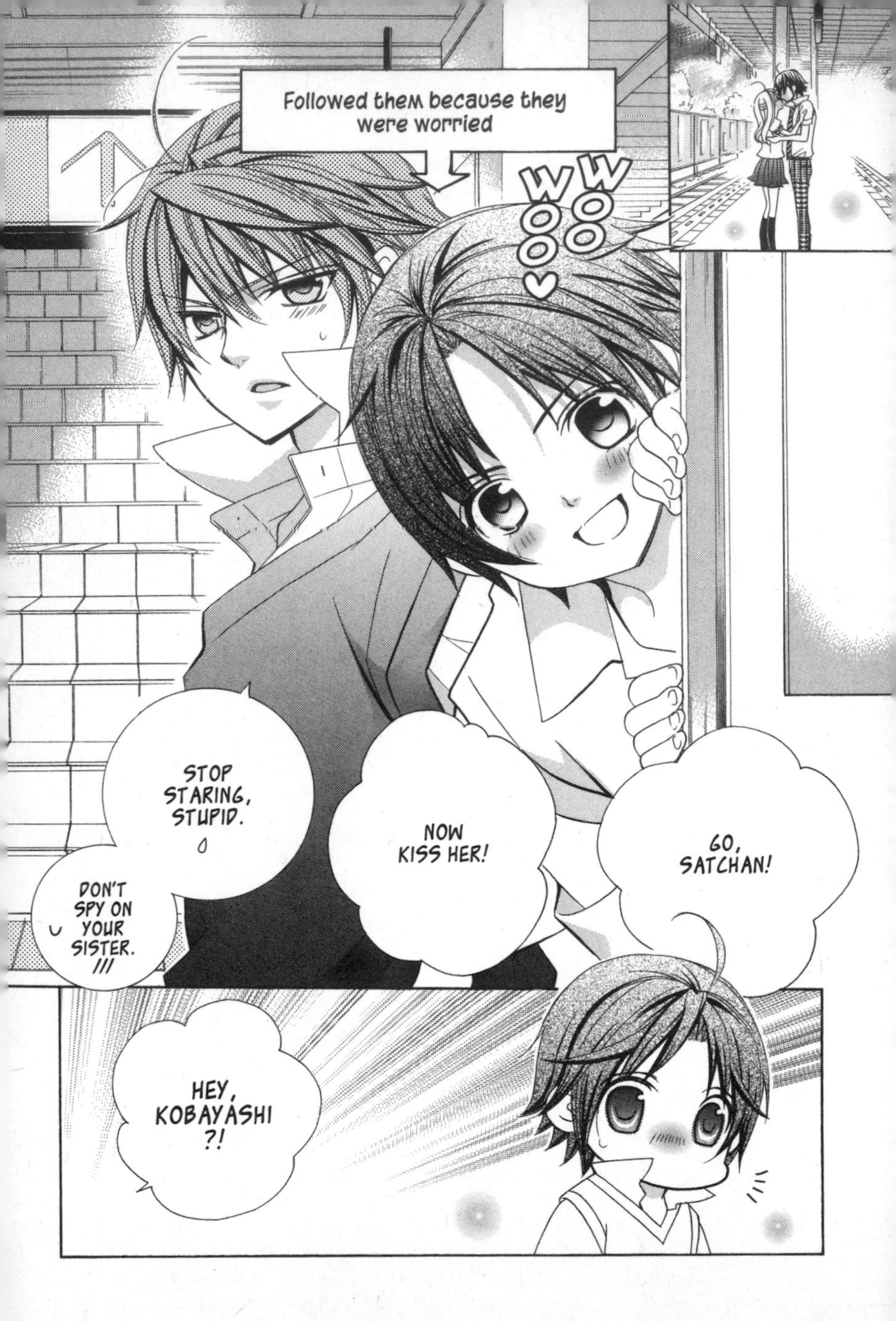

Followed them because they were worried
WOOO WOOO♥
GO, SATCHAN!
NOW KISS HER!
STOP STARING, STUPID.
DON'T SPY ON YOUR SISTER.
HEY, KOBAYASHI ?!

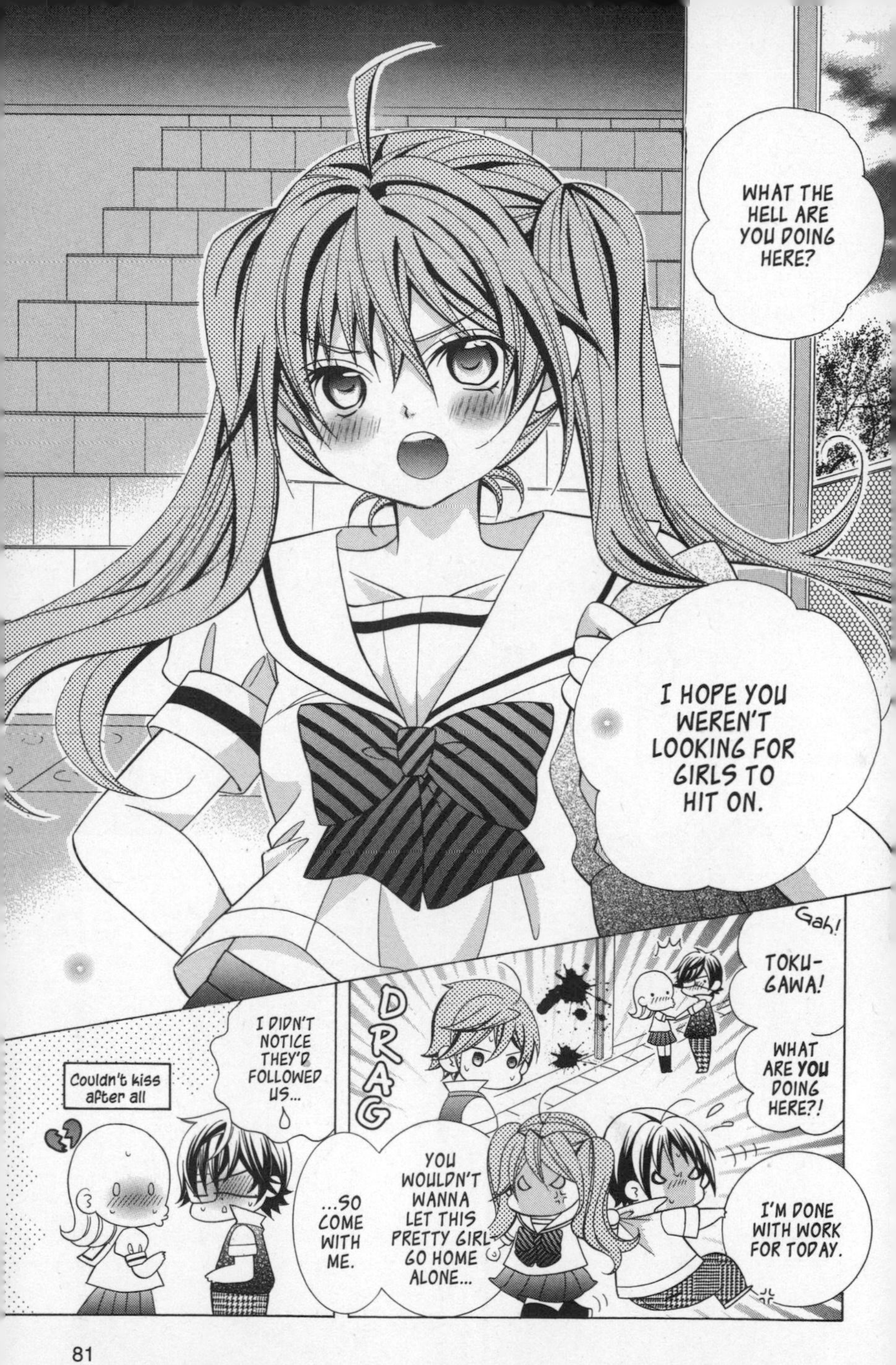
WHAT THE HELL ARE YOU DOING HERE?
I HOPE YOU WEREN'T LOOKING FOR GIRLS TO HIT ON.
Gah!
TOKU-GAWA!
WHAT ARE YOU DOING HERE?!
I'M DONE WITH WORK FOR TODAY.
YOU WOULDN'T WANNA LET THIS PRETTY GIRL GO HOME ALONE...
...SO COME WITH ME.
DRAG
I DIDN'T NOTICE THEY'D FOLLOWED US...
Couldn't kiss after all

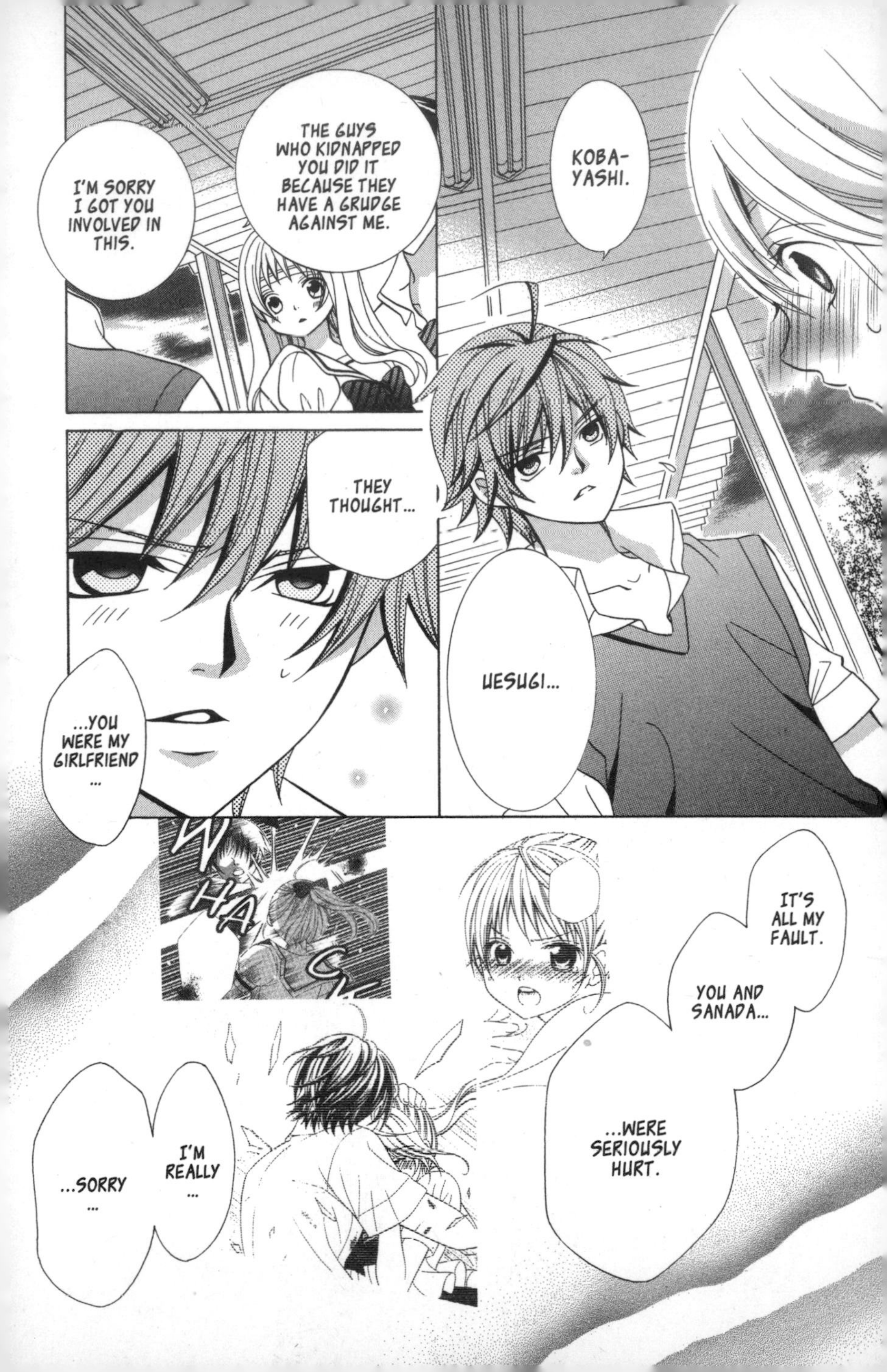
KOBA-YASHI.
UESUGI...
THE GUYS WHO KIDNAPPED YOU DID IT BECAUSE THEY HAVE A GRUDGE AGAINST ME.
I'M SORRY I GOT YOU INVOLVED IN THIS.
THEY THOUGHT...
...YOU WERE MY GIRLFRIEND ...
IT'S ALL MY FAULT.
YOU AND SANADA...
...WERE SERIOUSLY HURT.
I'M REALLY ...
...SORRY ...

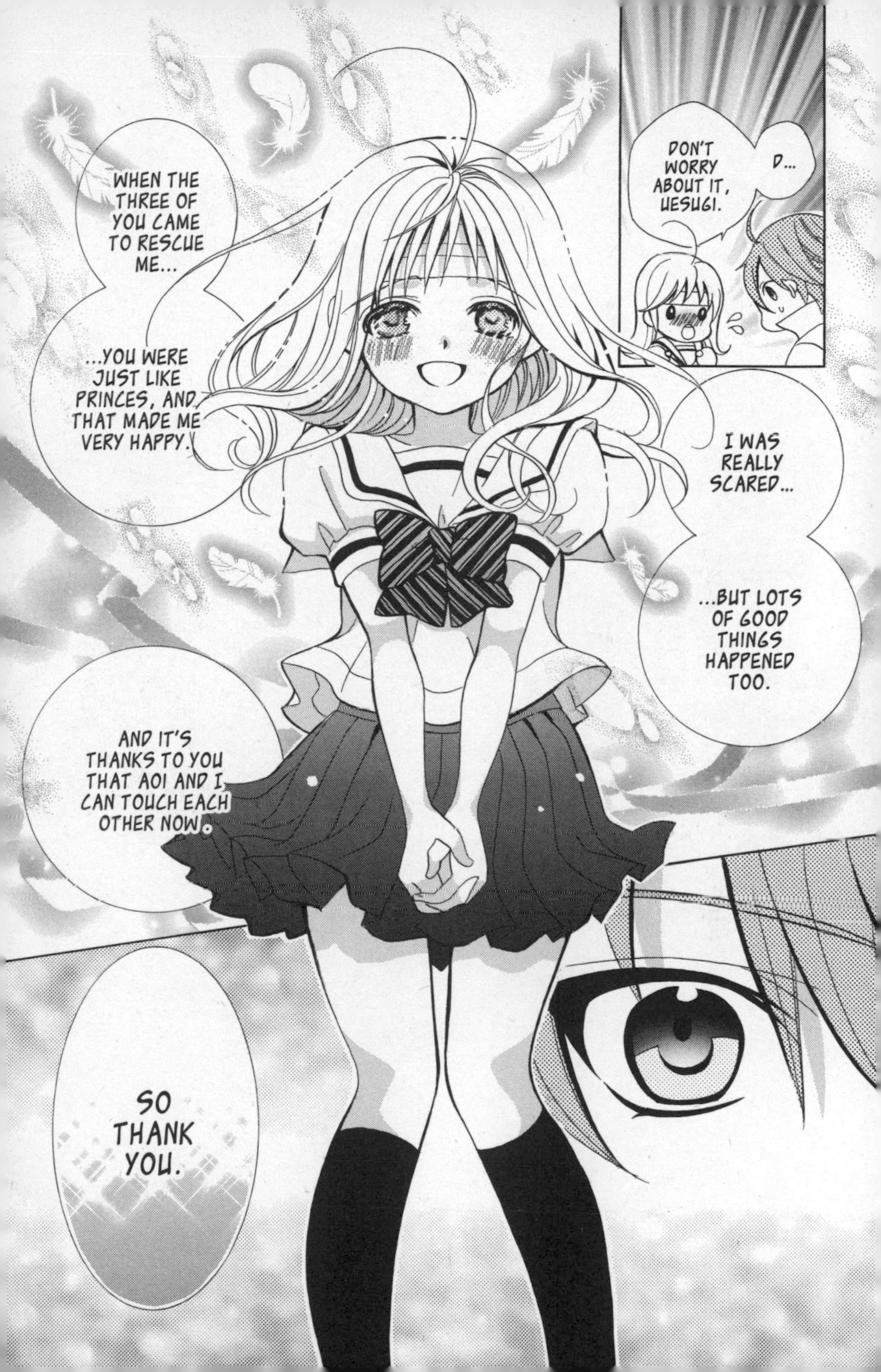
D...
DON'T WORRY ABOUT IT, UESUGI.
WHEN THE THREE OF YOU CAME TO RESCUE ME...
...YOU WERE JUST LIKE PRINCES, AND THAT MADE ME VERY HAPPY.
I WAS REALLY SCARED...
...BUT LOTS OF GOOD THINGS HAPPENED TOO.
AND IT'S THANKS TO YOU THAT AOI AND I CAN TOUCH EACH OTHER NOW.
SO THANK YOU.

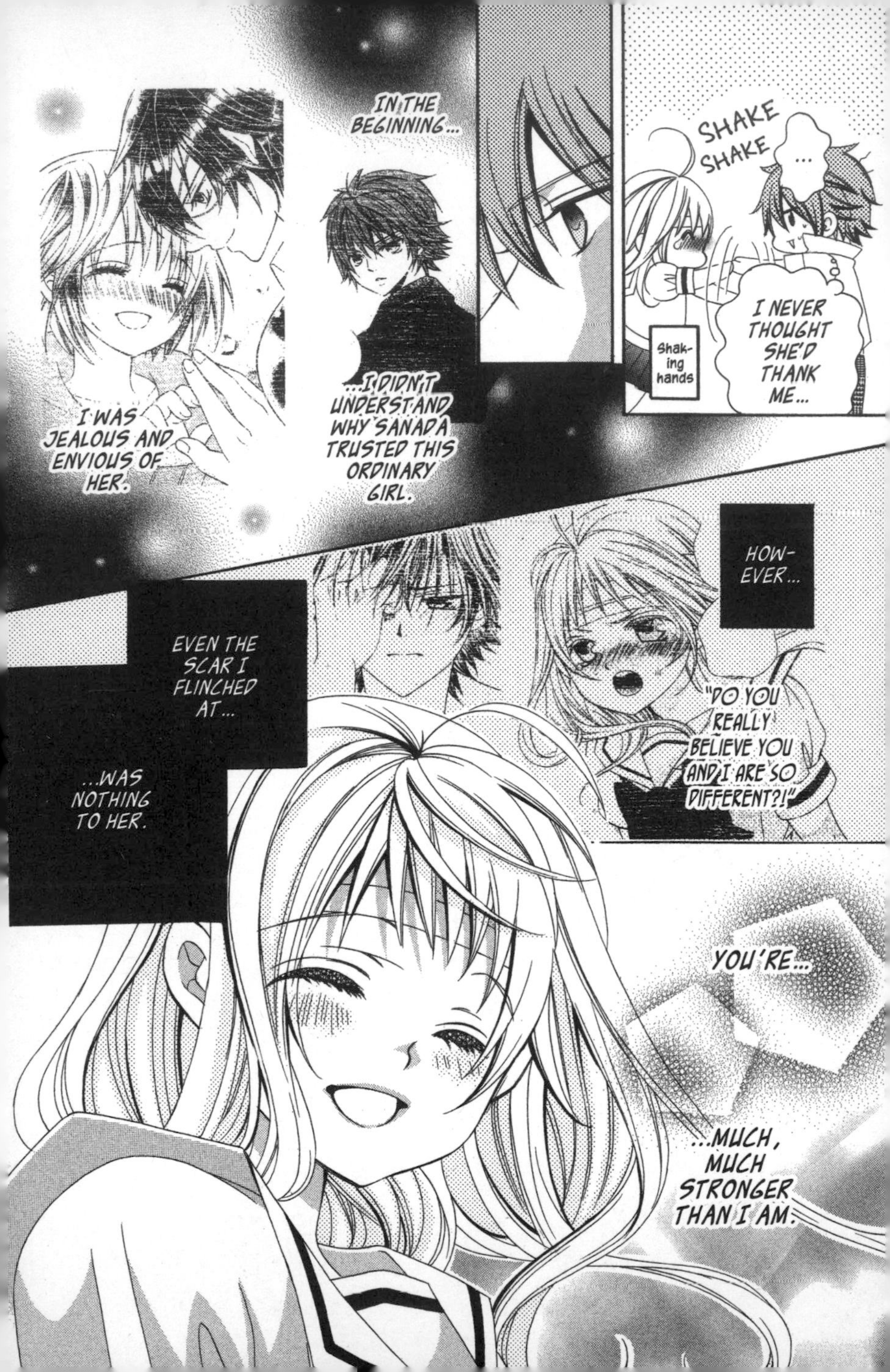
SHAKE SHAKE
...
Shaking hands
I NEVER THOUGHT SHE'D THANK ME...
IN THE BEGINNING...
...I DIDN'T UNDERSTAND WHY SANADA TRUSTED THIS ORDINARY GIRL.
I WAS JEALOUS AND ENVIOUS OF HER.
HOW-EVER...
"DO YOU REALLY BELIEVE YOU AND I ARE SO DIFFERENT?!"
EVEN THE SCAR I FLINCHED AT...
...WAS NOTHING TO HER.
YOU'RE...
...MUCH, MUCH STRONGER THAN I AM.

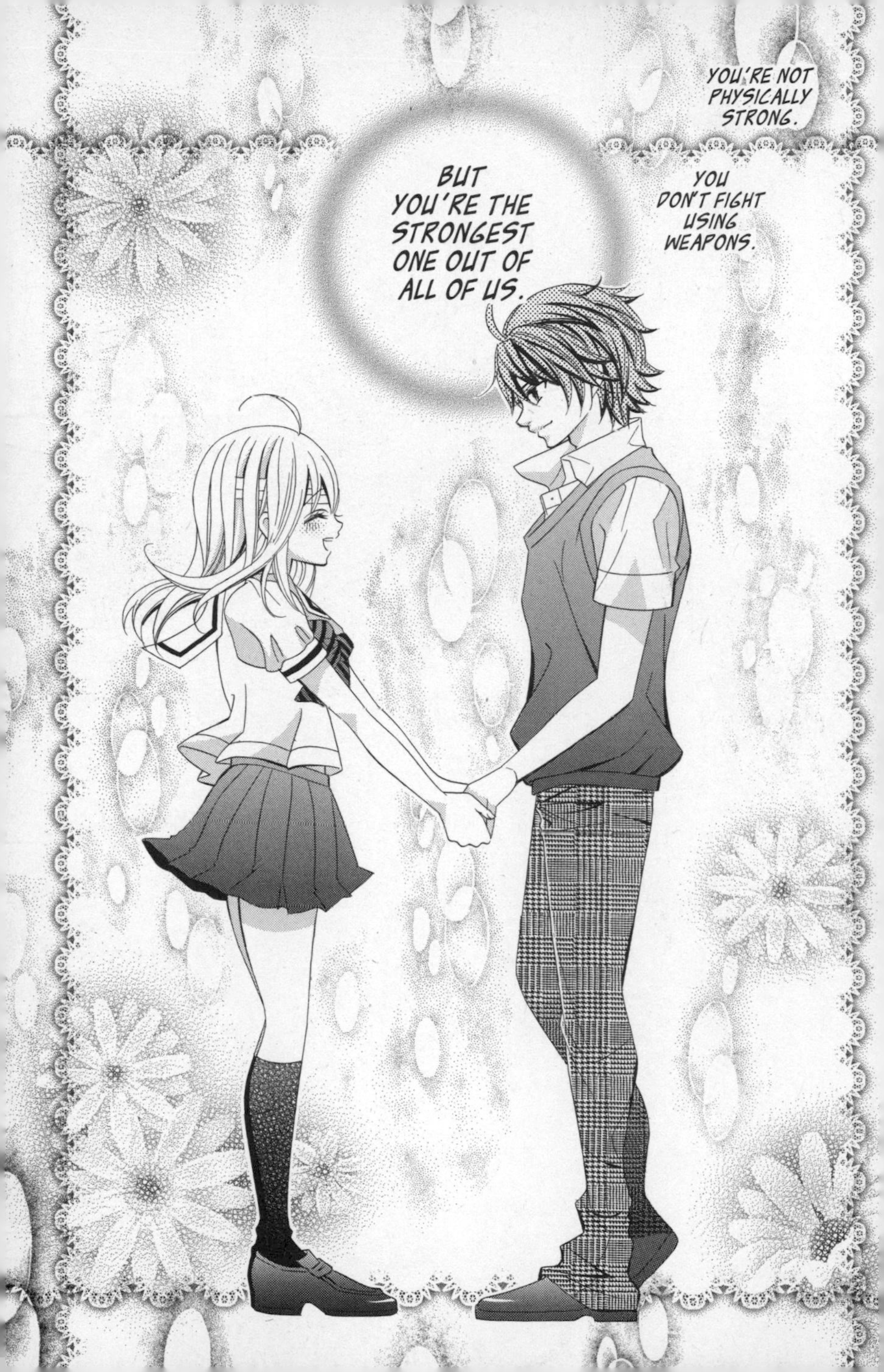
YOU'RE NOT PHYSICALLY STRONG.
YOU DON'T FIGHT USING WEAPONS.
BUT YOU'RE THE STRONGEST ONE OUT OF ALL OF US.

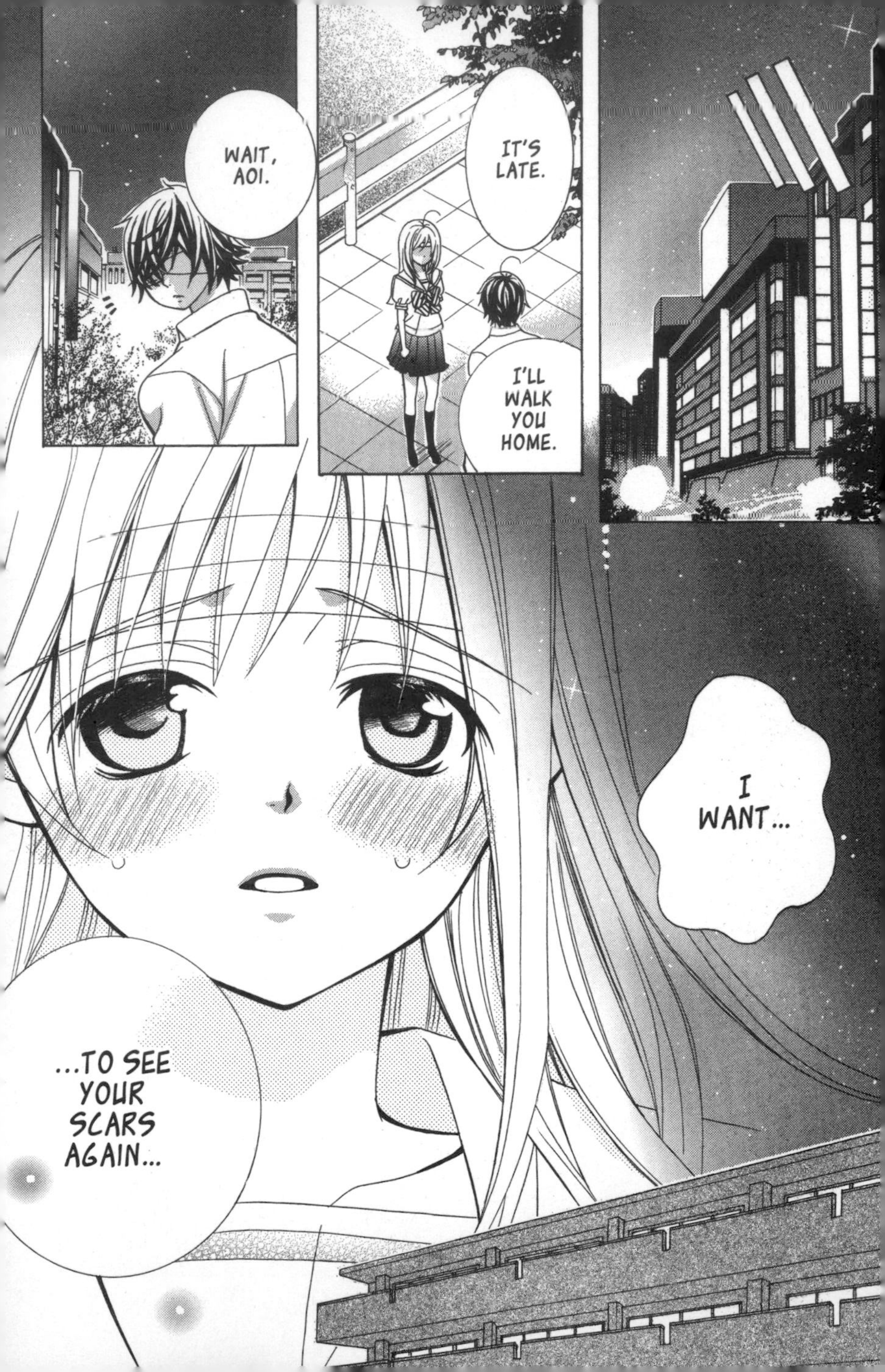
IT'S LATE.
I'LL WALK YOU HOME.
WAIT, AOI.
I WANT...
...TO SEE YOUR SCARS AGAIN...

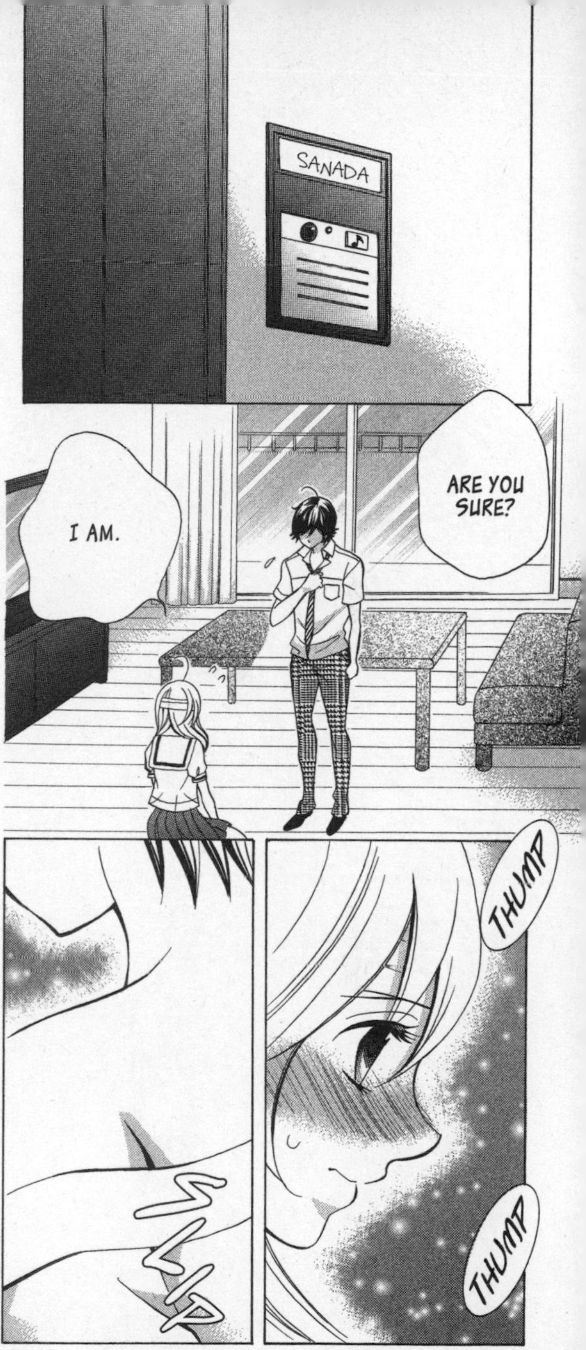
SANADA
ARE YOU SURE?
I AM.
THUMP
THUMP
SLIP

SPECIAL THANKS

Yuka Ito-sama,
Rieko Hirai-sama,
Kayoko Takahashi-sama,
Kawasaki-sama,
Nagisa Sato Sensei.

Rei Nanase Sensei,
Arisu Fujishiro Sensei,
Mumi Mimura Sensei,
Masayo Nagata-sama,
Naochan-sama,
Asuka Sakura Sensei
and many others.

Bookstore Dan Kinshicho Branch, Kinokuniya Shinjuku Branch, LIBRO Ikebukuro Branch, Kinokuniya Hankyu 32-Bangai Branch.

Sendai Hachimonjiya Bookstore, BOOKS HOSHINO Kintetsu Pass'e Branch, Asahiya Tennnoji MiO Branch, Kurashiki Kikuya Bookstore.

Salesperson:
Mizusawa-sama

Previous salesperson:
Honma-sama

Previous editor:
Nakata-sama

Current editor:
Shoji-sama

I also sincerely express my gratitude to everyone who picked up this volume.

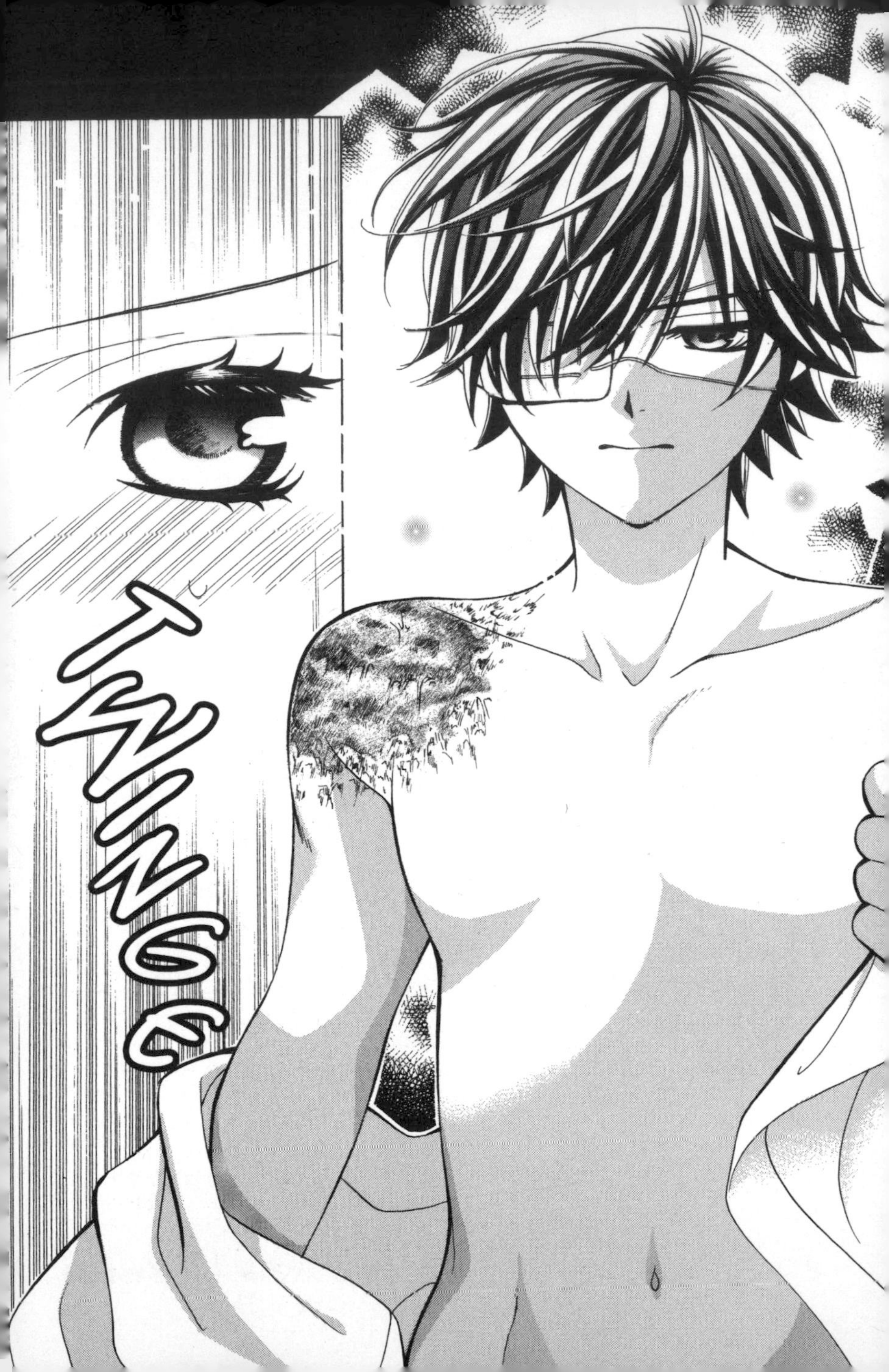
TWINGE

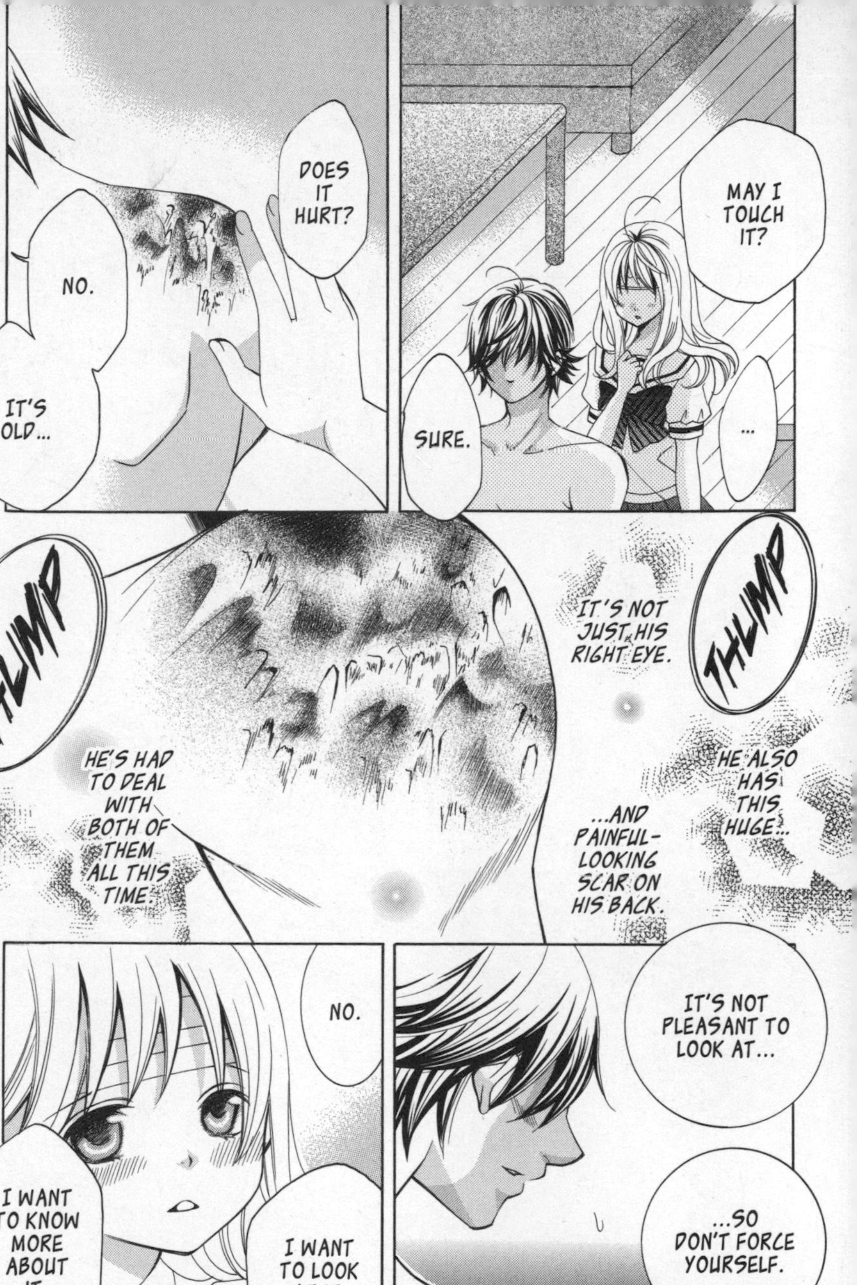
MAY I TOUCH IT?
...
SURE.
DOES IT HURT?
NO.
IT'S OLD...
THUMP
IT'S NOT JUST HIS RIGHT EYE.
HE ALSO HAS THIS HUGE...
...AND PAINFUL-LOOKING SCAR ON HIS BACK.
HE'S HAD TO DEAL WITH BOTH OF THEM ALL THIS TIME.
THUMP
IT'S NOT PLEASANT TO LOOK AT...
...SO DON'T FORCE YOURSELF.
NO.
I WANT TO LOOK AT IT.
I WANT TO KNOW MORE ABOUT IT.

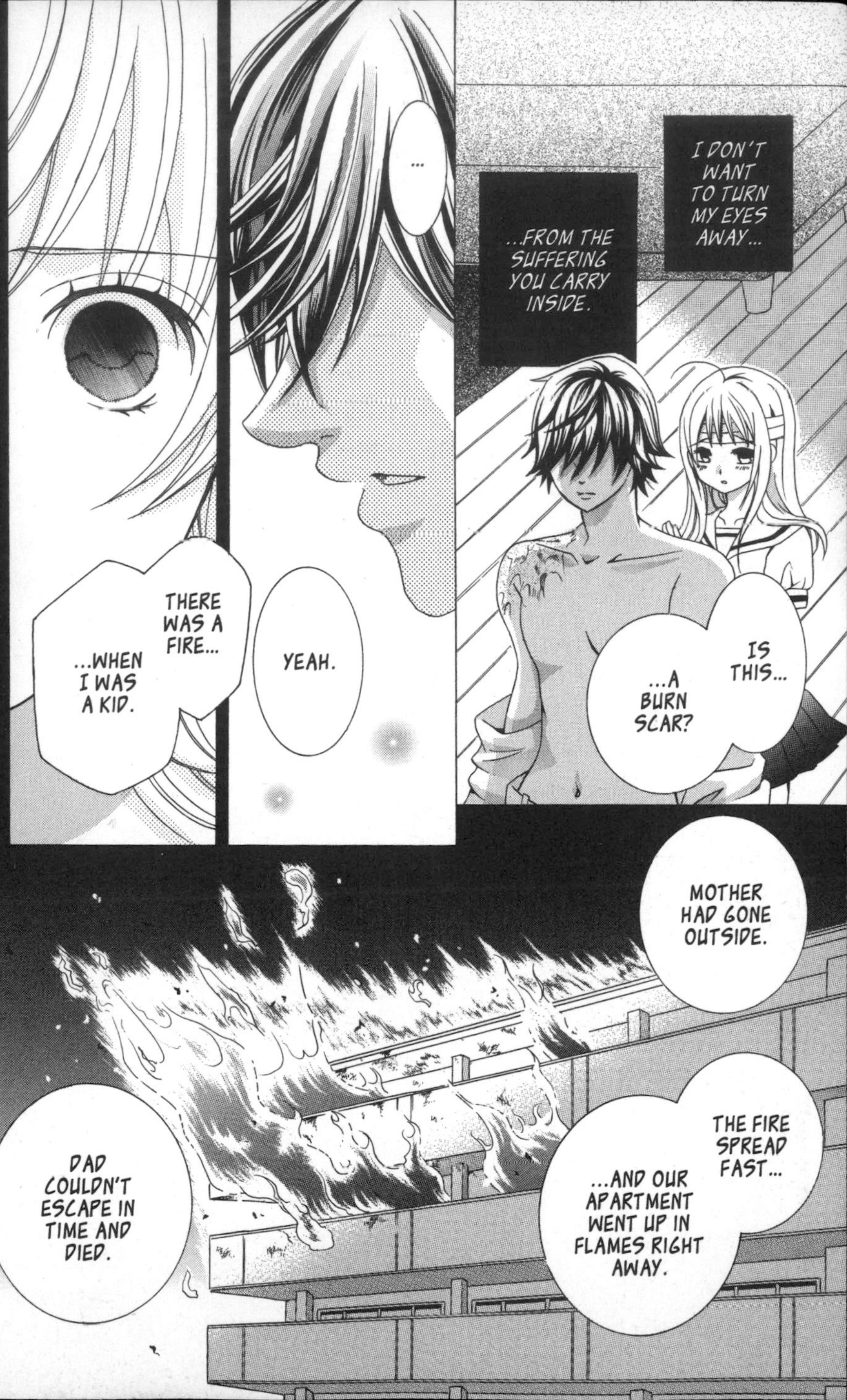
I DON'T WANT TO TURN MY EYES AWAY...
...FROM THE SUFFERING YOU CARRY INSIDE.
IS THIS...
...A BURN SCAR?
...
YEAH.
THERE WAS A FIRE...
...WHEN I WAS A KID.
MOTHER HAD GONE OUTSIDE.
THE FIRE SPREAD FAST...
...AND OUR APARTMENT WENT UP IN FLAMES RIGHT AWAY.
DAD COULDN'T ESCAPE IN TIME AND DIED.

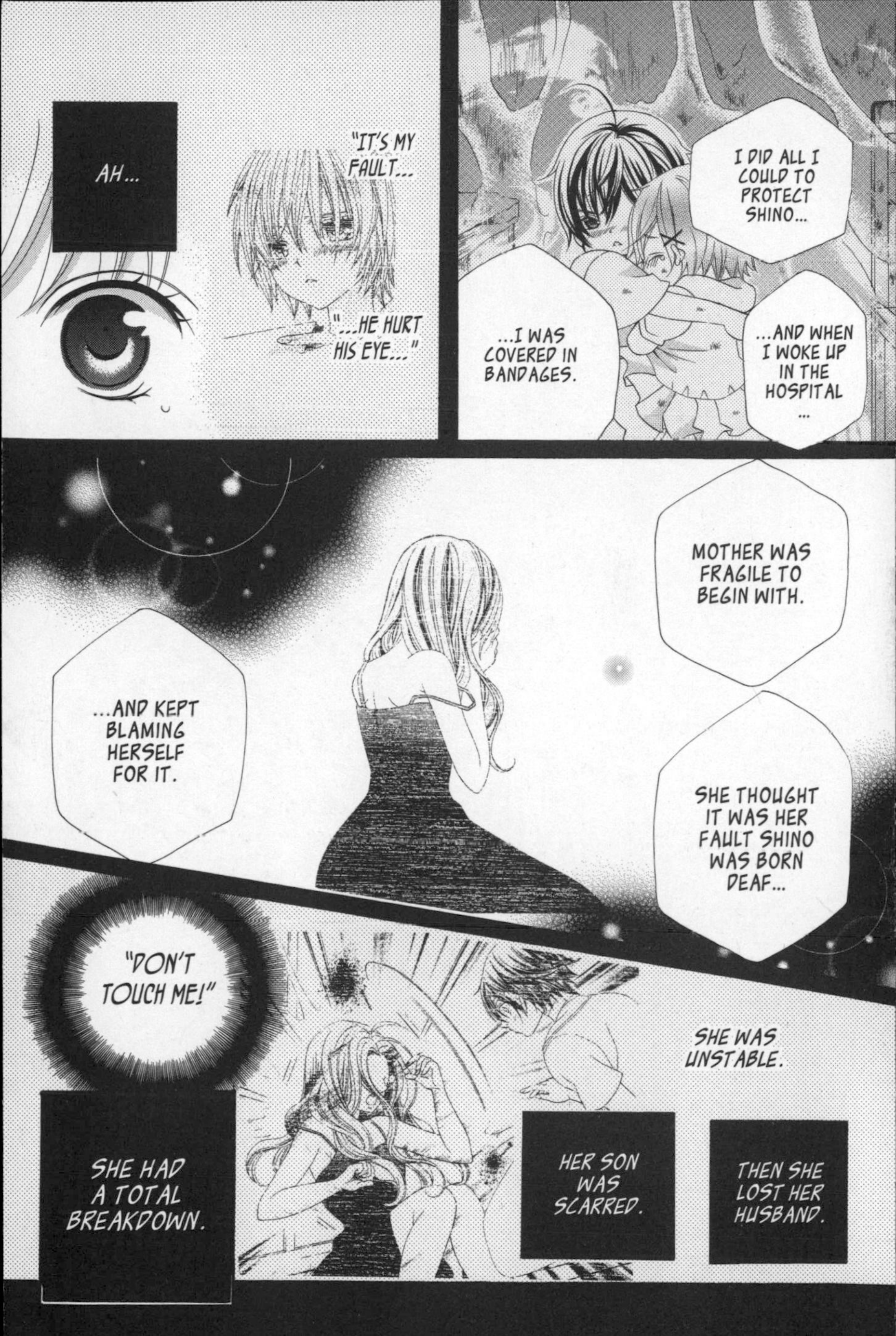
I DID ALL I COULD TO PROTECT SHINO...
...AND WHEN I WOKE UP IN THE HOSPITAL...
...I WAS COVERED IN BANDAGES.
"IT'S MY FAULT...
"...HE HURT HIS EYE..."
AH...
MOTHER WAS FRAGILE TO BEGIN WITH.
SHE THOUGHT IT WAS HER FAULT SHINO WAS BORN DEAF...
...AND KEPT BLAMING HERSELF FOR IT.
SHE WAS UNSTABLE.
THEN SHE LOST HER HUSBAND.
HER SON WAS SCARRED.
"DON'T TOUCH ME!"
SHE HAD A TOTAL BREAKDOWN.

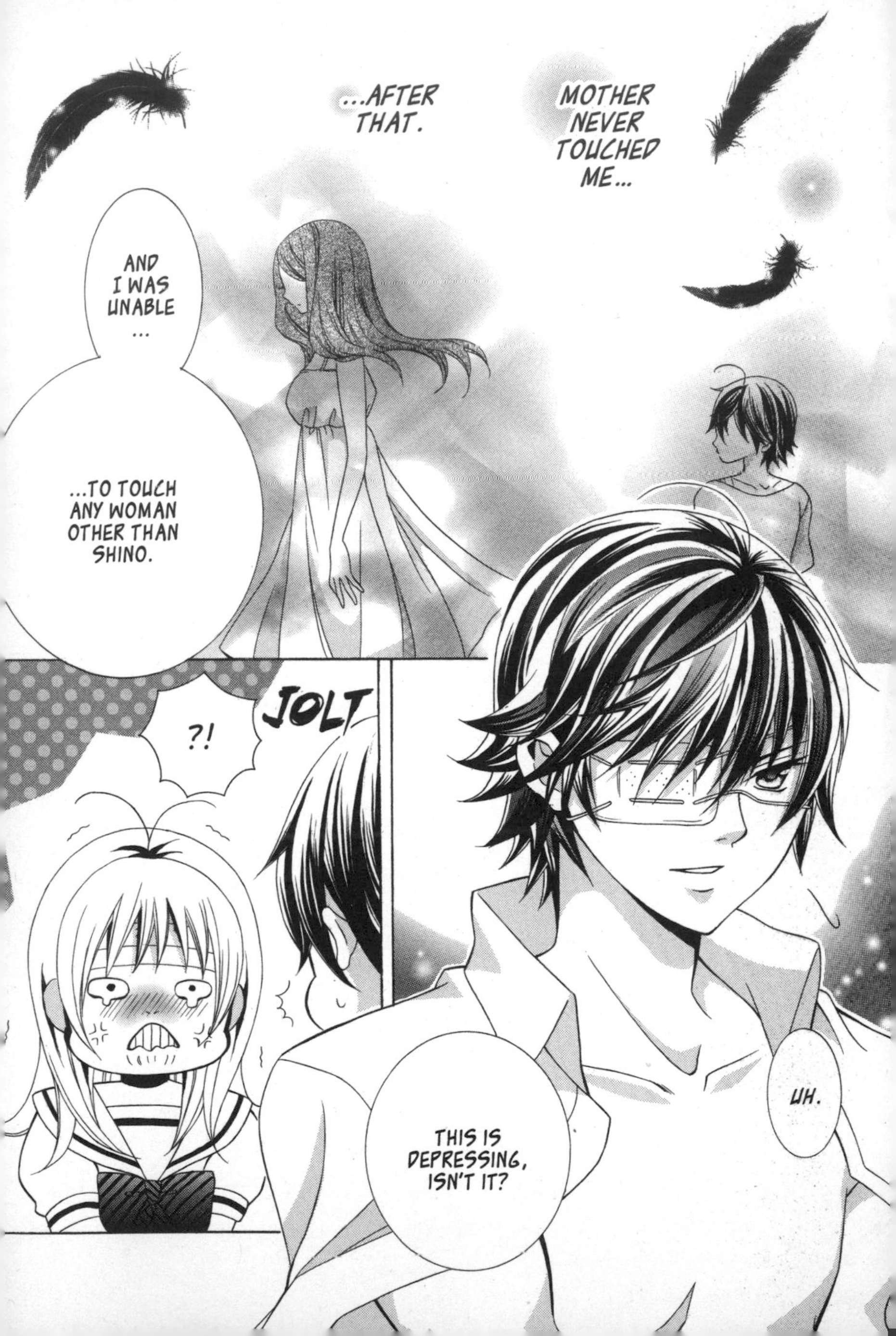
MOTHER NEVER TOUCHED ME...
...AFTER THAT.
AND I WAS UNABLE ...
...TO TOUCH ANY WOMAN OTHER THAN SHINO.
UH.
THIS IS DEPRESSING, ISN'T IT?
JOLT
?!

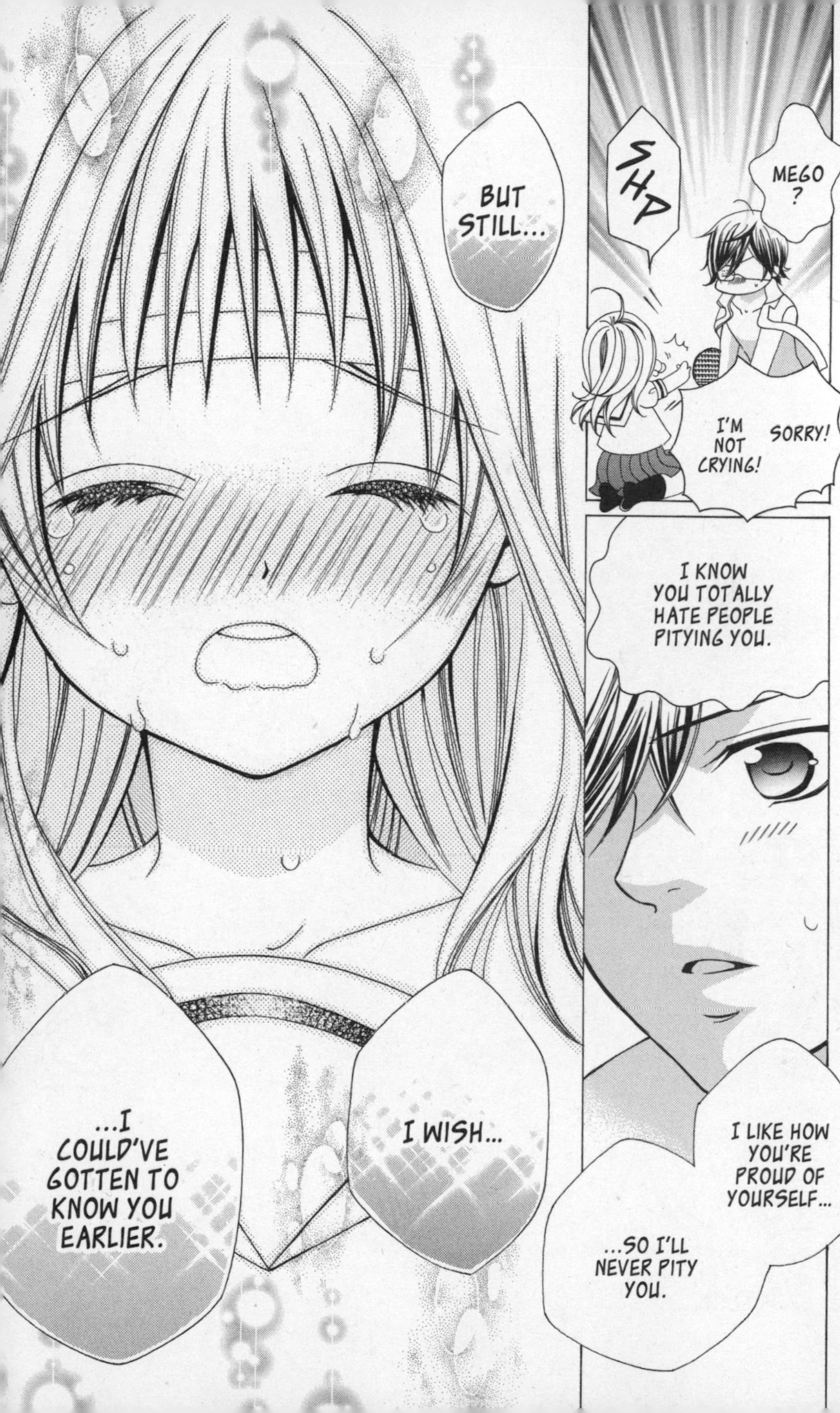
MEGO?
SHP
SORRY!
I'M NOT CRYING!
I KNOW YOU TOTALLY HATE PEOPLE PITYING YOU.
I LIKE HOW YOU'RE PROUD OF YOURSELF...
...SO I'LL NEVER PITY YOU.
BUT STILL...
I WISH...
...I COULD'VE GOTTEN TO KNOW YOU EARLIER.

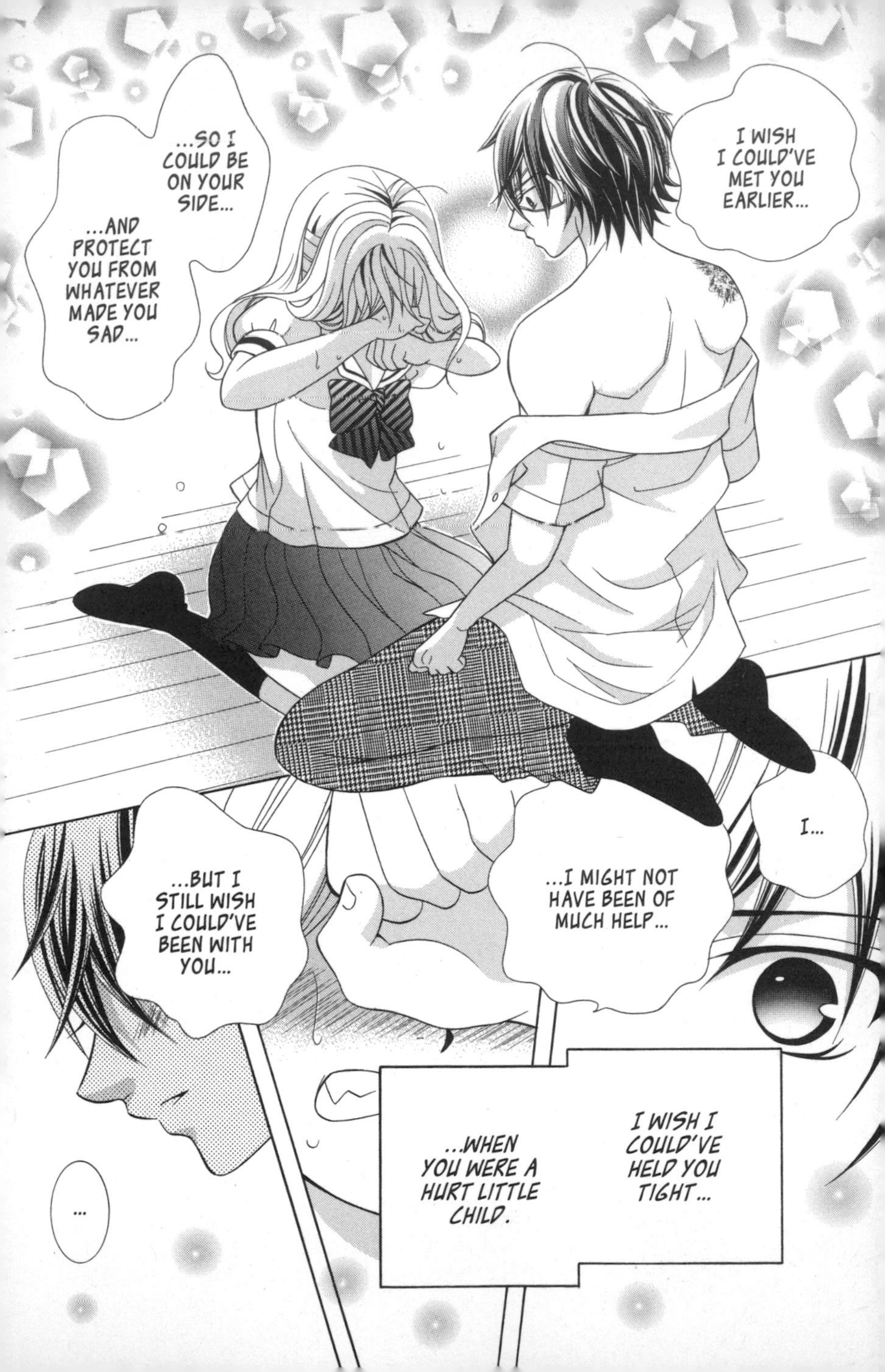
I WISH I COULD'VE MET YOU EARLIER...
...SO I COULD BE ON YOUR SIDE...
...AND PROTECT YOU FROM WHATEVER MADE YOU SAD...
I...
...I MIGHT NOT HAVE BEEN OF MUCH HELP...
...BUT I STILL WISH I COULD'VE BEEN WITH YOU...
I WISH I COULD'VE HELD YOU TIGHT...
...WHEN YOU WERE A HURT LITTLE CHILD.
...

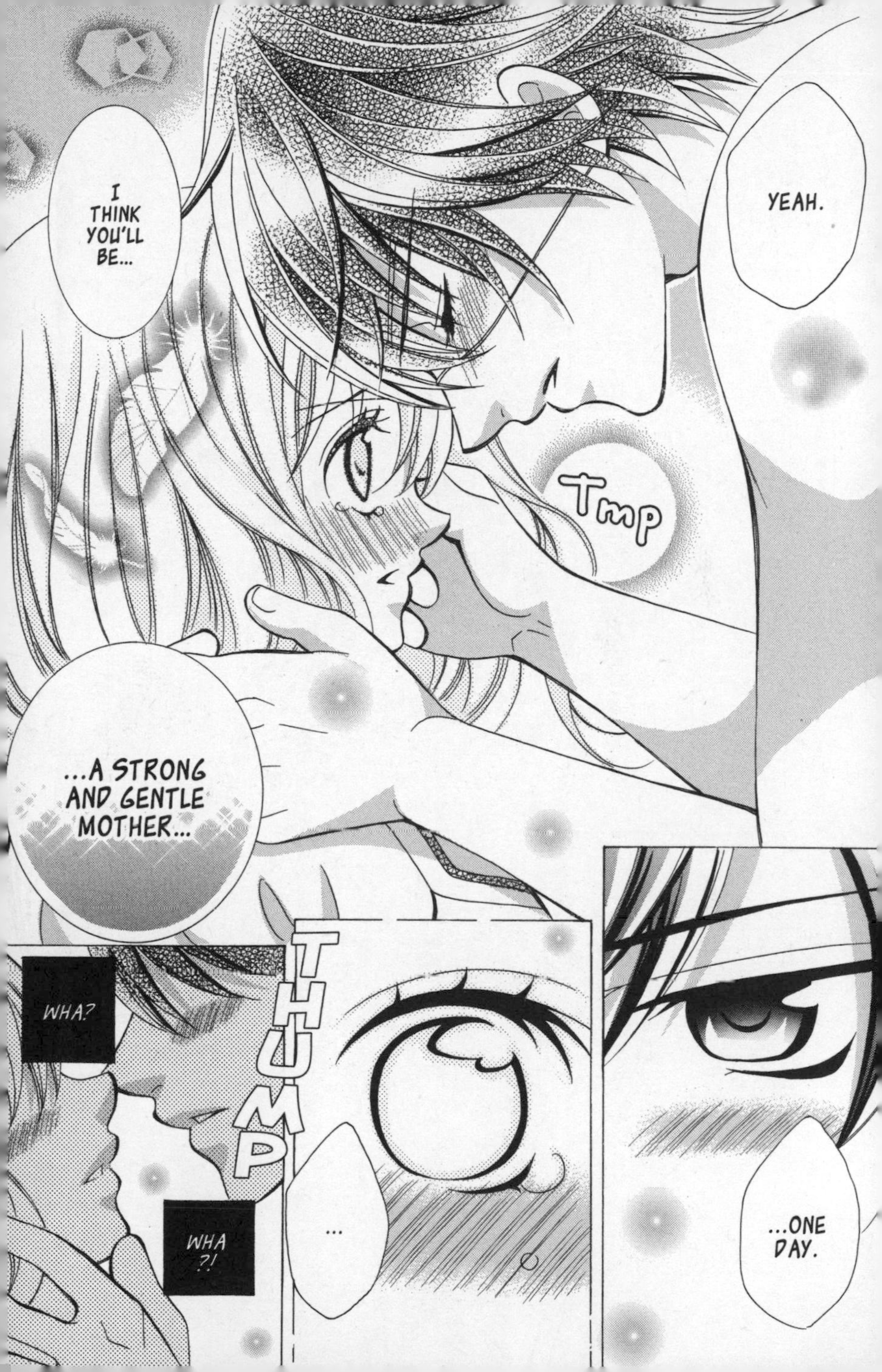
YEAH.
I THINK YOU'LL BE...
Tmp
...A STRONG AND GENTLE MOTHER...
...ONE DAY.
...
THUMP
WHA?
WHA ?!

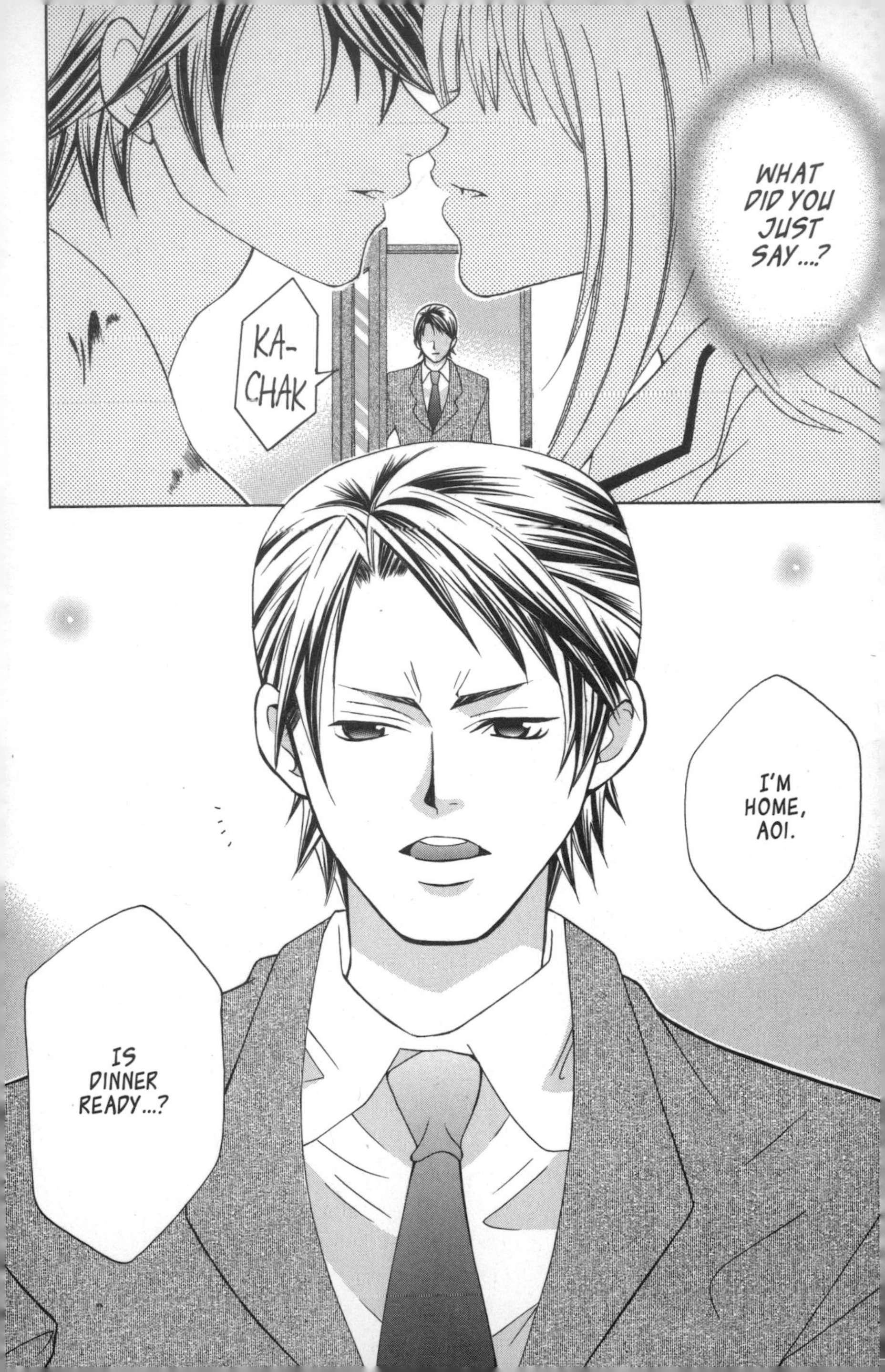
WHAT DID YOU JUST SAY...?
KA-CHAK
I'M HOME, AOI.
IS DINNER READY...?

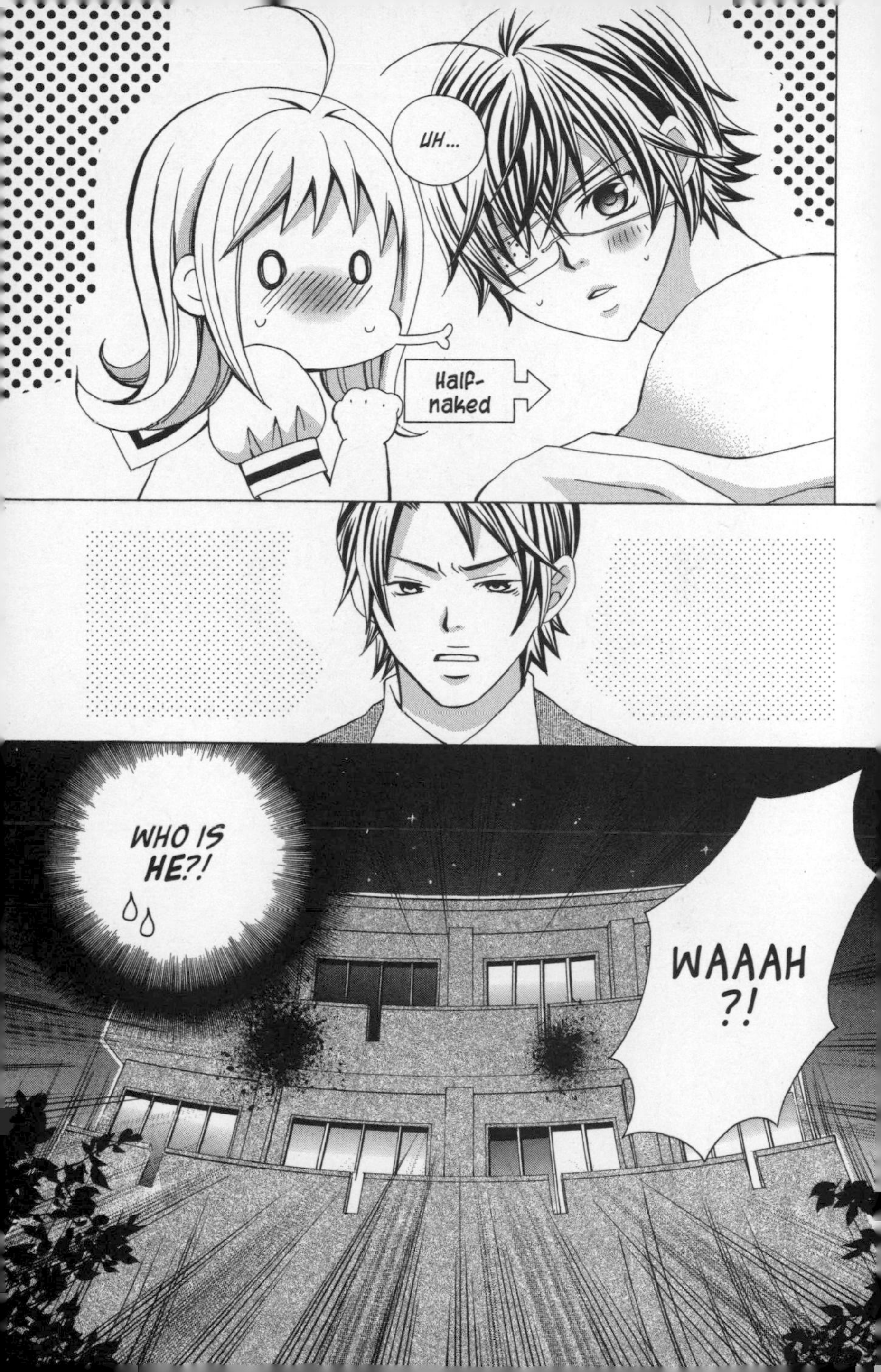
UH...
Half-naked
WAAAH ?!
WHO IS HE?!

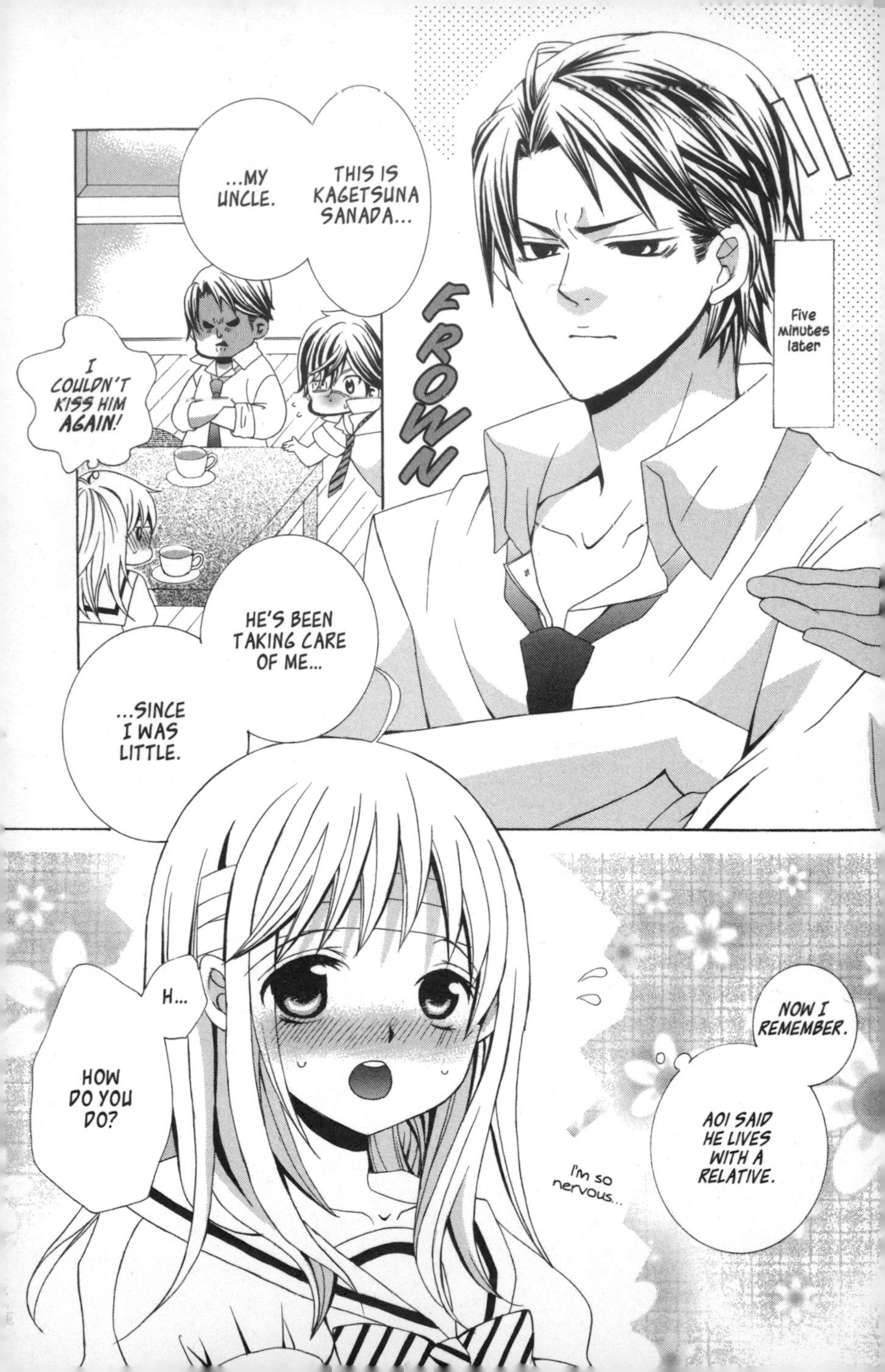
Five minutes later
FROWN
THIS IS KAGETSUNA SANADA...
...MY UNCLE.
I COULDN'T KISS HIM AGAIN!
HE'S BEEN TAKING CARE OF ME...
...SINCE I WAS LITTLE.
NOW I REMEMBER.
AOI SAID HE LIVES WITH A RELATIVE.
I'm so nervous...
H...
HOW DO YOU DO?

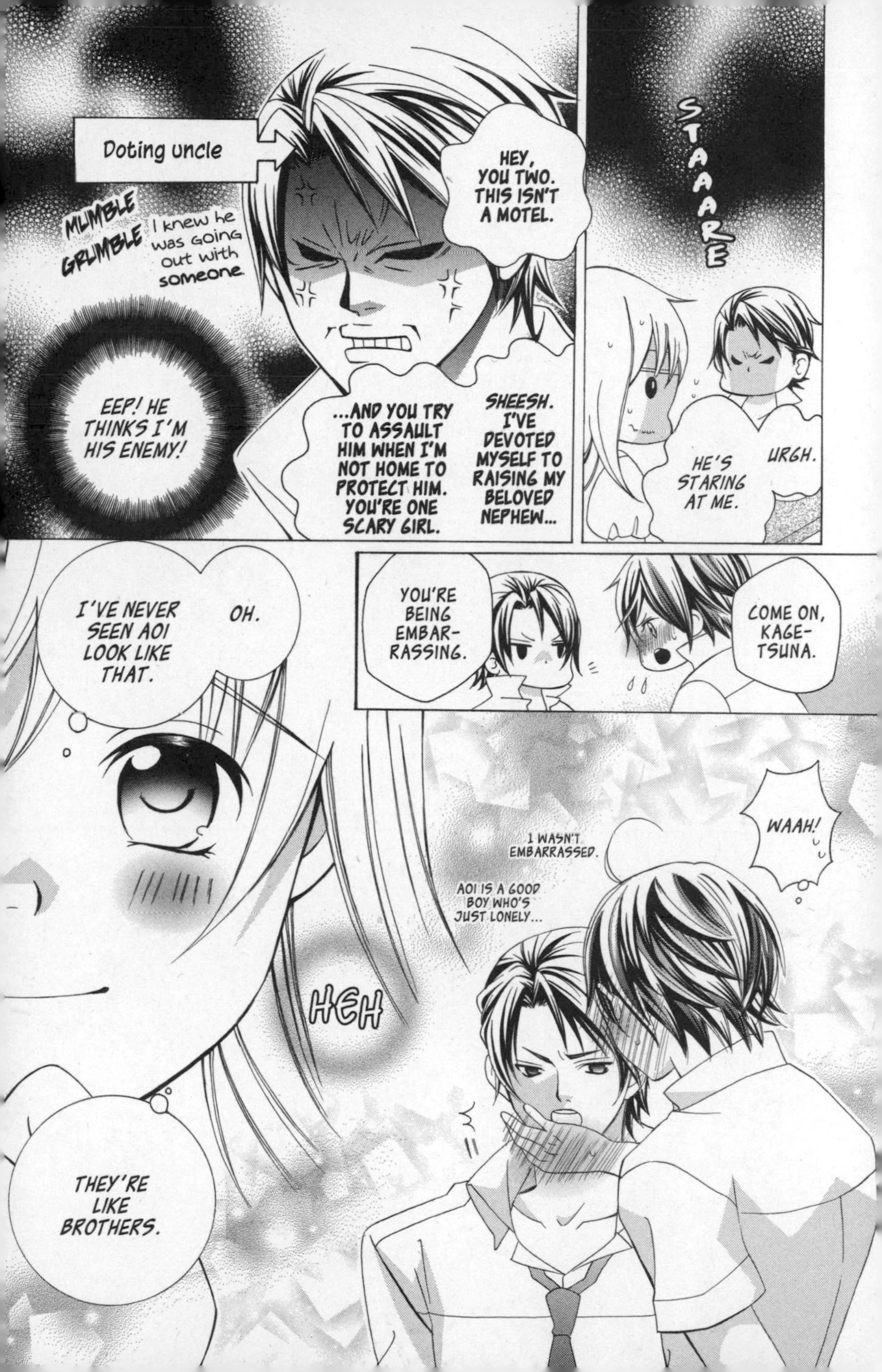
STAAARE
URGH.
HE'S STARING AT ME.
HEY, YOU TWO. THIS ISN'T A MOTEL.
SHEESH. I'VE DEVOTED MYSELF TO RAISING MY BELOVED NEPHEW...
...AND YOU TRY TO ASSAULT HIM WHEN I'M NOT HOME TO PROTECT HIM. YOU'RE ONE SCARY GIRL.
Doting uncle
MUMBLE GRUMBLE
I knew he was going out with someone.
EEP! HE THINKS I'M HIS ENEMY!
COME ON, KAGE-TSUNA.
YOU'RE BEING EMBARRASSING.
WAAH!
I WASN'T EMBARRASSED.
AOI IS A GOOD BOY WHO'S JUST LONELY...
HEH
OH.
I'VE NEVER SEEN AOI LOOK LIKE THAT.
THEY'RE LIKE BROTHERS.

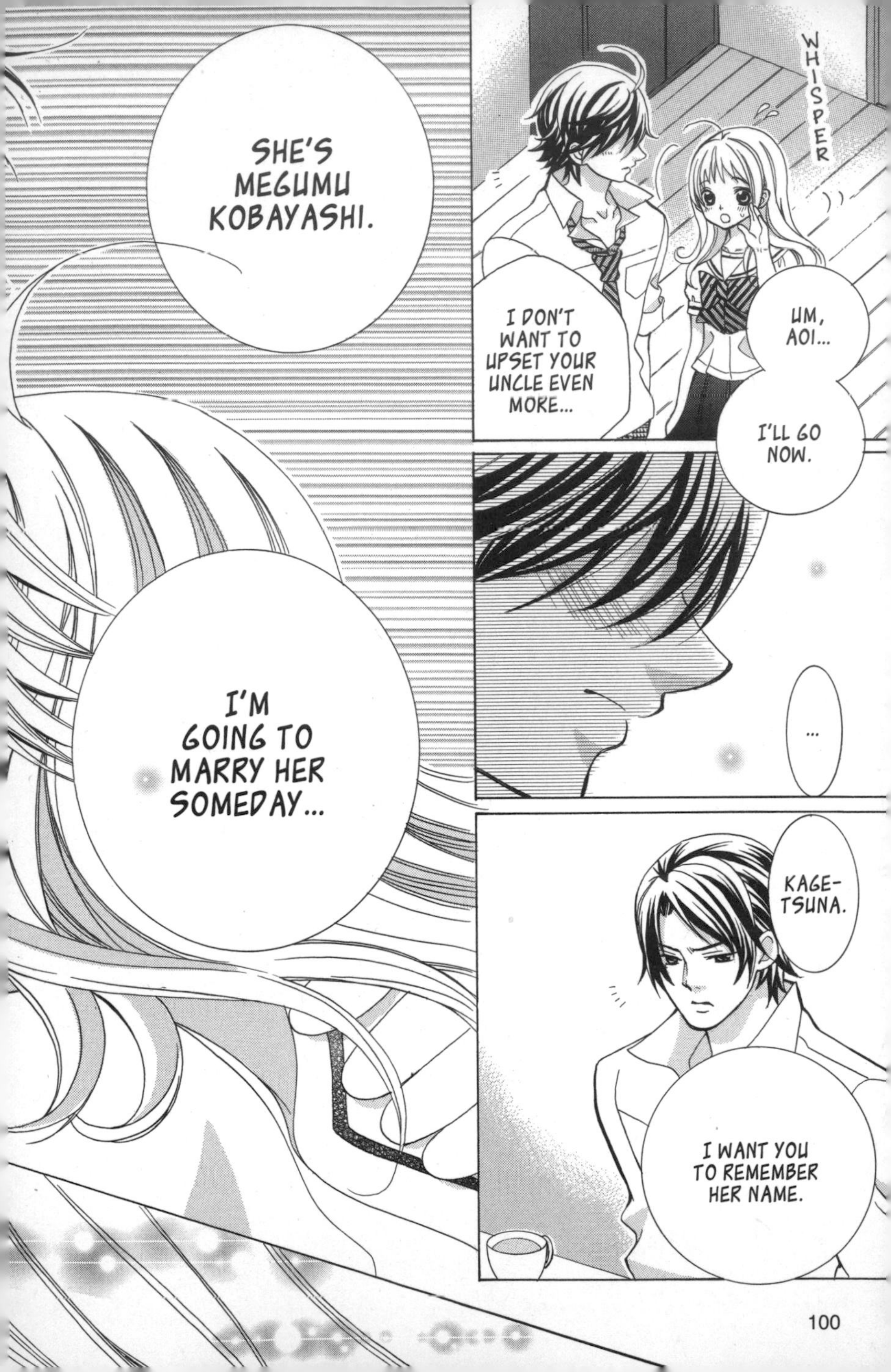

WHISPER
UM, AOI...
I DON'T WANT TO UPSET YOUR UNCLE EVEN MORE...
I'LL GO NOW.
...
KAGE-TSUNA.
I WANT YOU TO REMEMBER HER NAME.
SHE'S MEGUMU KOBAYASHI.
I'M GOING TO MARRY HER SOMEDAY...

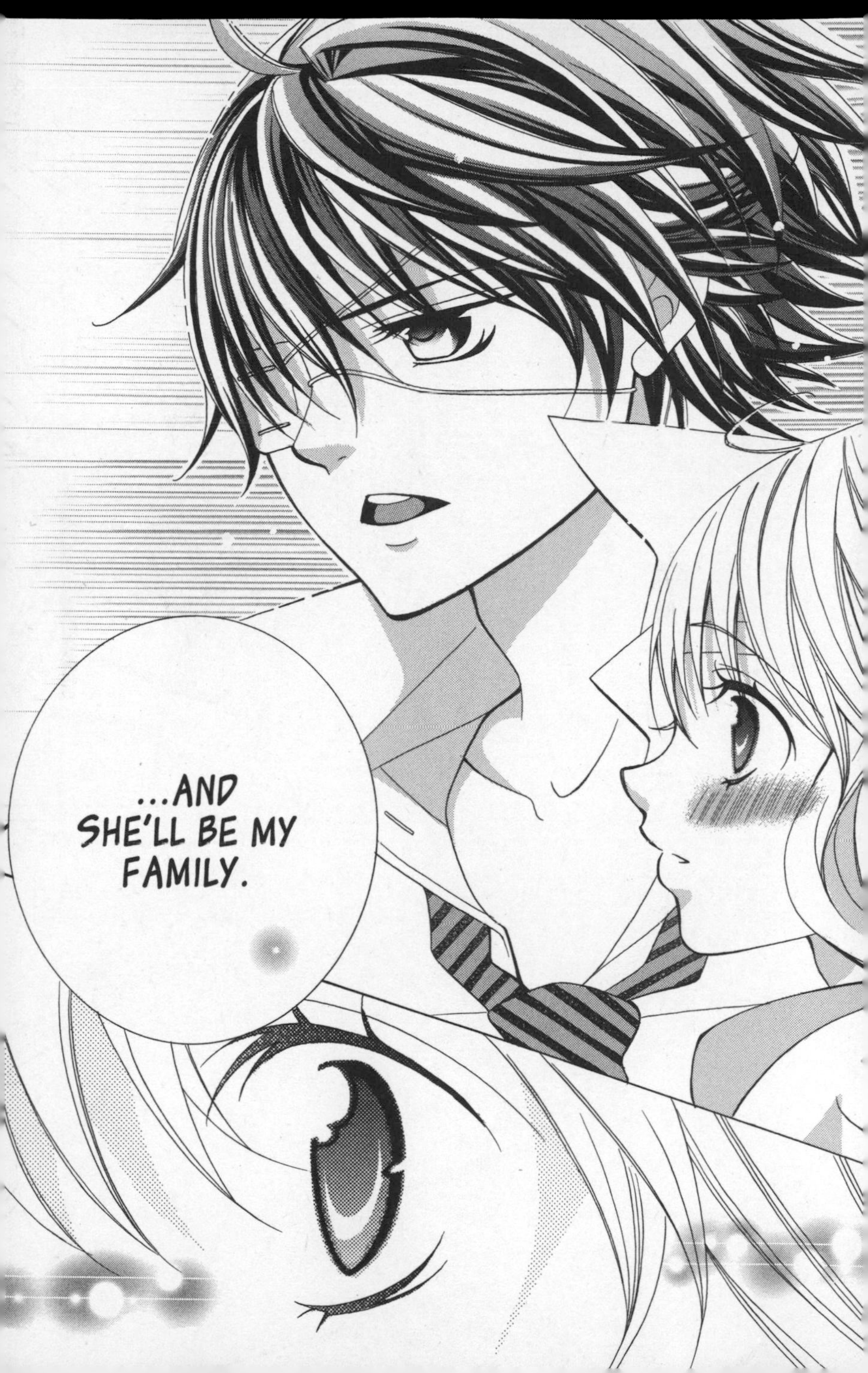
...AND SHE'LL BE MY FAMILY.

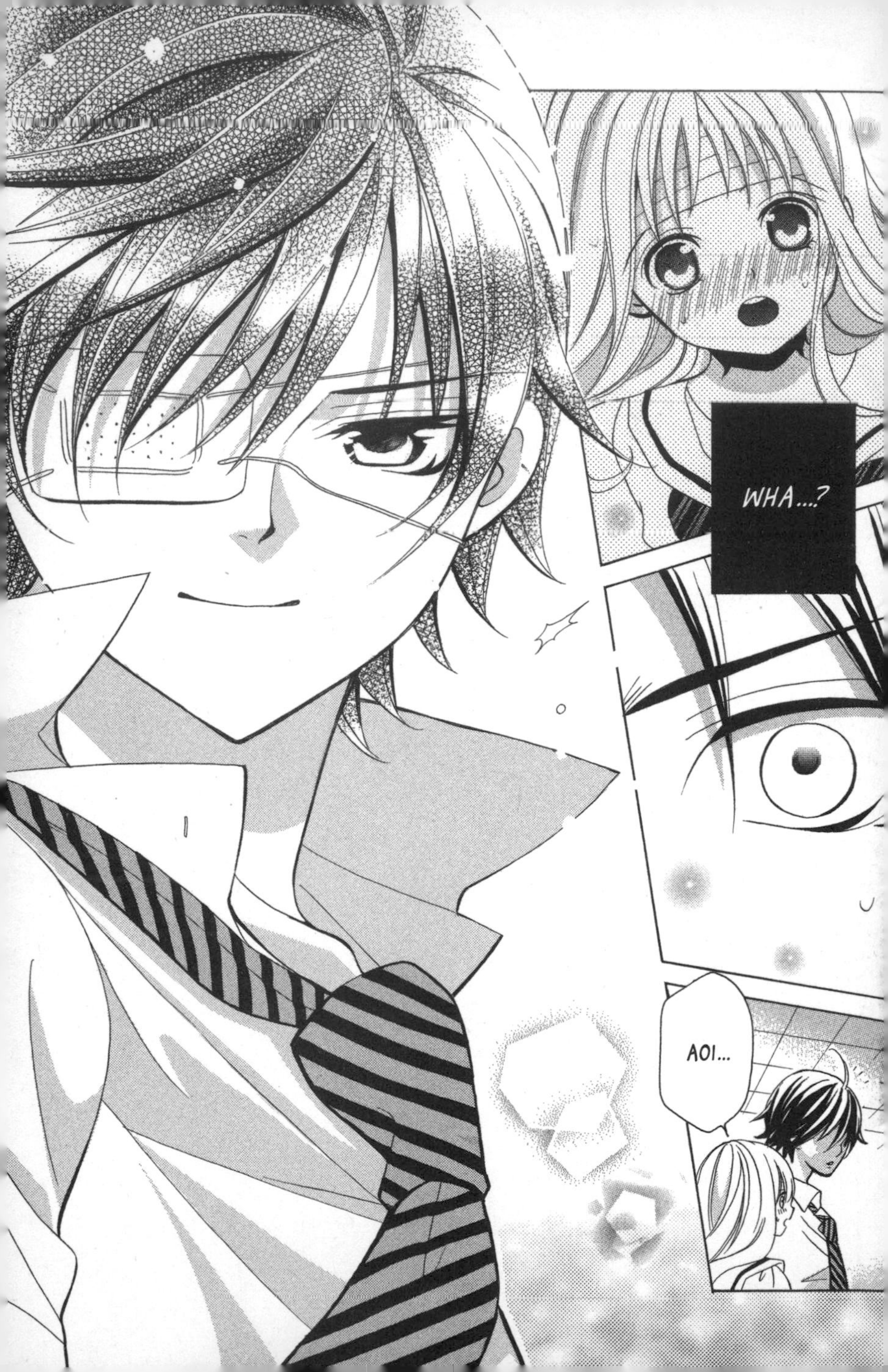
WHA...?
AOI...

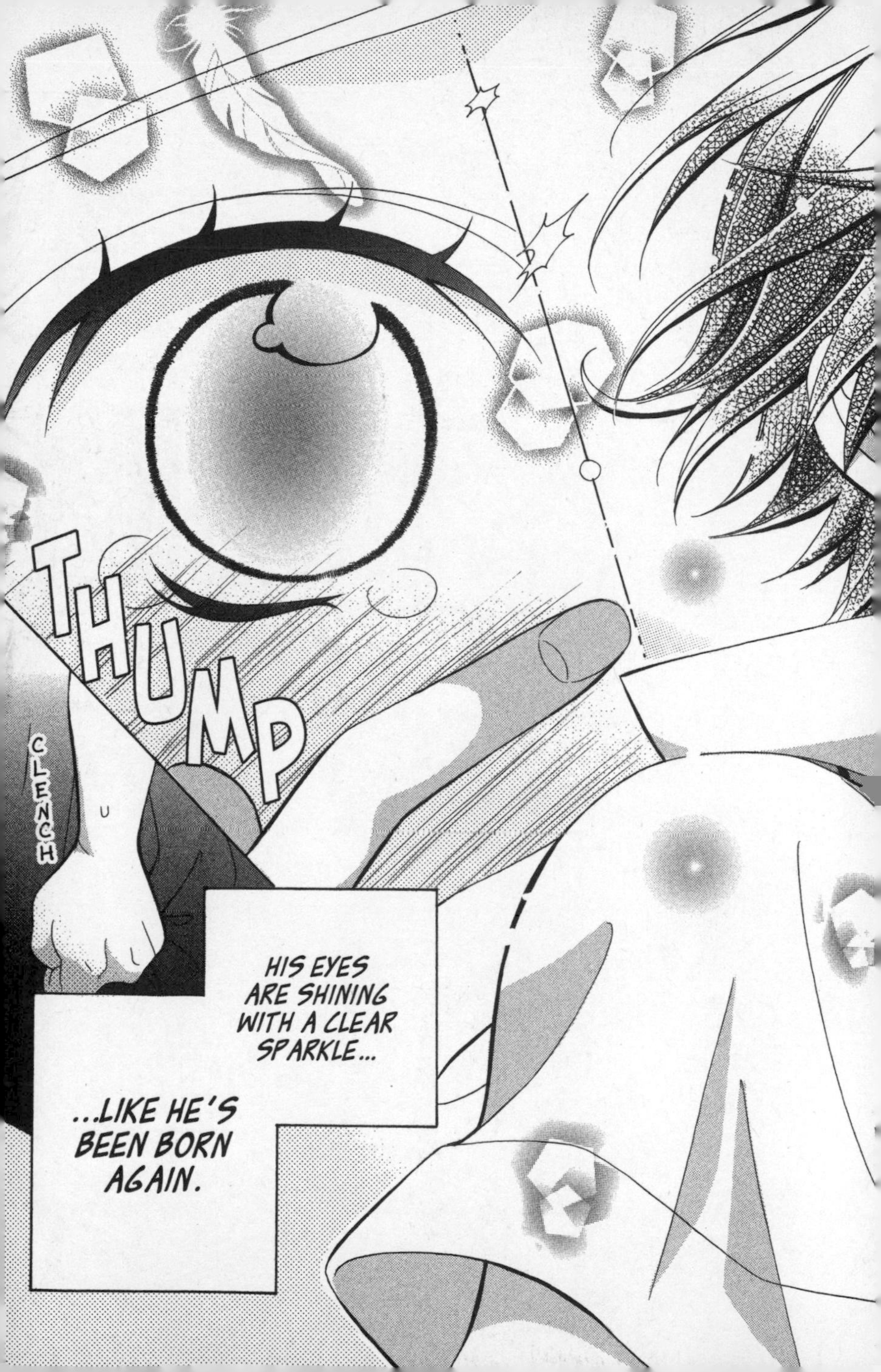
THUMP
CLENCH
HIS EYES ARE SHINING WITH A CLEAR SPARKLE...
...LIKE HE'S BEEN BORN AGAIN.

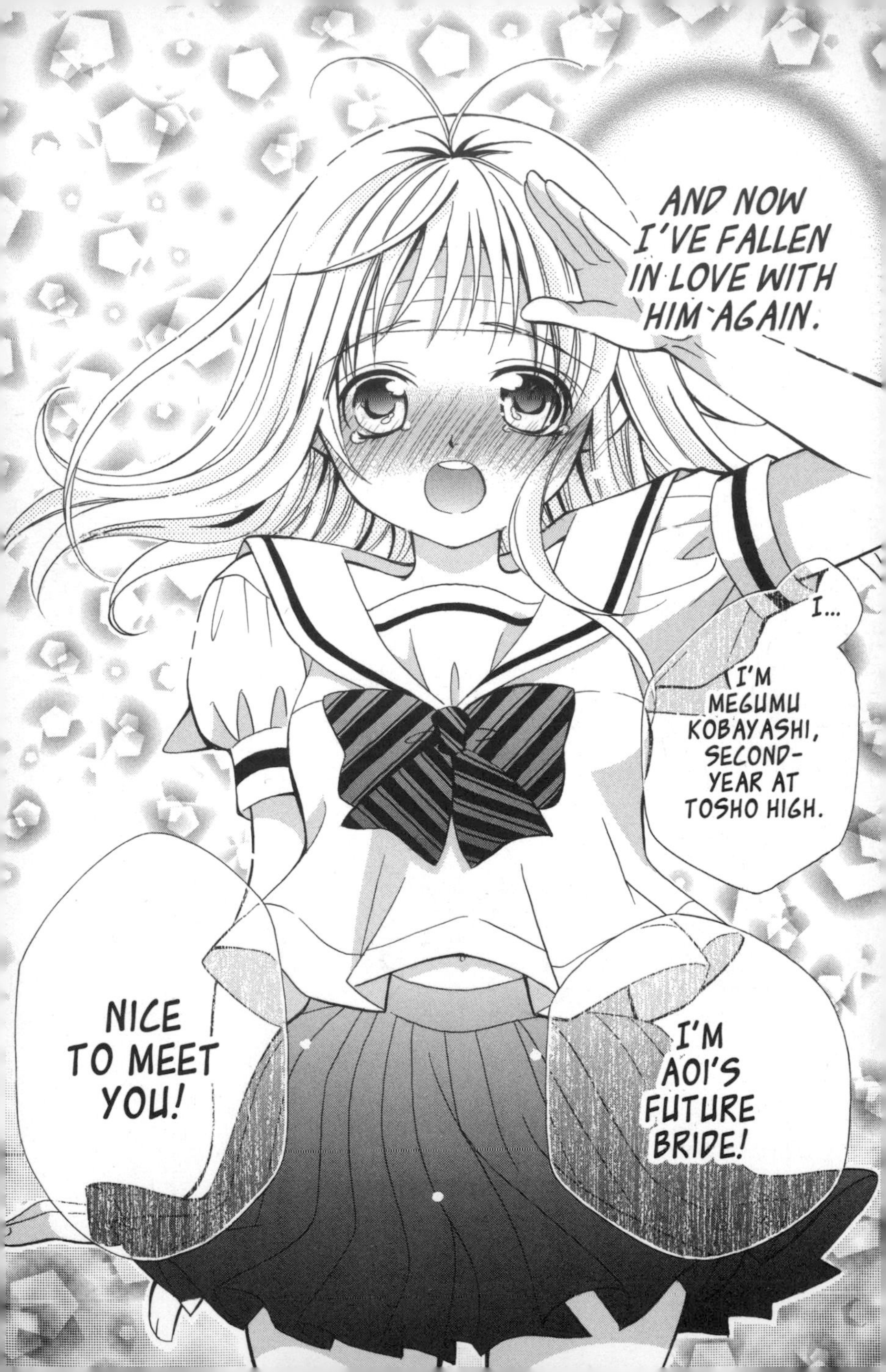
AND NOW I'VE FALLEN IN LOVE WITH HIM AGAIN.
I...
I'M MEGUMU KOBAYASHI, SECOND-YEAR AT TOSHO HIGH.
I'M AOI'S FUTURE BRIDE!
NICE TO MEET YOU!

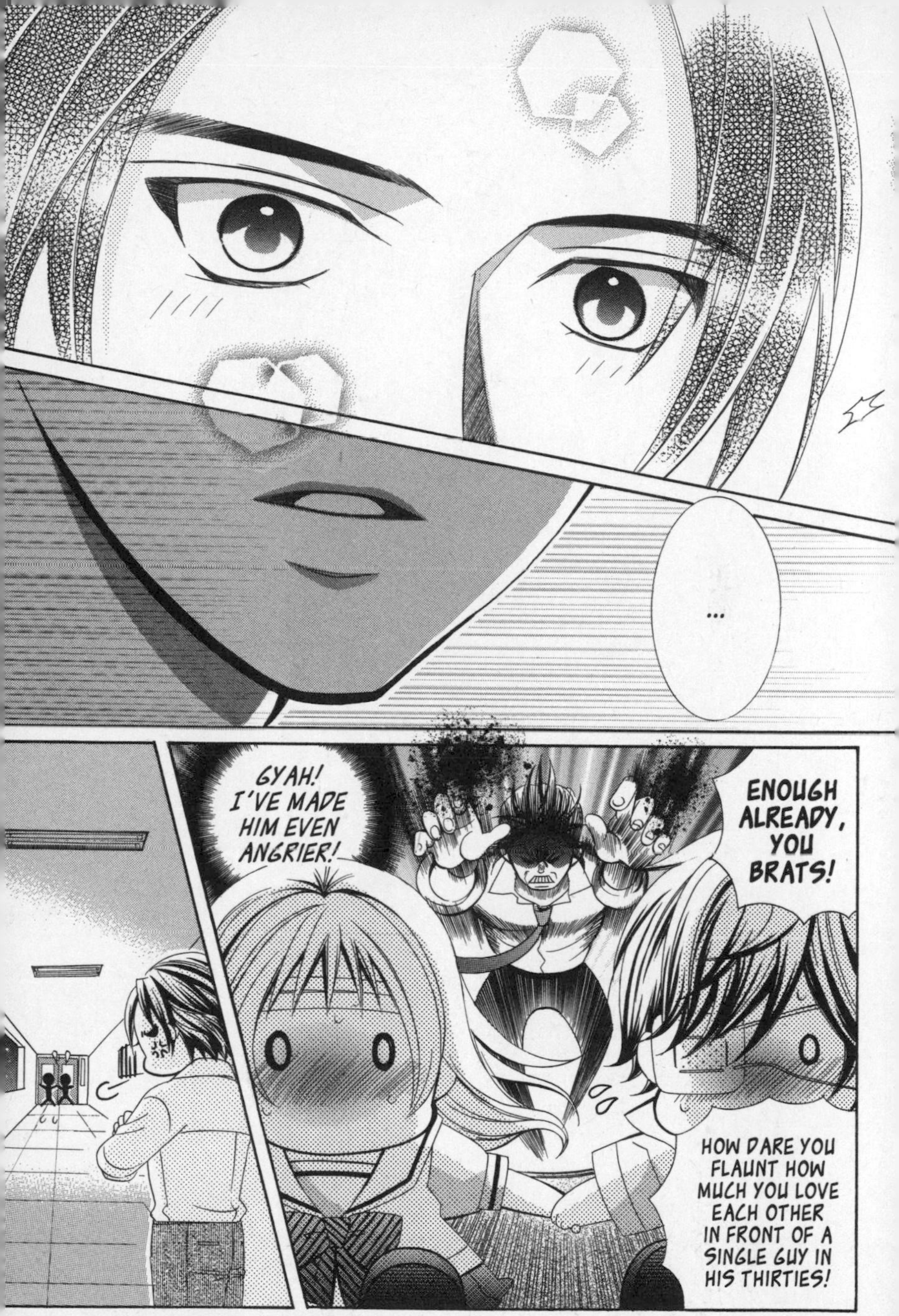
...
ENOUGH ALREADY, YOU BRATS!
GYAH! I'VE MADE HIM EVEN ANGRIER!
HOW DARE YOU FLAUNT HOW MUCH YOU LOVE EACH OTHER IN FRONT OF A SINGLE GUY IN HIS THIRTIES!

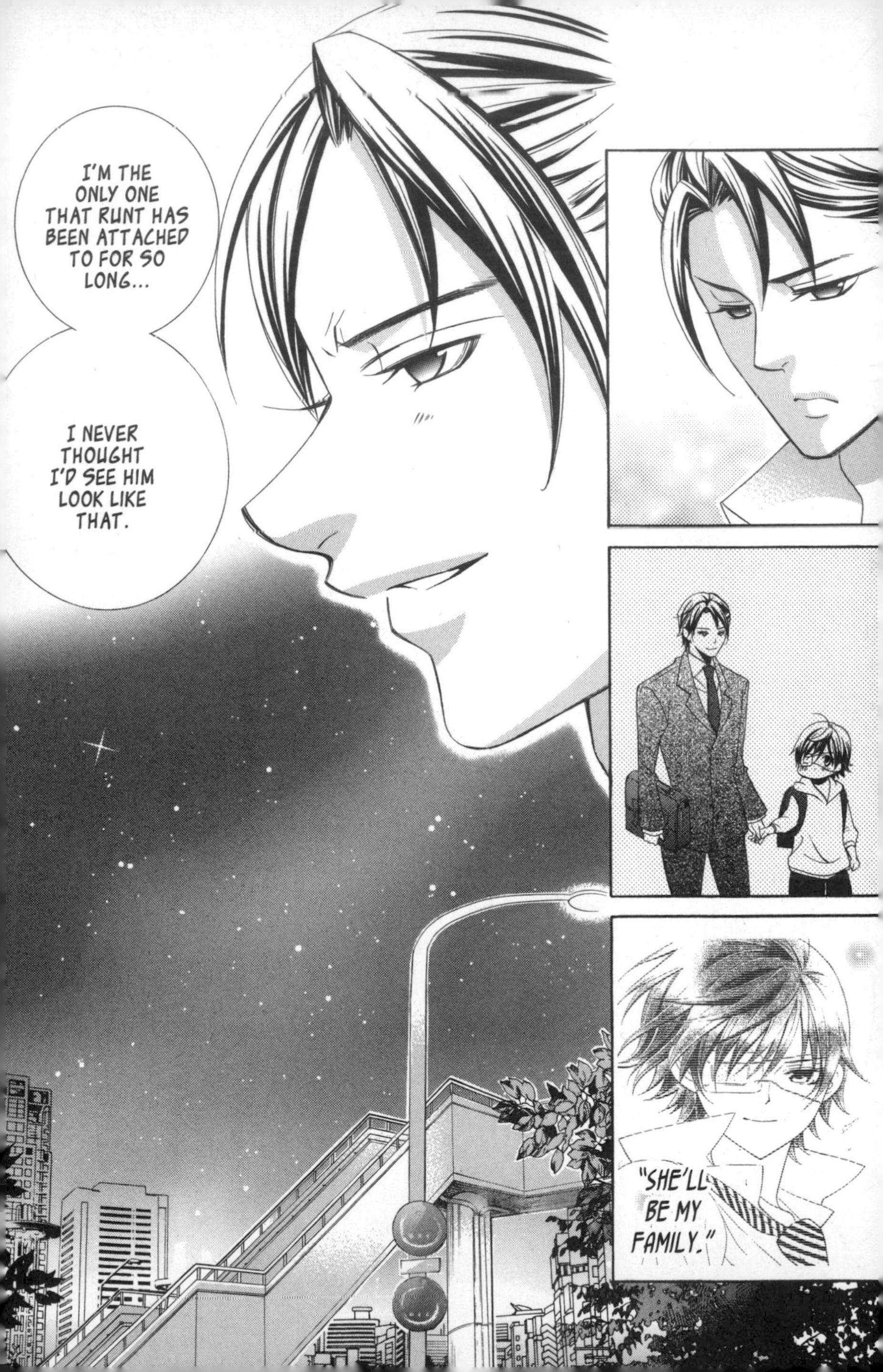
"SHE'LL BE MY FAMILY."
I'M THE ONLY ONE THAT RUNT HAS BEEN ATTACHED TO FOR SO LONG...
I NEVER THOUGHT I'D SEE HIM LOOK LIKE THAT.

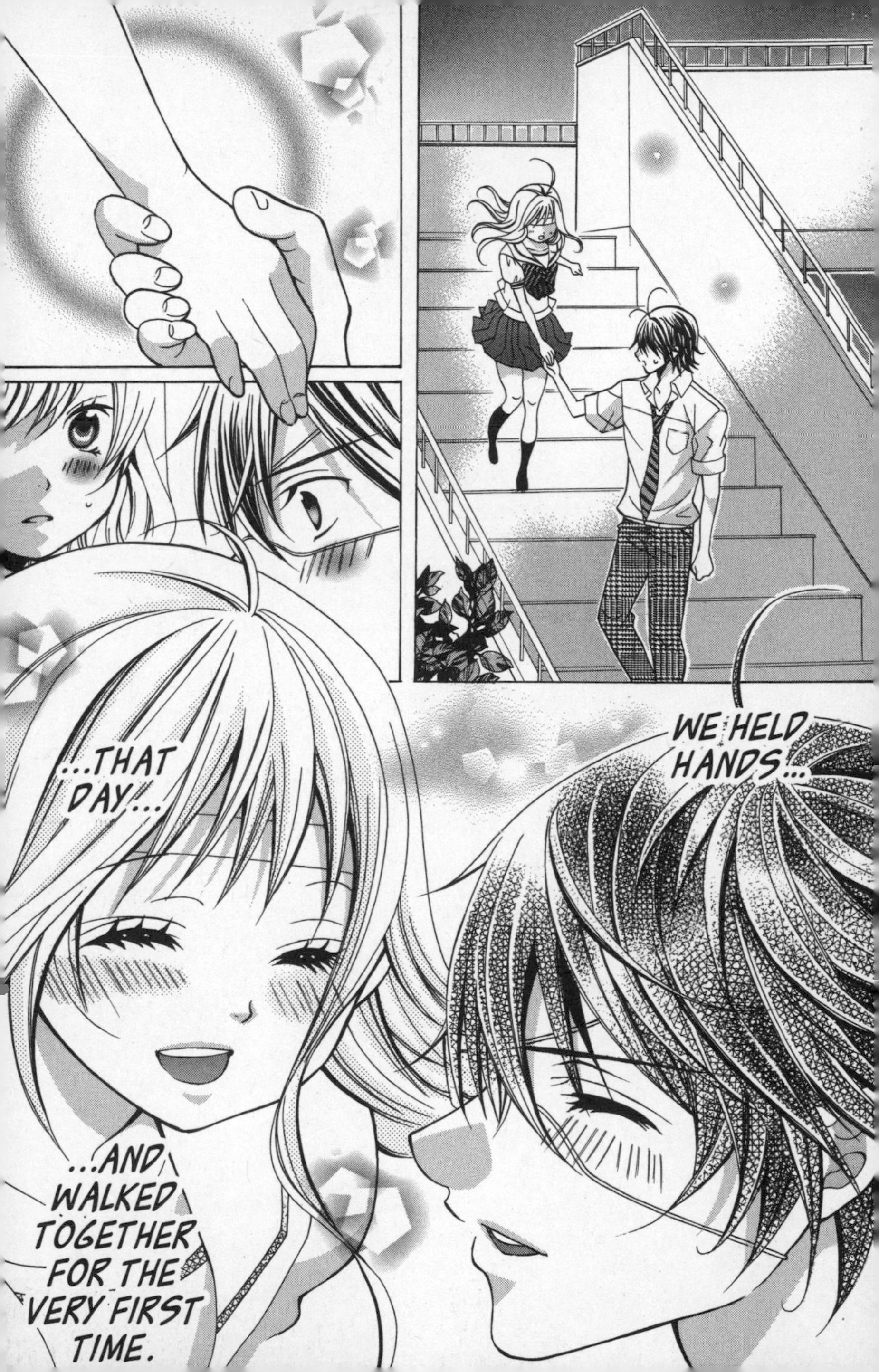
WE HELD HANDS...
...THAT DAY...
...AND WALKED TOGETHER FOR THE VERY FIRST TIME.

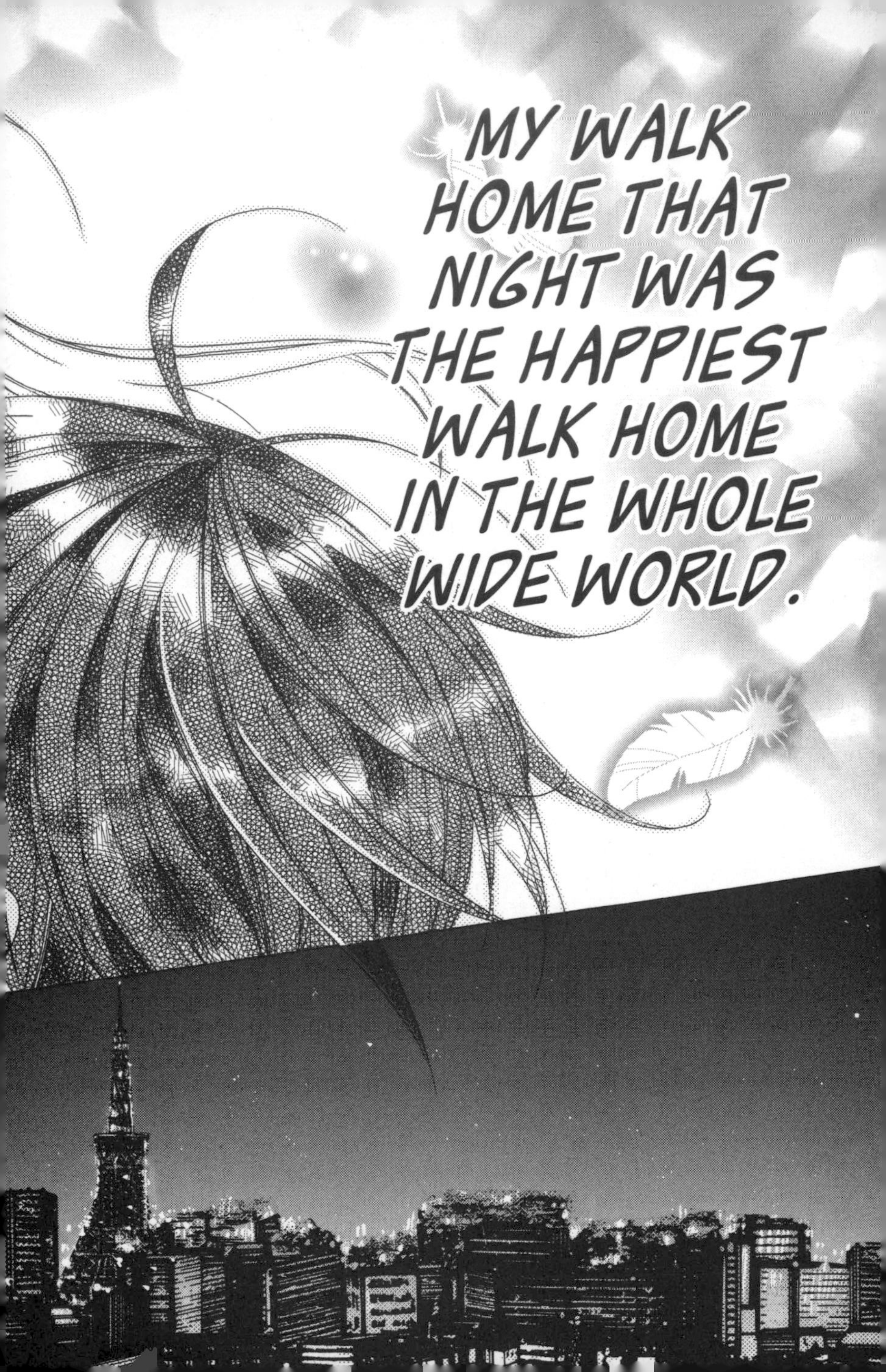
MY WALK HOME THAT NIGHT WAS THE HAPPIEST WALK HOME IN THE WHOLE WIDE WORLD.

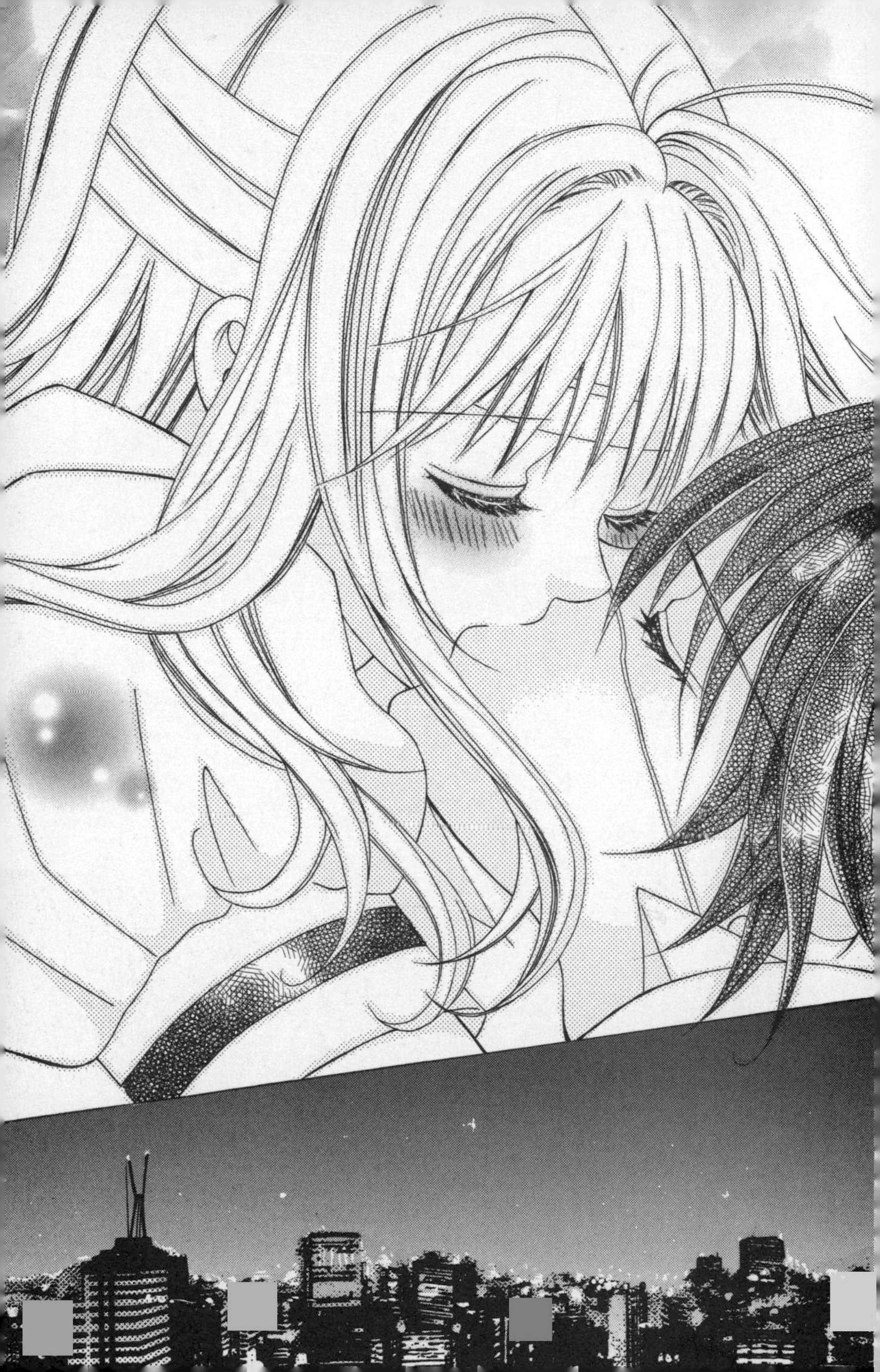

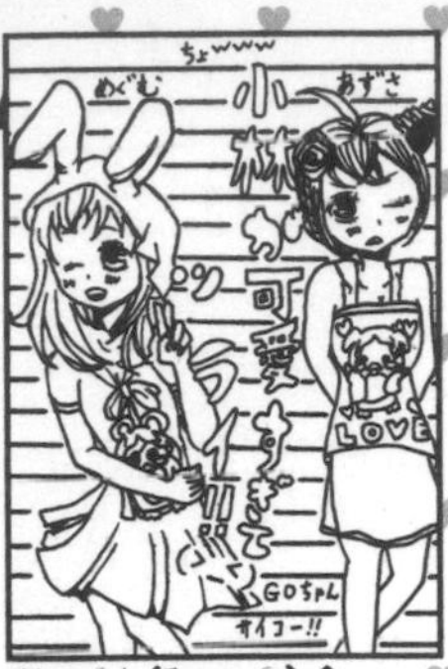

Ringo ☆ (Toyama) ↑
Ed.: The strongest couple!!

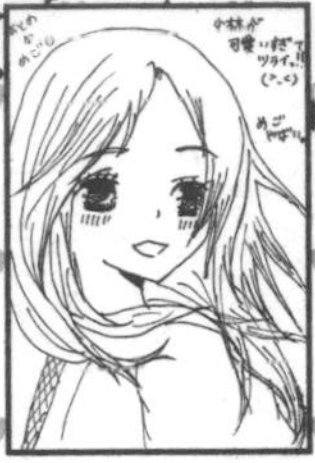

Mizuki Kawano (Hiroshima) ←
Ed.: The grown-up Mego looks super beautiful!!

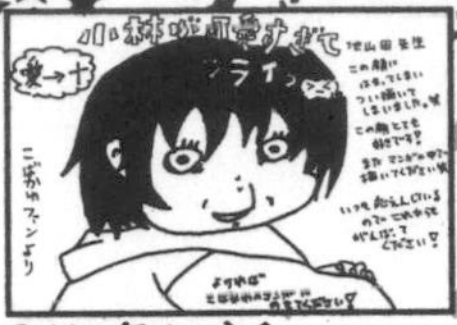

Pokky (Tokyo) ↑
Ed.: I was surprised by this expression too. (><)

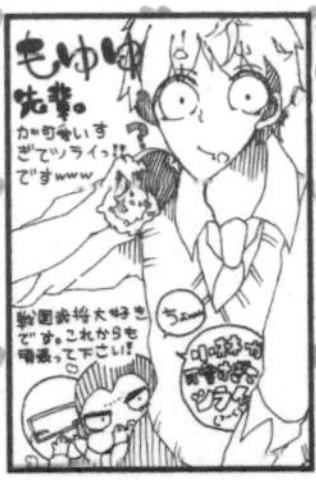

Daisy (Nagasaki) ←
Ed.: D-didn't think someone would draw Moyuyu!!

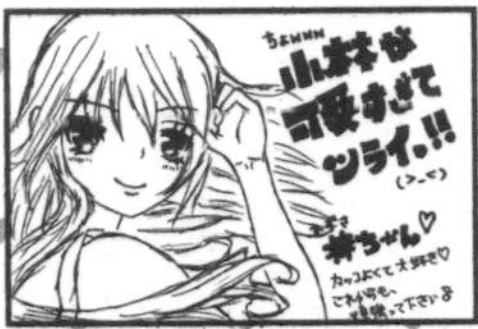
小林が可愛すぎてツライ。!!

Miku (Ibaraki) ↑
Ed.: Azusa is cool and cute!

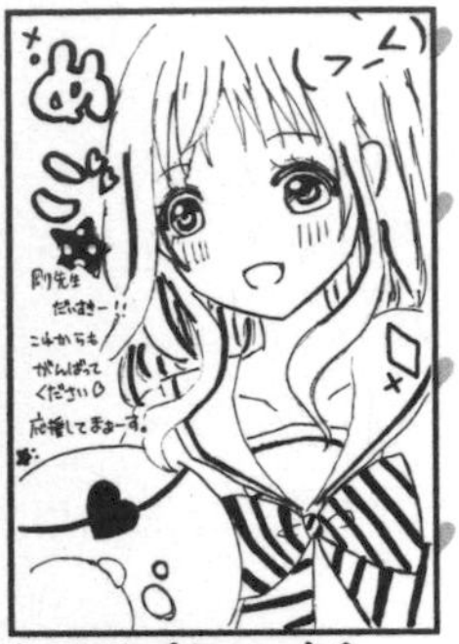

Aoi Saito (Kagawa) ↑
Ed.: Both Mego and the eye-patch penguin are super cute!!

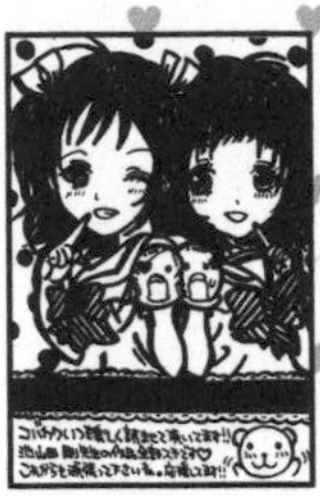

Tenten (Hyogo) ←
Ed.: A lovely two-shot!!

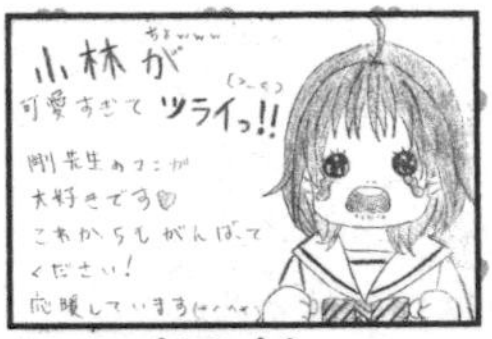
小林が
可愛すぎてツライっ!!

Ao-chan (Chiba) ↑
Ed.: I remember Megumu looking like this!!

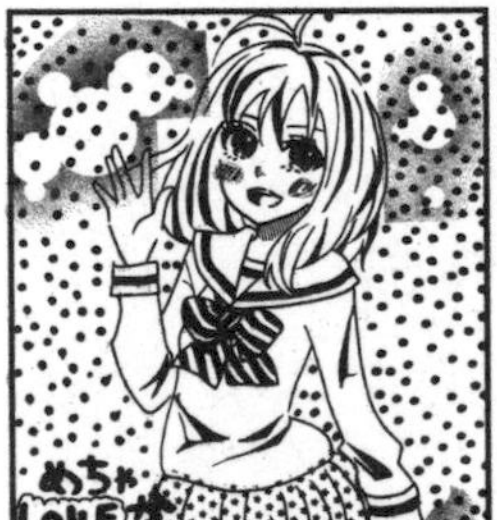
めちゃLOVE
めご

Kamui Okamukku (Saitama) ←
Ed.: Mego looks so cute!

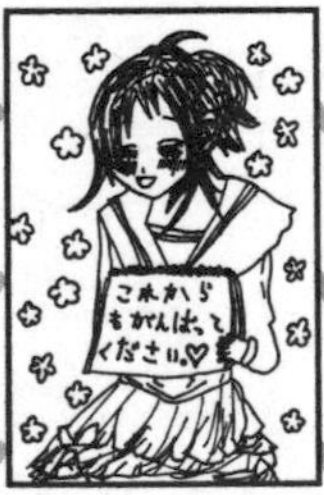
これからもがんばってください。♡

Aa-chan (Hyogo) ←
Ed.: Yes! We'll do our best!!!

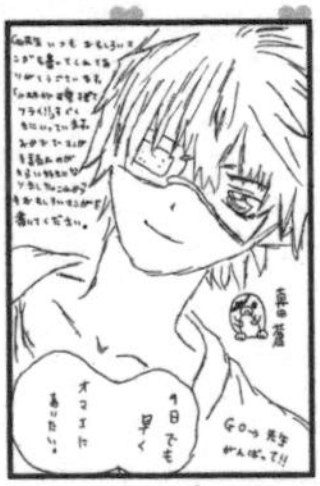

Haru-chan (Tottori) ↑
Ed.: Aoi's gentle smile. ♥

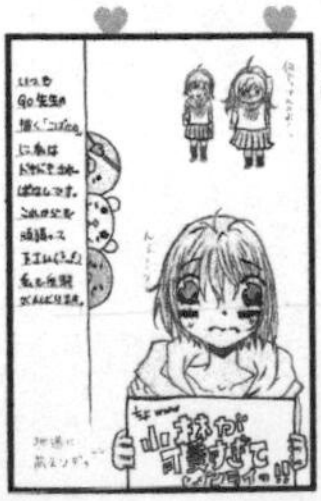

Naru (Nagasaki) ←
Ed.: Thanks for advertising!!

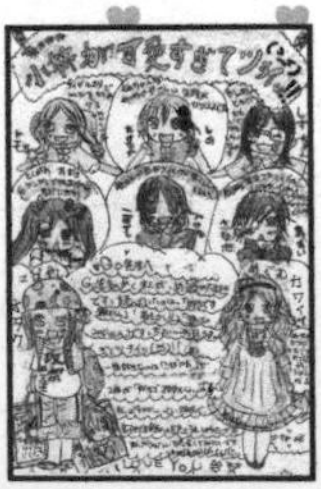

Kobakawa LOVE (Kumamoto) ←
Ed.: Everyone's so cute, it hurts!!

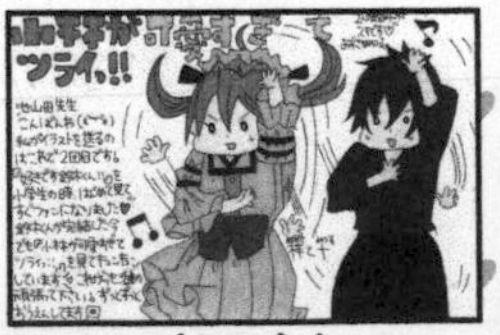

Nakamori (Chiba) ↑
Ed.: Let's go to an arcade together!!

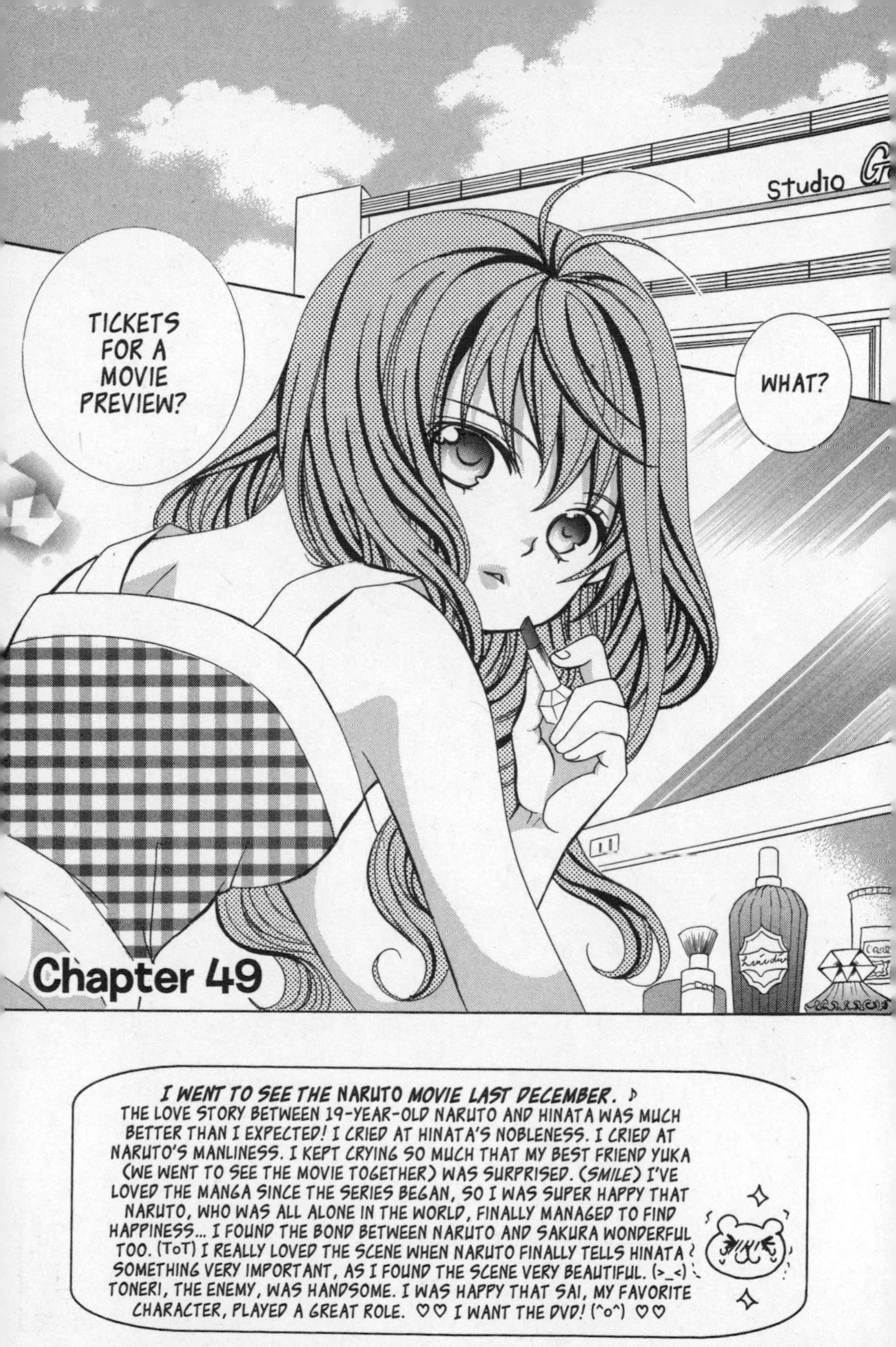
Studio
WHAT?
TICKETS FOR A MOVIE PREVIEW?

Chapter 49

I WENT TO SEE THE NARUTO *MOVIE LAST DECEMBER.* ♪
THE LOVE STORY BETWEEN 19-YEAR-OLD NARUTO AND HINATA WAS MUCH BETTER THAN I EXPECTED! I CRIED AT HINATA'S NOBLENESS. I CRIED AT NARUTO'S MANLINESS. I KEPT CRYING SO MUCH THAT MY BEST FRIEND YUKA (WE WENT TO SEE THE MOVIE TOGETHER) WAS SURPRISED. (SMILE) I'VE LOVED THE MANGA SINCE THE SERIES BEGAN, SO I WAS SUPER HAPPY THAT NARUTO, WHO WAS ALL ALONE IN THE WORLD, FINALLY MANAGED TO FIND HAPPINESS... I FOUND THE BOND BETWEEN NARUTO AND SAKURA WONDERFUL TOO. (ToT) I REALLY LOVED THE SCENE WHEN NARUTO FINALLY TELLS HINATA SOMETHING VERY IMPORTANT, AS I FOUND THE SCENE VERY BEAUTIFUL. (>_<) TONERI, THE ENEMY, WAS HANDSOME. I WAS HAPPY THAT SAI, MY FAVORITE CHARACTER, PLAYED A GREAT ROLE. ♡♡ I WANT THE DVD! (^o^) ♡♡

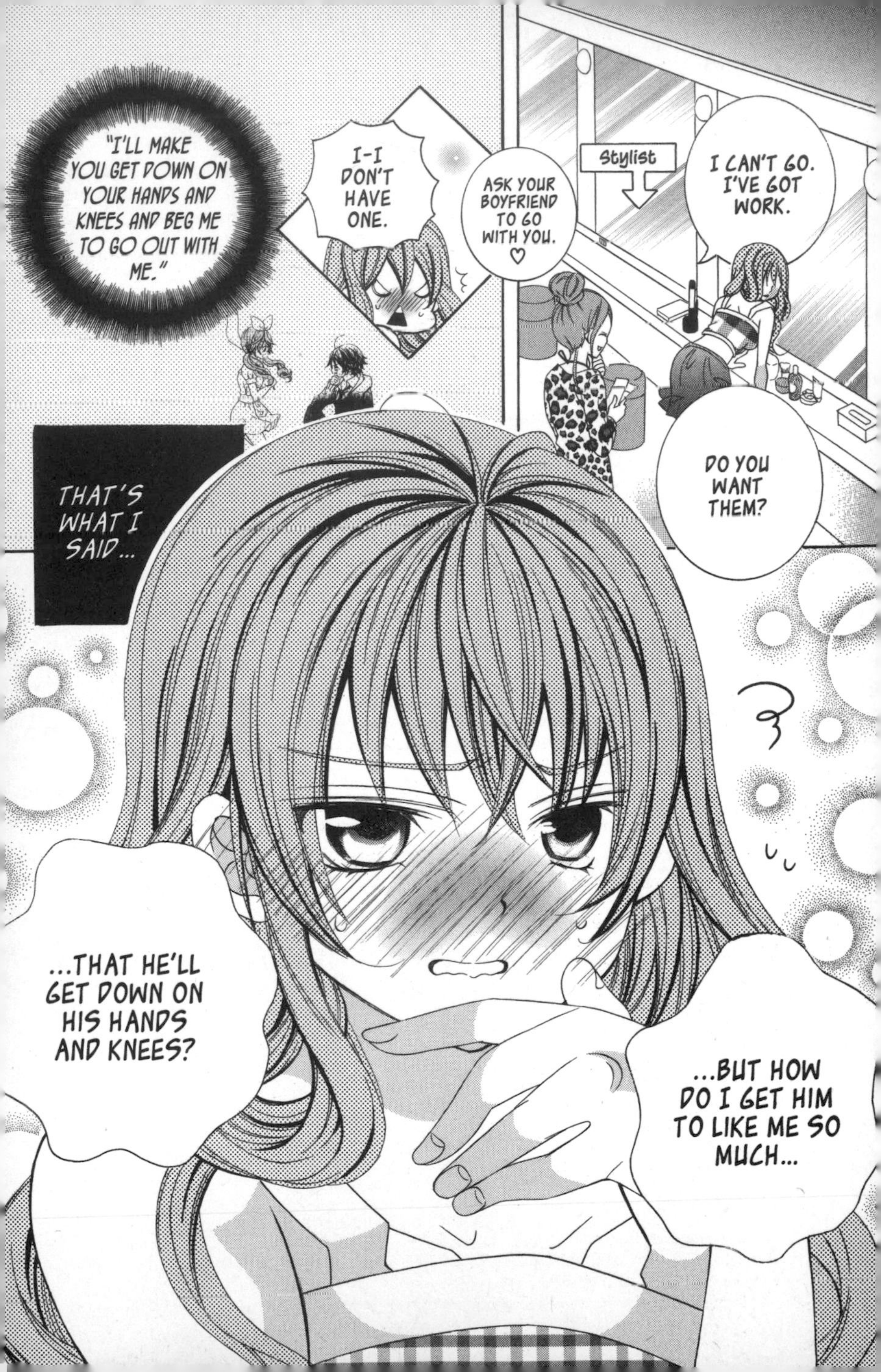
Stylist
I CAN'T GO. I'VE GOT WORK.
ASK YOUR BOYFRIEND TO GO WITH YOU. ♡
DO YOU WANT THEM?
I-I DON'T HAVE ONE.
"I'LL MAKE YOU GET DOWN ON YOUR HANDS AND KNEES AND BEG ME TO GO OUT WITH ME."
THAT'S WHAT I SAID...
...BUT HOW DO I GET HIM TO LIKE ME SO MUCH...
...THAT HE'LL GET DOWN ON HIS HANDS AND KNEES?

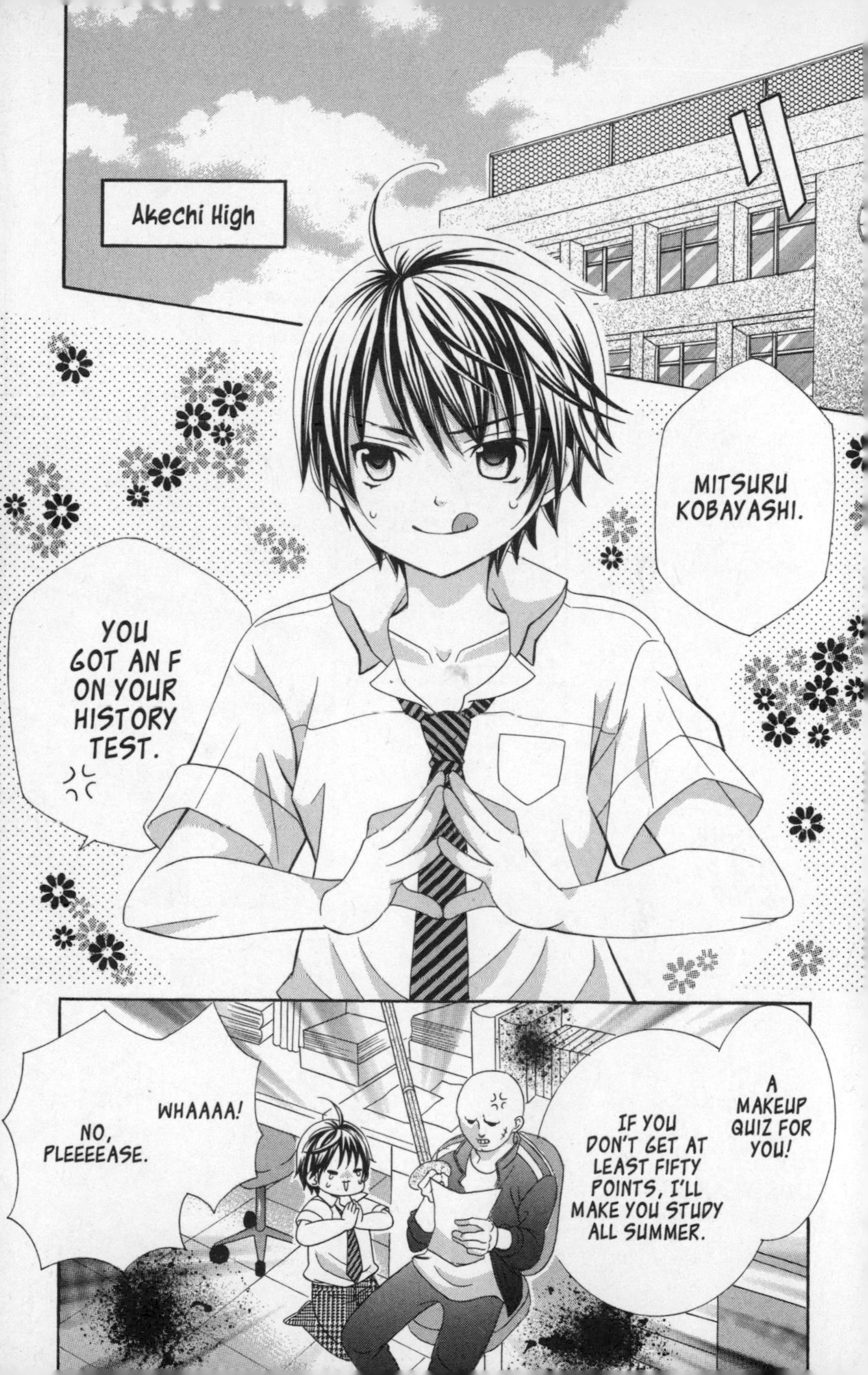
Akechi High
MITSURU KOBAYASHI.
YOU GOT AN F ON YOUR HISTORY TEST.
A MAKEUP QUIZ FOR YOU!
IF YOU DON'T GET AT LEAST FIFTY POINTS, I'LL MAKE YOU STUDY ALL SUMMER.
WHAAAA!
NO, PLEEEEASE.

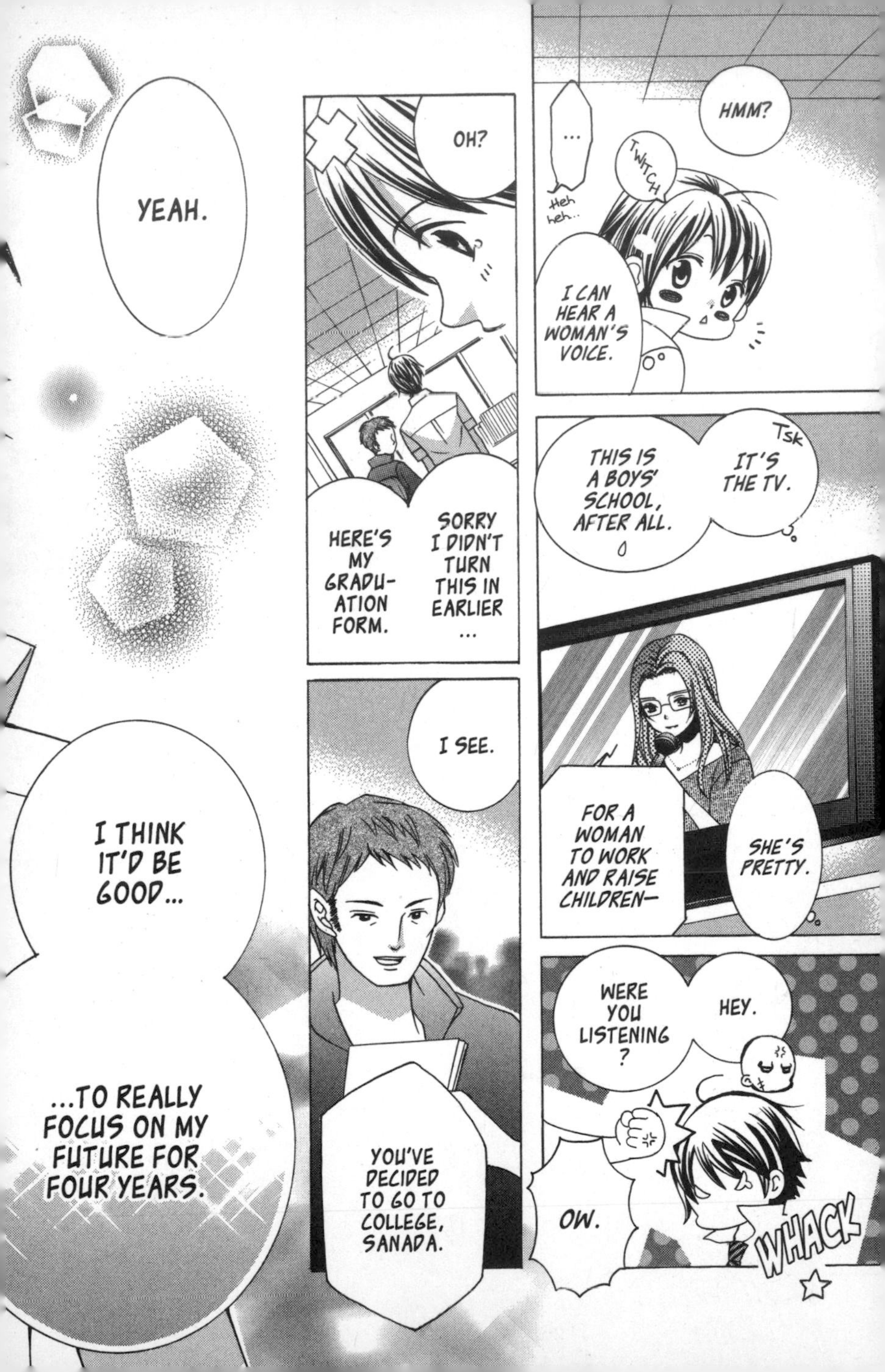
HMM?
TWITCH
...
Heh heh...
I CAN HEAR A WOMAN'S VOICE.
Tsk
IT'S THE TV.
THIS IS A BOYS' SCHOOL, AFTER ALL.
FOR A WOMAN TO WORK AND RAISE CHILDREN—
SHE'S PRETTY.
HEY.
WERE YOU LISTENING?
WHACK
OW.
OH?
SORRY I DIDN'T TURN THIS IN EARLIER...
HERE'S MY GRADUATION FORM.
I SEE.
YOU'VE DECIDED TO GO TO COLLEGE, SANADA.
YEAH.
I THINK IT'D BE GOOD...
...TO REALLY FOCUS ON MY FUTURE FOR FOUR YEARS.

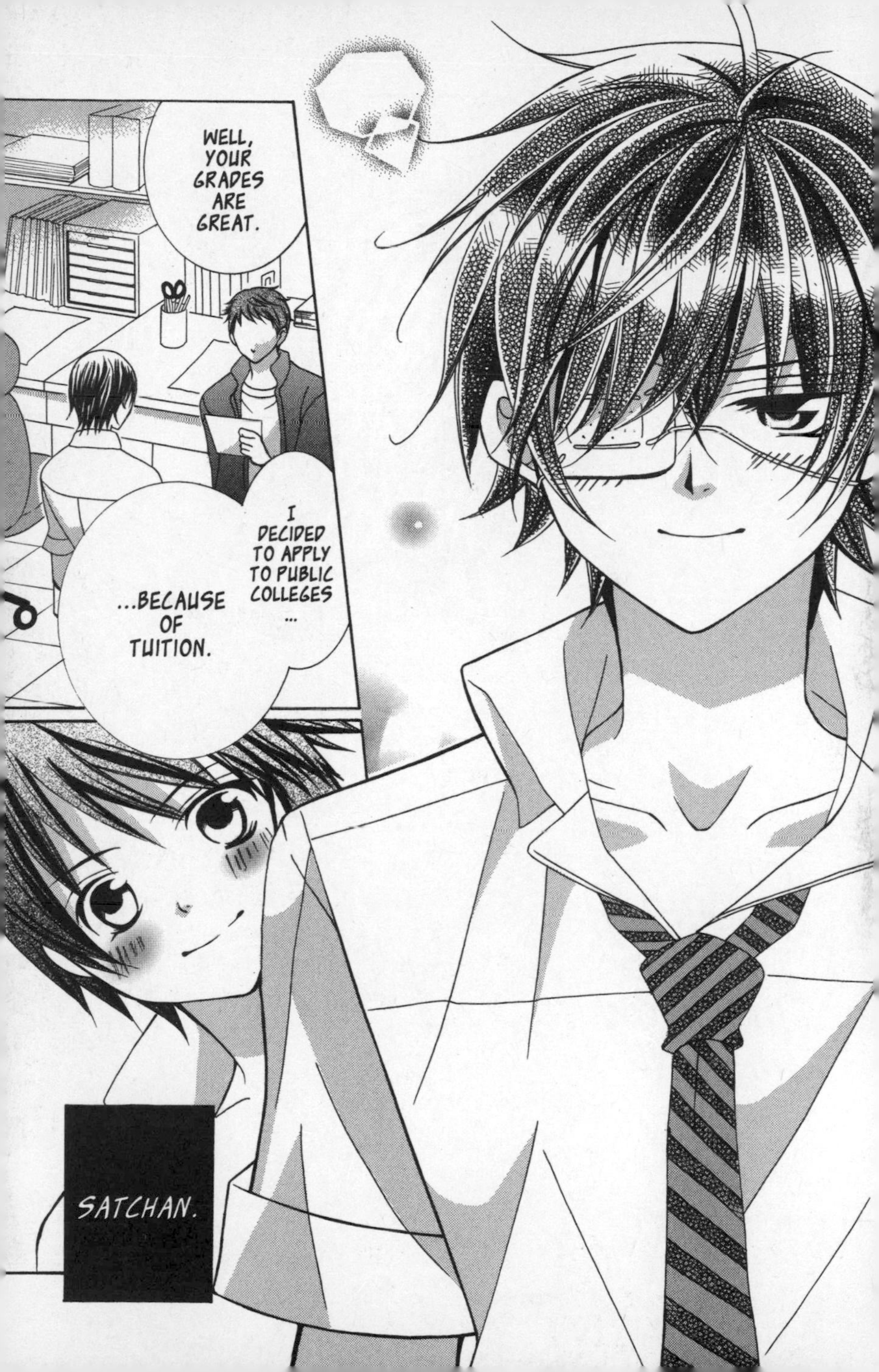
WELL, YOUR GRADES ARE GREAT.
I DECIDED TO APPLY TO PUBLIC COLLEGES ...
...BECAUSE OF TUITION.
SATCHAN.

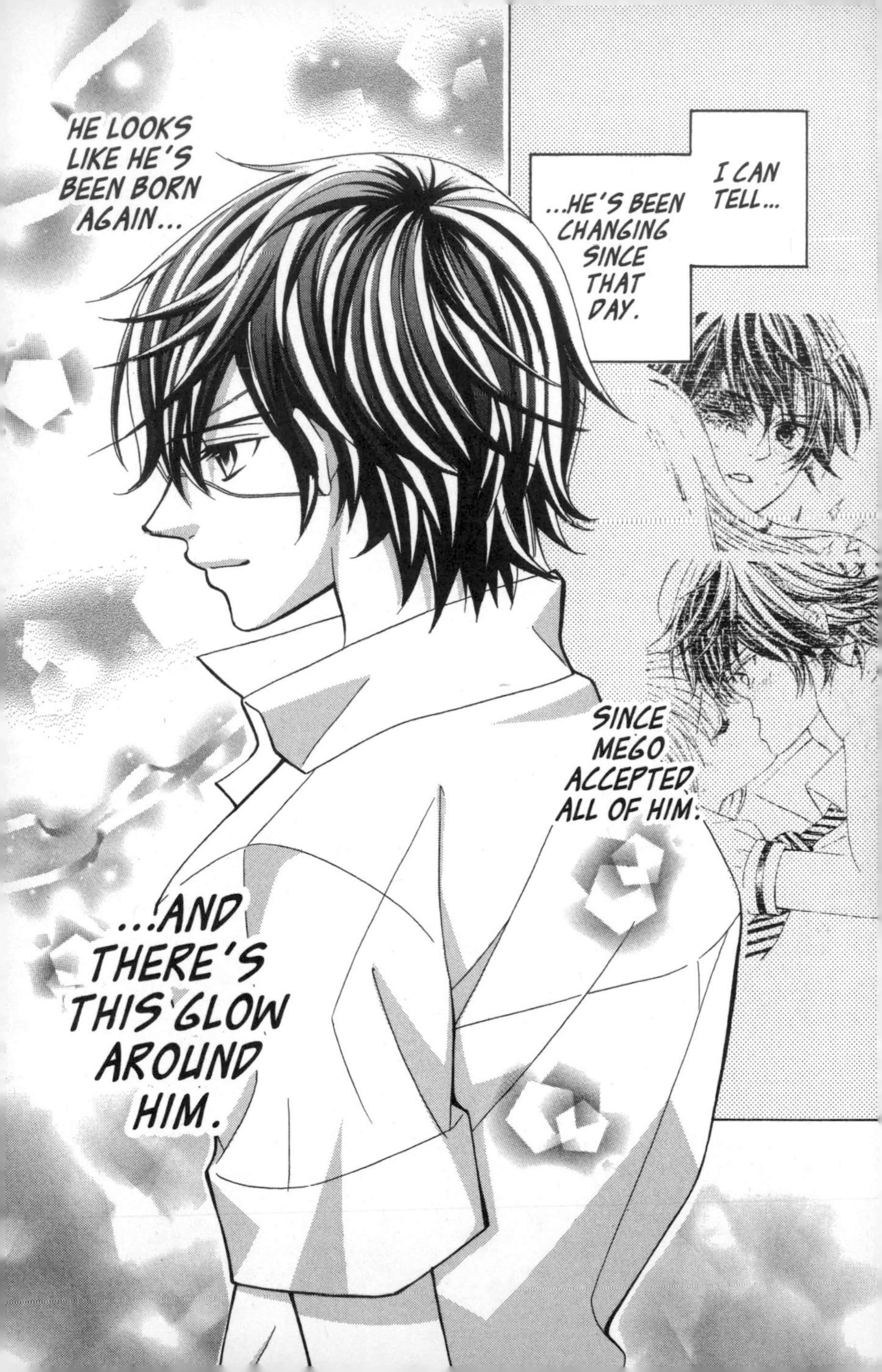
I CAN TELL...
...HE'S BEEN CHANGING SINCE THAT DAY.
SINCE MEGO ACCEPTED ALL OF HIM.
HE LOOKS LIKE HE'S BEEN BORN AGAIN...
...AND THERE'S THIS GLOW AROUND HIM.

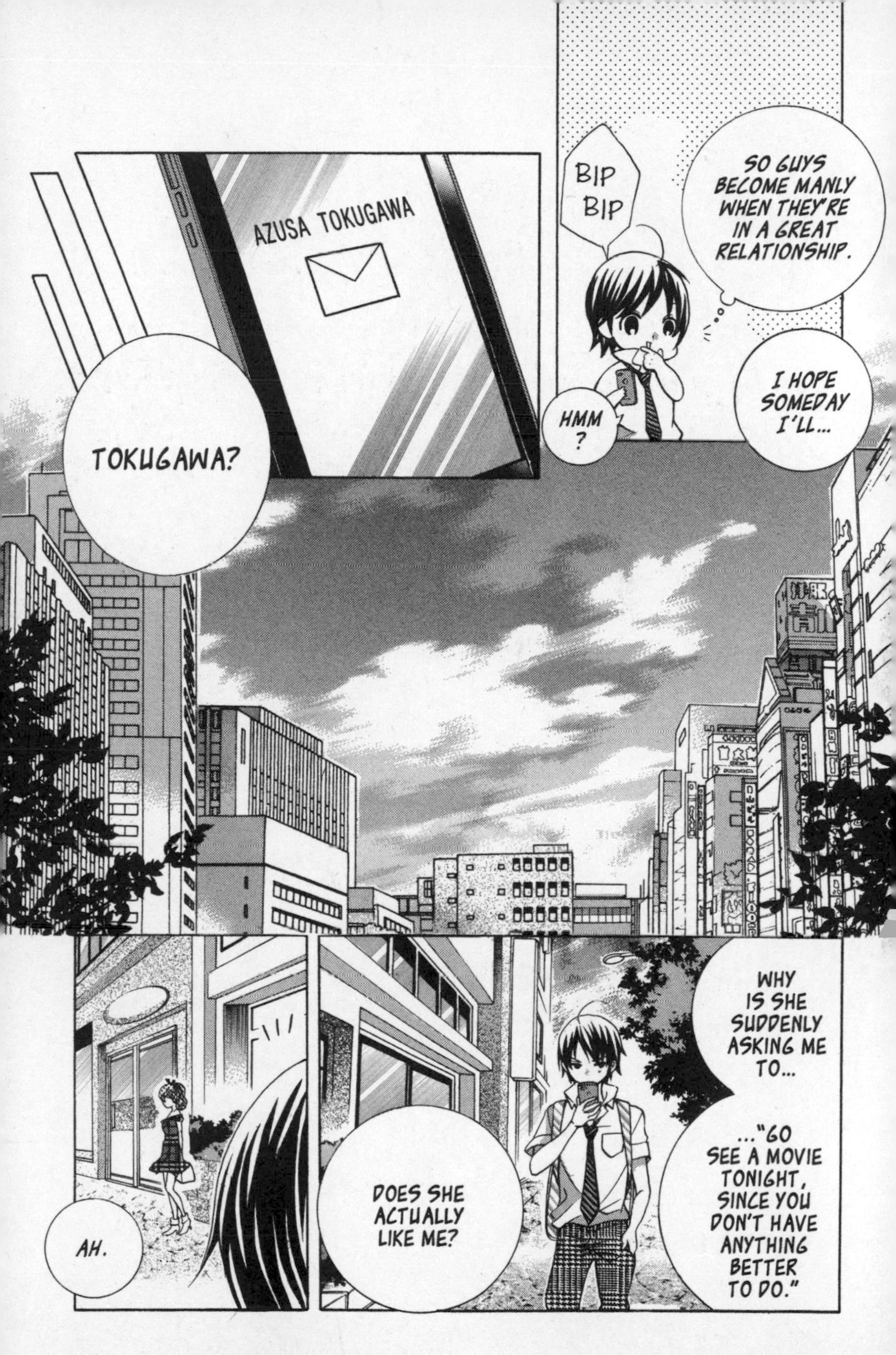
SO GUYS BECOME MANLY WHEN THEY'RE IN A GREAT RELATIONSHIP.
BIP BIP
I HOPE SOMEDAY I'LL...
HMM?
AZUSA TOKUGAWA
TOKUGAWA?
WHY IS SHE SUDDENLY ASKING ME TO...
..."GO SEE A MOVIE TONIGHT, SINCE YOU DON'T HAVE ANYTHING BETTER TO DO."
DOES SHE ACTUALLY LIKE ME?
AH.

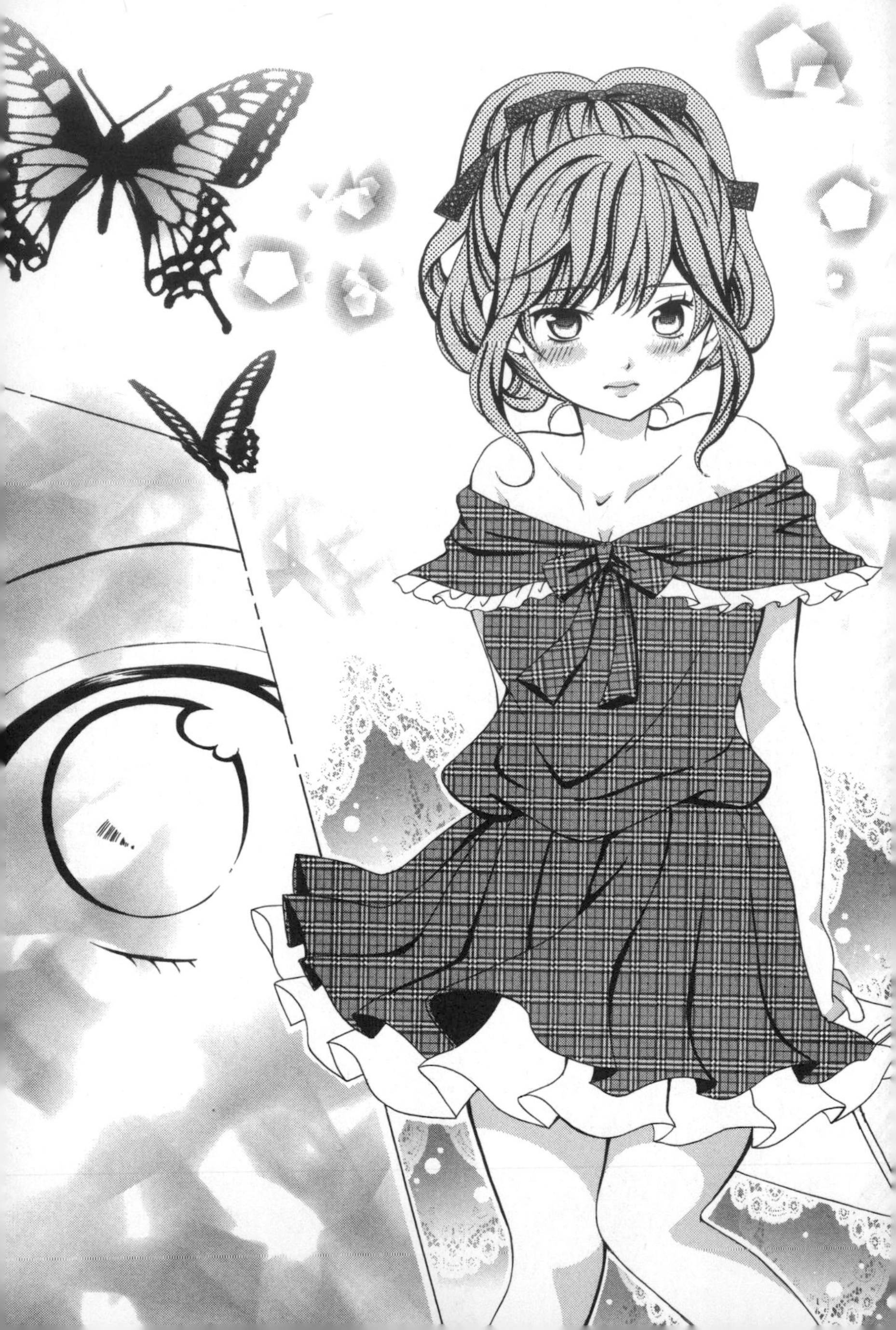

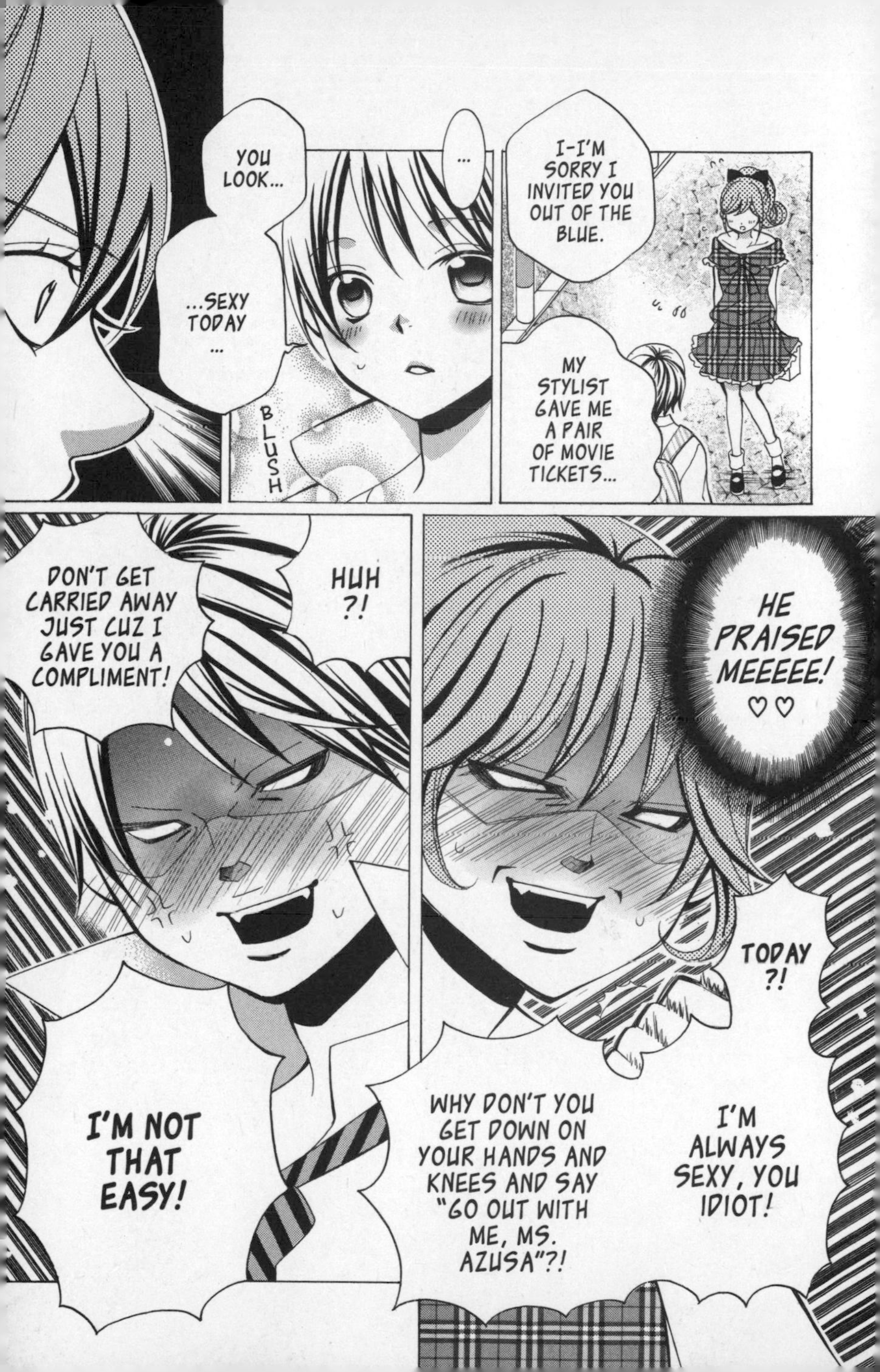
I-I'M SORRY I INVITED YOU OUT OF THE BLUE.
MY STYLIST GAVE ME A PAIR OF MOVIE TICKETS...
...
BLUSH
YOU LOOK...
...SEXY TODAY ...
HE PRAISED MEEEEEE! ♡♡
TODAY ?!
I'M ALWAYS SEXY, YOU IDIOT!
WHY DON'T YOU GET DOWN ON YOUR HANDS AND KNEES AND SAY "GO OUT WITH ME, MS. AZUSA"?!
HUH ?!
DON'T GET CARRIED AWAY JUST CUZ I GAVE YOU A COMPLIMENT!
I'M NOT THAT EASY!

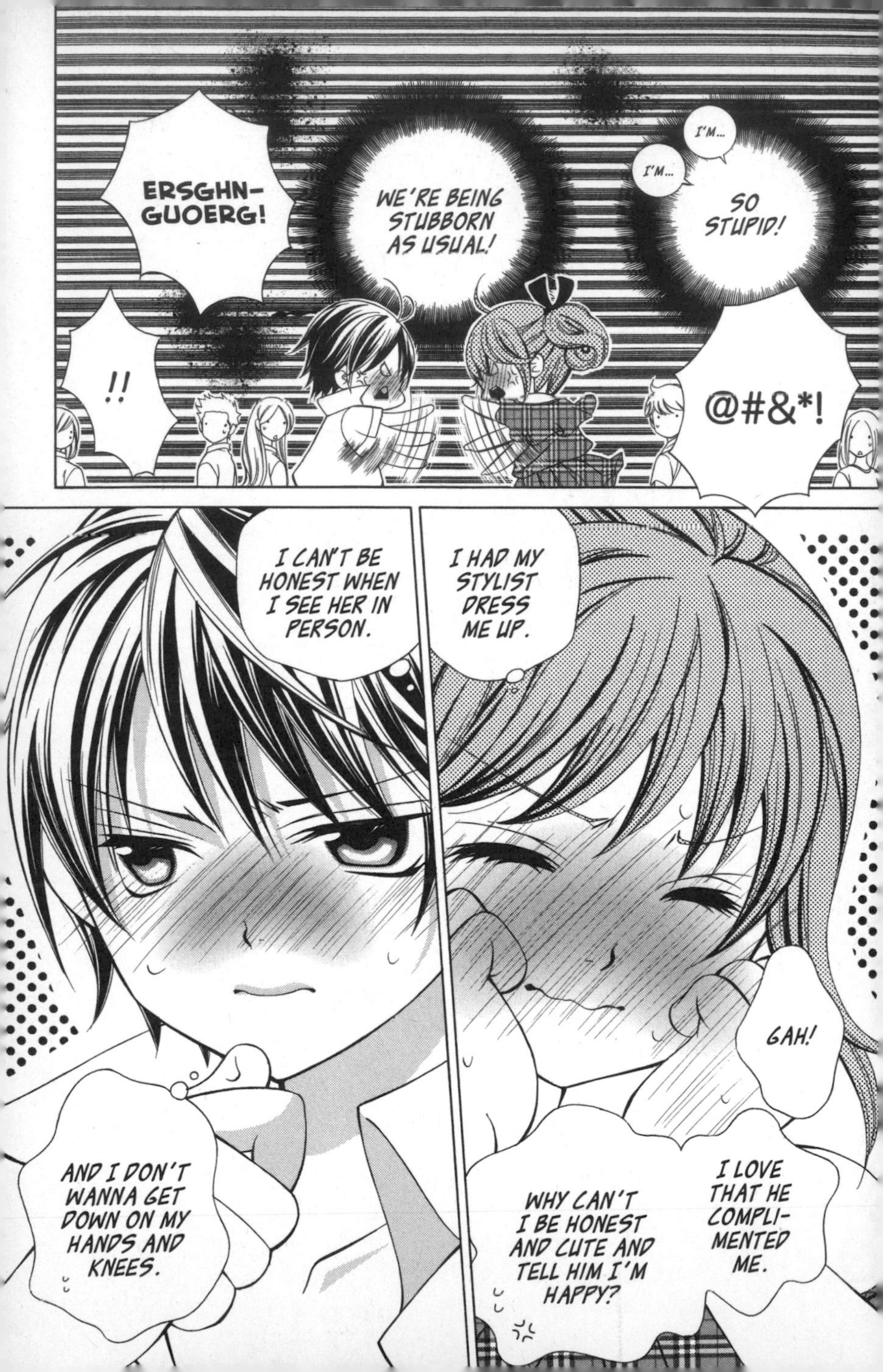
I'M...
I'M...
SO STUPID!
@#&*!
WE'RE BEING STUBBORN AS USUAL!
ERSGHN-GUOERG!
!!
I HAD MY STYLIST DRESS ME UP.
GAH!
I LOVE THAT HE COMPLI-MENTED ME.
WHY CAN'T I BE HONEST AND CUTE AND TELL HIM I'M HAPPY?
I CAN'T BE HONEST WHEN I SEE HER IN PERSON.
AND I DON'T WANNA GET DOWN ON MY HANDS AND KNEES.

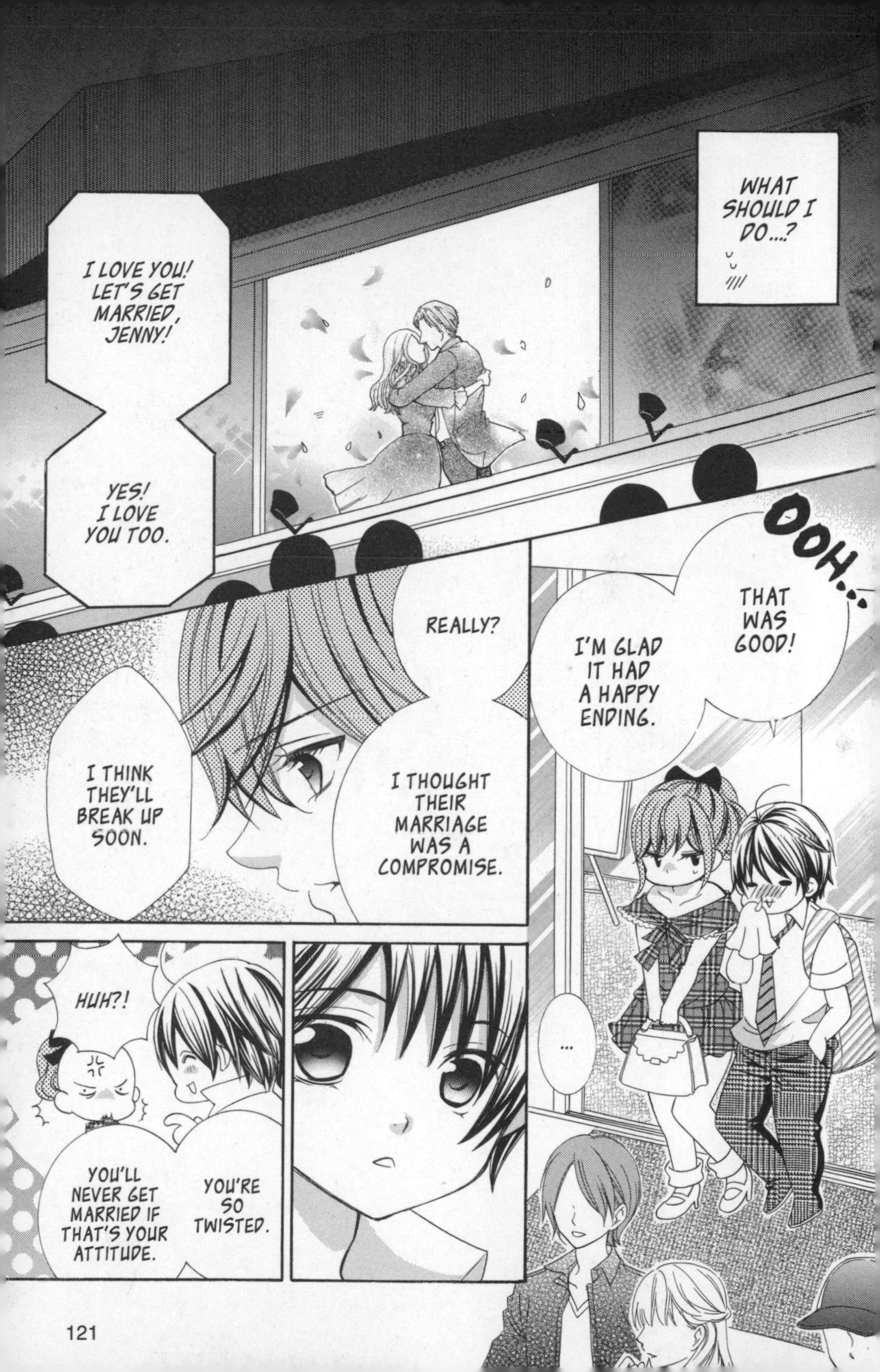
WHAT SHOULD I DO...?
I LOVE YOU! LET'S GET MARRIED, JENNY!
YES! I LOVE YOU TOO.
OOH...
THAT WAS GOOD!
I'M GLAD IT HAD A HAPPY ENDING.
...
REALLY?
I THOUGHT THEIR MARRIAGE WAS A COMPROMISE.
I THINK THEY'LL BREAK UP SOON.
HUH?!
YOU'RE SO TWISTED.
YOU'LL NEVER GET MARRIED IF THAT'S YOUR ATTITUDE.

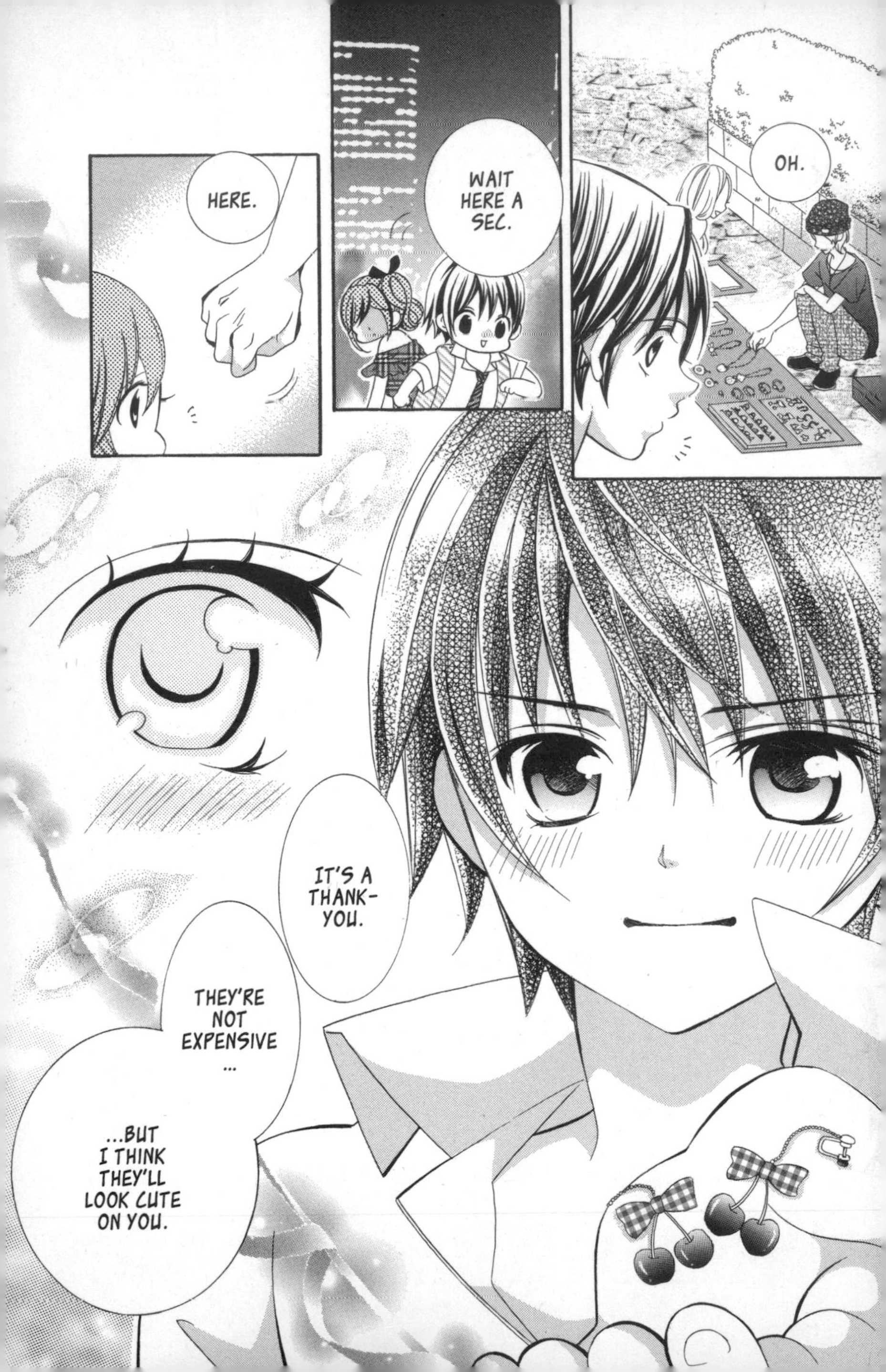
OH.
WAIT HERE A SEC.
HERE.
IT'S A THANK-YOU.
THEY'RE NOT EXPENSIVE...
...BUT I THINK THEY'LL LOOK CUTE ON YOU.

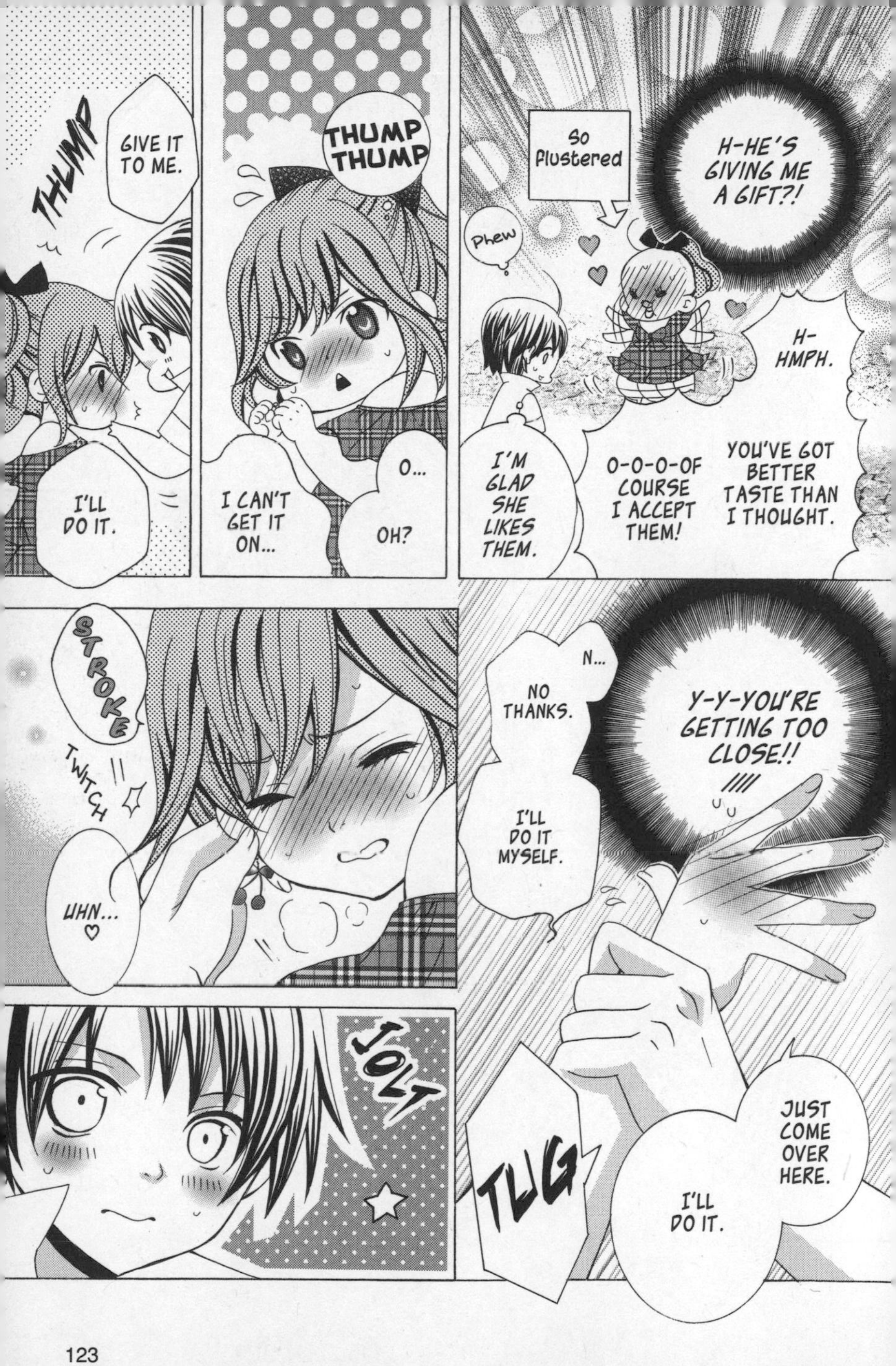
H-HE'S GIVING ME A GIFT?!
So flustered
Phew
H- HMPH.
YOU'VE GOT BETTER TASTE THAN I THOUGHT.
O-O-O-OF COURSE I ACCEPT THEM!
I'M GLAD SHE LIKES THEM.
THUMP THUMP
O...
OH?
I CAN'T GET IT ON...
GIVE IT TO ME.
THUMP
I'LL DO IT.
N...
NO THANKS.
Y-Y-YOU'RE GETTING TOO CLOSE!!
I'LL DO IT MYSELF.
JUST COME OVER HERE.
I'LL DO IT.
TUG
STROKE
TWITCH
UHN... ♡
JOLT

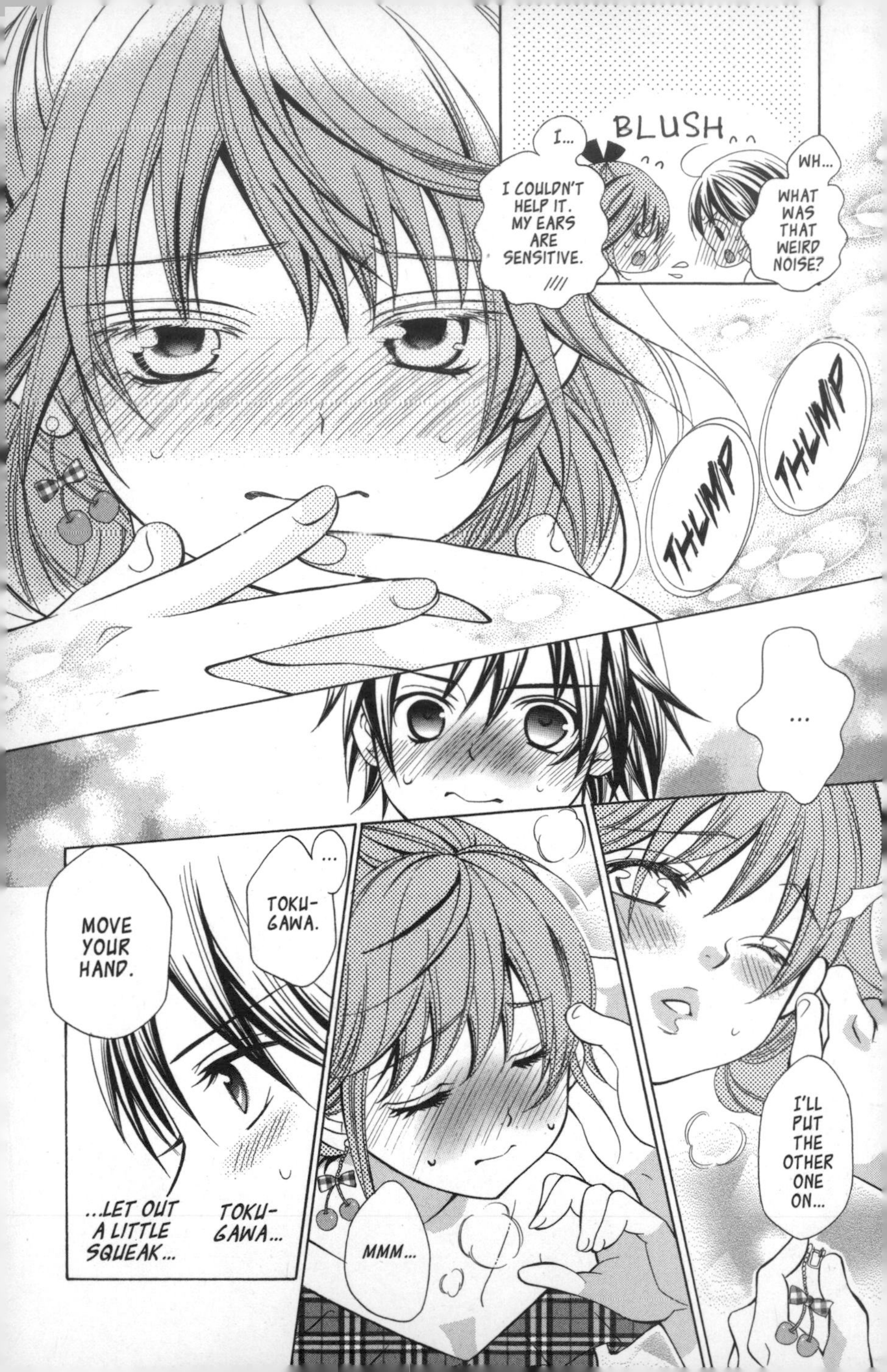
WH... WHAT WAS THAT WEIRD NOISE?
BLUSH
I...
I COULDN'T HELP IT. MY EARS ARE SENSITIVE.
THUMP
THUMP
...
I'LL PUT THE OTHER ONE ON...
MMM...
... TOKU-GAWA.
MOVE YOUR HAND.
TOKU-GAWA...
...LET OUT A LITTLE SQUEAK...

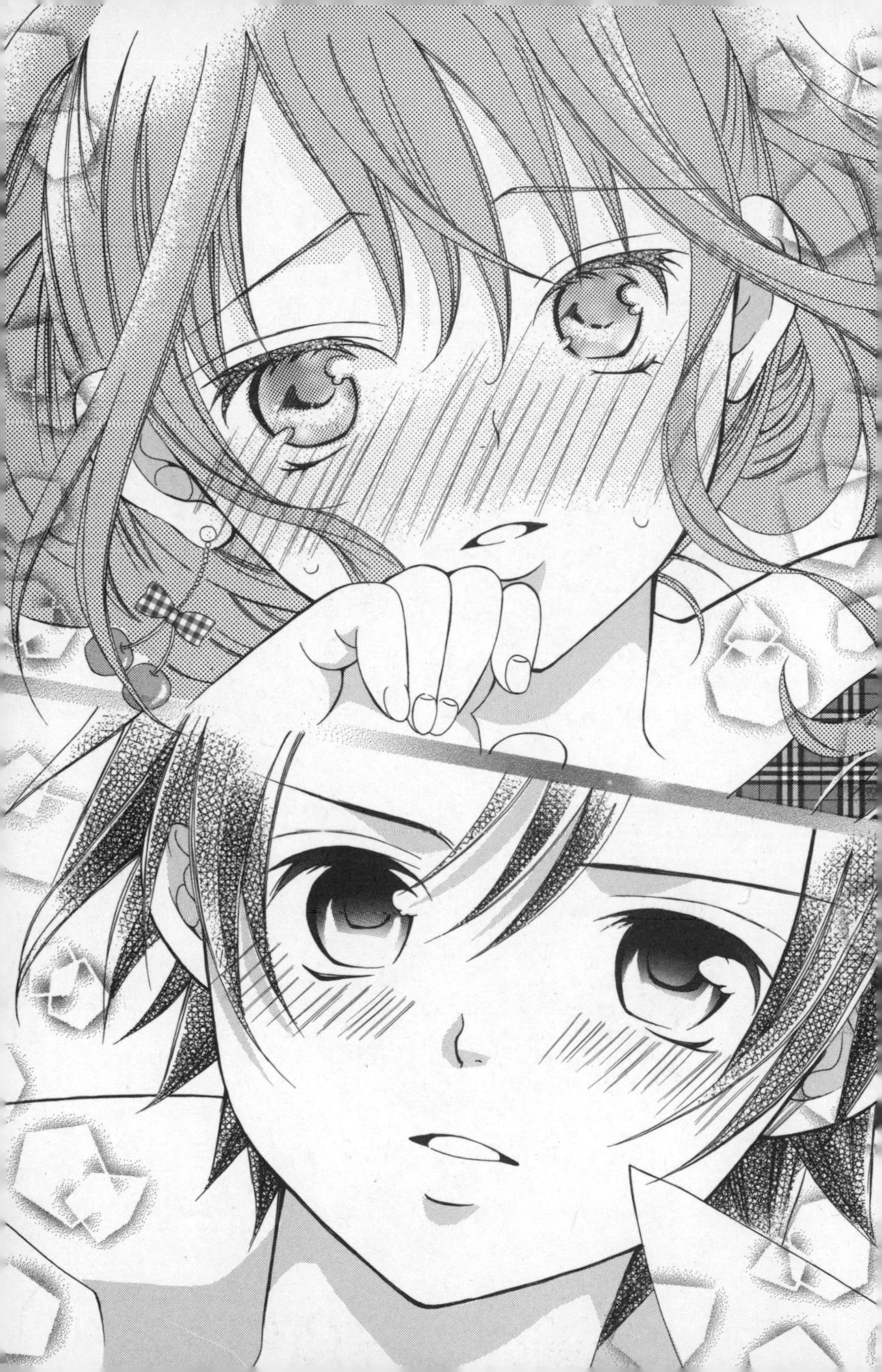

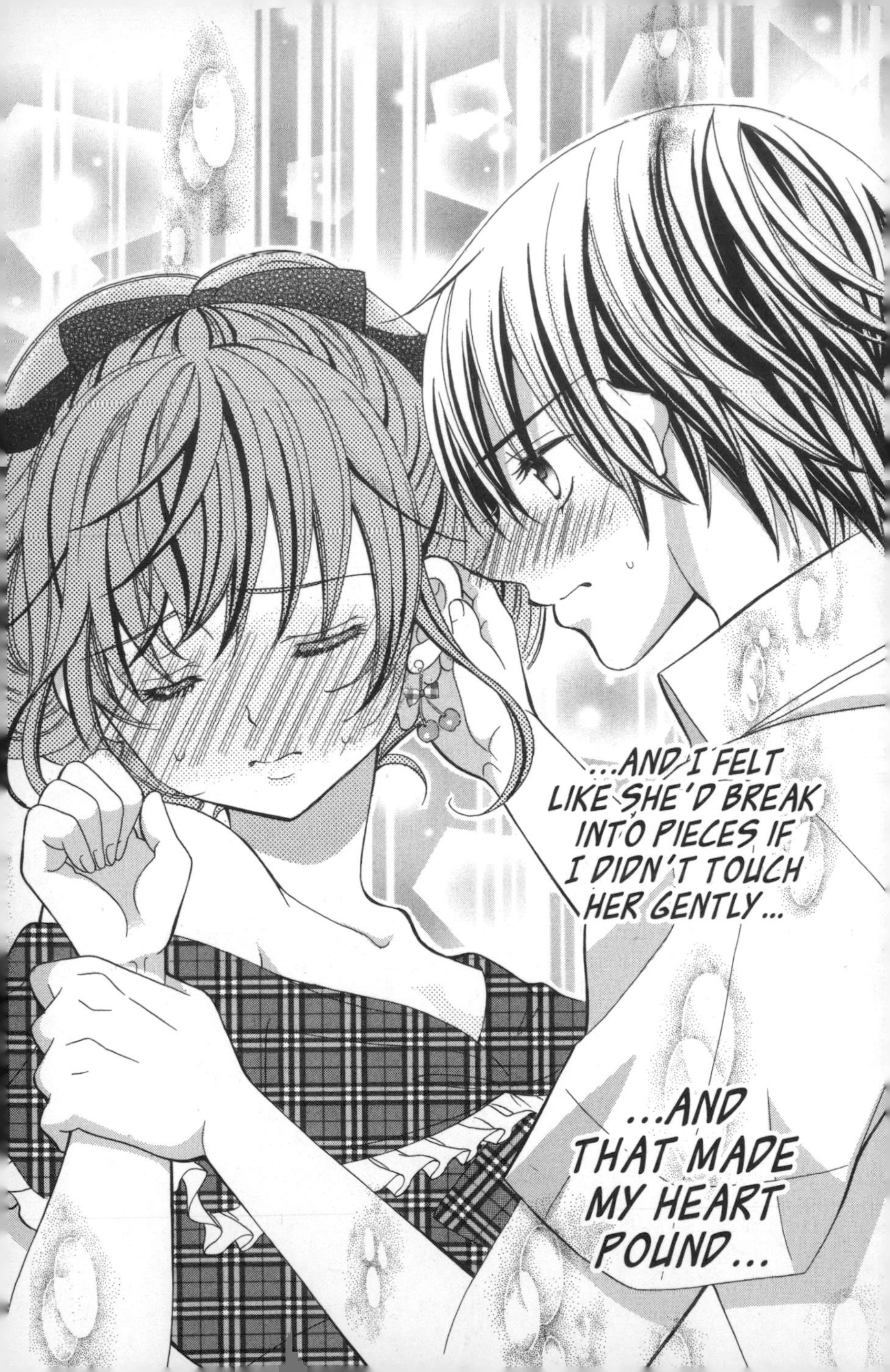
...AND I FELT LIKE SHE'D BREAK INTO PIECES IF I DIDN'T TOUCH HER GENTLY...
...AND THAT MADE MY HEART POUND...

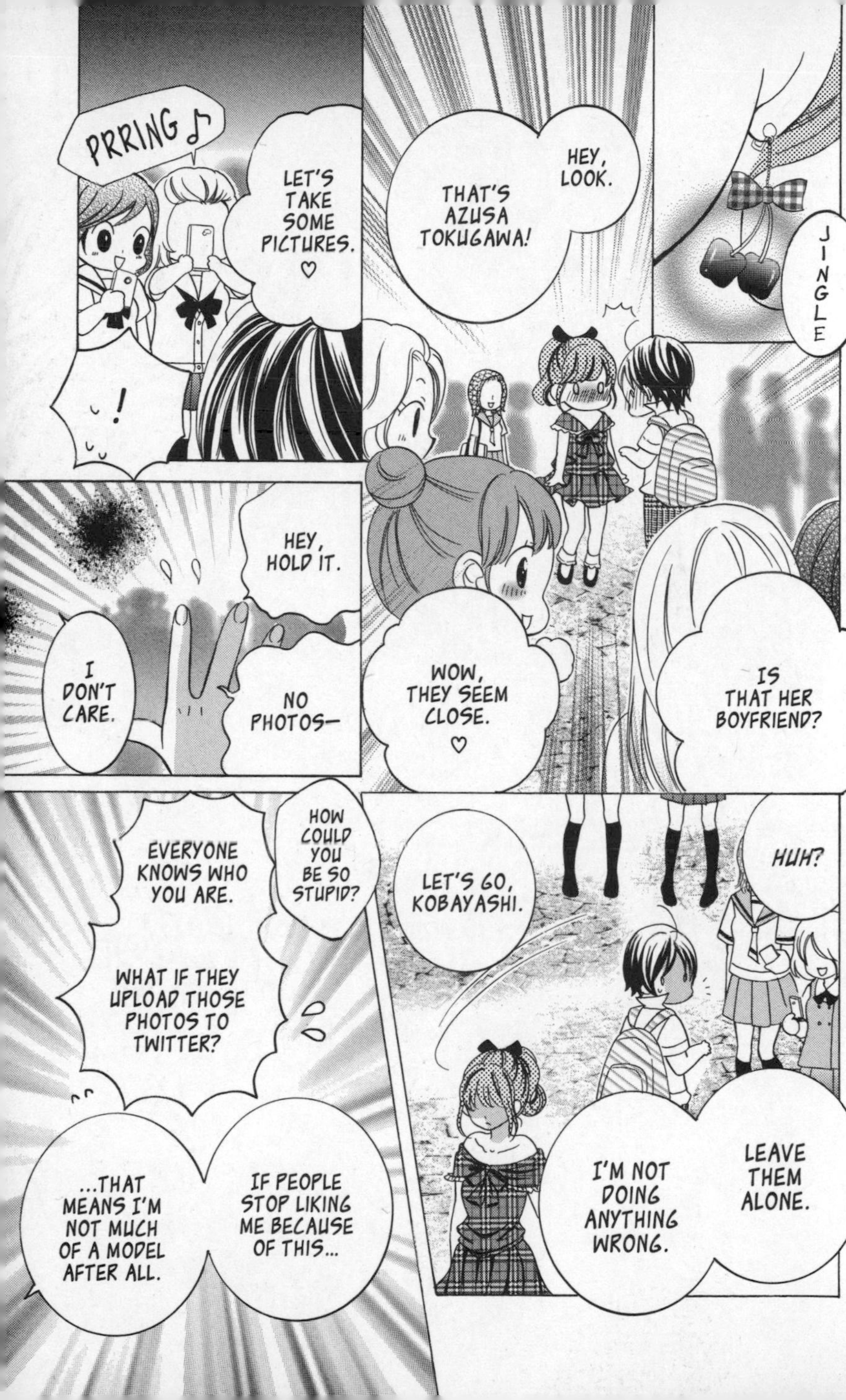
JINGLE
HEY, LOOK.
THAT'S AZUSA TOKUGAWA!
IS THAT HER BOYFRIEND?
WOW, THEY SEEM CLOSE. ♡
PRRING ♪
LET'S TAKE SOME PICTURES. ♡
HEY, HOLD IT.
NO PHOTOS—
I DON'T CARE.
HUH?
LET'S GO, KOBAYASHI.
LEAVE THEM ALONE.
I'M NOT DOING ANYTHING WRONG.
HOW COULD YOU BE SO STUPID?
EVERYONE KNOWS WHO YOU ARE.
WHAT IF THEY UPLOAD THOSE PHOTOS TO TWITTER?
IF PEOPLE STOP LIKING ME BECAUSE OF THIS...
...THAT MEANS I'M NOT MUCH OF A MODEL AFTER ALL.

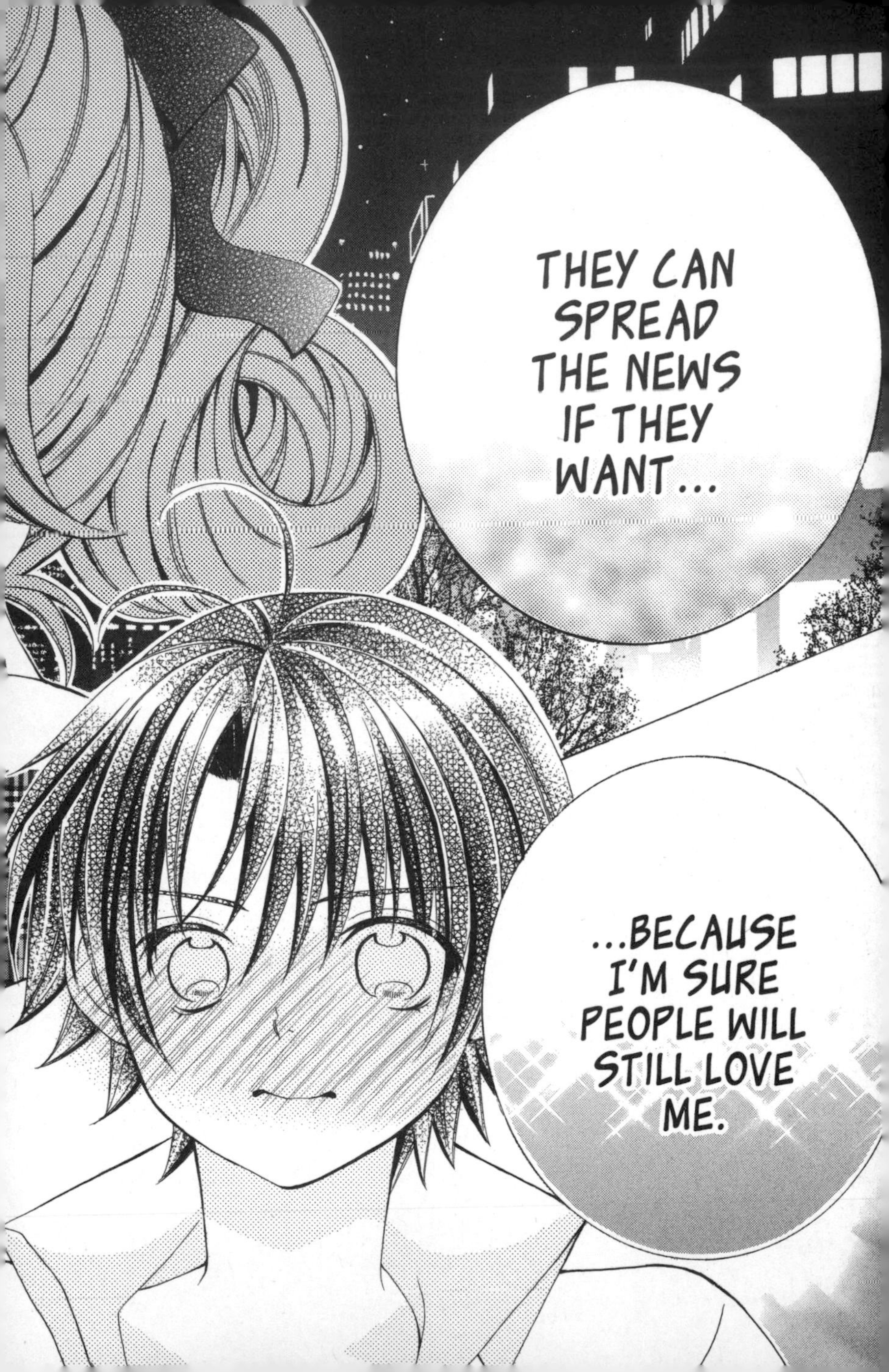
THEY CAN SPREAD THE NEWS IF THEY WANT...
...BECAUSE I'M SURE PEOPLE WILL STILL LOVE ME.

WHAT'S WRONG WITH GOING OUT WITH THE GUY I REALLY LOVE?
I'VE GOT NOTHING TO BE ASHAMED OF.
I'M PROUD OF IT, ACTUALLY.

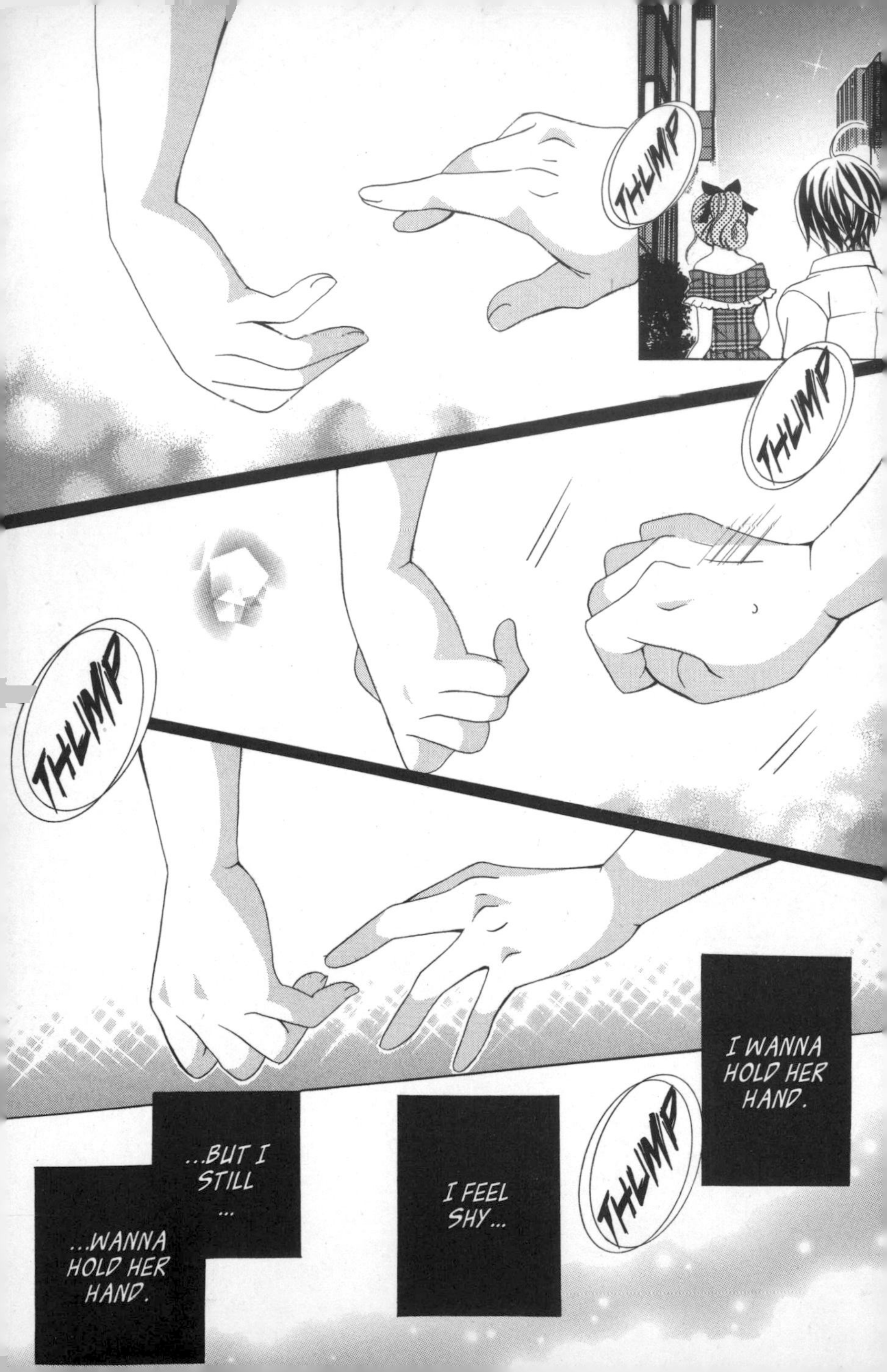
THUMP
THUMP
THUMP
I WANNA HOLD HER HAND.
THUMP
I FEEL SHY...
...BUT I STILL ...
...WANNA HOLD HER HAND.

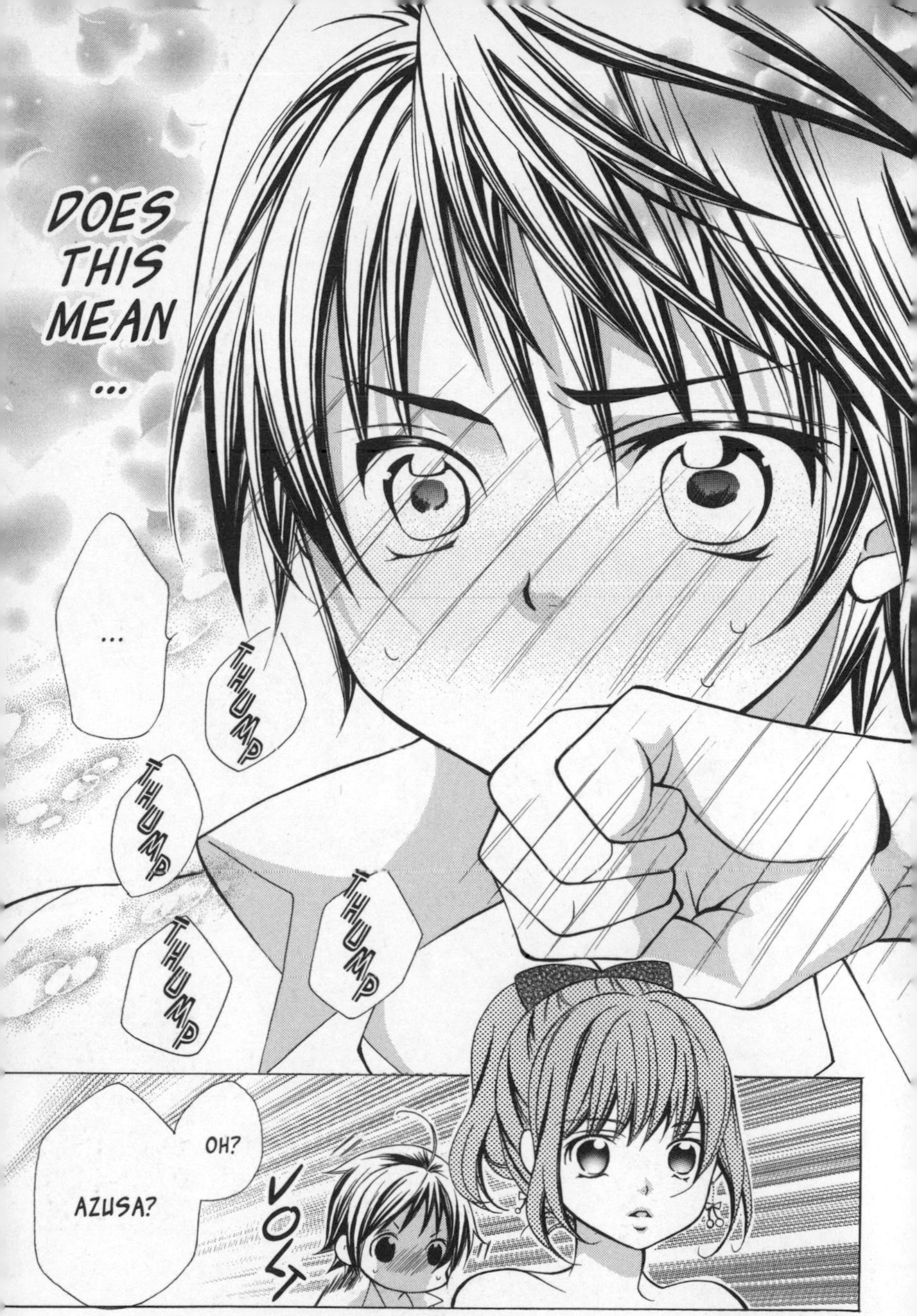
DOES THIS MEAN ...
...
THUMP
THUMP
THUMP
THUMP
OH?
AZUSA?
VOLT

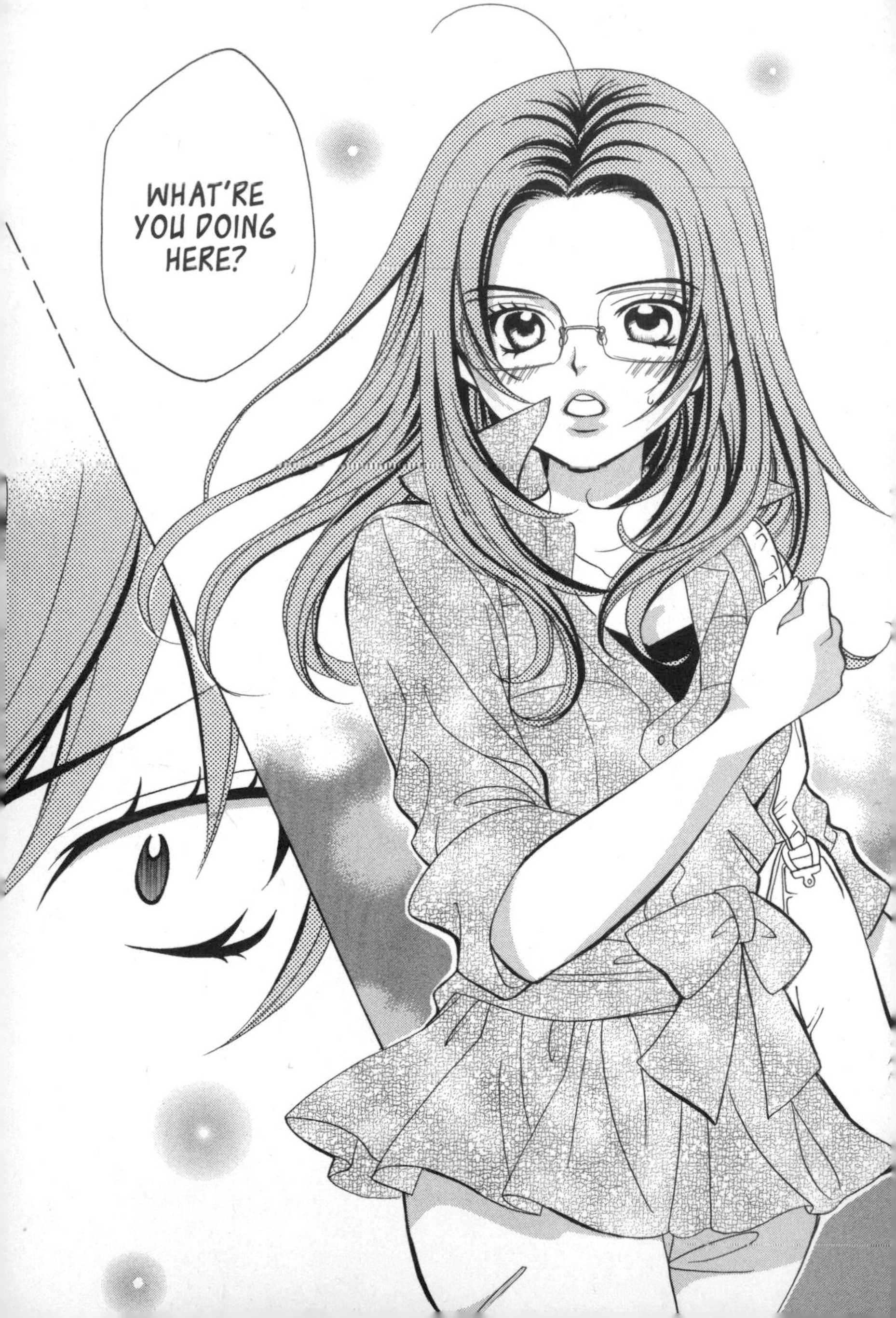
WHAT'RE YOU DOING HERE?

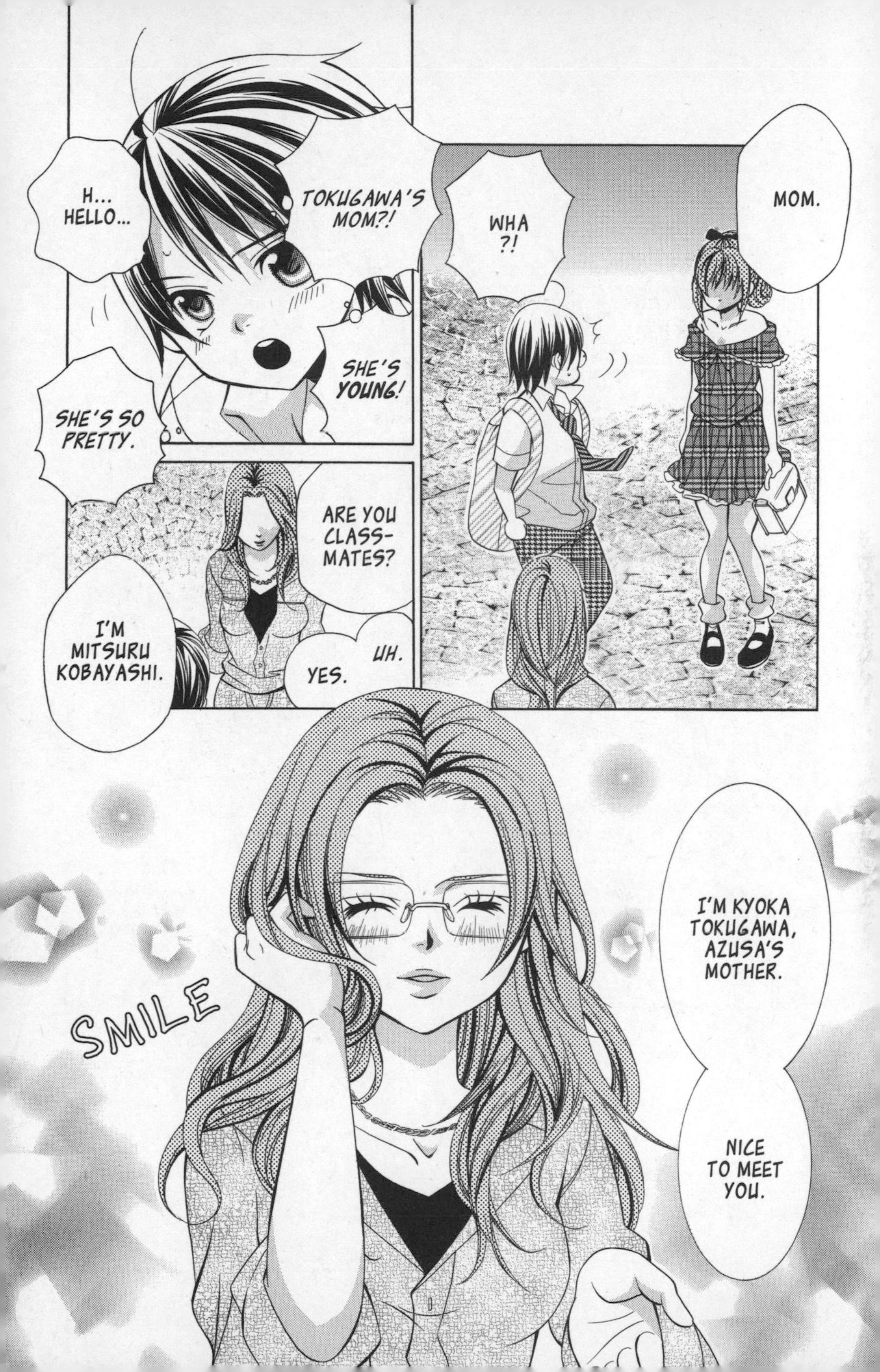
MOM.
WHA ?!
TOKUGAWA'S MOM?!
H... HELLO...
SHE'S YOUNG!
SHE'S SO PRETTY.
ARE YOU CLASSMATES?
UH. YES.
I'M MITSURU KOBAYASHI.
I'M KYOKA TOKUGAWA, AZUSA'S MOTHER.
NICE TO MEET YOU.
SMILE

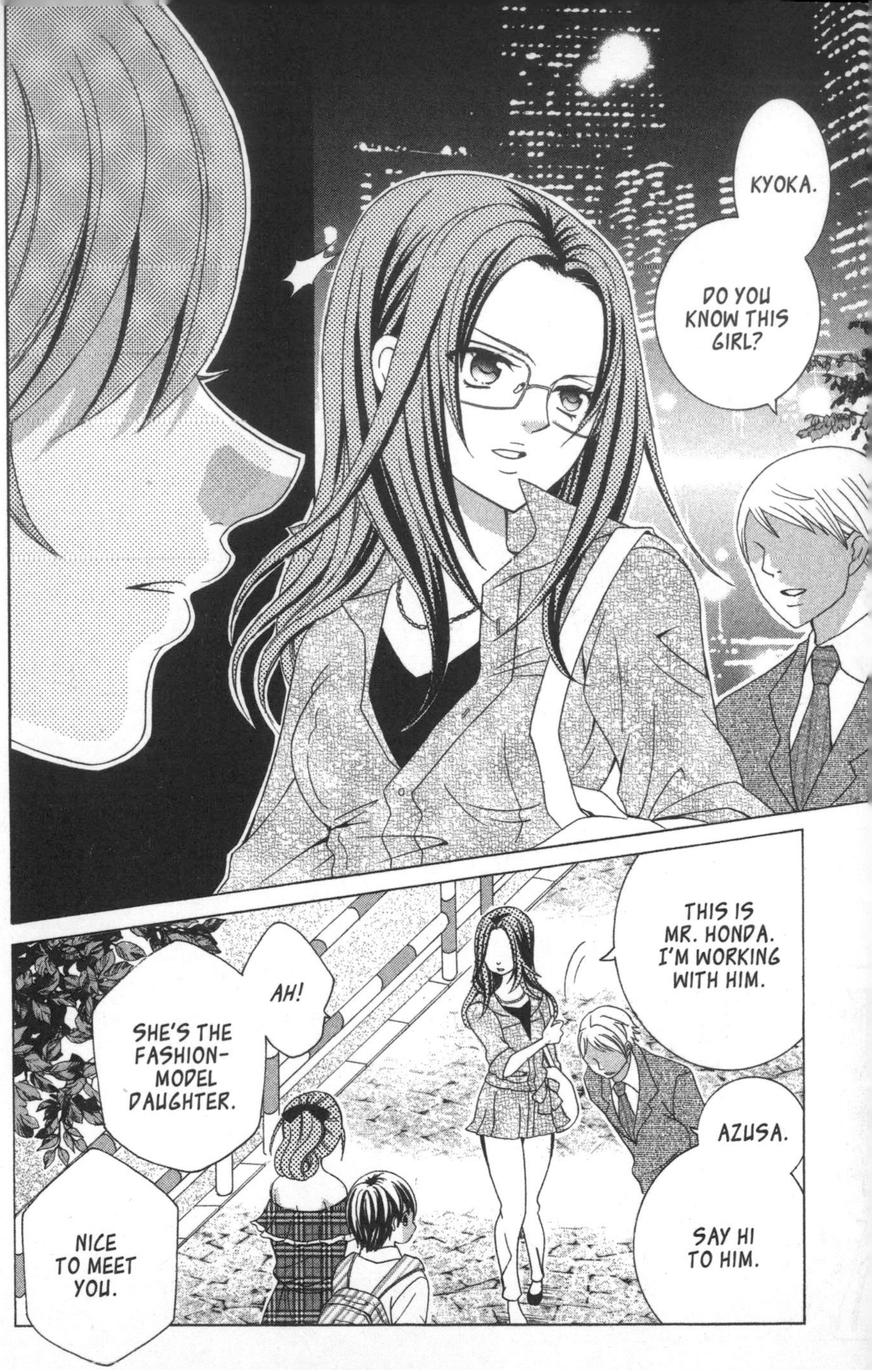
KYOKA.
DO YOU KNOW THIS GIRL?
THIS IS MR. HONDA. I'M WORKING WITH HIM.
AZUSA.
SAY HI TO HIM.
AH!
SHE'S THE FASHION-MODEL DAUGHTER.
NICE TO MEET YOU.

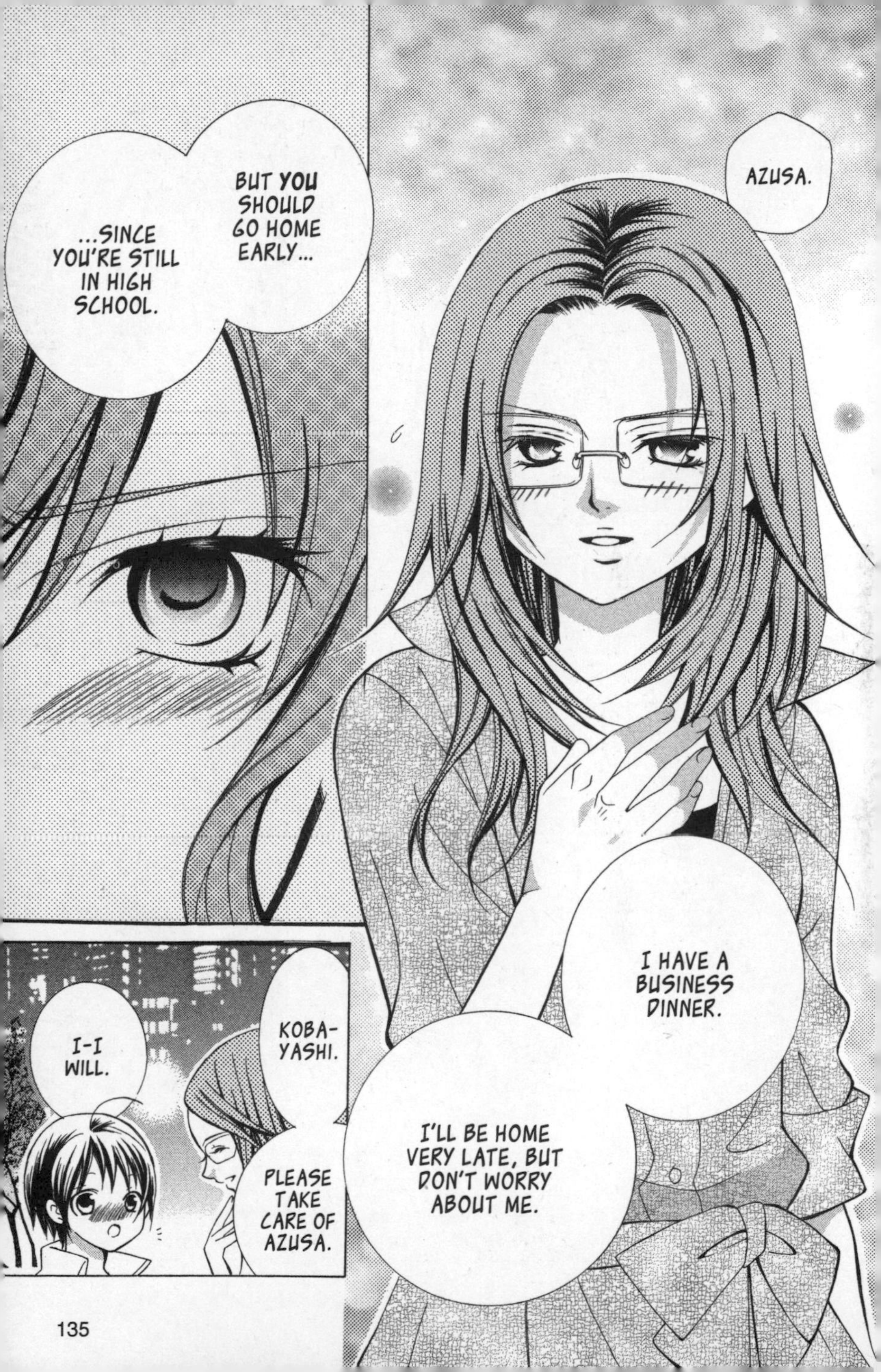
AZUSA.
I HAVE A BUSINESS DINNER.
I'LL BE HOME VERY LATE, BUT DON'T WORRY ABOUT ME.
BUT YOU SHOULD GO HOME EARLY...
...SINCE YOU'RE STILL IN HIGH SCHOOL.
KOBA-YASHI.
PLEASE TAKE CARE OF AZUSA.
I-I WILL.

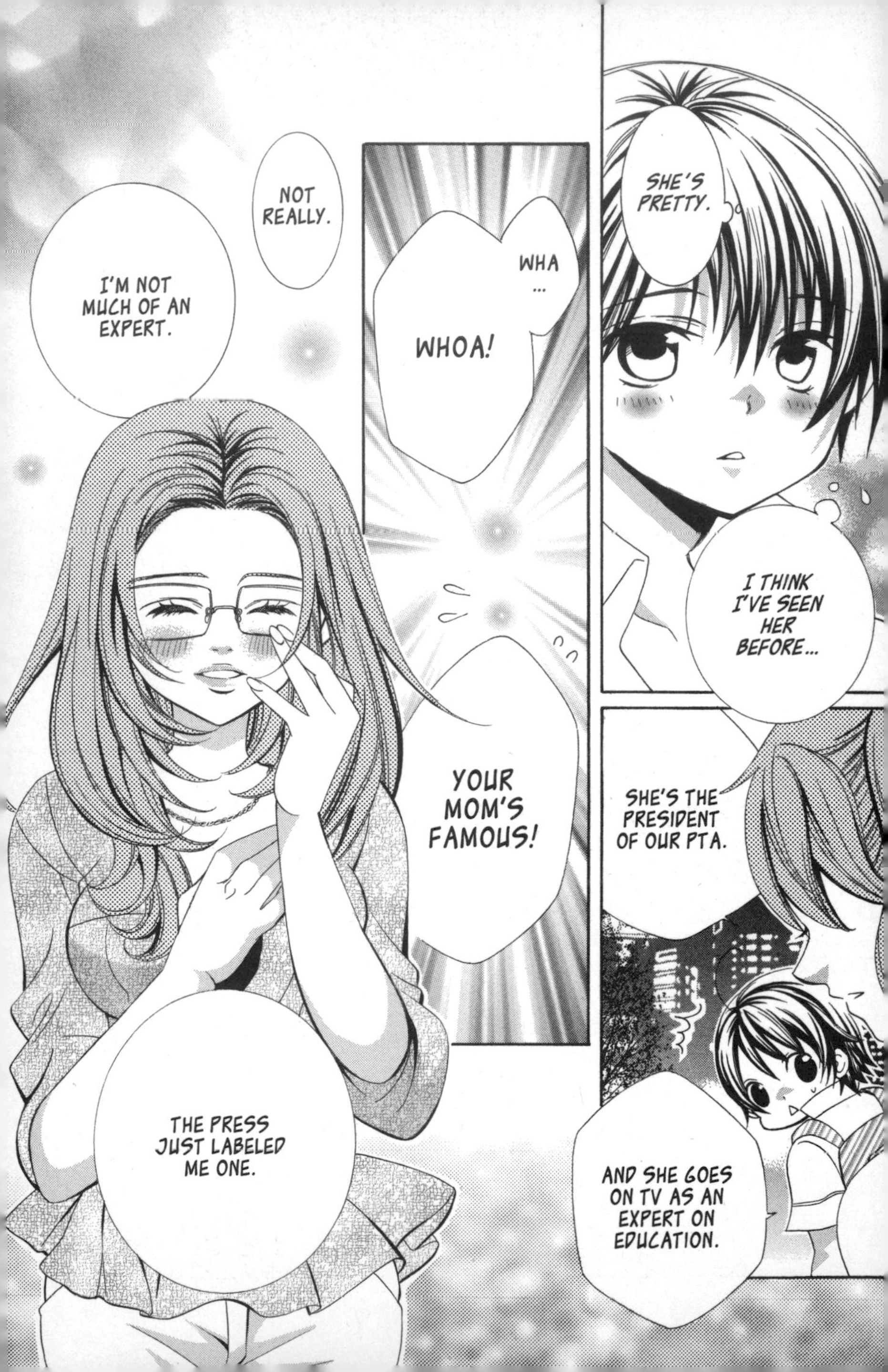
SHE'S PRETTY.
I THINK I'VE SEEN HER BEFORE...
SHE'S THE PRESIDENT OF OUR PTA.
AND SHE GOES ON TV AS AN EXPERT ON EDUCATION.
WHA...
WHOA!
YOUR MOM'S FAMOUS!
NOT REALLY.
I'M NOT MUCH OF AN EXPERT.
THE PRESS JUST LABELED ME ONE.

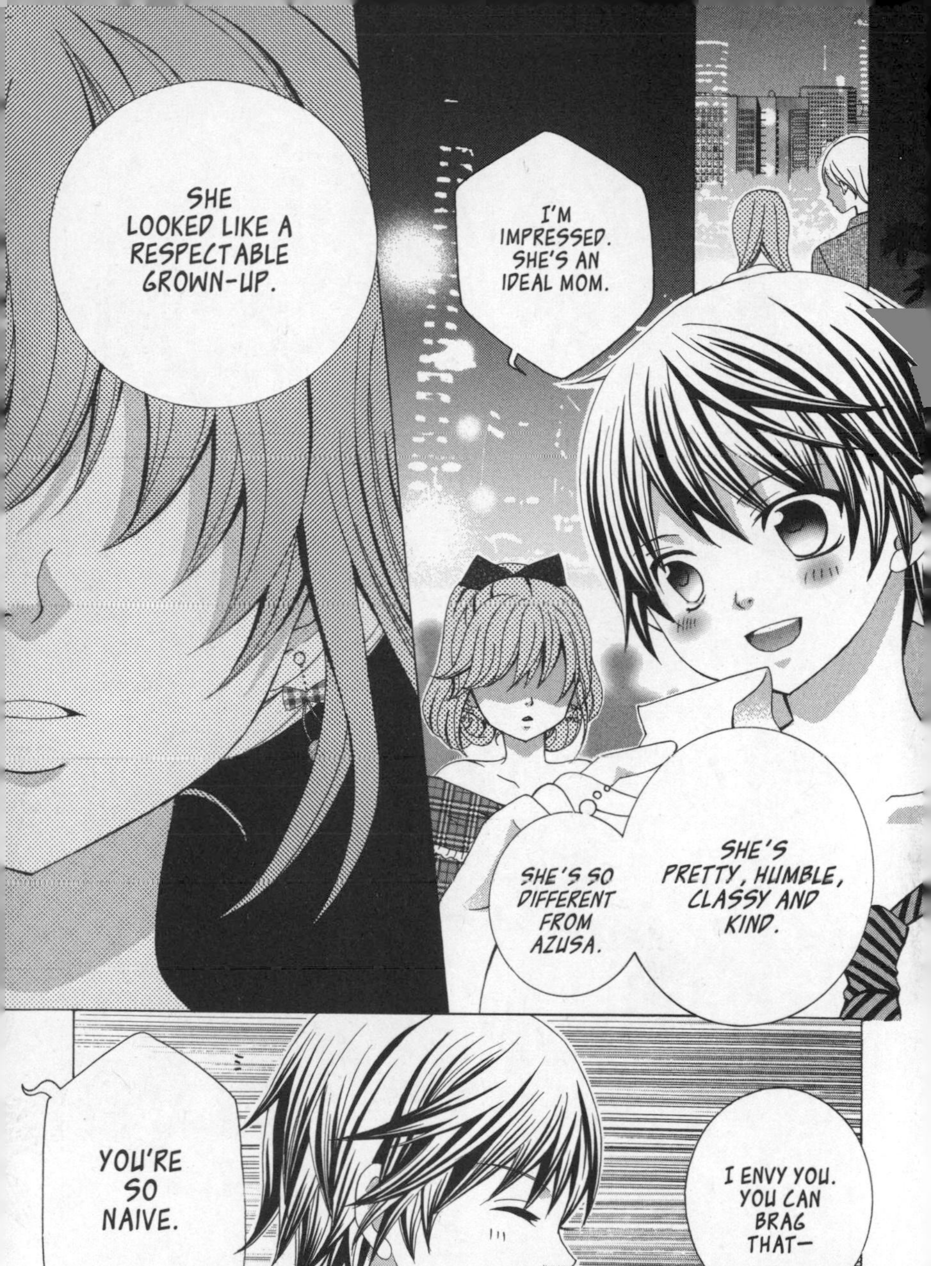
I'M IMPRESSED. SHE'S AN IDEAL MOM.
SHE'S PRETTY, HUMBLE, CLASSY AND KIND.
SHE'S SO DIFFERENT FROM AZUSA.
SHE LOOKED LIKE A RESPECTABLE GROWN-UP.
I ENVY YOU. YOU CAN BRAG THAT—
YOU'RE SO NAIVE.

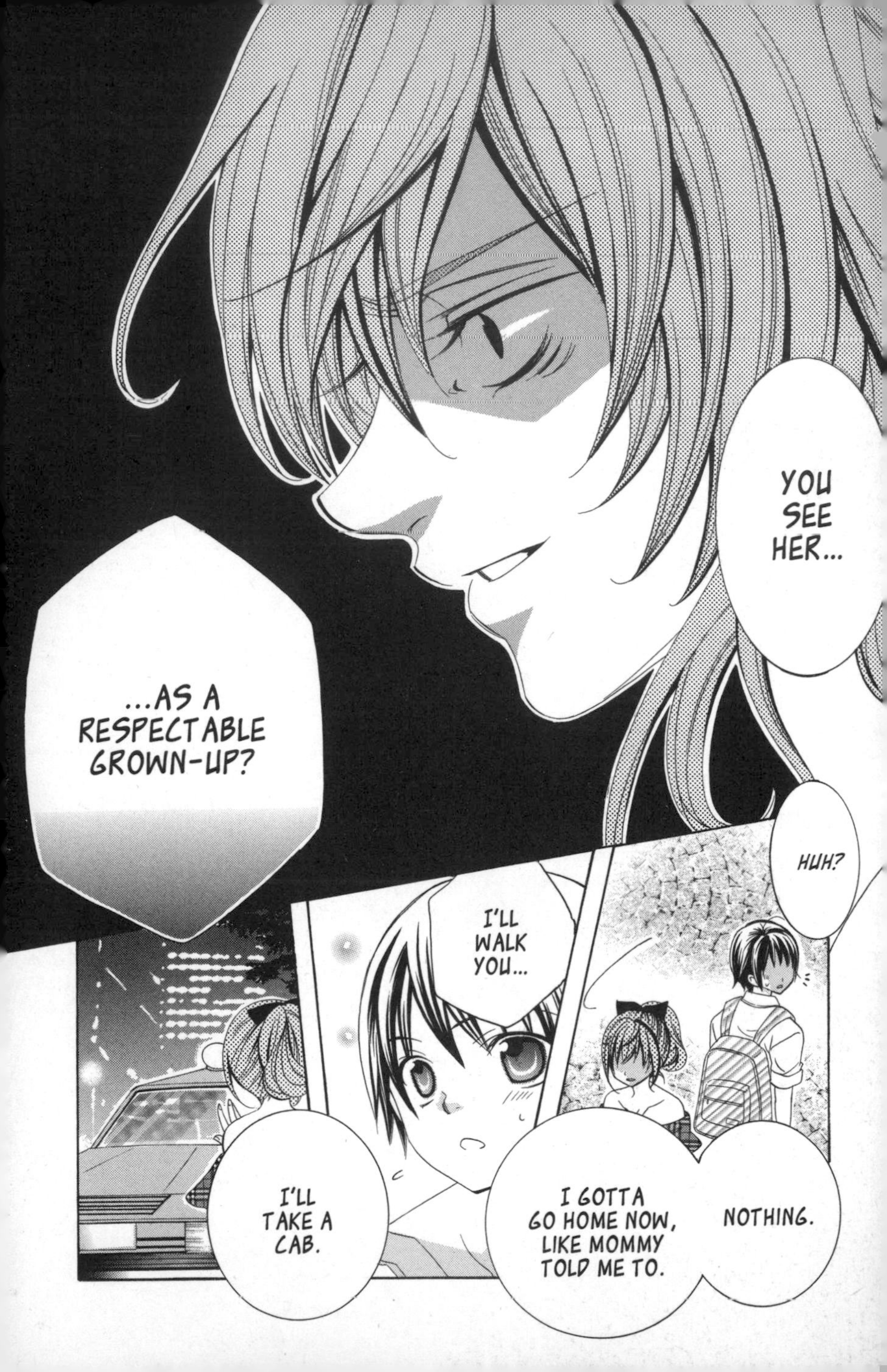
YOU SEE HER...
...AS A RESPECTABLE GROWN-UP?
HUH?
NOTHING.
I'LL WALK YOU...
I GOTTA GO HOME NOW, LIKE MOMMY TOLD ME TO.
I'LL TAKE A CAB.

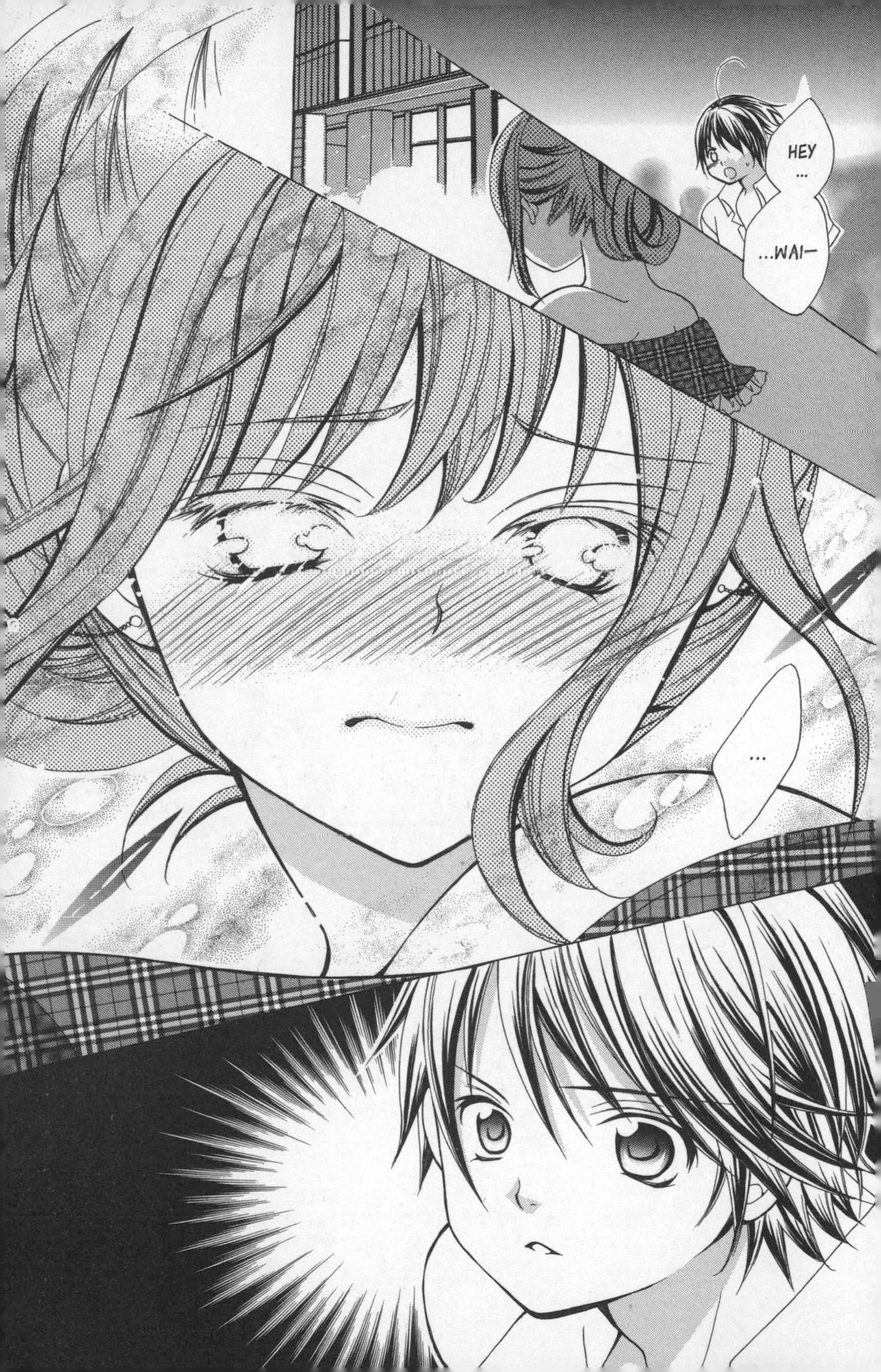
HEY ...
...WAI—
...

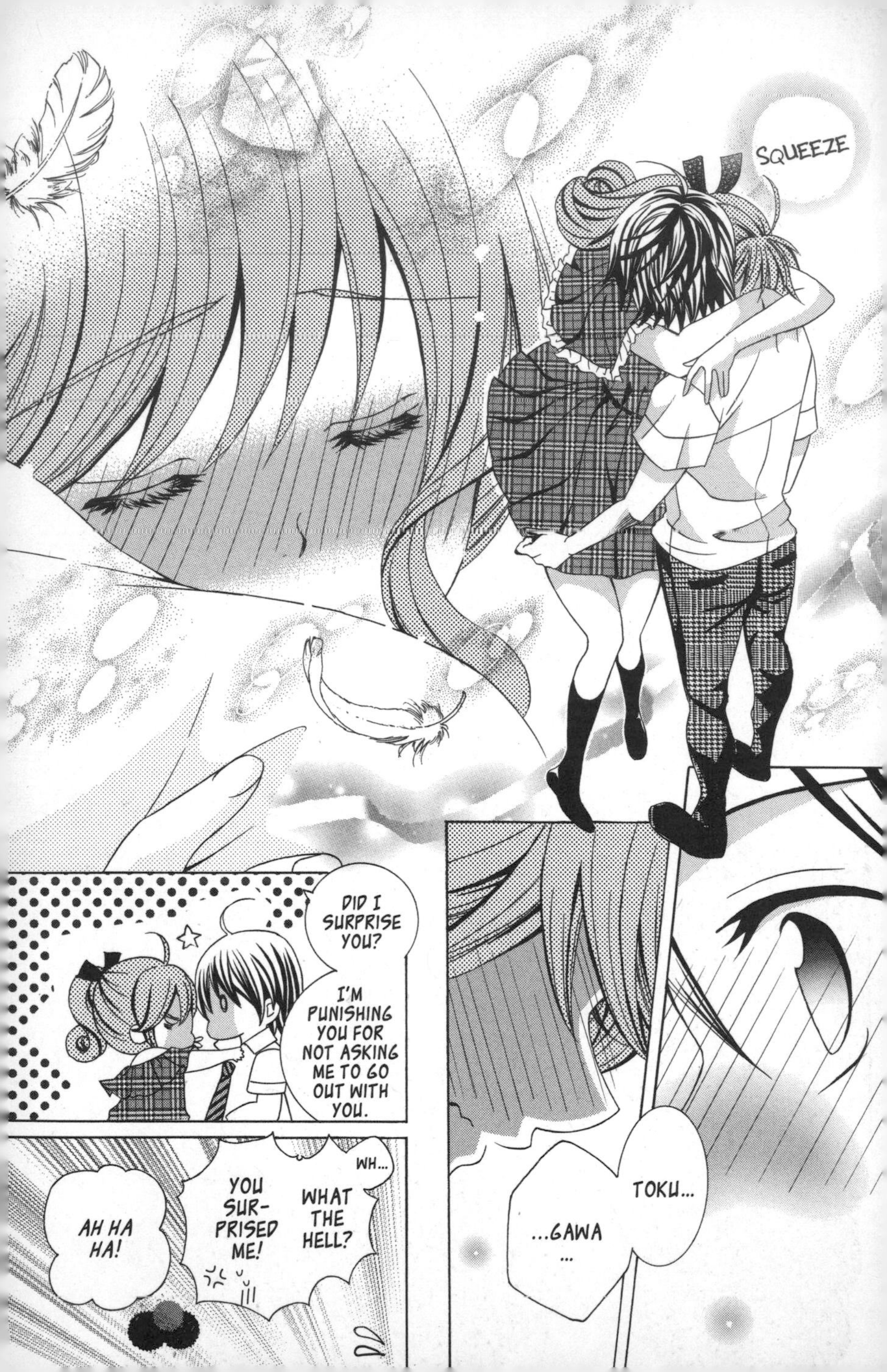
SQUEEZE
TOKU...
...GAWA ...
DID I SURPRISE YOU?
I'M PUNISHING YOU FOR NOT ASKING ME TO GO OUT WITH YOU.
WH...
WHAT THE HELL?
YOU SUR-PRISED ME!
AH HA HA!

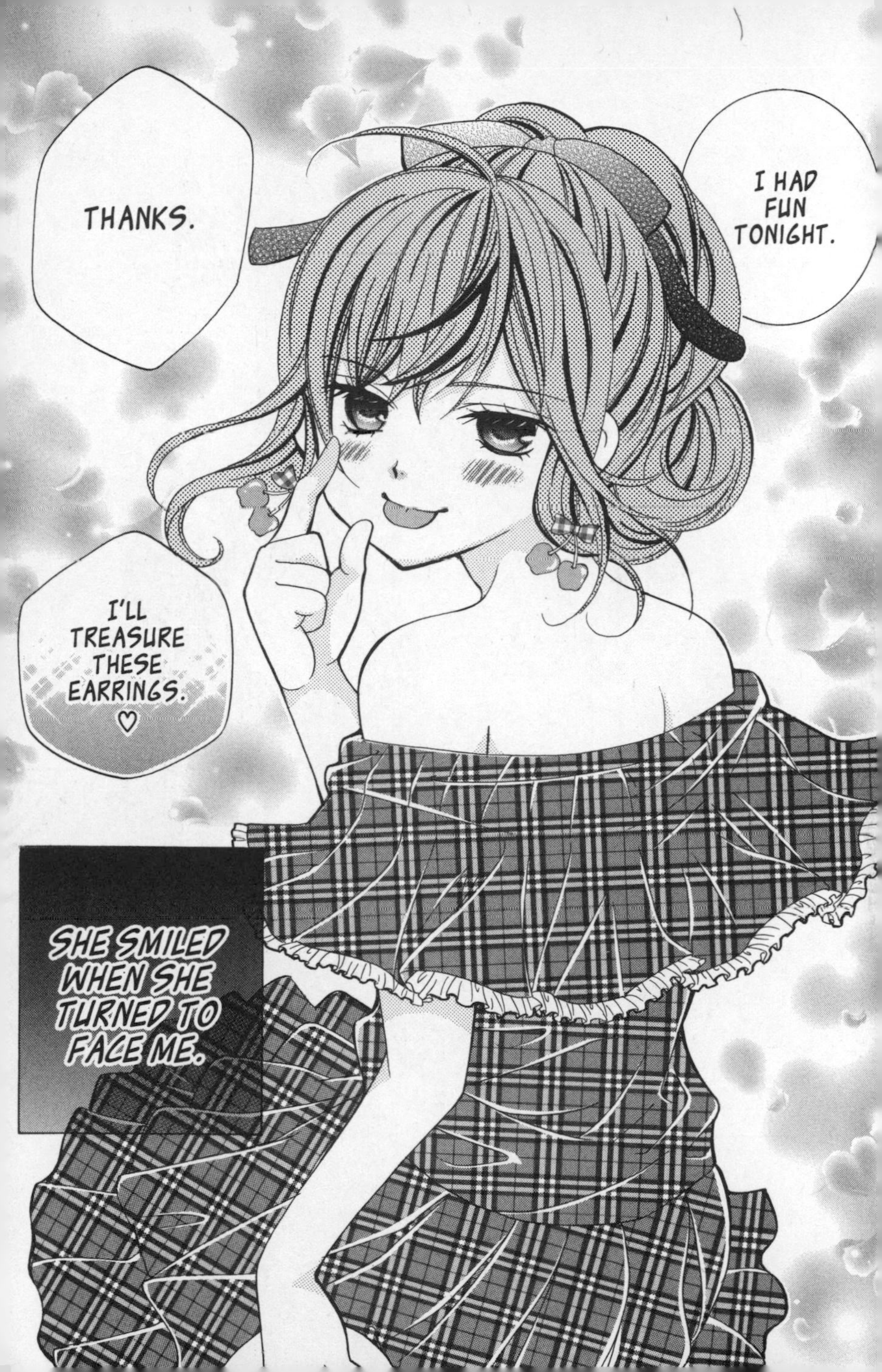
I HAD FUN TONIGHT.
THANKS.
I'LL TREASURE THESE EARRINGS. ♡
SHE SMILED WHEN SHE TURNED TO FACE ME.

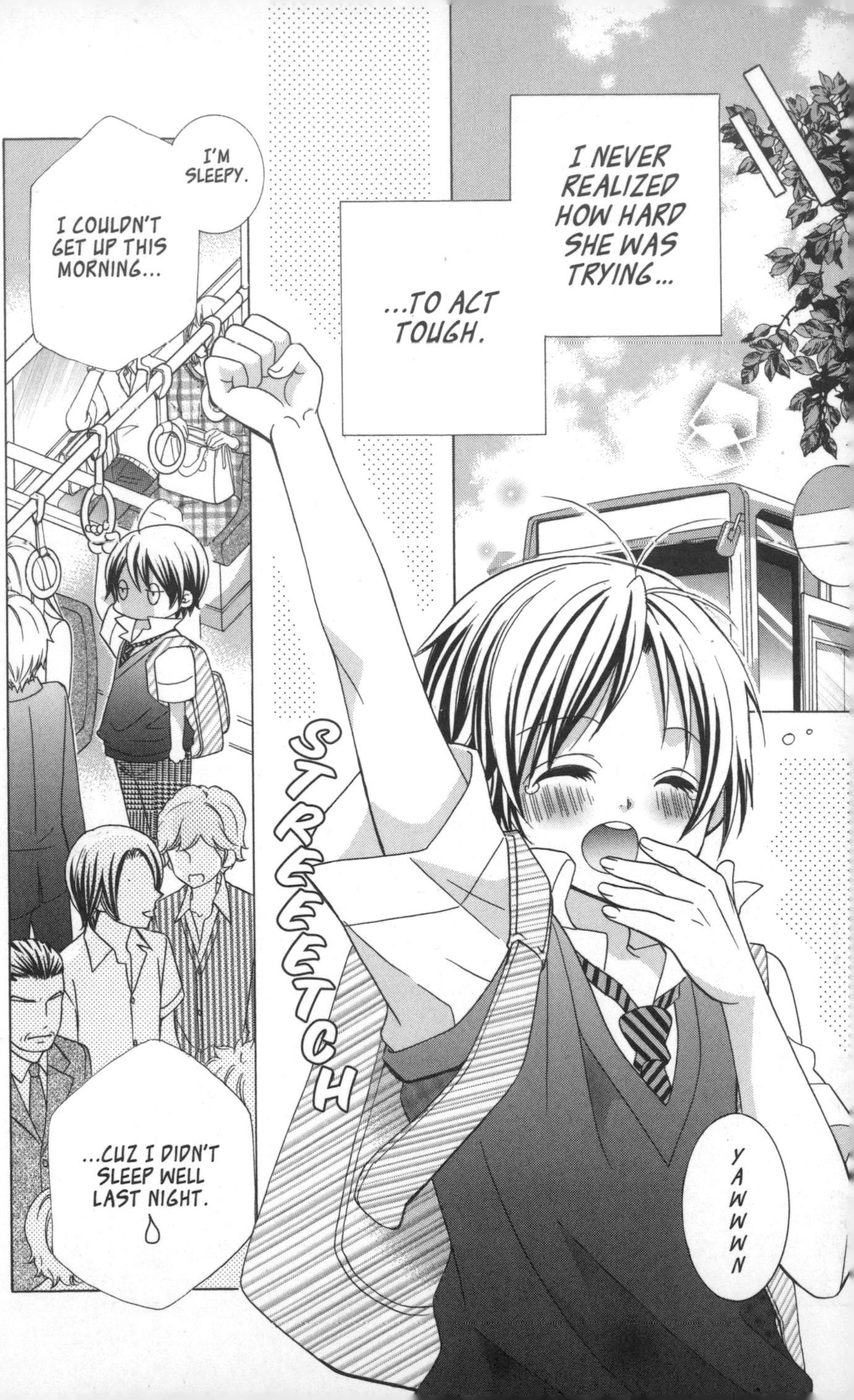
I NEVER REALIZED HOW HARD SHE WAS TRYING...
...TO ACT TOUGH.
STRETCH
YAWWWN
I'M SLEEPY.
I COULDN'T GET UP THIS MORNING...
...CUZ I DIDN'T SLEEP WELL LAST NIGHT.

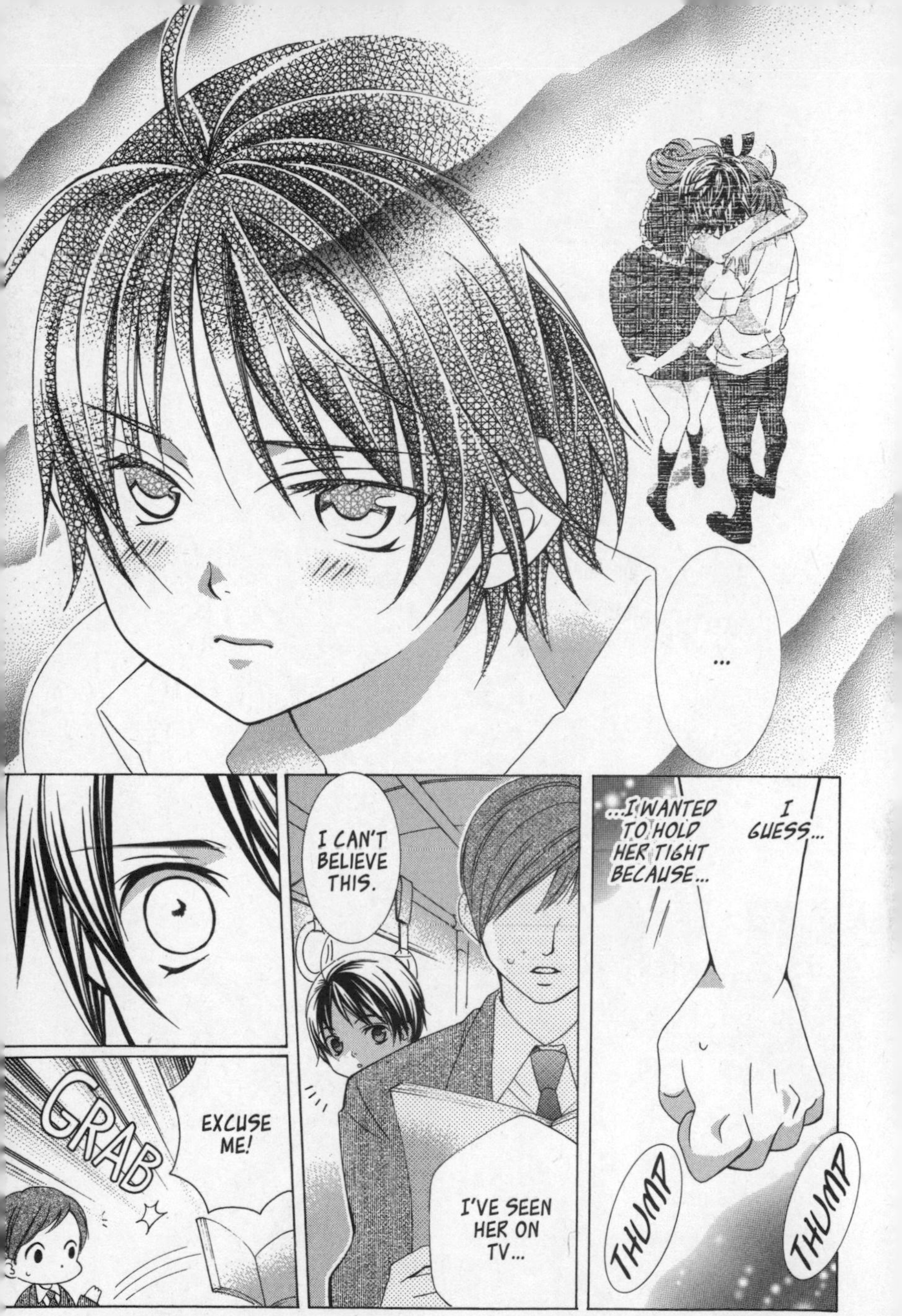
...
I GUESS...
...I WANTED TO HOLD HER TIGHT BECAUSE...
THUMP
THUMP
I CAN'T BELIEVE THIS.
I'VE SEEN HER ON TV...
GRAB
EXCUSE ME!

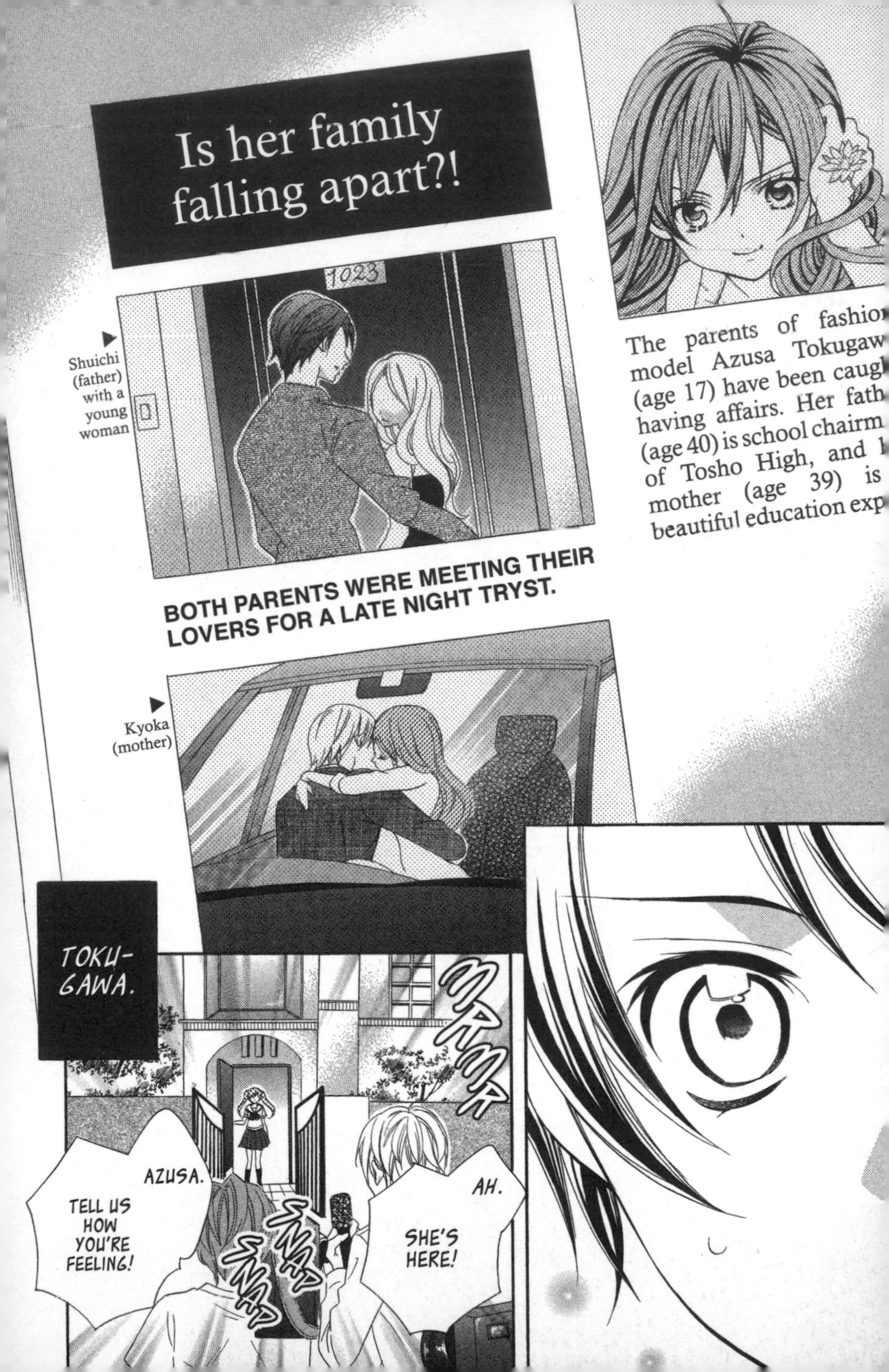

Is her family falling apart?!
The parents of fashio
model Azusa Tokugaw
(age 17) have been caug
having affairs. Her fath
(age 40) is school chairm
of Tosho High, and
mother (age 39) is
beautiful education exp
1023
Shuichi (father) with a young woman
BOTH PARENTS WERE MEETING THEIR LOVERS FOR A LATE NIGHT TRYST.
Kyoka (mother)
TOKU-GAWA.
MRMR
AH.
SHE'S HERE!
AZUSA.
TELL US HOW YOU'RE FEELING!
SNAP
SNAP

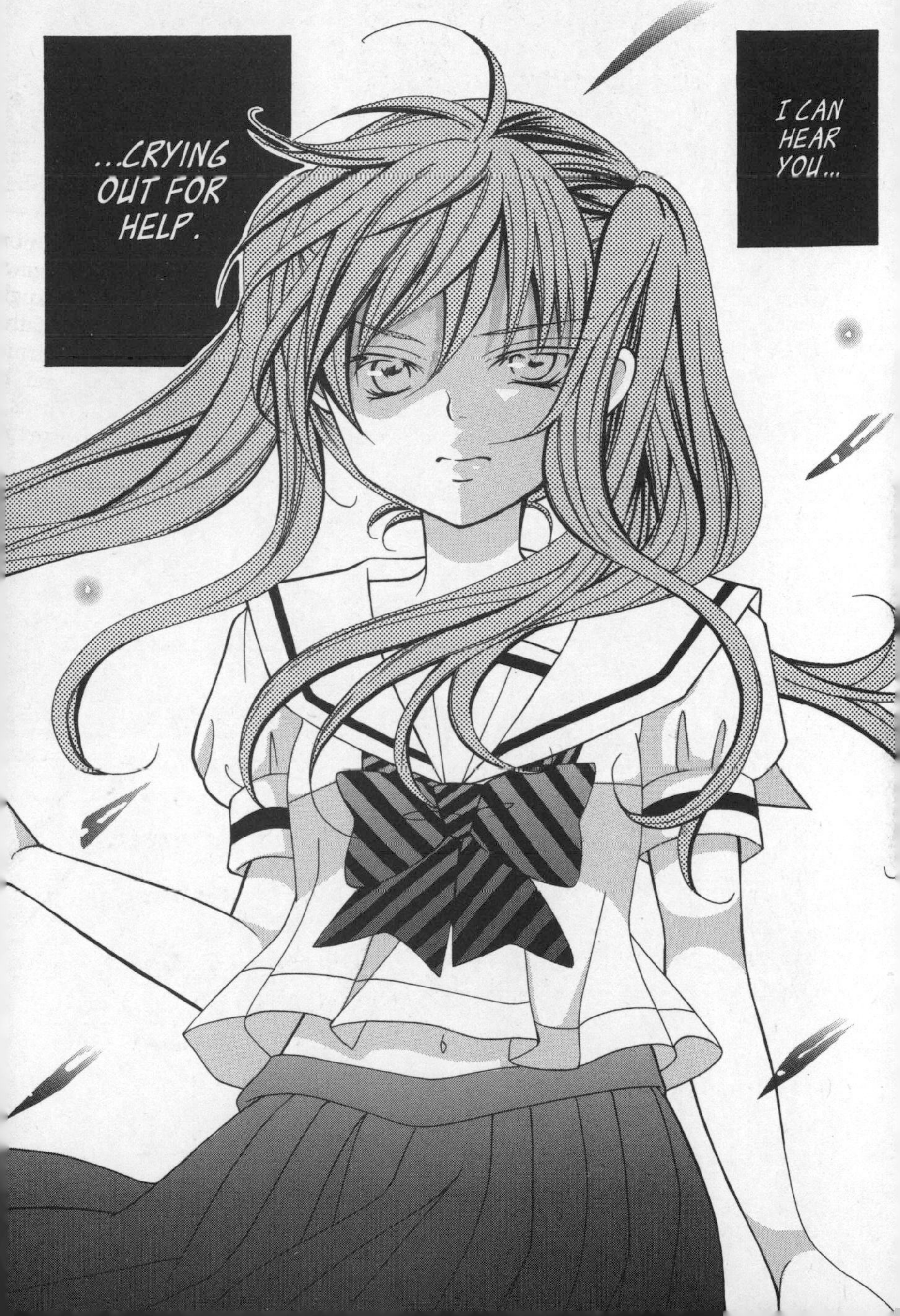
I CAN HEAR YOU...
...CRYING OUT FOR HELP.

Chapter 50

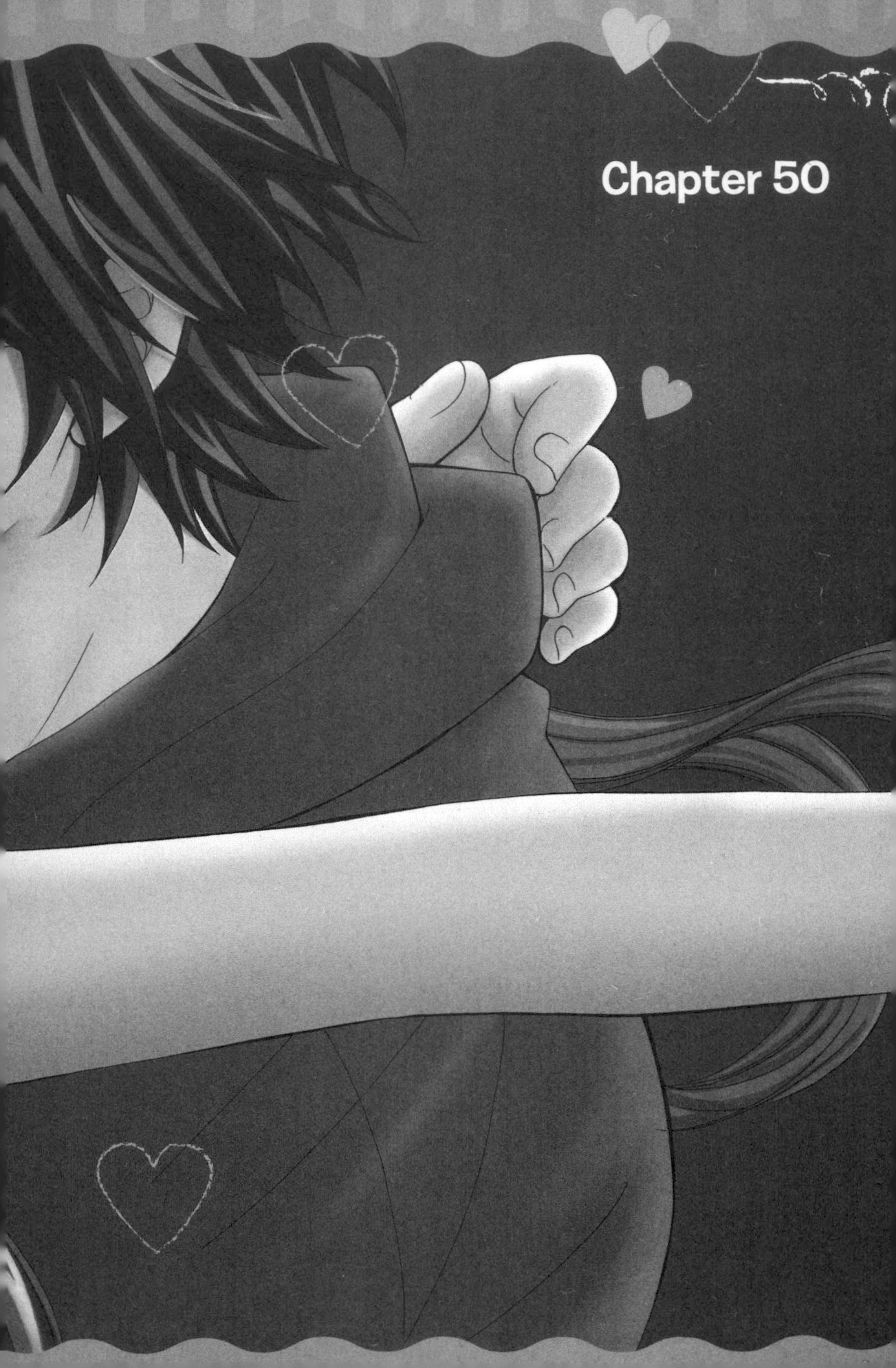

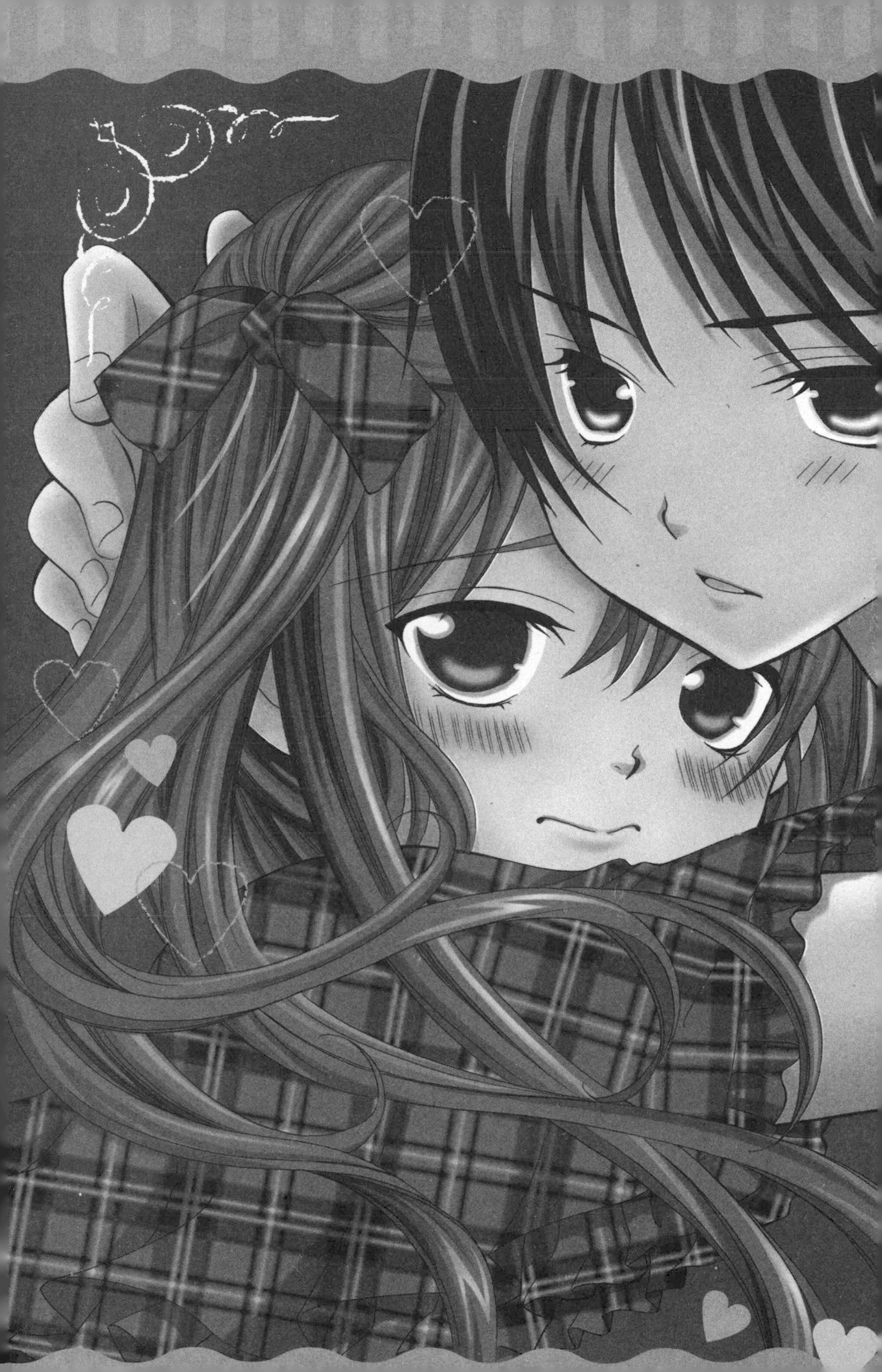

So Cute It Hurts!!

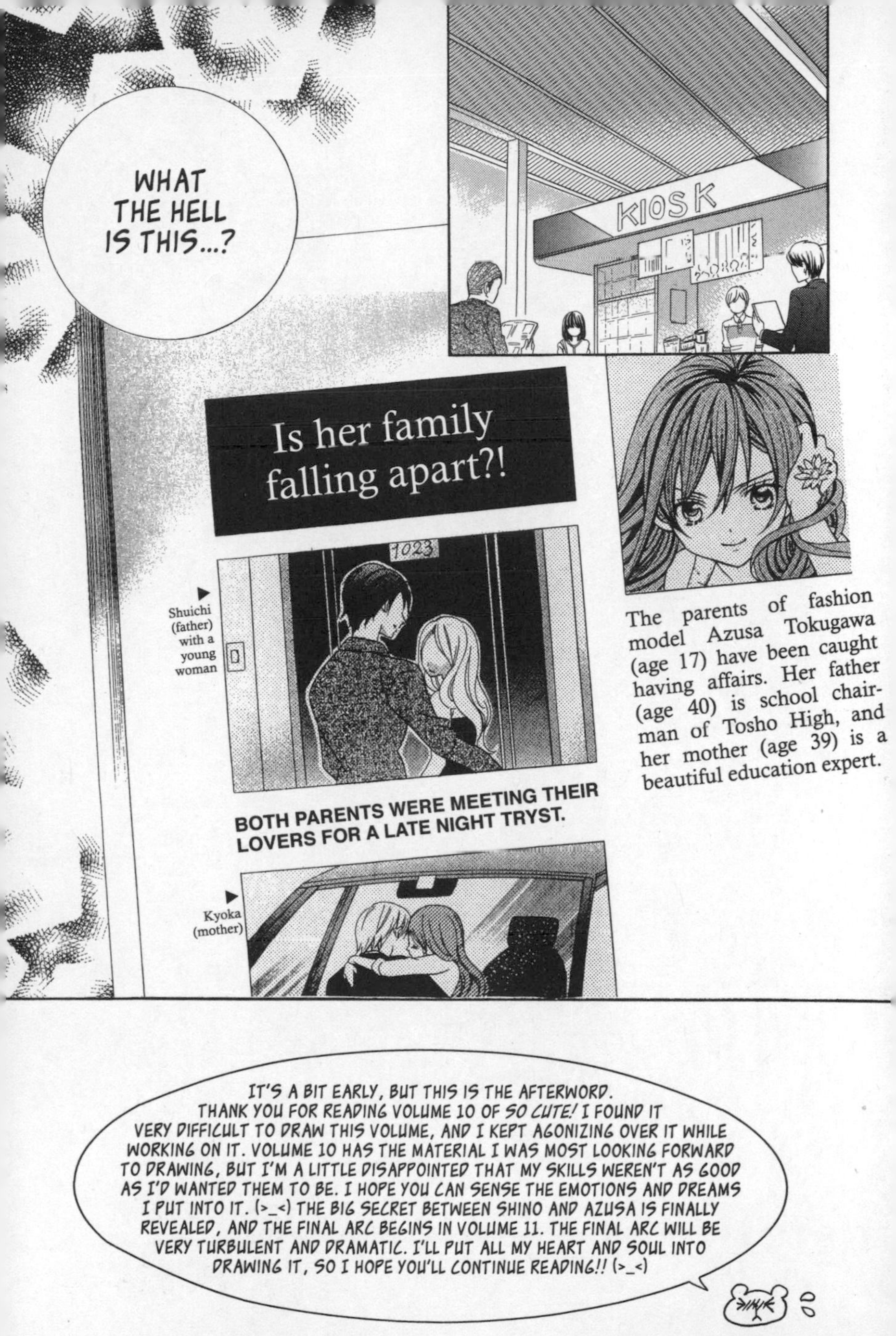
WHAT THE HELL IS THIS...?
Is her family falling apart?!
The parents of fashion model Azusa Tokugawa (age 17) have been caught having affairs. Her father (age 40) is school chairman of Tosho High, and her mother (age 39) is a beautiful education expert.
Shuichi (father) with a young woman
BOTH PARENTS WERE MEETING THEIR LOVERS FOR A LATE NIGHT TRYST.
Kyoka (mother)

IT'S A BIT EARLY, BUT THIS IS THE AFTERWORD. THANK YOU FOR READING VOLUME 10 OF *SO CUTE!* I FOUND IT VERY DIFFICULT TO DRAW THIS VOLUME, AND I KEPT AGONIZING OVER IT WHILE WORKING ON IT. VOLUME 10 HAS THE MATERIAL I WAS MOST LOOKING FORWARD TO DRAWING, BUT I'M A LITTLE DISAPPOINTED THAT MY SKILLS WEREN'T AS GOOD AS I'D WANTED THEM TO BE. I HOPE YOU CAN SENSE THE EMOTIONS AND DREAMS I PUT INTO IT. (>_<) THE BIG SECRET BETWEEN SHINO AND AZUSA IS FINALLY REVEALED, AND THE FINAL ARC BEGINS IN VOLUME 11. THE FINAL ARC WILL BE VERY TURBULENT AND DRAMATIC. I'LL PUT ALL MY HEART AND SOUL INTO DRAWING IT, SO I HOPE YOU'LL CONTINUE READING!! (>_<)

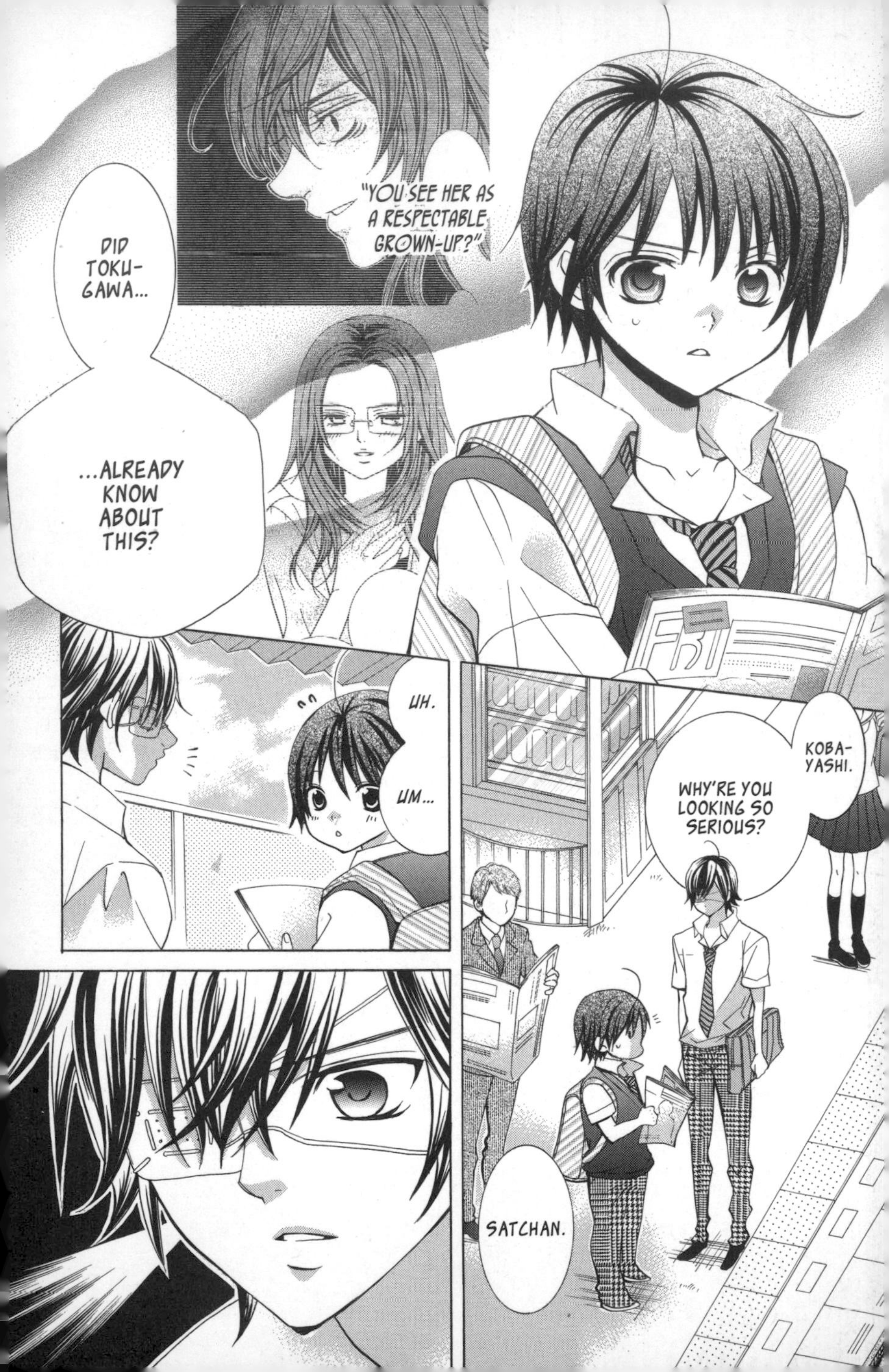
"YOU SEE HER AS A RESPECTABLE GROWN-UP?"
DID TOKU-GAWA...
...ALREADY KNOW ABOUT THIS?
KOBA-YASHI.
WHY'RE YOU LOOKING SO SERIOUS?
SATCHAN.
UH.
UM...

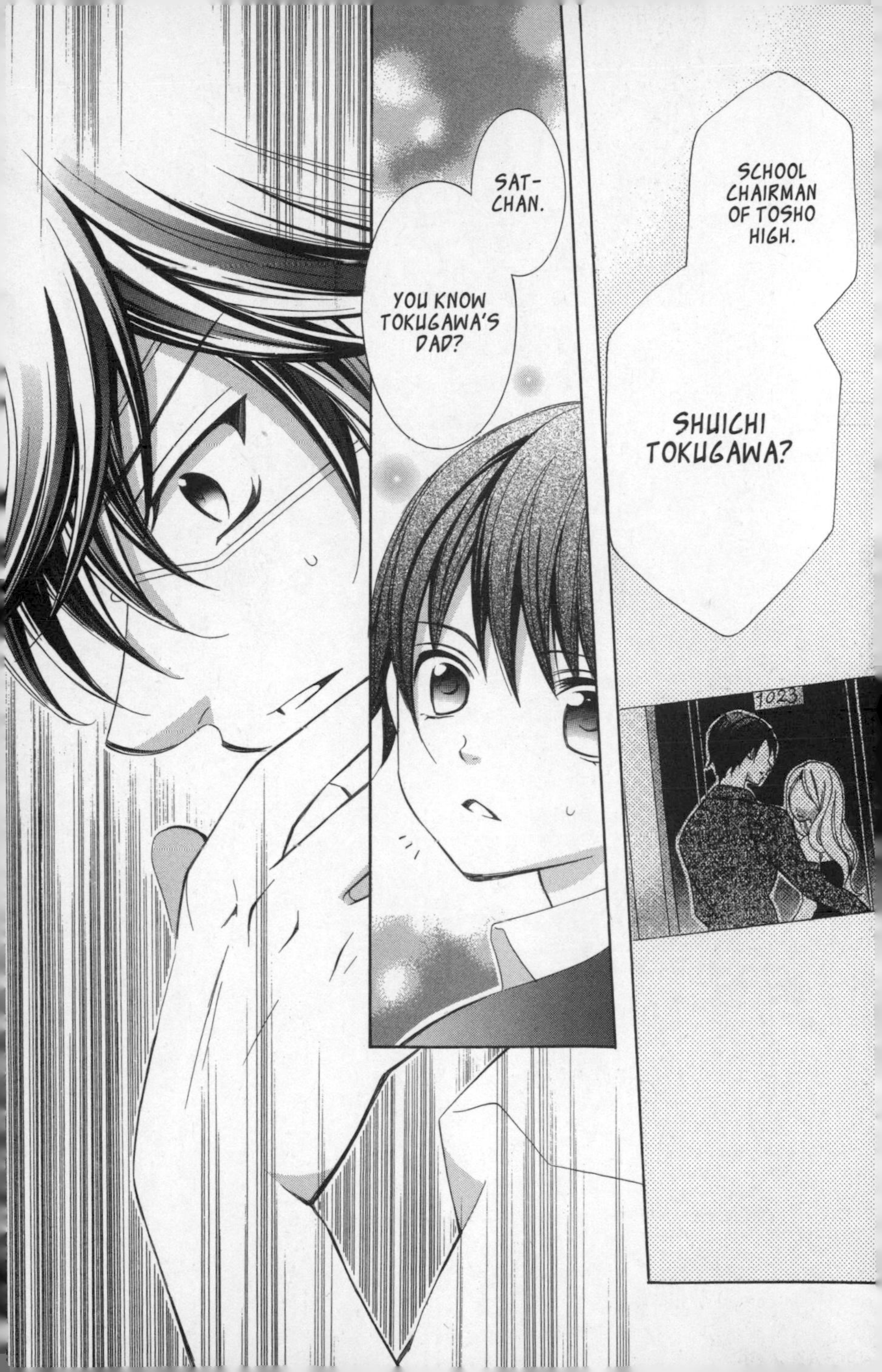
SCHOOL CHAIRMAN OF TOSHO HIGH.
SHUICHI TOKUGAWA?
1023
SAT-CHAN.
YOU KNOW TOKUGAWA'S DAD?

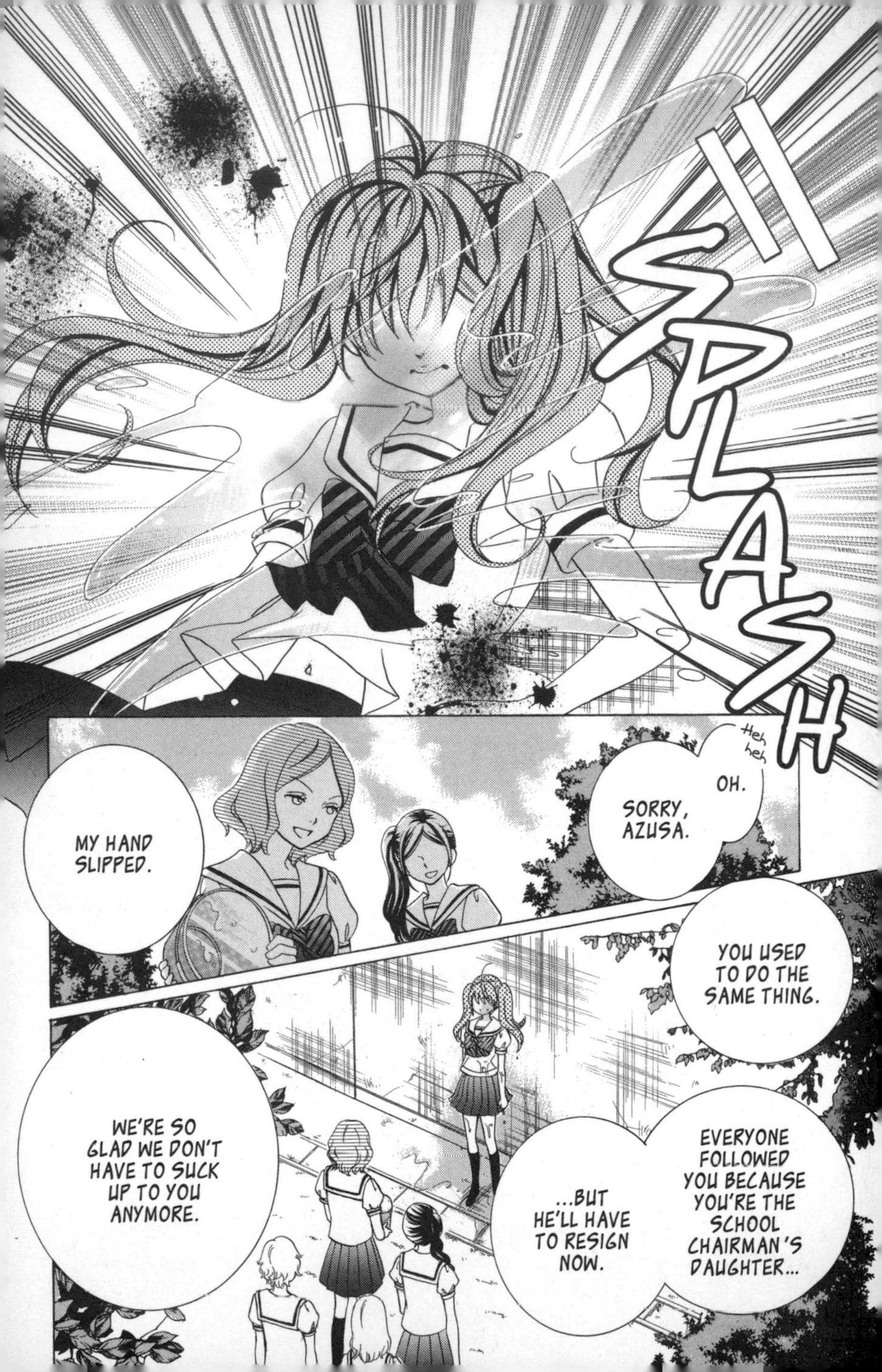
SPLASH
Heh heh
OH.
SORRY, AZUSA.
MY HAND SLIPPED.
YOU USED TO DO THE SAME THING.
EVERYONE FOLLOWED YOU BECAUSE YOU'RE THE SCHOOL CHAIRMAN'S DAUGHTER...
...BUT HE'LL HAVE TO RESIGN NOW.
WE'RE SO GLAD WE DON'T HAVE TO SUCK UP TO YOU ANYMORE.

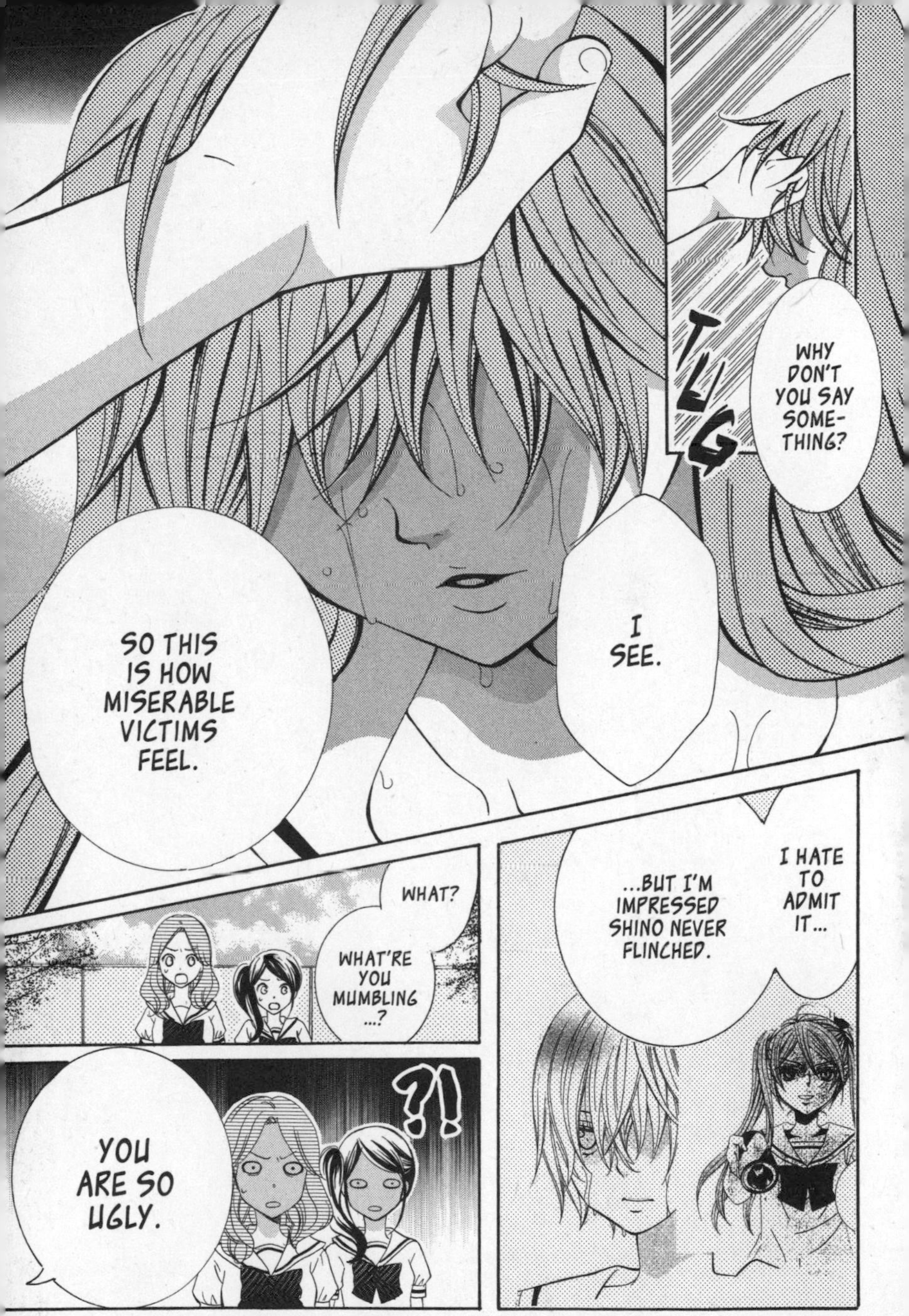
TUG
WHY DON'T YOU SAY SOME-THING?
I SEE.
SO THIS IS HOW MISERABLE VICTIMS FEEL.
I HATE TO ADMIT IT...
...BUT I'M IMPRESSED SHINO NEVER FLINCHED.
WHAT?
WHAT'RE YOU MUMBLING ...?
?!
YOU ARE SO UGLY.

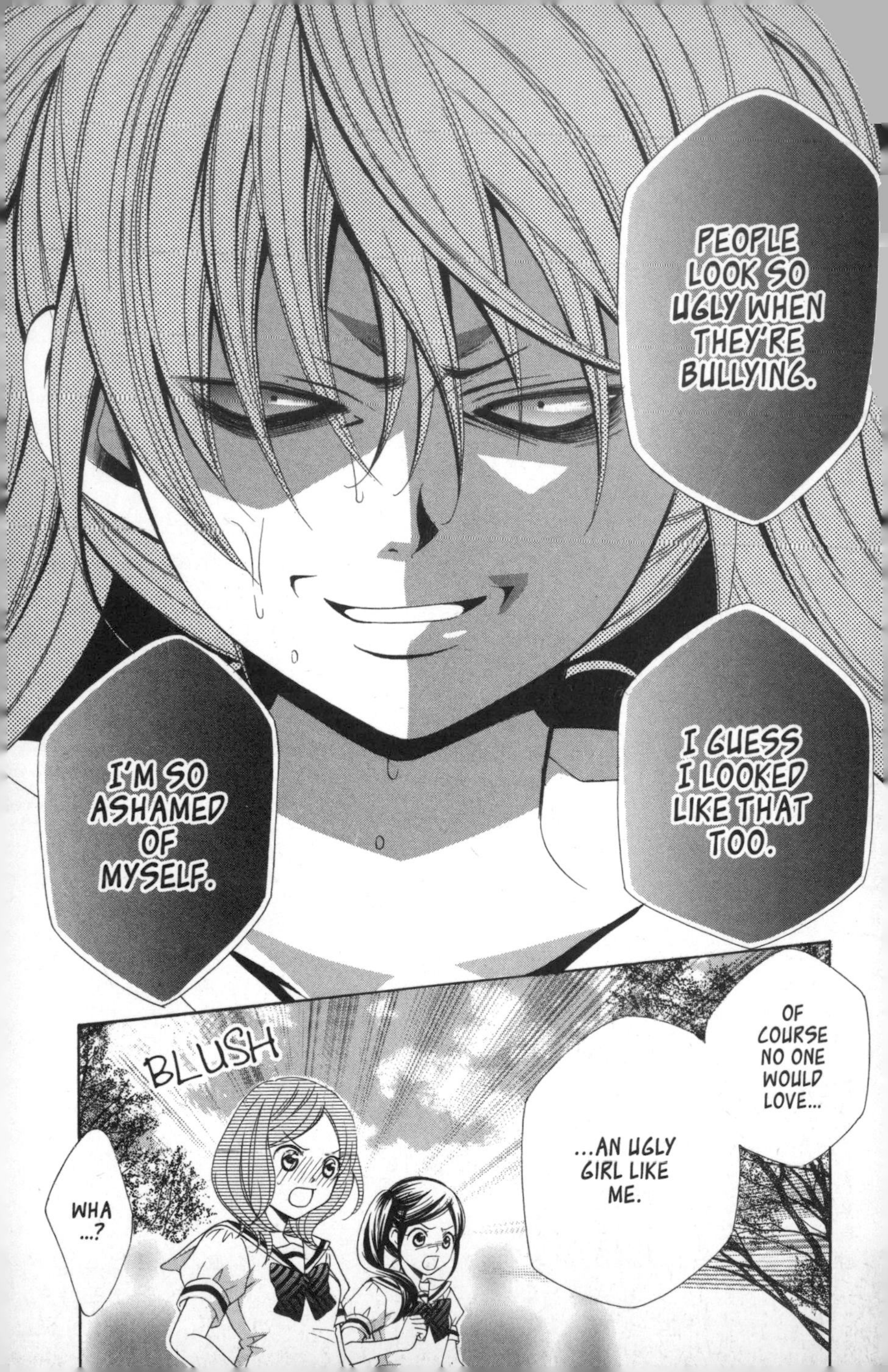
PEOPLE LOOK SO UGLY WHEN THEY'RE BULLYING.
I GUESS I LOOKED LIKE THAT TOO.
I'M SO ASHAMED OF MYSELF.
OF COURSE NO ONE WOULD LOVE...
...AN UGLY GIRL LIKE ME.
BLUSH
WHA ...?

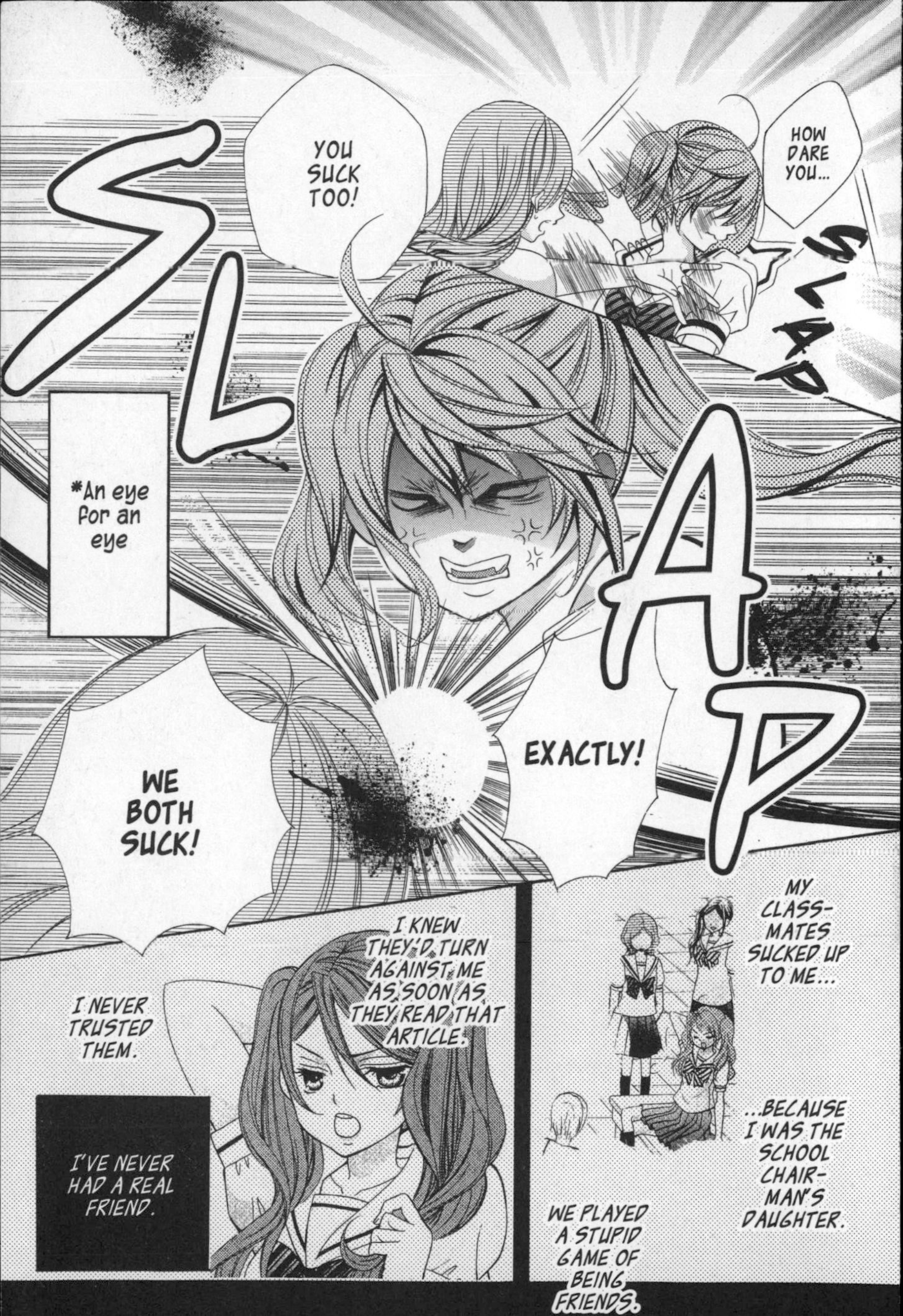
HOW DARE YOU...
SLAP
YOU SUCK TOO!
SLAP
EXACTLY!
WE BOTH SUCK!
*An eye for an eye
MY CLASS-MATES SUCKED UP TO ME...
...BECAUSE I WAS THE SCHOOL CHAIR-MAN'S DAUGHTER.
WE PLAYED A STUPID GAME OF BEING FRIENDS.
I KNEW THEY'D TURN AGAINST ME AS SOON AS THEY READ THAT ARTICLE.
I NEVER TRUSTED THEM.
I'VE NEVER HAD A REAL FRIEND.

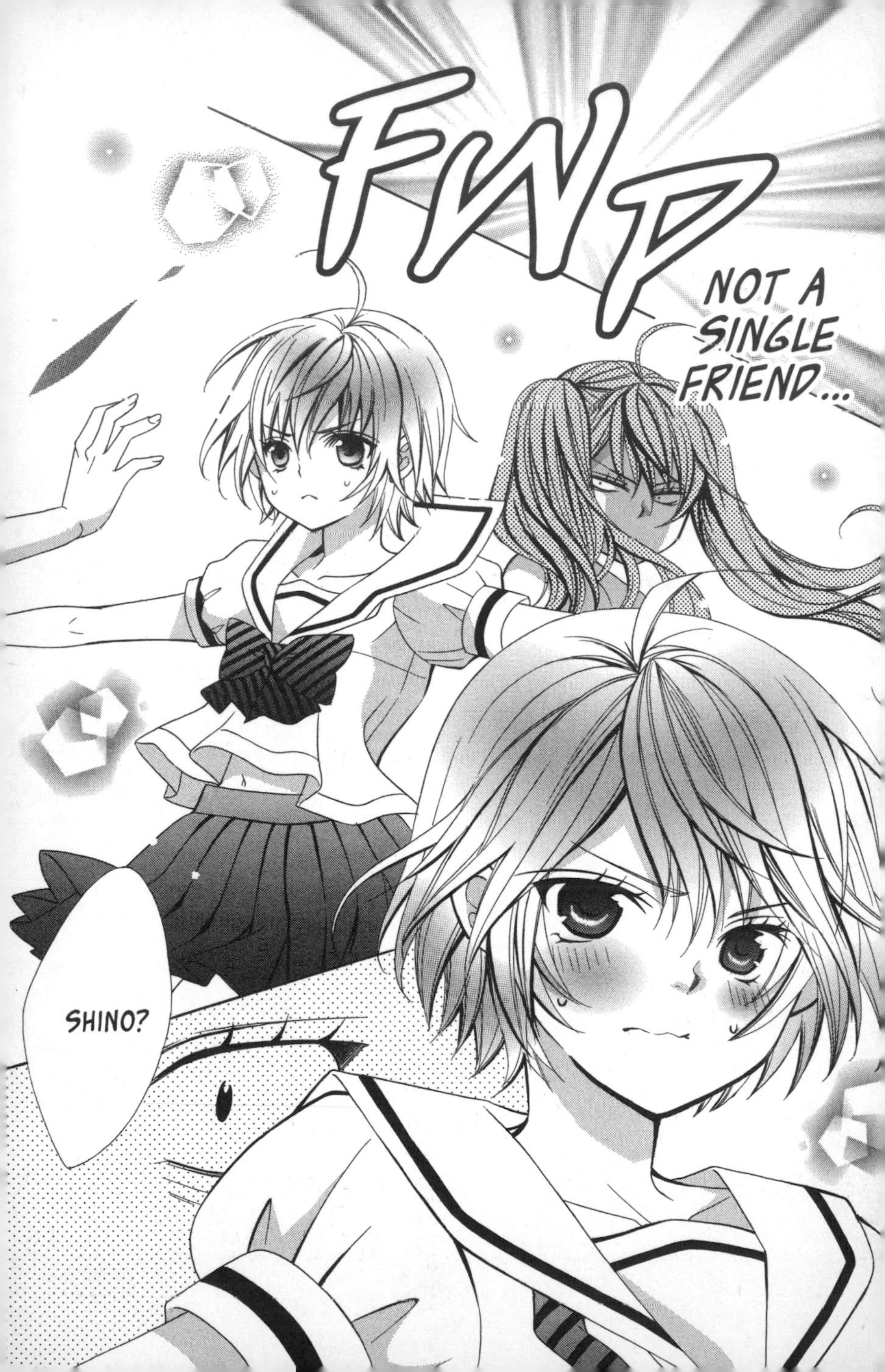
FWP
NOT A SINGLE FRIEND...
SHINO?

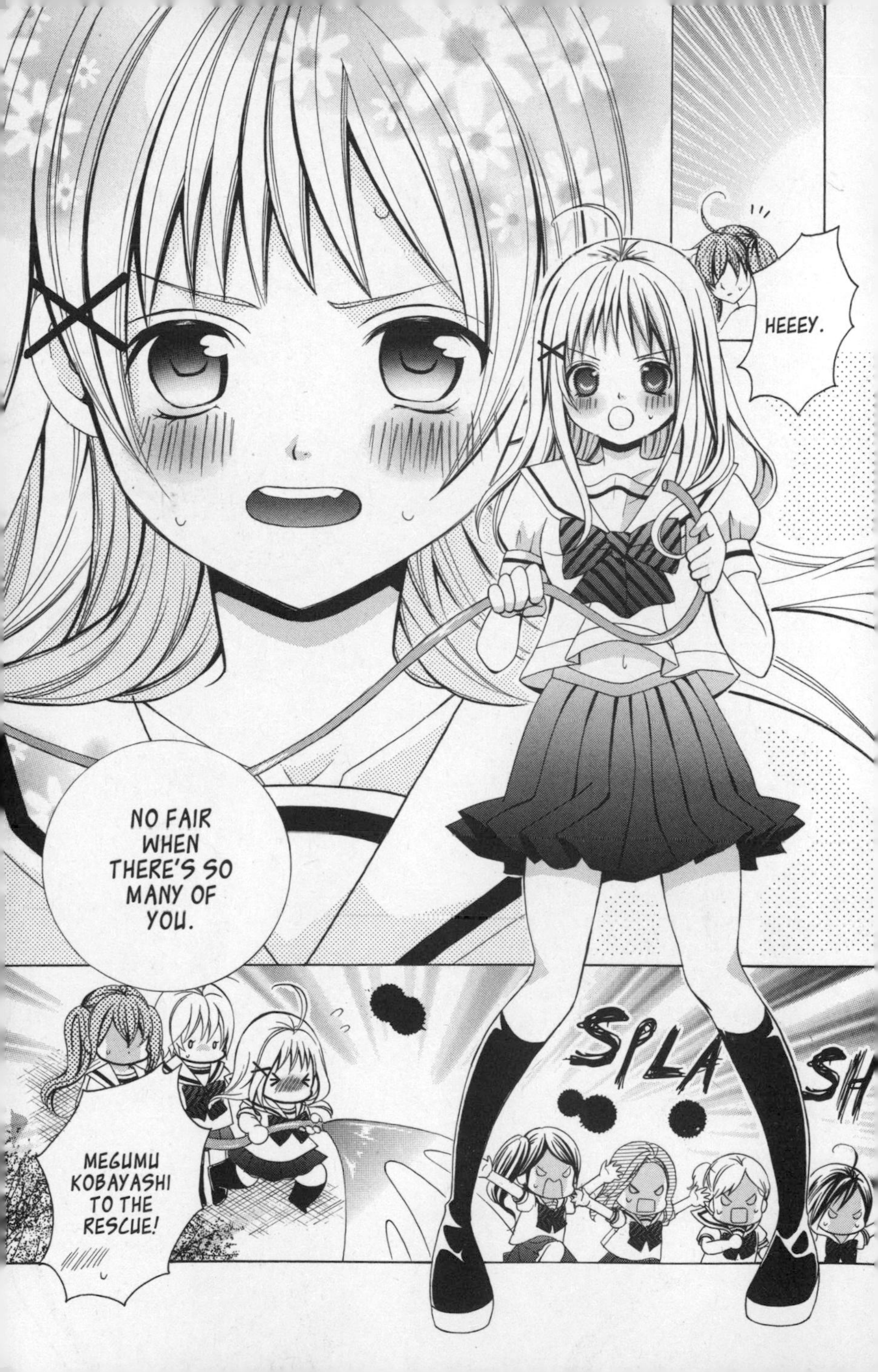
HEEEY.
NO FAIR WHEN THERE'S SO MANY OF YOU.
SPLASH
MEGUMU KOBAYASHI TO THE RESCUE!

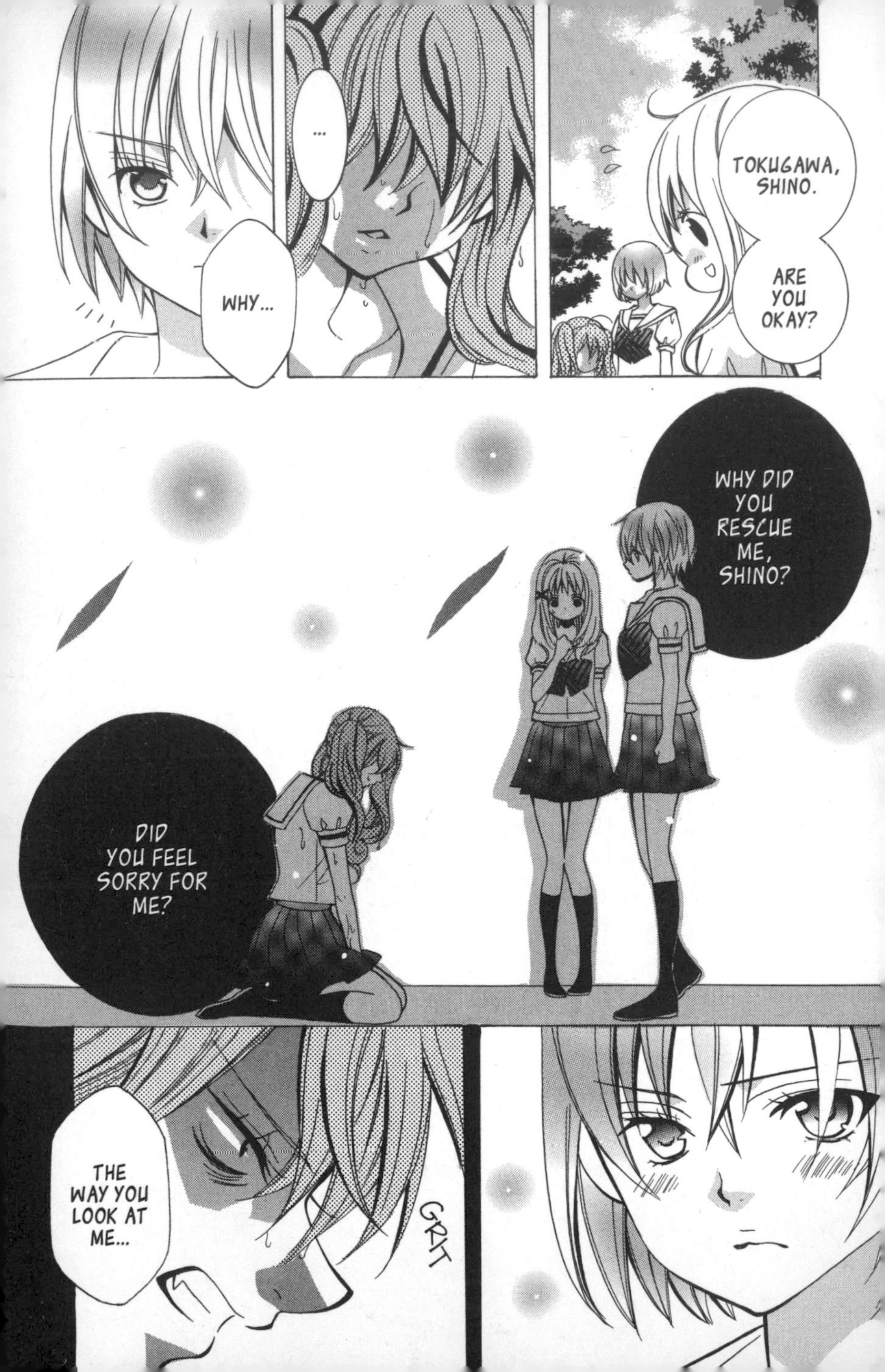
TOKUGAWA, SHINO.
ARE YOU OKAY?
...
WHY...
WHY DID YOU RESCUE ME, SHINO?
DID YOU FEEL SORRY FOR ME?
THE WAY YOU LOOK AT ME...
GRIT

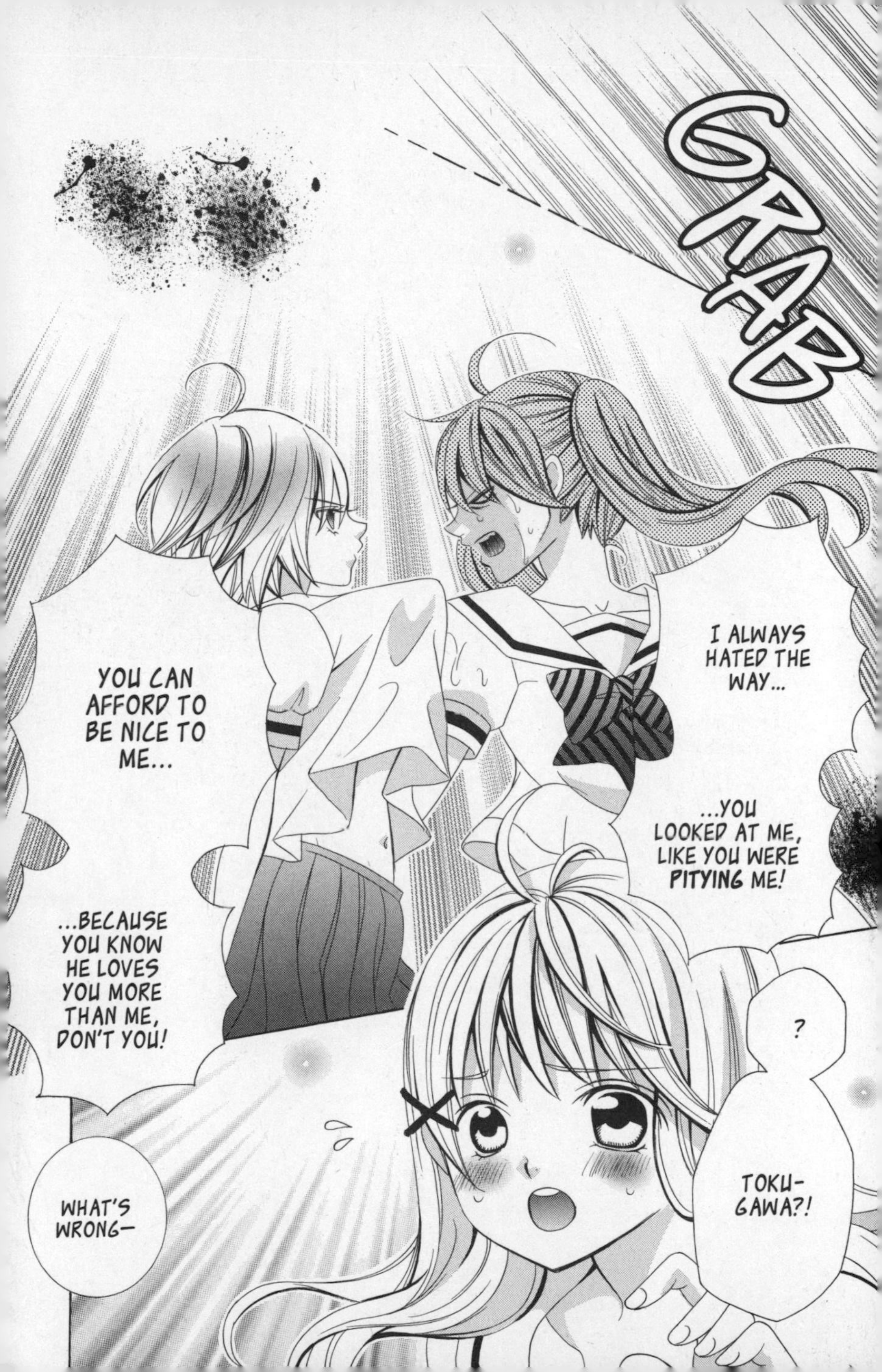
GRAB
I ALWAYS HATED THE WAY...
...YOU LOOKED AT ME, LIKE YOU WERE PITYING ME!
YOU CAN AFFORD TO BE NICE TO ME...
...BECAUSE YOU KNOW HE LOVES YOU MORE THAN ME, DON'T YOU!
?
TOKU-GAWA?!
WHAT'S WRONG—

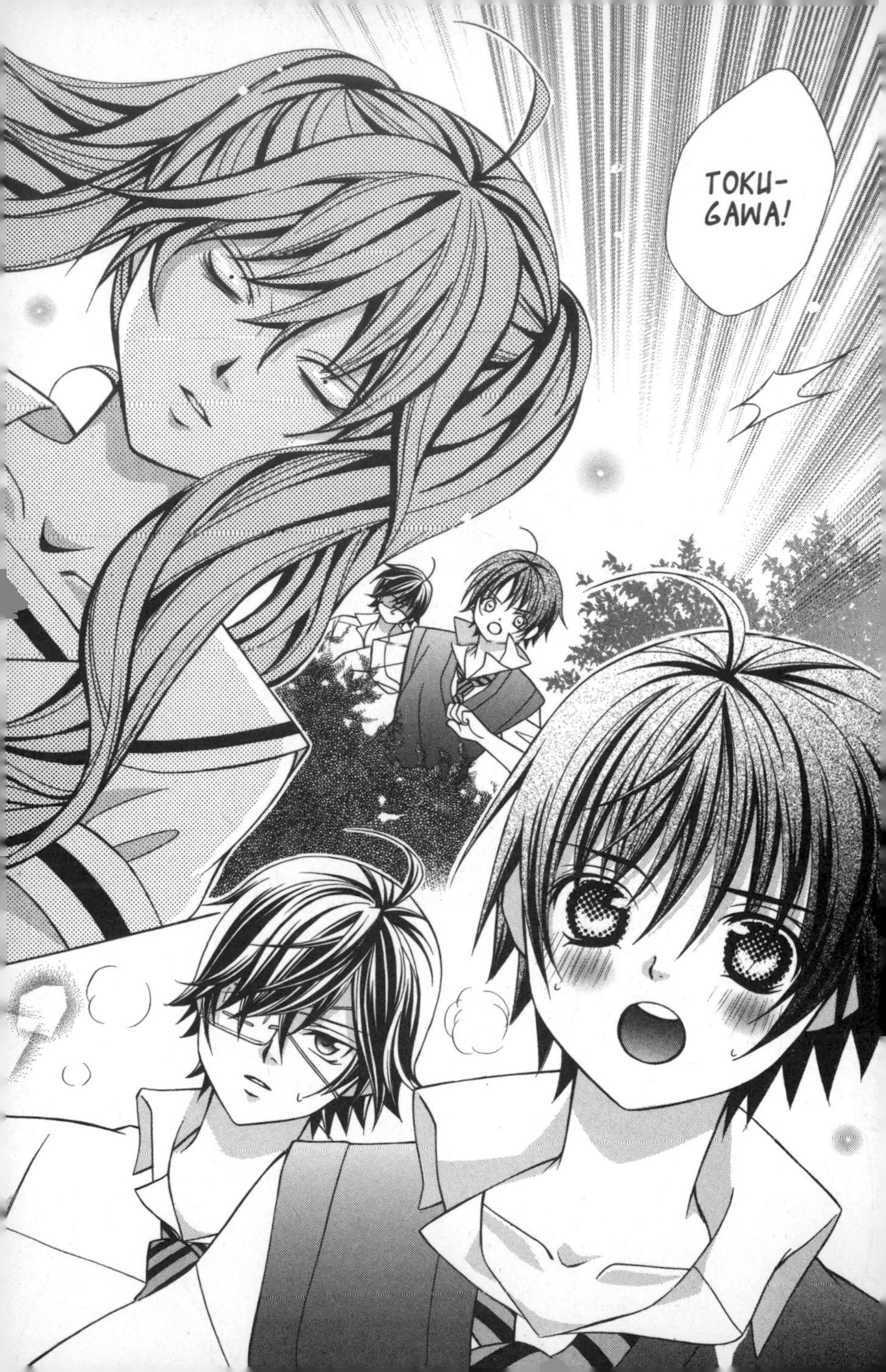
TOKU-GAWA!

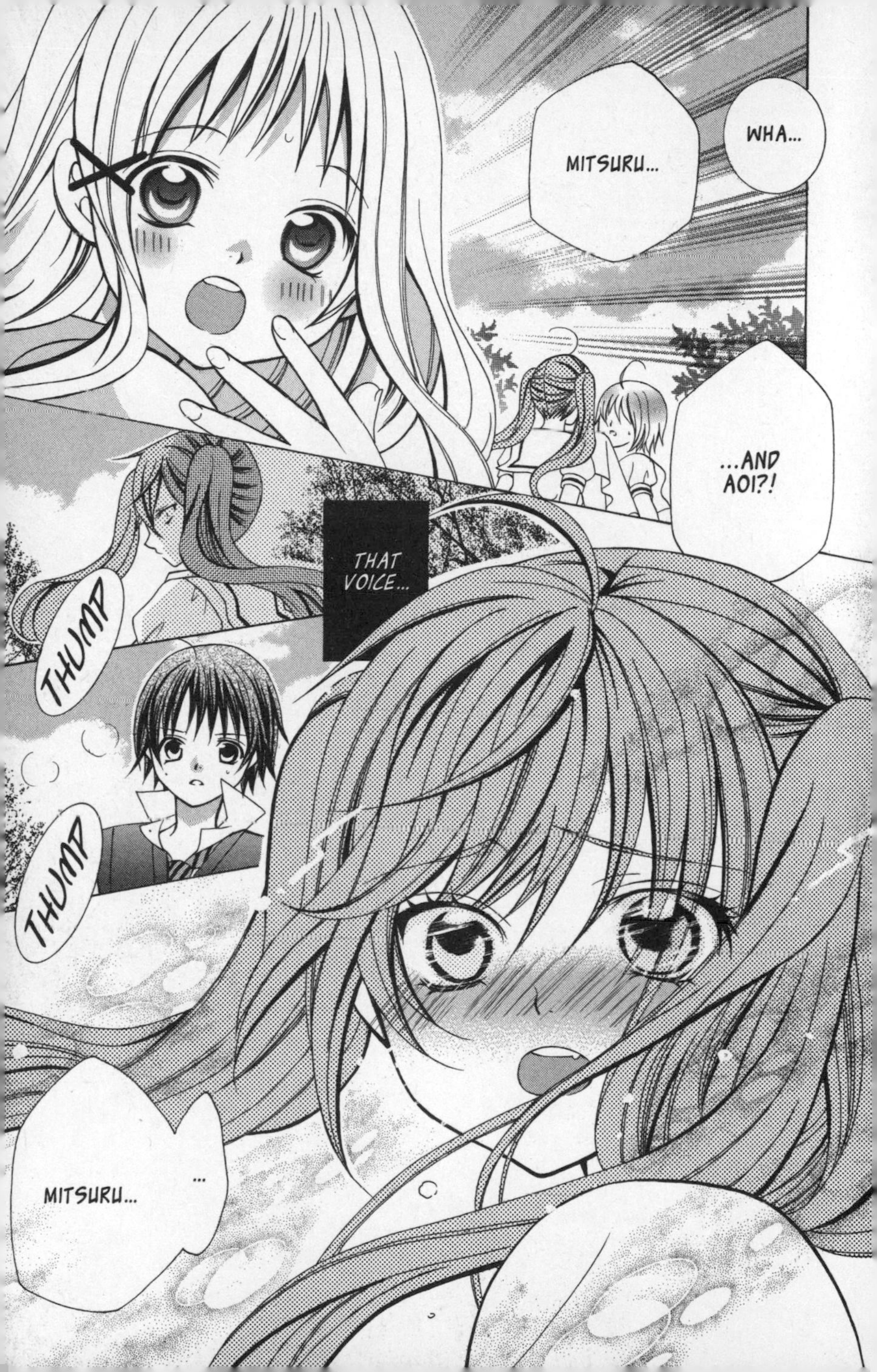

WHA...
MITSURU...
...AND AOI?!
THAT VOICE...
THUMP
THUMP
...
MITSURU...

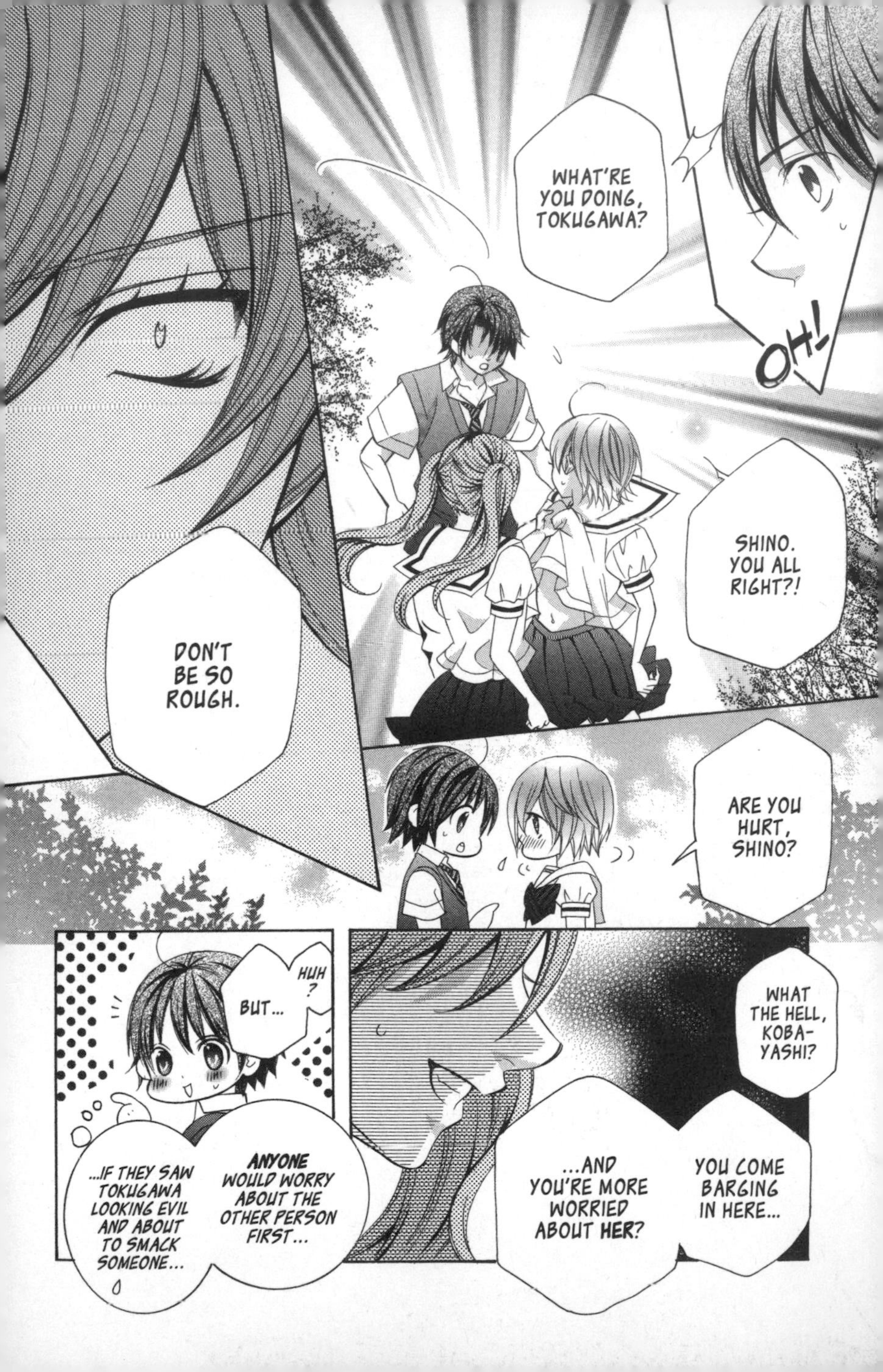
WHAT'RE YOU DOING, TOKUGAWA?
OH!
SHINO. YOU ALL RIGHT?!
DON'T BE SO ROUGH.
ARE YOU HURT, SHINO?
WHAT THE HELL, KOBA-YASHI?
YOU COME BARGING IN HERE...
...AND YOU'RE MORE WORRIED ABOUT HER?
HUH?
BUT...
ANYONE WOULD WORRY ABOUT THE OTHER PERSON FIRST...
...IF THEY SAW TOKUGAWA LOOKING EVIL AND ABOUT TO SMACK SOMEONE...

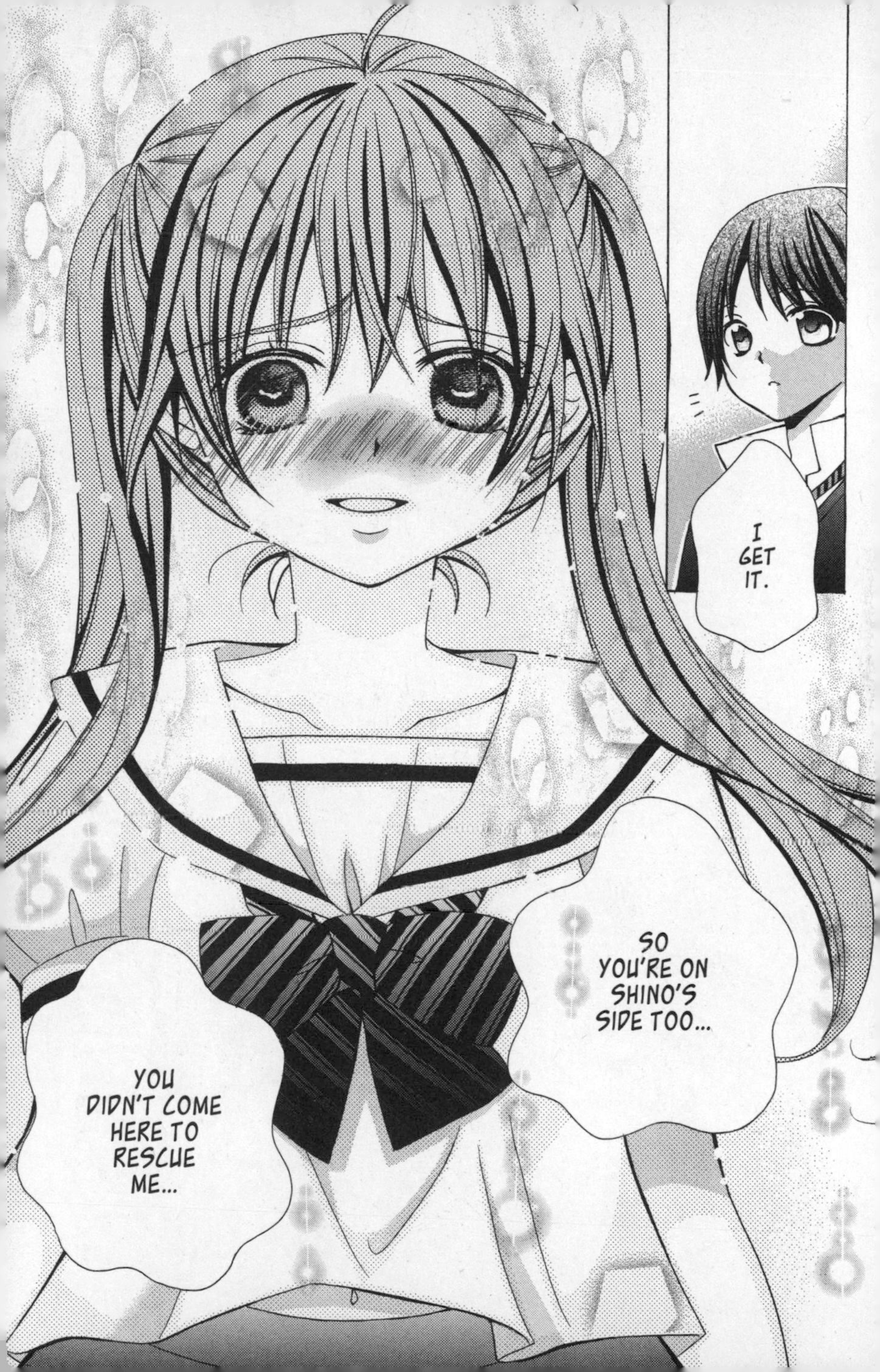
I GET IT.
SO YOU'RE ON SHINO'S SIDE TOO...
YOU DIDN'T COME HERE TO RESCUE ME...

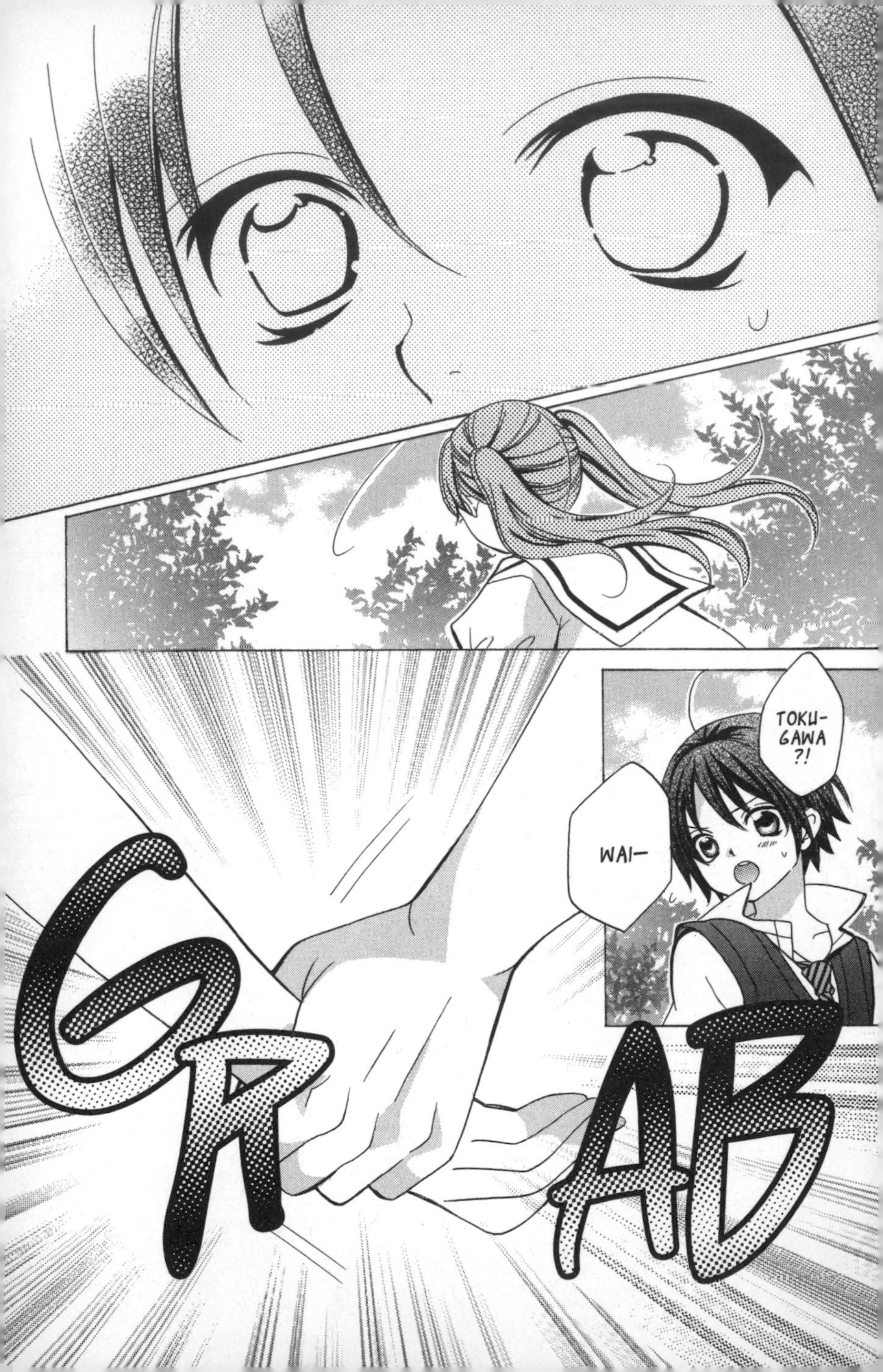
TOKU-
GAWA
?!
WAI—
GRAB

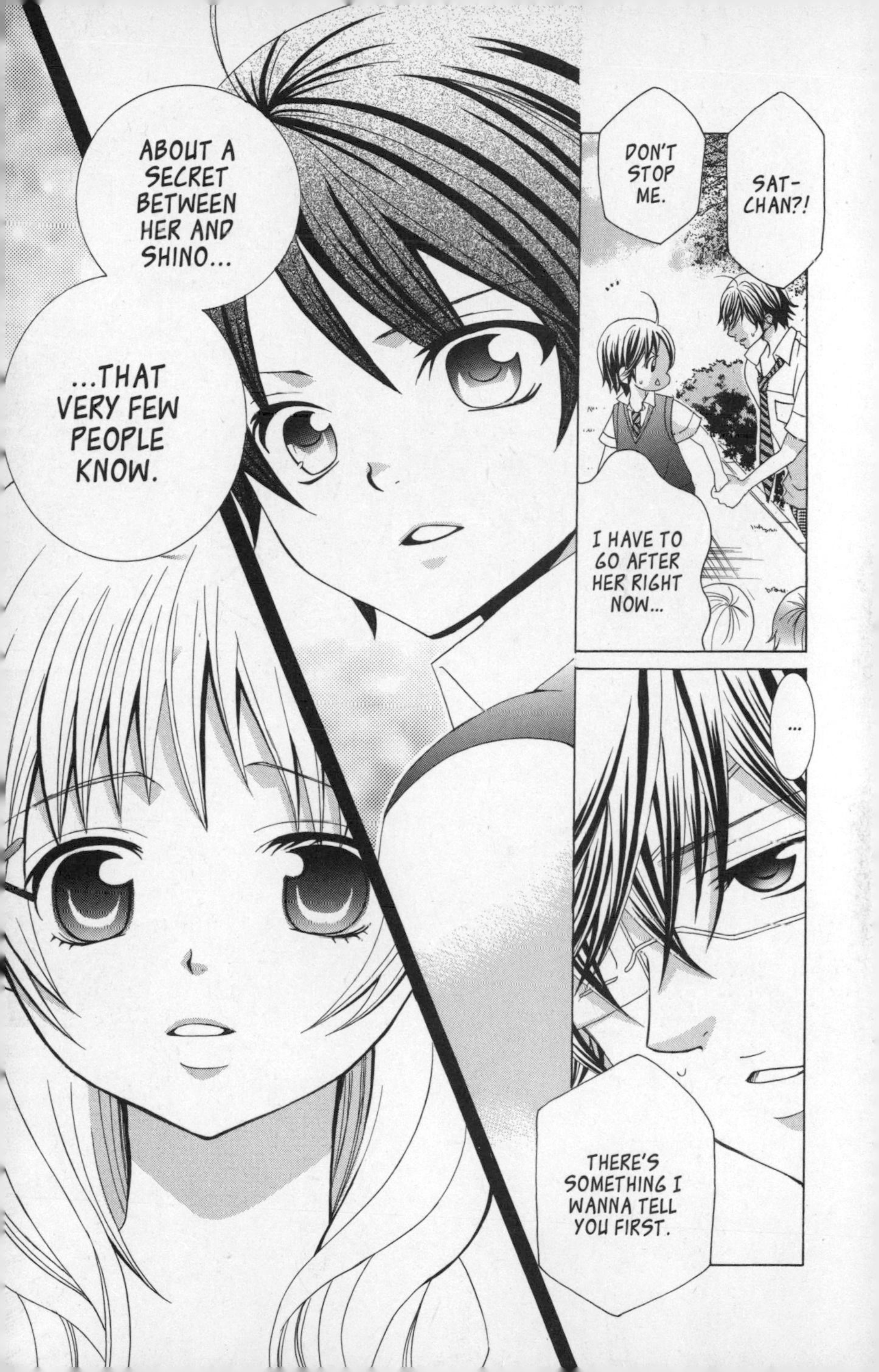
SAT-CHAN?!
DON'T STOP ME.
...
I HAVE TO GO AFTER HER RIGHT NOW...
...
THERE'S SOMETHING I WANNA TELL YOU FIRST.
ABOUT A SECRET BETWEEN HER AND SHINO...
...THAT VERY FEW PEOPLE KNOW.

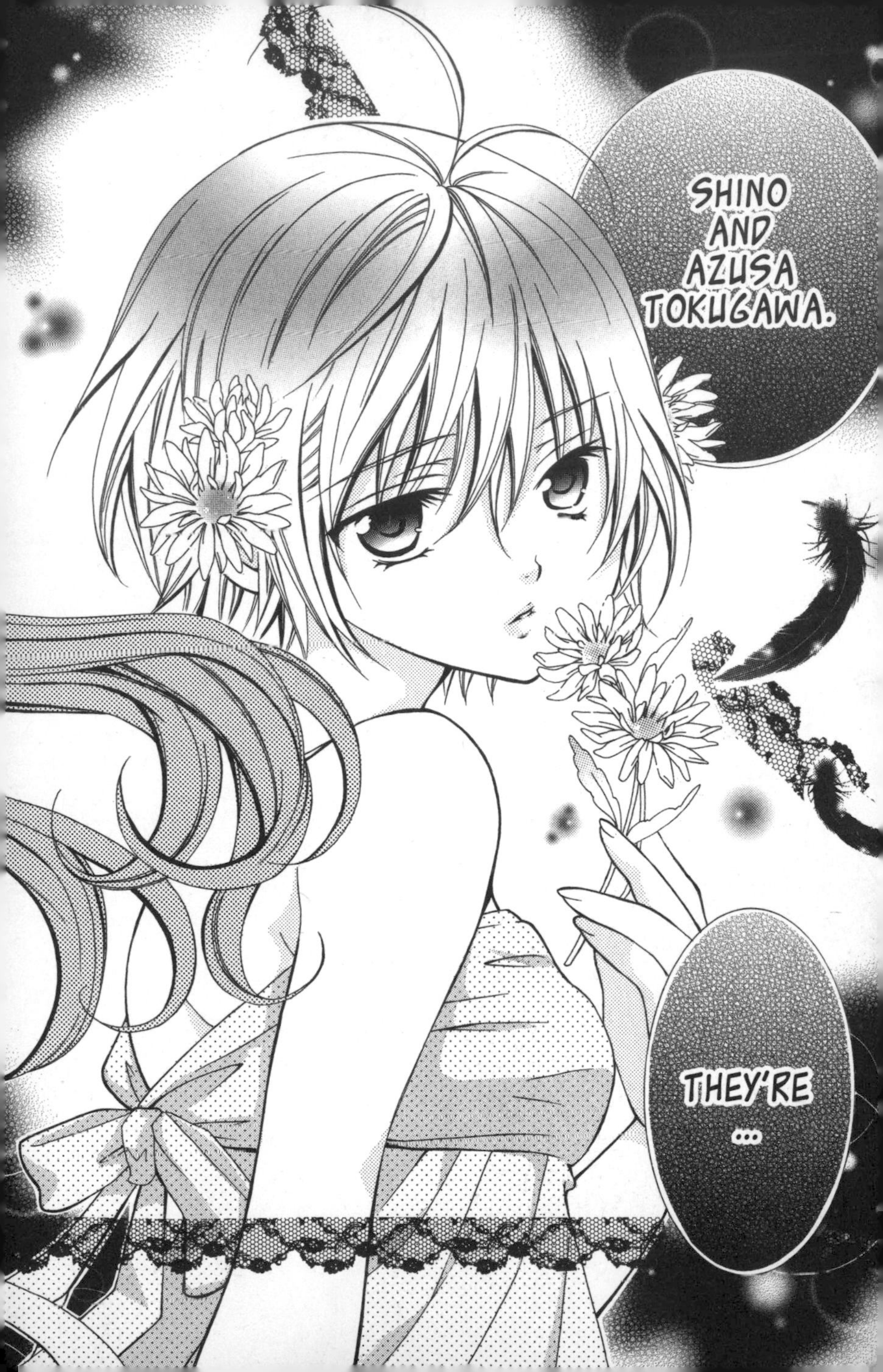
SHINO AND AZUSA TOKUGAWA.
THEY'RE ...

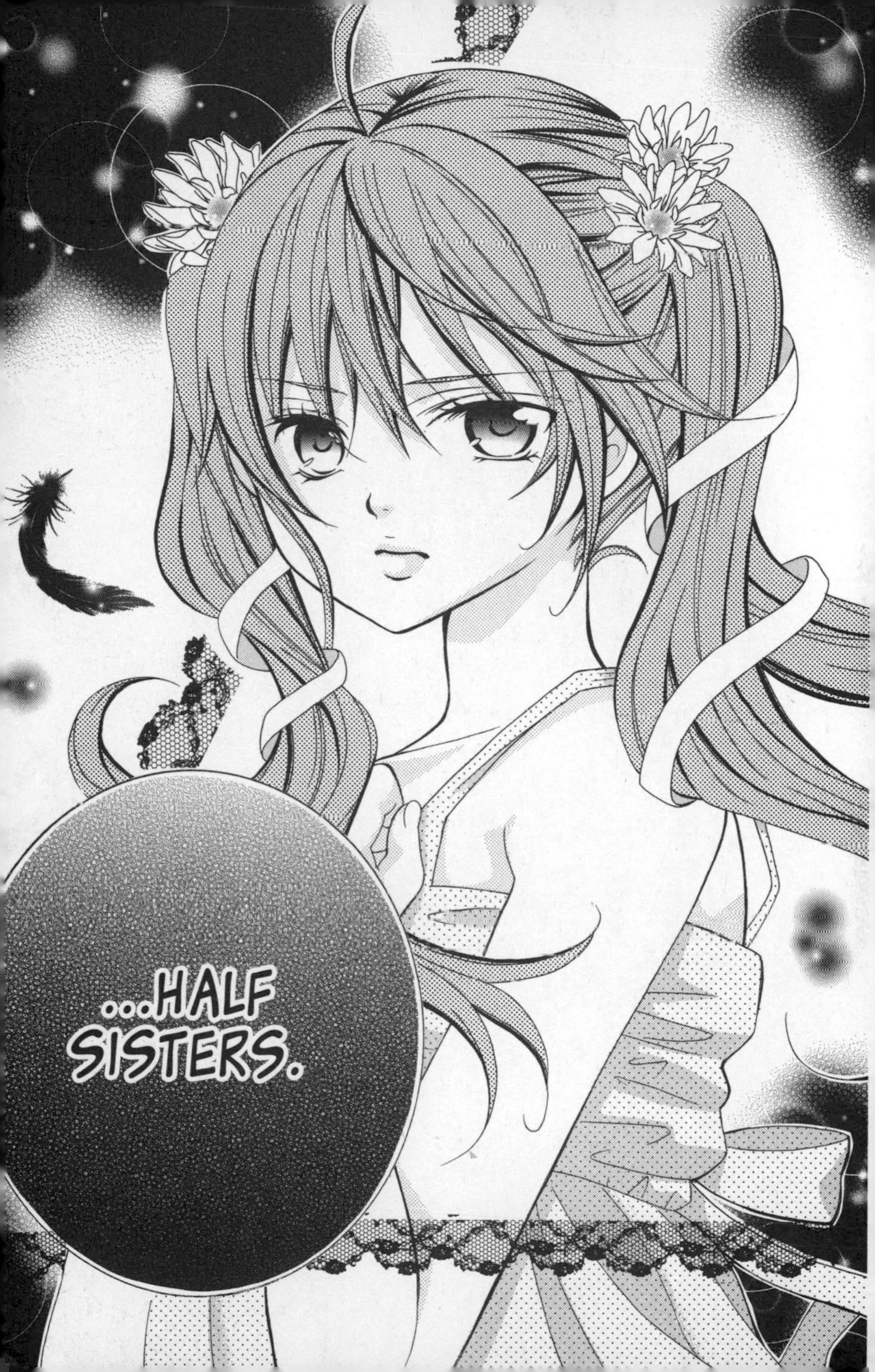
...HALF SISTERS.

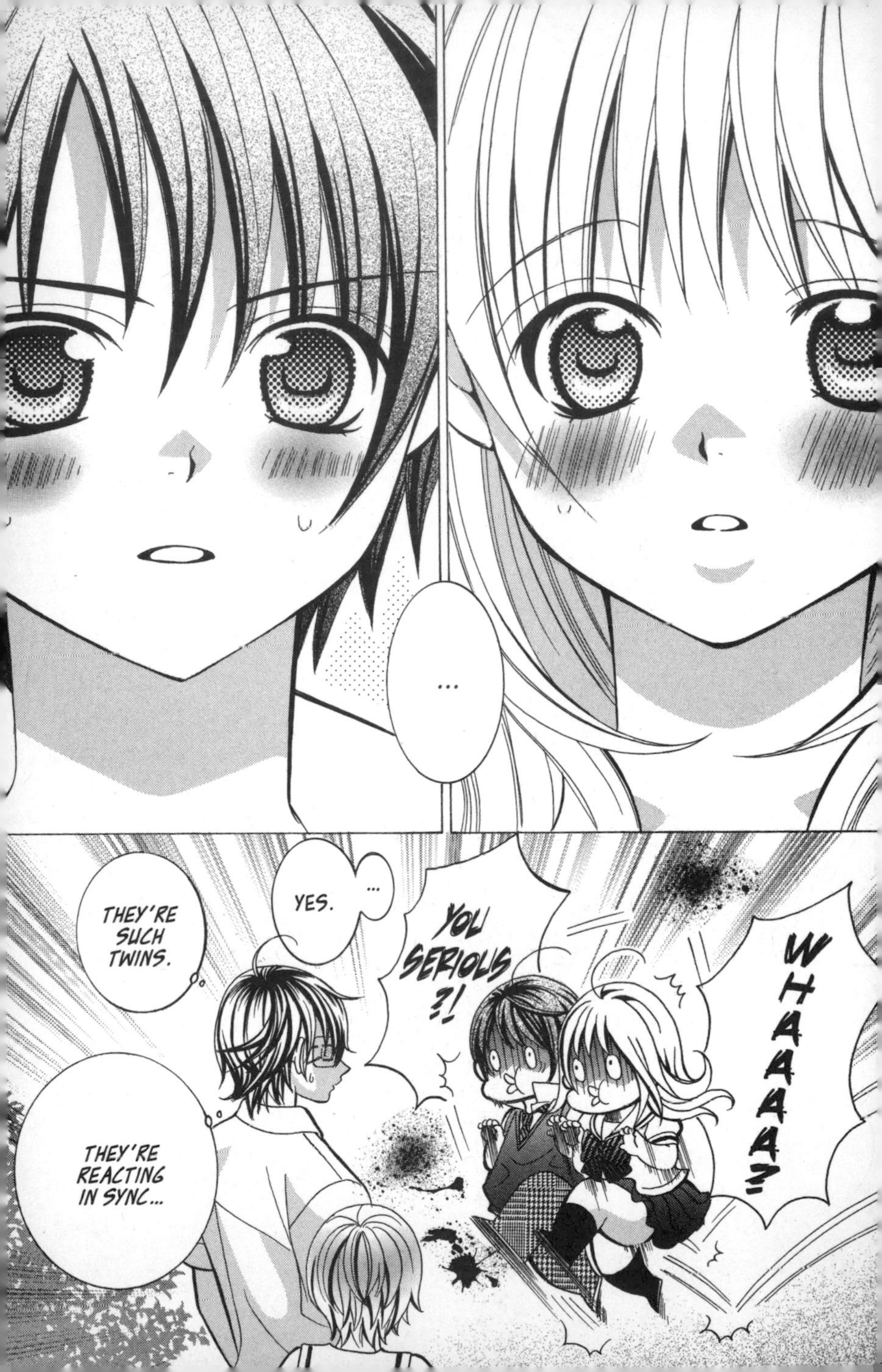
...
WHAAAAA?
YOU SERIOUS?!
...
YES.
THEY'RE SUCH TWINS.
THEY'RE REACTING IN SYNC...

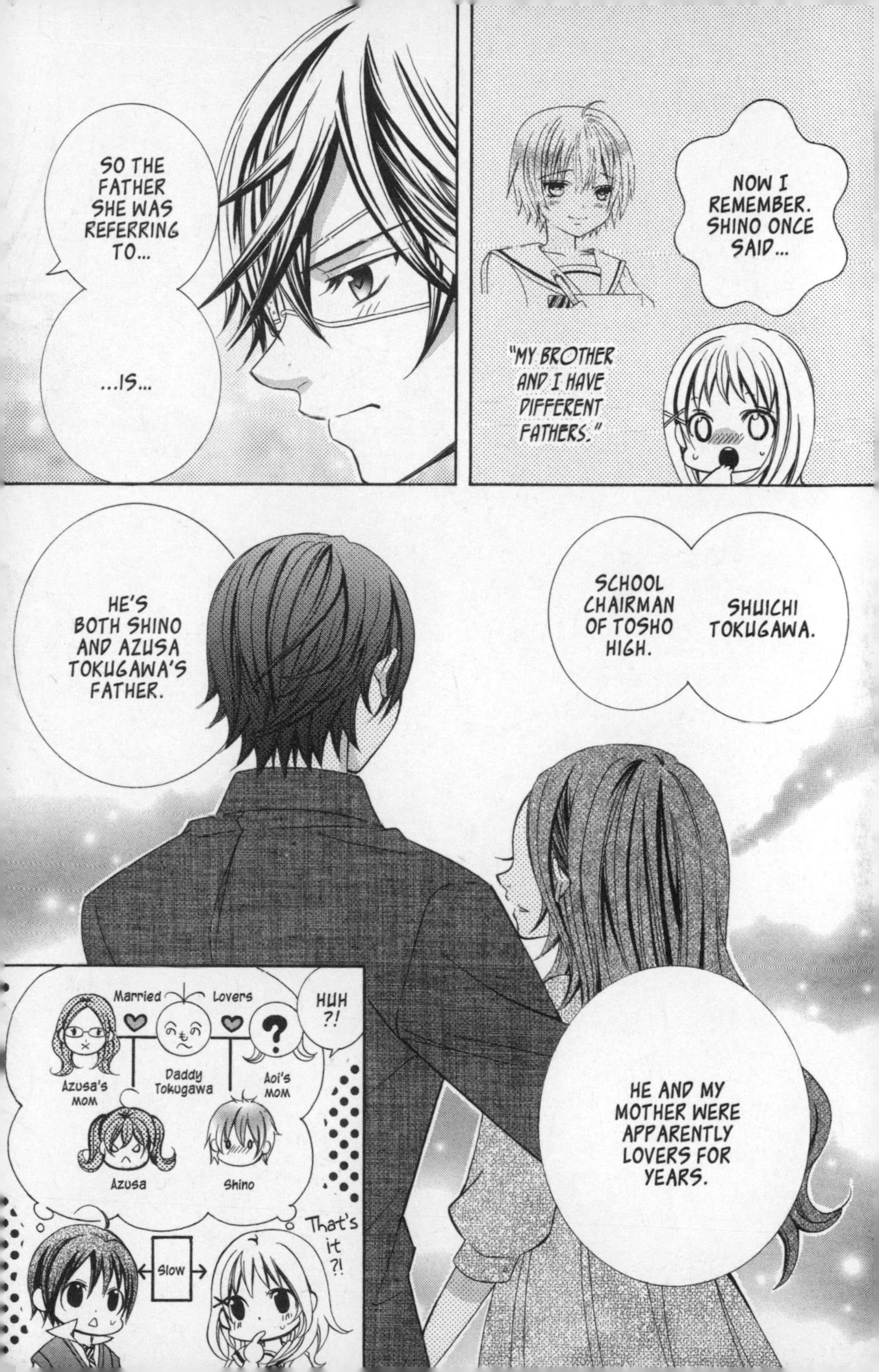
NOW I REMEMBER. SHINO ONCE SAID...
"MY BROTHER AND I HAVE DIFFERENT FATHERS."
SO THE FATHER SHE WAS REFERRING TO...
...IS...
SHUICHI TOKUGAWA.
SCHOOL CHAIRMAN OF TOSHO HIGH.
HE'S BOTH SHINO AND AZUSA TOKUGAWA'S FATHER.
HE AND MY MOTHER WERE APPARENTLY LOVERS FOR YEARS.
HUH ?!
Married
Lovers
Azusa's MOM
Daddy Tokugawa
Aoi's MOM
Azusa
Shino
That's it ?!
Slow

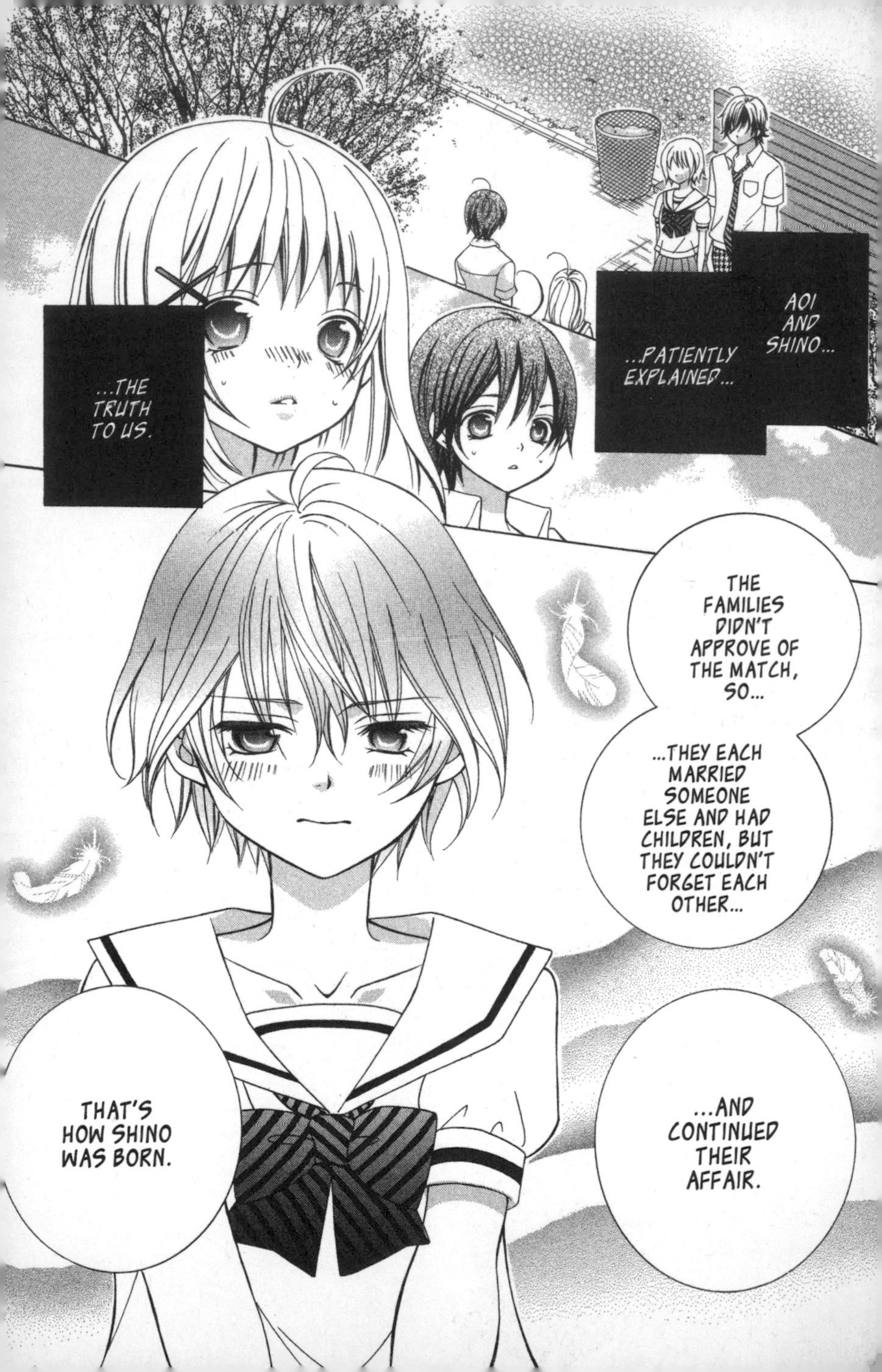
AOI AND SHINO...
...PATIENTLY EXPLAINED...
...THE TRUTH TO US.
THE FAMILIES DIDN'T APPROVE OF THE MATCH, SO...
...THEY EACH MARRIED SOMEONE ELSE AND HAD CHILDREN, BUT THEY COULDN'T FORGET EACH OTHER...
...AND CONTINUED THEIR AFFAIR.
THAT'S HOW SHINO WAS BORN.

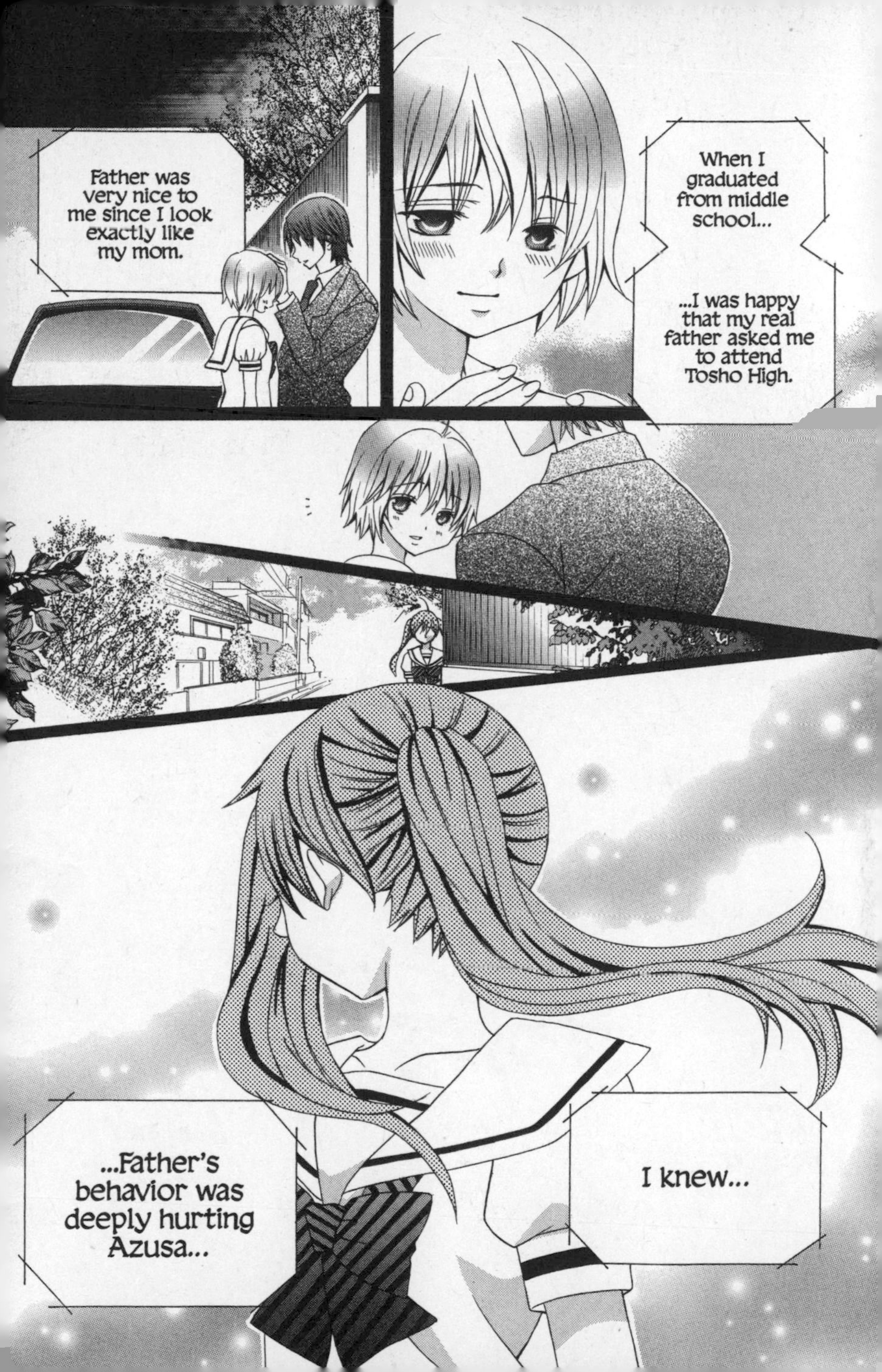
When I graduated from middle school...
...I was happy that my real father asked me to attend Tosho High.
Father was very nice to me since I look exactly like my mom.
I knew...
...Father's behavior was deeply hurting Azusa...

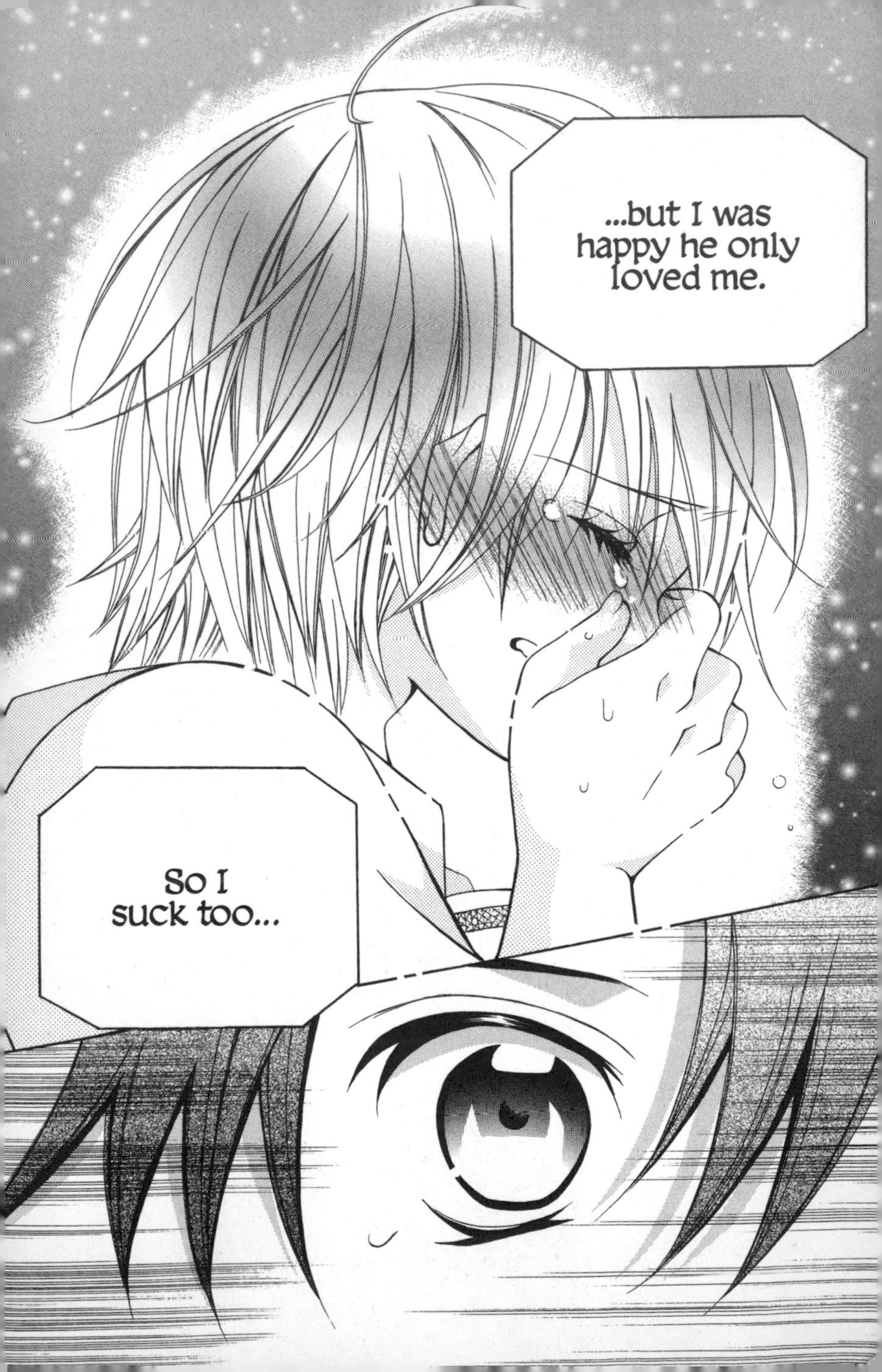
...but I was happy he only loved me.
So I suck too...

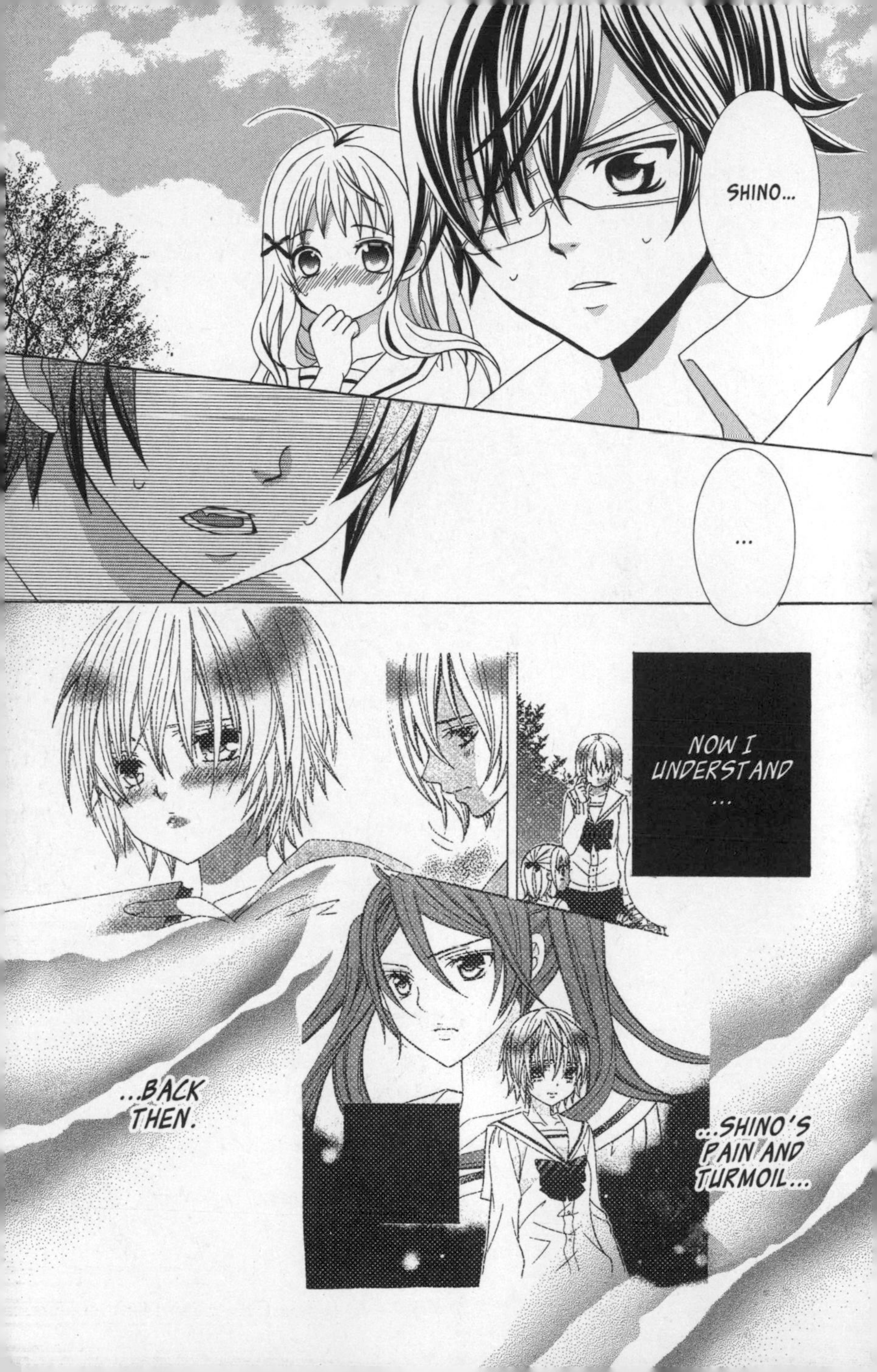
SHINO...
...
NOW I UNDERSTAND ...
...SHINO'S PAIN AND TURMOIL...
...BACK THEN.

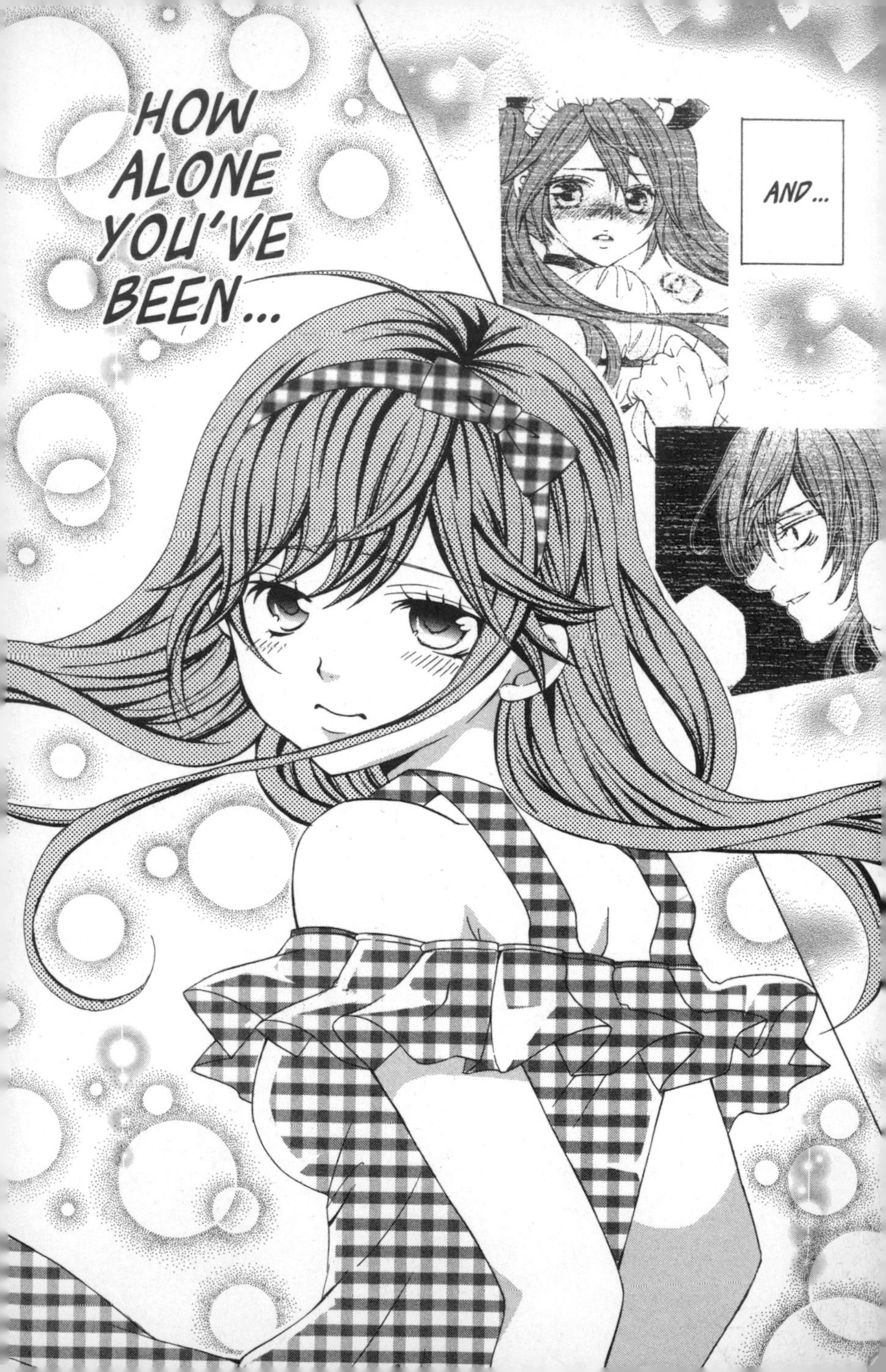
AND...
HOW ALONE YOU'VE BEEN...

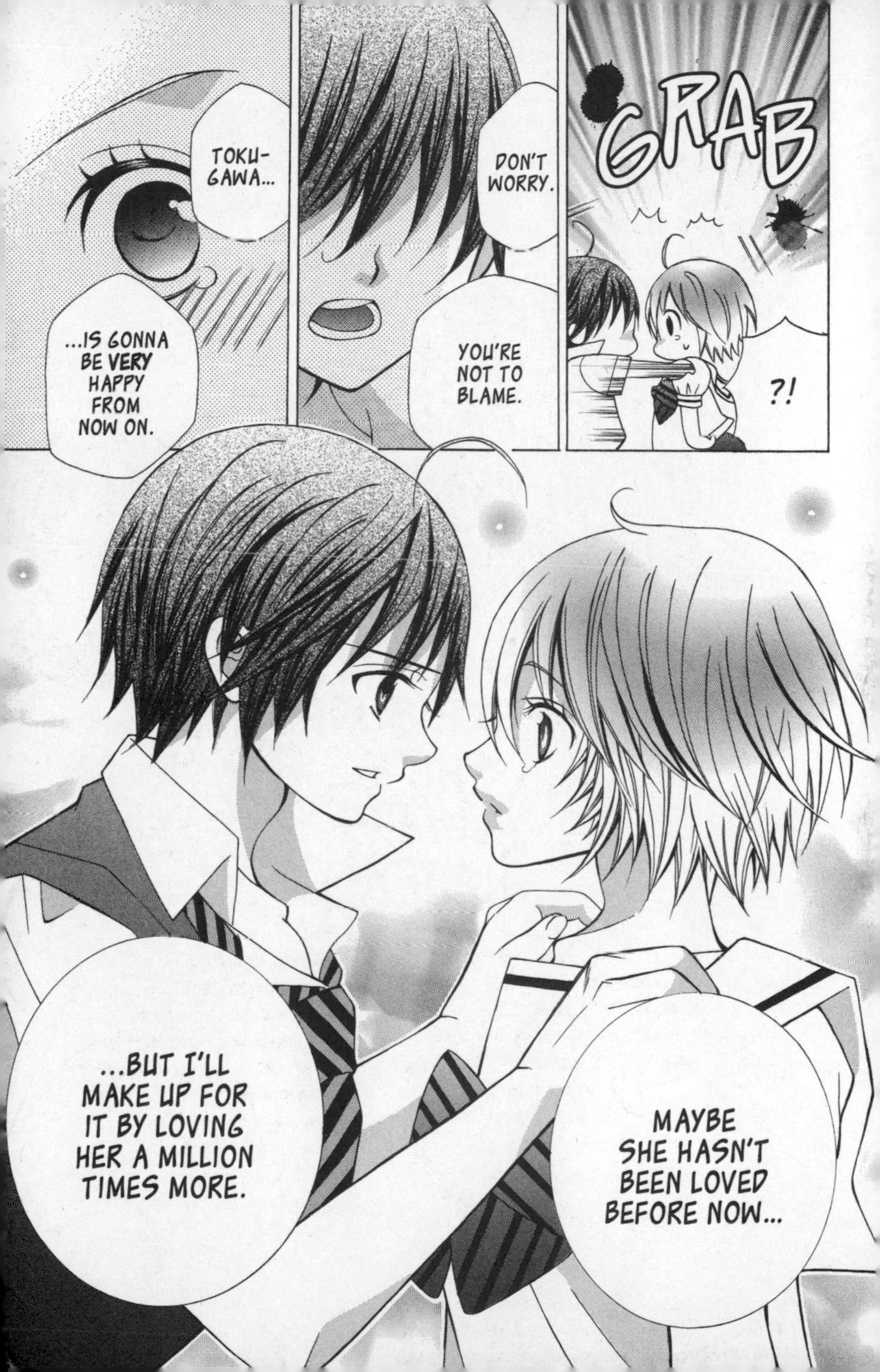
GRAB
?!
DON'T WORRY.
YOU'RE NOT TO BLAME.
TOKU-GAWA...
...IS GONNA BE VERY HAPPY FROM NOW ON.
MAYBE SHE HASN'T BEEN LOVED BEFORE NOW...
...BUT I'LL MAKE UP FOR IT BY LOVING HER A MILLION TIMES MORE.

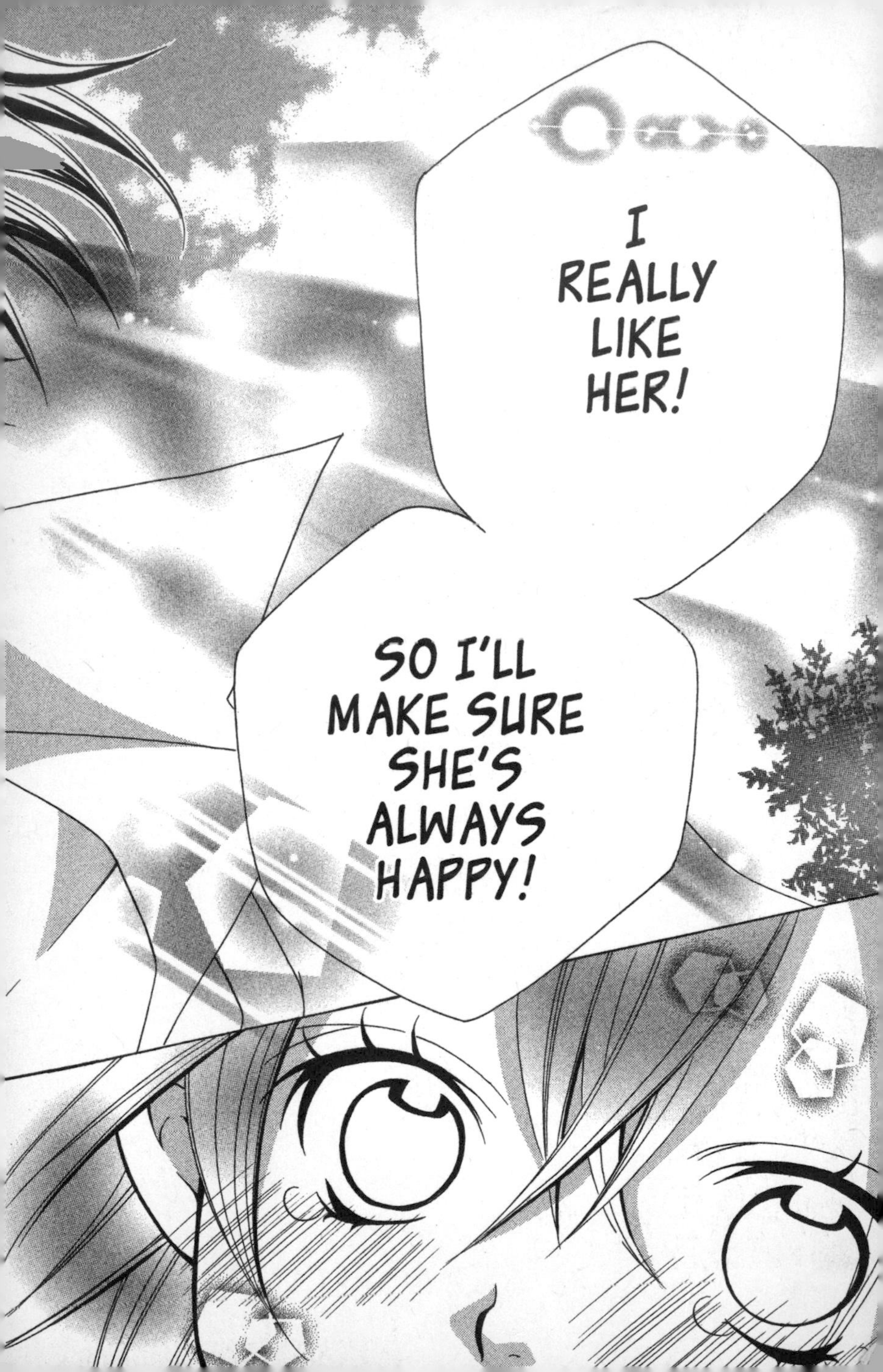
I REALLY LIKE HER!
SO I'LL MAKE SURE SHE'S ALWAYS HAPPY!

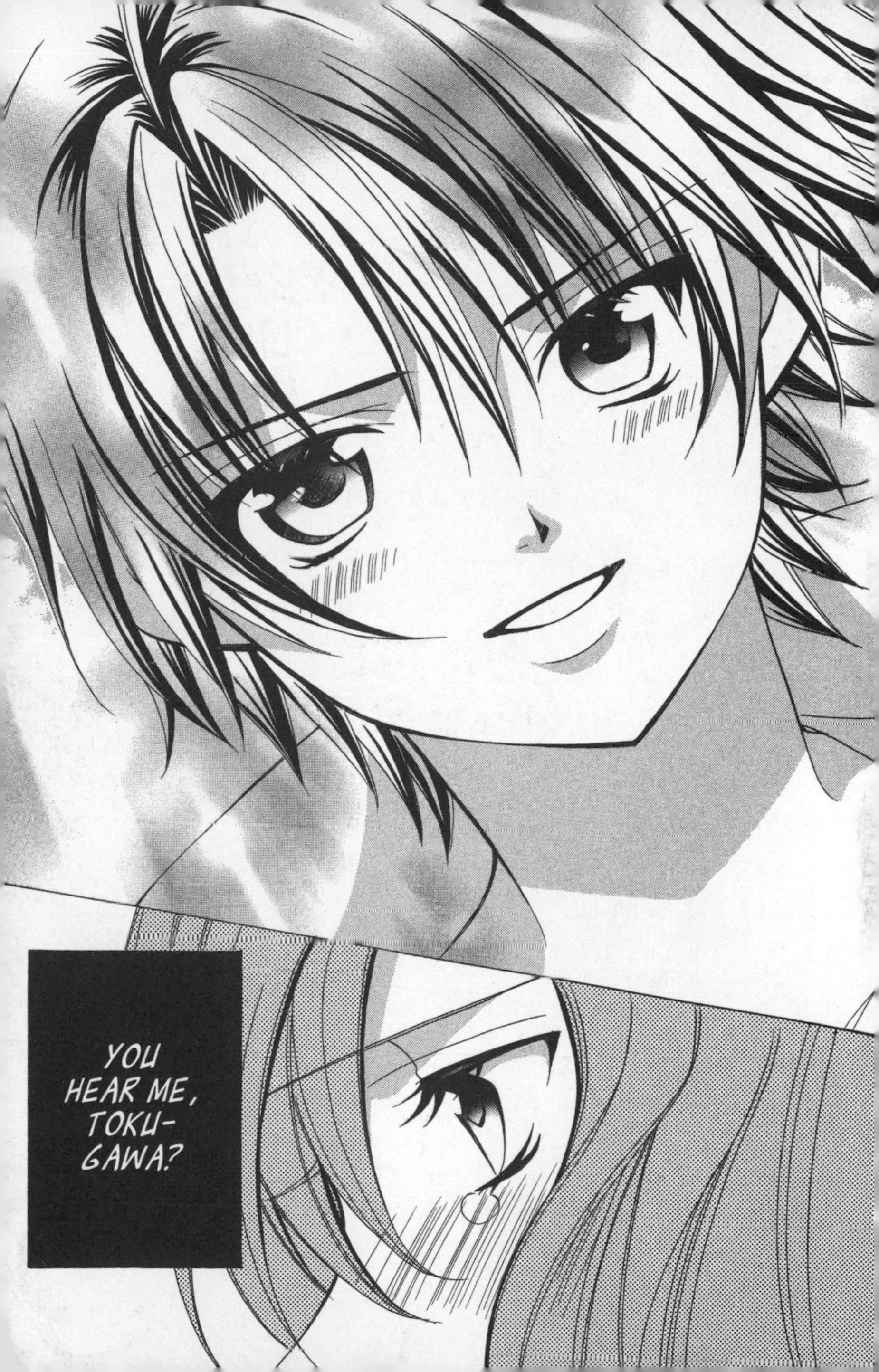
YOU HEAR ME, TOKU-GAWA?

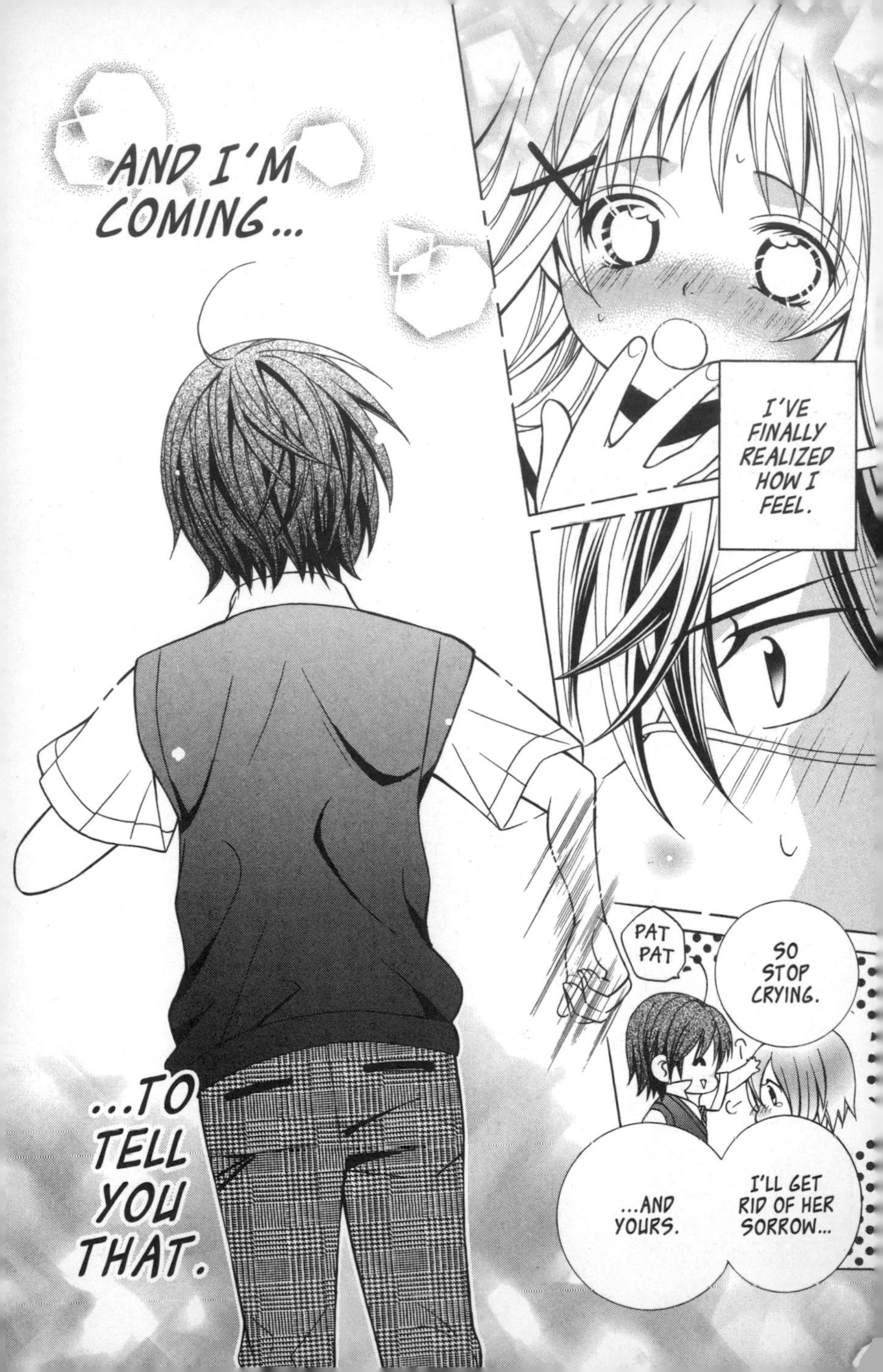
I'VE FINALLY REALIZED HOW I FEEL.
PAT PAT
SO STOP CRYING.
I'LL GET RID OF HER SORROW...
...AND YOURS.
AND I'M COMING...
...TO TELL YOU THAT.

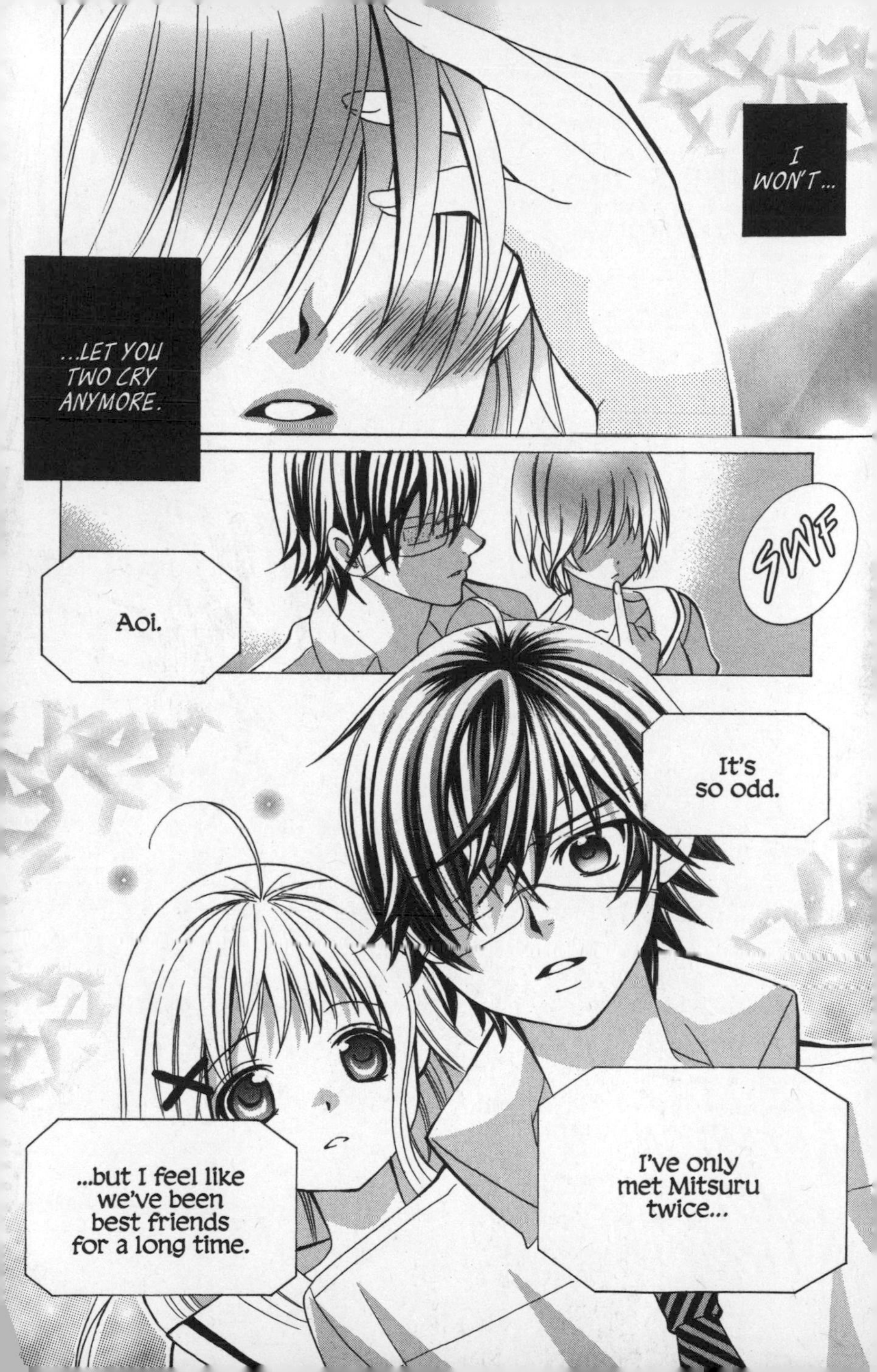
I WON'T...
...LET YOU TWO CRY ANYMORE.
SWF
Aoi.
It's so odd.
I've only met Mitsuru twice...
...but I feel like we've been best friends for a long time.

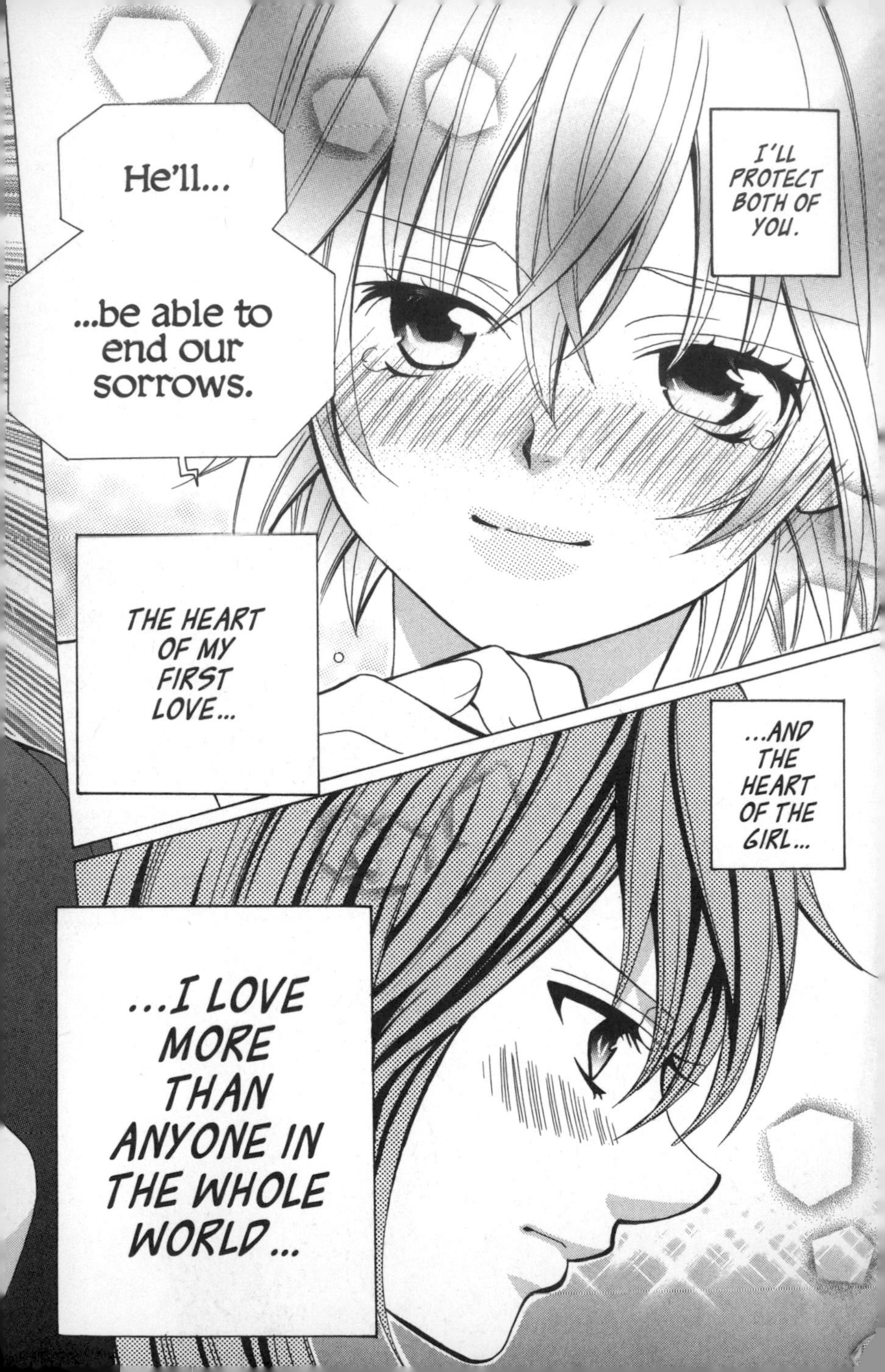
I'LL PROTECT BOTH OF YOU.
He'll...
...be able to end our sorrows.
THE HEART OF MY FIRST LOVE...
...AND THE HEART OF THE GIRL...
...I LOVE MORE THAN ANYONE IN THE WHOLE WORLD...

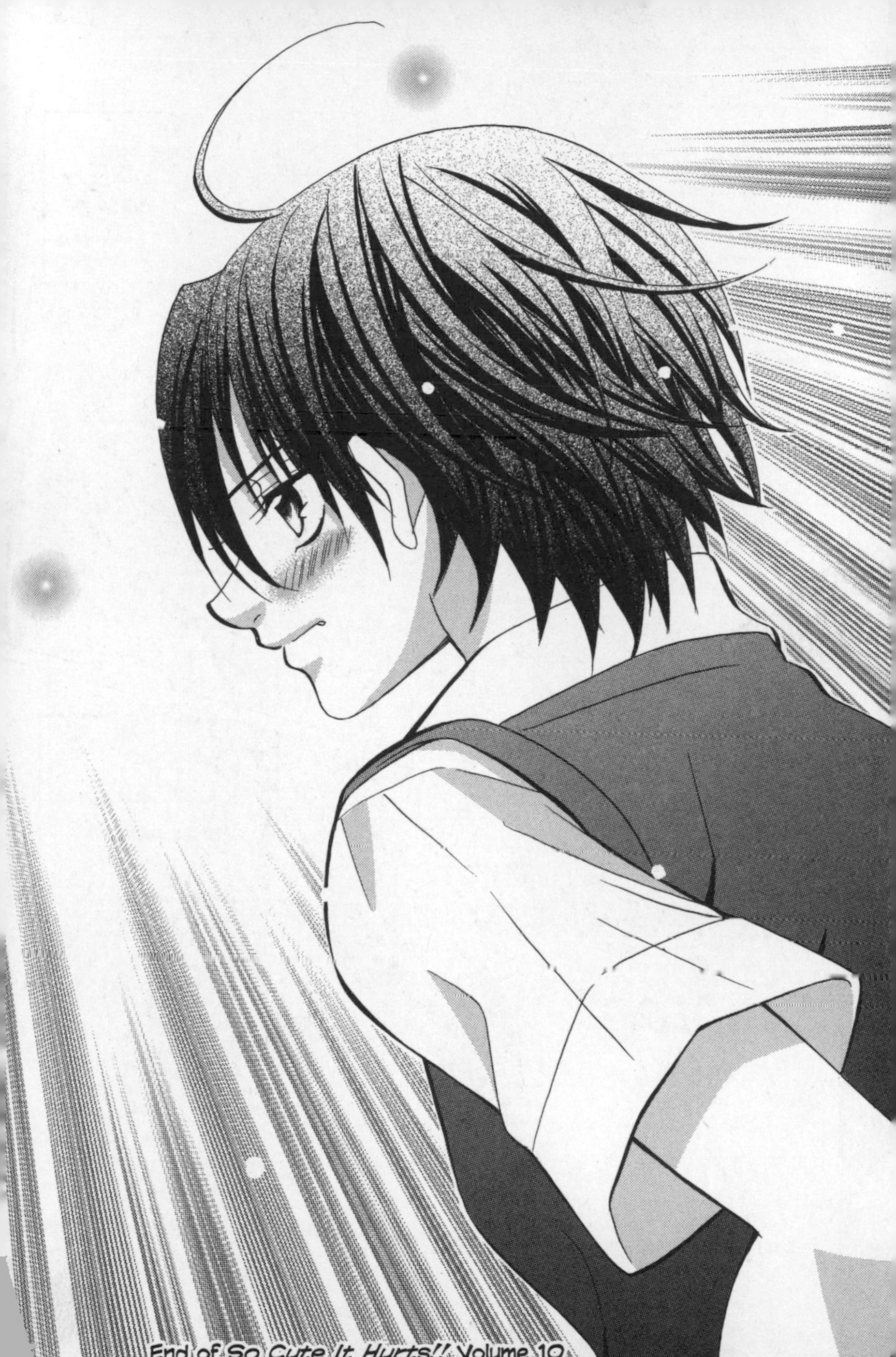

End of So Cute It Hurts!! Volume 10

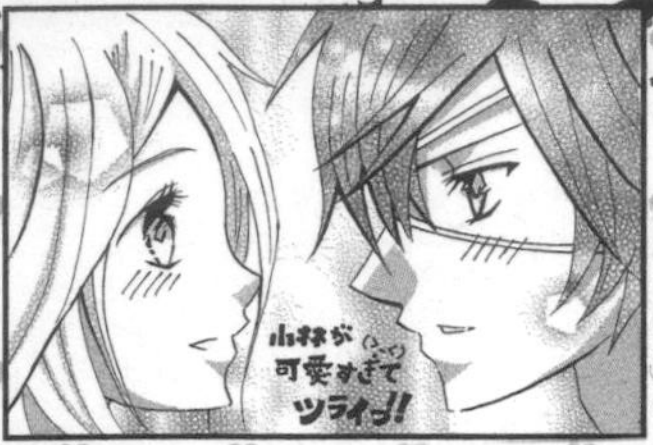
小林が可愛すぎてツライッ!!

Saya Kitano (Saitama) ←
Ed.: You can tell they love each other. ♥

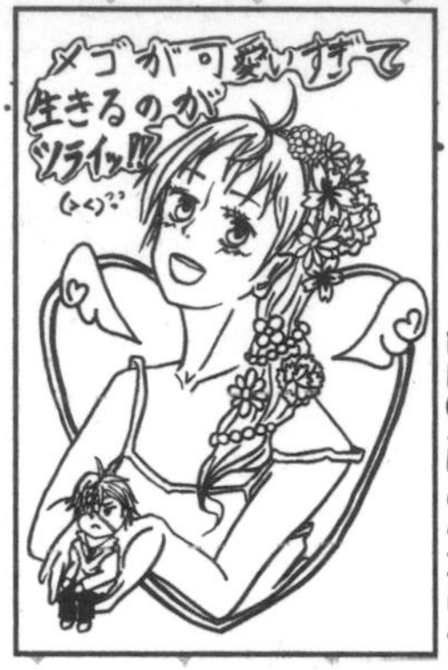
メゴが可愛いすぎて生きるのがツライッ!!

Rio Hashida (Nagasaki) ←
Ed.: This drawing is so lovely I'm finding it hard to survive!!

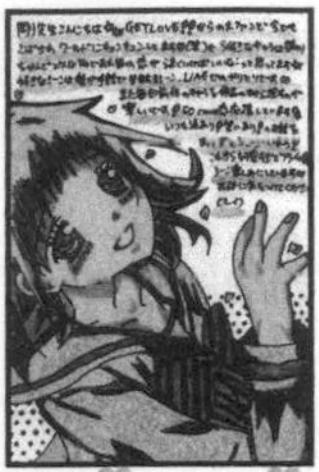

Maa-chan (Kyoto) ←
Ed.: This Mego really looks like an angel!!

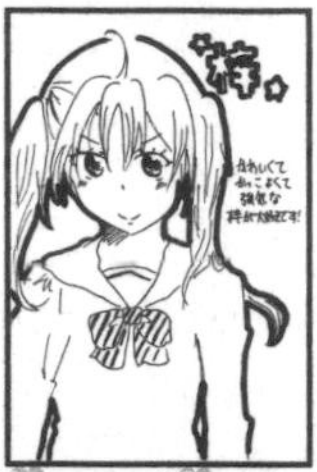

Kuroneko (Chiba) ↑
Ed.: You look cool, Azusa!!

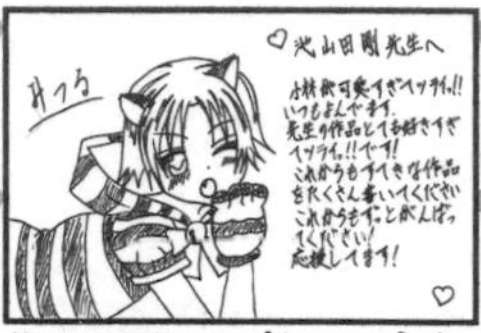

Manami Hirata (Toyama) ↑
Ed.: Mitsuru the cat is cute, meow. ♥

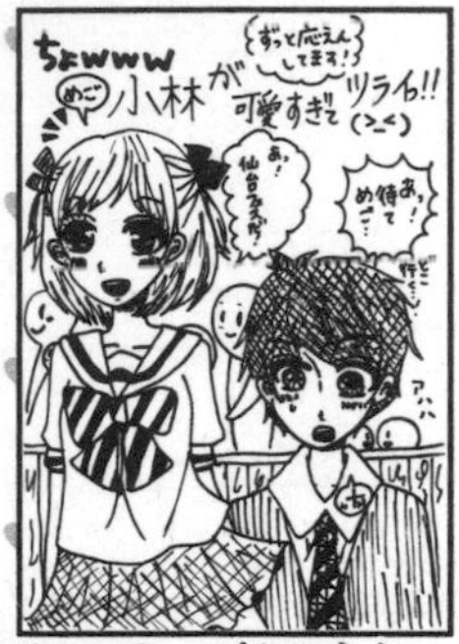
ちょwww
めご 小林が可愛すぎてツライ!!
ずっと応えんしてます!

Karen Omori (Chiba) ↑
Ed.: Reminds me of their first date!

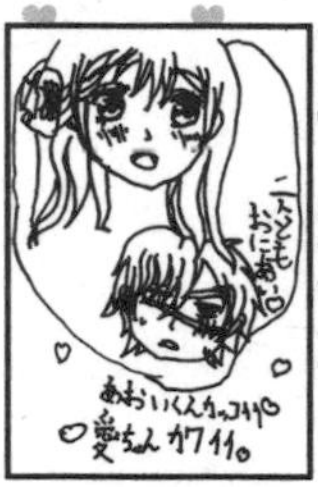

Yuha Hayasaka (Miyagi) ←
Ed.: Yes, these two are made for each other. ♥

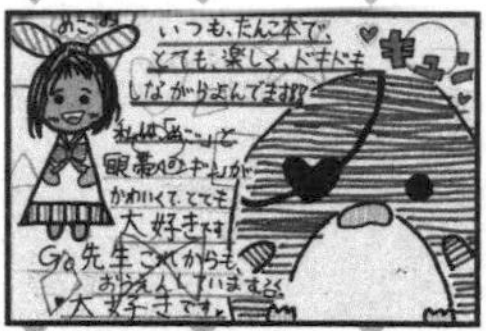

Orange ♡ (Oita) ↑
Ed.: Here's the eye-patch penguin!!

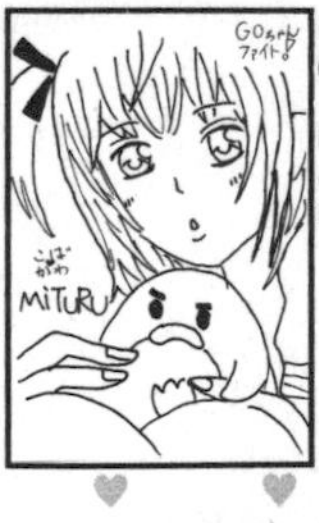
MiTURU

Umi Kubota (Shizuoka) ←
Ed.: Mitsuru's cross-dressing is the best!!

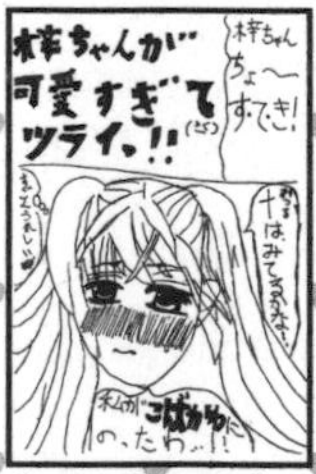
梓ちゃんが可愛すぎてツライっ!!

Cocoa Omura ↑ (Aomori)
Ed.: The shy-looking Azusa is super cute!!

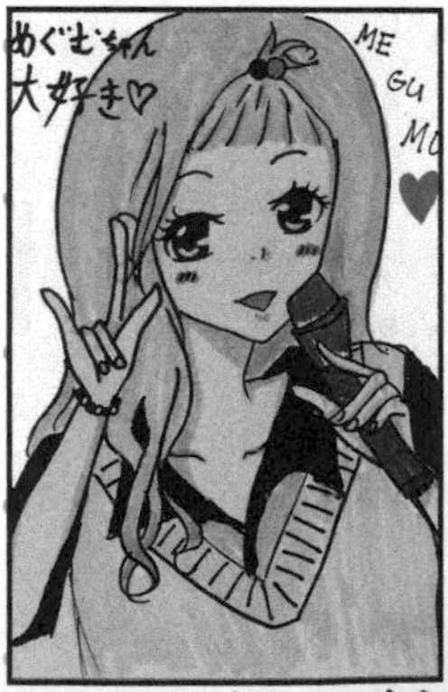
めぐむちゃん大好き♡
ME
GU
MI

Minori Kanpei (Hiroshima) ↑
Ed.: What's she singing?

Send your fan mail to:

Go Ikeyamada
c/o Shojo Beat
VIZ Media, LLC
P.O. Box 77010
San Francisco, CA 94107

Thanks to all of you, here's volume 10 of *So Cute!* I'm grateful that everyone's cheering me on. ♥ I'm very happy that you send me letters!! One reader who's been following me since I debuted (she was in junior high then) wrote me a letter saying she's gotten married and had a baby and would like her child to read my manga someday. She said she loved the heroes when she was in junior high, but she feels differently when she reads those manga now as an adult, and she hopes someone like Mego will appear and gently kiss her child's scars. I was so happy reading the letter that I cried. I'll do my absolute best so I can draw manga that all of you can read with your children when they grow up (*ToT) !!

Go Ikeyamada is a Gemini from Miyagi Prefecture whose hobbies include taking naps and watching movies. Her debut manga *Get Love!!* appeared in *Shojo Comic* in 2002, and her current work *So Cute It Hurts!!* (*Kobayashi ga Kawai Suguite Tsurai!!*) is being published by VIZ Media.

SO C[

Shojo Beat Edition

STORY AND ART BY
GO IKEYAMADA

English Translation & Adaptation/Tomo Kimura
Touch-Up Art & Lettering/Joanna Estep
Design/Izumi Evers
Editor/Pancha Diaz

KOBAYASHI GA KAWAISUGITE TSURAI!! Vol.10
by Go IKEYAMADA
© 2012 Go IKEYAMADA
All rights reserved.
Original Japanese edition published by SHOGAKUKAN.
English translation rights in the United States of America, Canada,
the United Kingdom and Ireland arranged with SHOGAKUKAN.

The stories, characters and incidents mentioned in
this publication are entirely fictional.

Printed in the U.S.A.

Published by VIZ Media, LLC
P.O. Box 77010
San Francisco, CA 94107

10 9 8 7 6 5 4 3 2 1
First printing, December 2016

www.viz.com   www.shojobeat.com